A-Level

Mathematics

for Edexcel
Mechanics 2

CGP
~ books
like no others!

CGP

The Complete Course for Edexcel M2

Contents

Chapter 3

Work, Energy and Power

Chapter 4

Collisions

Chapter 5

Statics

Reference

About this book

In this book you'll find...

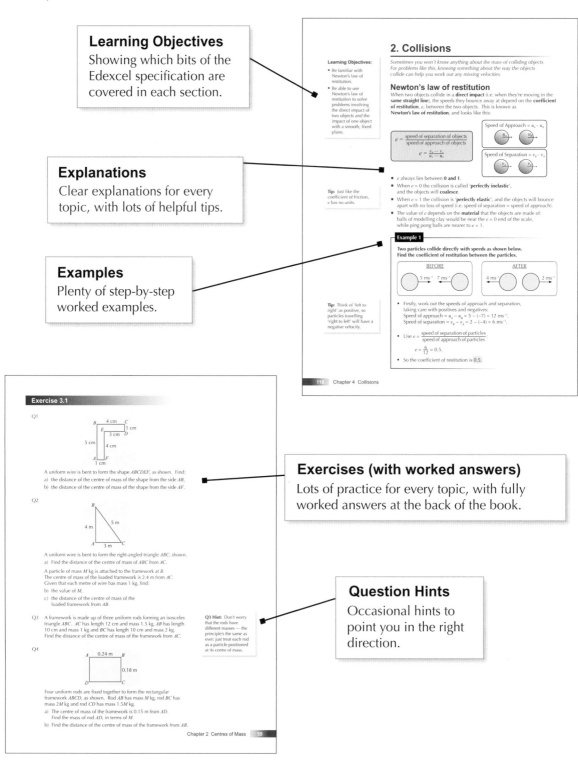

Learning Objectives
Showing which bits of the Edexcel specification are covered in each section.

Explanations
Clear explanations for every topic, with lots of helpful tips.

Examples
Plenty of step-by-step worked examples.

Exercises (with worked answers)
Lots of practice for every topic, with fully worked answers at the back of the book.

Question Hints
Occasional hints to point you in the right direction.

Review Exercises
Mixed questions covering the whole chapter, with fully worked answers.

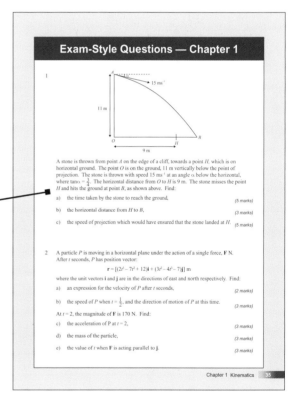
Exam-Style Questions
Questions in the same style as the ones you'll get in the exam, with worked solutions and mark schemes.

Formula Sheet
Contains all the formulas you'll be given in the M2 exam.

Glossary
All the definitions you need to know for the exam, plus other useful words.

Practice Exam Papers (on CD-ROM)
Two printable exam papers, with fully worked answers and mark schemes.

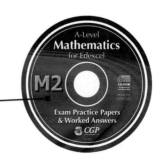

Published by CGP

Editors:
David Ryan, Lyn Setchell, Jonathan Wray, Dawn Wright.

Contributors:
Michael Coe, Barbara Mascetti, Rosemary Rogers.

ISBN: 978 1 84762 810 7

With thanks to Janet Dickinson and Glenn Rogers for the proofreading.
With thanks to Alastair Duncombe for the reviewing.

Printed by Elanders Ltd, Newcastle upon Tyne.
Clipart from Corel®

1. Projectiles

A projectile is an object which has been projected (e.g. thrown or fired) through the air.

When you're doing projectile questions, you'll have to consider the motion of the projectile in two dimensions. That means you'll have to split the projectile's velocity into its horizontal and vertical components, then use the constant acceleration equations to find out more information about the projectile's motion.

Learning Objectives:

- Be able to resolve a body's velocity into its horizontal and vertical components.
- Be able to perform calculations involving projectile motion.

The two components of velocity

When you project a body through the air with **initial speed u**, at an **angle of θ** to the horizontal, it will move along a **curved path**:

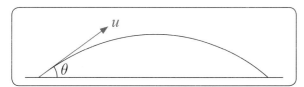

You can use trigonometry to resolve the body's initial velocity into its **horizontal** and **vertical components**:

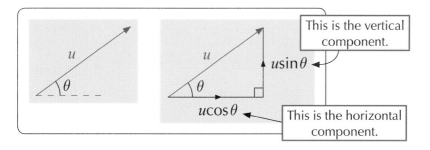

This is the vertical component.

This is the horizontal component.

Tip: You can split the projectile's velocity at any point along its path into horizontal and vertical components — as long as you know its speed and direction at that particular point.

Example 1

A ball is thrown with initial speed 9 ms⁻¹ at an angle of 40° above the horizontal. Find the horizontal and vertical components of the ball's initial velocity.

- Resolving horizontally:
    Horizontal component = $9\cos 40° = 6.89$ ms⁻¹ (3 s.f.)

- Resolving vertically:
    Vertical component = $9\sin 40° = 5.79$ ms⁻¹ (3 s.f.)

Given the horizontal and vertical components of a projectile's velocity, you can find its **speed** using **Pythagoras' theorem**.
You can find its **direction of motion** using **trigonometry**.

Tip: A projectile's trajectory is just the path that it moves along.

Example 2

At a particular point on its trajectory, a particle has velocity v, with horizontal component 7 ms⁻¹ and vertical component –4 ms⁻¹.

Find the particle's speed, v, and direction of motion at this point.

- Draw a diagram to show the particle's motion.

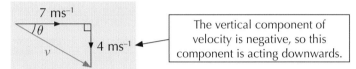

The vertical component of velocity is negative, so this component is acting downwards.

- Using Pythagoras' theorem:

$$v = \sqrt{7^2 + (-4)^2} = 8.06 \text{ ms}^{-1} \text{ (3 s.f.)}$$

- Using trigonometry:

$$\theta = \tan^{-1}\left(\tfrac{4}{7}\right) = 29.7° \text{ (3 s.f.) below the horizontal}$$

Exercise 1.1

Q1 Each of the following diagrams shows the speed of a projectile and the angle its velocity makes with the horizontal. In each case, find the horizontal and vertical components of the projectile's velocity.

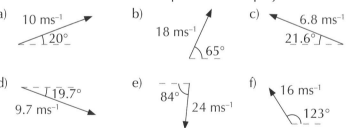

a) 10 ms⁻¹ 20°

b) 18 ms⁻¹ 65°

c) 6.8 ms⁻¹ 21.6°

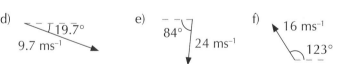

d) 19.7° 9.7 ms⁻¹

e) 84° 24 ms⁻¹

f) 16 ms⁻¹ 123°

Q2 A particle is moving with speed 8 ms⁻¹ at an angle of 35° to the horizontal. Find the horizontal and vertical components of its velocity.

Q3 A rocket is fired vertically upwards with speed 45 ms⁻¹. Find the horizontal and vertical components of its initial velocity.

Q4 A body is fired at an angle α to the horizontal with speed 22 kmh⁻¹. Find the horizontal and vertical components of its initial velocity, giving your answer in metres per second.

Q5   A ball is thrown with velocity **v**, with horizontal component 6 ms^{-1} and vertical component 8 ms^{-1}.
Find the speed and direction of projection of the ball.

Q6   A particle moves with velocity **u**. The horizontal component of **u** is 17 ms^{-1} and the vertical component is -2.5 ms^{-1}.
Find the magnitude and direction of **u**.

The constant acceleration equations

- In M2, you'll model a projectile as moving only under the influence of **gravity** (i.e. there'll be **no external forces** acting on it).
- You'll also model the projectile as a **particle** — i.e. its weight acts from a single point, so its dimensions don't matter.
- Because the projectile is modelled as moving only under the influence of gravity, the only acceleration the projectile will experience will be **acceleration due to gravity** ($g = 9.8$ **ms**$^{-2}$).
- Acceleration due to gravity acts **vertically downwards**, so will only affect the **vertical component** of the projectile's velocity.
- The **horizontal component** of velocity will remain **constant** throughout motion.
- Another modelling assumption you can make is that the projectile moves in a **two-dimensional vertical plane** — i.e. it doesn't swerve from side to side. For example, in the diagram of the projectile's path on page 1, the projectile stays flat on the page — it doesn't move towards you (out of the page) or away from you (into the page).
- To answer a projectiles question, split all the vector quantities you know — **velocity**, **acceleration** and **displacement** — into their **horizontal** and **vertical components**. Then you can deal with the two components **separately** using the *uvast* **equations** from M1.
- The thing that connects the two components is **time** — this will be the same no matter what direction you're resolving in.

Tip: An external force is any force acting on a body other than the body's weight — e.g. air resistance, friction, tension etc.

The Constant Acceleration Equations

$$v = u + at$$

$$s = ut + \frac{1}{2}at^2$$

$$s = \left(\frac{u + v}{2}\right)t$$

$$v^2 = u^2 + 2as$$

$$s = vt - \frac{1}{2}at^2$$

u = initial speed (or velocity) in ms^{-1}
v = final speed (or velocity) in ms^{-1}
a = acceleration in ms^{-2}
s = displacement in m
t = time that passes in s (seconds)

Remember — these equations only work if the acceleration is **constant**.

Tip: The *uvast* equations only work for motion in a straight line. Using them for projectiles means that you consider the horizontal and vertical components of motion separately.

Example 1

A particle is projected with initial speed 18 ms⁻¹ from a
point on horizontal ground, at an angle of 40° above the
horizontal. Find the particle's distance from its point of
projection 1.8 seconds after it is projected.

Tip: Subscripts $_x$ and $_y$
are often used to denote
the horizontal and
vertical components of
a vector respectively. So
here s_x is the particle's
horizontal displacement
and s_y is the particle's
vertical displacement.

- Consider the horizontal and vertical motion separately.

- Resolving horizontally, taking right as positive:

$$u = 18\cos 40°, \quad a = 0, \quad s = s_x, \quad t = 1.8$$

Using $s = ut + \frac{1}{2}at^2$:

$$s_x = (18\cos 40° \times 1.8) + 0$$
$$= 24.8198...$$

- Resolving vertically, taking up as positive:

$$u = 18\sin 40°, \quad a = -9.8, \quad s = s_y, \quad t = 1.8$$

Using $s = ut + \frac{1}{2}at^2$:

$$s_y = (18\sin 40° \times 1.8) + (\frac{1}{2} \times -9.8 \times 1.8^2)$$
$$= 4.9503...$$

- So the particle has travelled 24.8198... metres horizontally and
4.9503... metres vertically. Use Pythagoras' theorem to find the
particle's distance from its starting point:

$$\text{distance} = \sqrt{(24.8198...)^2 + (4.9503...)^2}$$
$$= 25.3 \text{ m (3 s.f.)}$$

4.9503... m

24.8198... m

Example 2

A ball is kicked from a point on horizontal ground. The initial velocity
of the ball is 23 ms⁻¹, at an angle α to the horizontal.
The ball reaches a maximum vertical height above the ground of 4.8 m.
Find the value of α.

Tip: When the
ball reaches its
maximum height, the
vertical component
of its velocity will
momentarily be zero.

- Resolving vertically, taking up as positive:

$$u = 23\sin \alpha, \quad v = 0, \quad a = -9.8, \quad s = 4.8$$

Using $v^2 = u^2 + 2as$:

$$0 = (23\sin \alpha)^2 + (2 \times -9.8 \times 4.8)$$
$$0 = 529\sin^2\alpha - 94.08$$
$$\sin^2\alpha = 94.08 \div 529$$
$$= 0.1778...$$
$$\sin \alpha = 0.4217...$$
$$\Rightarrow \alpha = 24.9° \text{ (3 s.f.)}$$

Example 3

A stone is thrown horizontally with speed 10 ms⁻¹ from a height of 2 m above horizontal ground.

a) Find the speed and direction of motion of the stone after 0.5 seconds.

- Consider the vertical and horizontal motion separately.
- Resolving vertically, taking down as positive:

    $u = 0, \quad v = v_y, \quad a = 9.8, \quad t = 0.5$

    Using $v = u + at$:

    $v_y = 9.8 \times 0.5 = 4.9 \text{ ms}^{-1}$

Tip: The stone is thrown horizontally, so the vertical component of its initial velocity is zero.

- The horizontal component of velocity is constant, as there is no acceleration horizontally, so $v_x = u_x = 10 \text{ ms}^{-1}$.

- You can now find the speed and direction of motion of the stone at this time.

    $v = \sqrt{10^2 + (-4.9)^2}$

    $= 11.1 \text{ ms}^{-1}$ (3 s.f.)

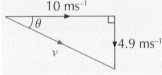

    $\tan\theta = \dfrac{4.9}{10}$

    $\Rightarrow \theta = 26.1°$ (3 s.f.) below the horizontal

b) Find the horizontal distance the stone travels before landing on the ground.

- First, you need to find the length of time that the stone is in the air before it lands.

- Resolving vertically, taking down as positive:

    $u = 0, \quad a = 9.8, \quad s = 2, \quad t = t$

    Using $s = ut + \frac{1}{2}at^2$:

    $2 = \frac{1}{2} \times 9.8 \times t^2$

    $t^2 = 0.4081...$

    $\Rightarrow t = 0.6388...$ s

Tip: You may see similar questions asked as 'find the horizontal range of the stone.'

Tip: The length of time the projectile is in the air is usually referred to as the 'time of flight'.

- Now you know how long the stone is in the air, you can find how far it travels horizontally in this time.

- Resolving horizontally, taking right as positive:

    $u = 10, \quad a = 0, \quad s = s, \quad t = 0.6388...$

    Using $s = ut + \frac{1}{2}at^2$:

    $s = 10 \times 0.6388... = 6.39$ m (3 s.f.)

Example 4

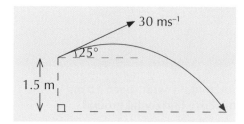

A cricket ball is thrown from a point 1.5 m above flat horizontal ground. The initial velocity of the ball is 30 ms⁻¹ at an angle of 25° to the horizontal, as shown.

a) Find the maximum height the ball reaches above the ground.

- Resolving vertically, taking up as positive:

  $u = 30\sin 25°$, $v = 0$, $a = -9.8$, $s = s$

  Using $v^2 = u^2 + 2as$:

  $$0 = (30\sin 25°)^2 + (2 \times -9.8 \times s)$$
  $$s = 160.745... \div 19.6$$
  $$= 8.201...$$

- So the ball travels 8.201... metres upwards from its point of projection. So its maximum height above the ground is:

  $$8.201... + 1.5 = \boxed{9.70 \text{ m (3 s.f.)}}$$

b) Find the horizontal distance travelled by the ball before it lands.

Tip: The ball is thrown from 1.5 m above the ground, so when it lands, its vertical displacement from its point of projection will be –1.5 m, i.e. 1.5 m below the level of projection.

- Resolving vertically, taking up as positive:

  $u = 30\sin 25°$, $a = -9.8$, $s = -1.5$, $t = t$

  Using $s = ut + \frac{1}{2}at^2$:

  $$-1.5 = (30\sin 25° \times t) + (\tfrac{1}{2} \times -9.8 \times t^2)$$
  $$4.9t^2 - (12.67...)t - 1.5 = 0$$

  Using the quadratic formula:

  $$t = \frac{12.67... \pm \sqrt{(-12.67...)^2 - (4 \times 4.9 \times -1.5)}}{9.8}$$
  $$\Rightarrow t = -0.113... \text{ or } t = 2.700...$$

- Time can't be negative, so take $t = 2.700...$ seconds.

- Now, resolving horizontally:

  $u = 30\cos 25°$, $a = 0$, $s = s$, $t = 2.700...$

  Using $s = ut + \frac{1}{2}at^2$:

  $$s = 30\cos 25° \times 2.700...$$
  $$= \boxed{73.4 \text{ m (3 s.f.)}}$$

c) Find the length of time the ball is at least 5 m above the ground.

- Resolving vertically, taking up as positive:

$$u = 30\sin 25°, \quad a = -9.8, \quad s = 3.5, \quad t = t$$

Using $s = ut + \frac{1}{2}at^2$:

$$3.5 = (30\sin 25° \times t) + (\frac{1}{2} \times -9.8 \times t^2)$$

$$4.9t^2 - (12.67...)t + 3.5 = 0$$

Using the quadratic formula:

$$t = \frac{12.67... \pm \sqrt{(-12.67...)^2 - (4 \times 4.9 \times 3.5)}}{9.8}$$

$$\Rightarrow t = 0.314... \quad \text{or} \quad t = 2.273...$$

Tip: Because the ball is thrown from 1.5 m above the ground, it only has to travel 3.5 m to reach a height of 5 m above ground level.

- So the ball is exactly 5 m above the ground 0.314... seconds after being thrown, and again 2.273... seconds after being thrown:

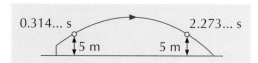

- The length of time that the ball is at least 5 m above the ground is therefore:

$$2.273... - 0.314... = \boxed{1.96 \text{ s (3 s.f.)}}$$

Example 5

A golf ball is struck from a point A on a horizontal plane. When the ball has moved a horizontal distance x, its height above the plane is y. The ball is modelled as a particle projected with initial speed u ms⁻¹ at an angle α above the horizontal.

a) Show that $y = x\tan\alpha - \dfrac{gx^2}{2u^2\cos^2\alpha}$.

- Resolving horizontally, taking right as positive:

$$u_x = u\cos\alpha, \quad a = 0, \quad s = x, \quad t = t$$

Using $s = ut + \frac{1}{2}at^2$:

$$x = u\cos\alpha \times t$$

Rearrange to make t the subject:

$$t = \frac{x}{u\cos\alpha} \quad \text{— call this equation ①}$$

- Resolving vertically, taking up as positive:

$$u_y = u\sin\alpha, \quad a = -g, \quad s = y, \quad t = t$$

Using $s = ut + \frac{1}{2}at^2$:

$$y = (u\sin\alpha \times t) - \frac{1}{2}gt^2 \quad \text{— call this equation ②}$$

Tip: It would be a massive pain to rearrange equation 2 to make t the subject, so you're better off doing it to equation 1.

- t is the same horizontally and vertically, so you can substitute equation ① into equation ② and eliminate t:

$$y = \left(u\sin\alpha \times \frac{x}{u\cos\alpha}\right) - \frac{1}{2}g\left(\frac{x}{u\cos\alpha}\right)^2$$

$$= x\frac{\sin\alpha}{\cos\alpha} - \frac{1}{2}g\left(\frac{x^2}{u^2\cos^2\alpha}\right)$$

$$= x\tan\alpha - \frac{gx^2}{2u^2\cos^2\alpha} \quad \text{— as required.}$$

Tip: t doesn't appear in the formula you're given in the question, so you know that's what you should be trying to eliminate.

b) **The ball just passes over the top of a 10 m tall tree, which is 45 m from A. Given that $\alpha = 45°$, find the speed of the ball as it passes over the tree.**

- First of all, you need to find the ball's initial speed, u.
- Using the result from part a), and substituting $x = 45$ m, $y = 10$ m and $\alpha = 45°$:

$$y = x\tan\alpha - \frac{gx^2}{2u^2\cos^2\alpha}$$

$$10 = 45\tan45° - \frac{9.8 \times 45^2}{2u^2 \times \cos^2 45°}$$

$$10 = 45 - \frac{19\,845}{u^2}$$

$$\frac{19\,845}{u^2} = 35$$

$$\Rightarrow u = 23.811... \text{ ms}^{-1}$$

Tip: Once you've found the ball's initial velocity, you can resolve horizontally and vertically and use the *uvast* equations as usual.

- So the ball was struck with initial speed 23.811... ms^{-1}, at an angle of 45° above the horizontal.

- Resolving horizontally, taking right as positive:
$$v_x = u_x = (23.811...)\cos45°$$
$$= 16.837... \text{ ms}^{-1}$$

Tip: Remember that the horizontal component of velocity stays constant throughout the motion — so v_x always equals u_x.

- Resolving vertically, taking up as positive:
$$u = (23.811...)\sin45° = 16.837..., \quad v = v_y, \quad a = -9.8, \quad s = 10$$
Using $v^2 = u^2 + 2as$:
$$v_y^2 = (16.837...)^2 + (2 \times -9.8 \times 10)$$
$$= 87.5 \text{ m}^2\text{s}^{-2}$$

Tip: Don't bother square rooting to find v_y — you'll need to use v_y^2 in the next step. And don't worry about the weird m^{2}s^{-2} units — it's just because the speed it squared, so the units should be squared too.

- Now you can find the speed using Pythagoras' theorem:
$$\text{speed} = \sqrt{(16.837...)^2 + 87.5}$$
$$= 19.3 \text{ ms}^{-1} \text{ (3 s.f.)}$$

Q1

A projectile is launched from a point on horizontal ground with speed 15 ms^{-1} at an angle of 50° above the horizontal. Find:
a) the time taken for the projectile to reach its maximum height,
b) the maximum height the projectile reaches above the ground.

Q2 A stone is catapulted with speed 12 ms^{-1} at an angle of 37° above the horizontal. It hits a target 0.5 seconds after being fired. Find:
a) the stone's horizontal displacement 0.5 seconds after being fired,
b) the stone's vertical displacement 0.5 seconds after being fired,
c) the straight-line distance from the stone's point of projection to the target.

Q3 A ball is kicked from a point on a flat, horizontal field. It has initial speed 8 ms^{-1} and leaves the ground at an angle of 59°. Find:
a) the ball's time of flight,
b) the horizontal range of the ball.

Q4 A particle is projected at an angle θ above the horizontal with speed 18 ms^{-1}. Given that $\tan\theta = \sqrt{3}$, find:
a) the particle's speed 2 seconds after being projected,
b) the direction of motion of the particle at this time.

Q5

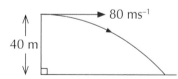

A bullet is fired horizontally at a speed of 80 ms^{-1} from the edge of a vertical cliff 40 m above sea level, as shown.
a) How long after being fired does the bullet hit the sea?
b) Find the horizontal distance from the bottom of the cliff to the point that the bullet hits the sea.

Q6

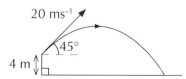

An object is fired from a point 4 m directly above flat, horizontal ground. It has initial speed 20 ms^{-1} at an angle of 45° above the horizontal. For how long is it higher than 11 m above the ground?

Q7

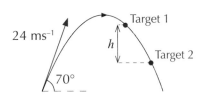

A ball is fired from a machine with speed 24 ms⁻¹ at an angle of 70° above the horizontal. The ball passes through a target 3 seconds after being fired, and then passes through a second target 4 seconds after being fired. Find h, the difference in height between the two targets.

Q8 A particle is projected from a point 0.6 m above flat, horizontal ground. The particle's initial speed is 7.5 ms⁻¹ at an angle of α above the horizontal. It reaches a maximum height of 2.8 m above the ground. Find the horizontal distance travelled by the particle in the first 1.2 seconds of its motion.

Q9 A ball is hit by a bat from a point on flat, horizontal ground. The ball leaves the ground with speed V ms⁻¹, at an angle of 56° above the horizontal. The ball lands a horizontal distance of 50 m away. Find the value of V.

Q10 Hint: Be careful with this one — the particle is fired at an angle below the horizontal.

Q10 A particle is fired from a point 16 m above flat, horizontal ground. The particle's initial speed is 3 ms⁻¹ at an angle of 7° below the horizontal. Find:
a) the horizontal range of the particle,
b) the speed and direction of the particle when it lands.

Q11 A golf ball is struck by a golf club from a point on flat, horizontal ground. It leaves the ground at an angle of 40° to the horizontal. 2 seconds after being struck, the ball is travelling upwards at an angle of 10° to the horizontal. Find:
a) the ball's speed of projection,
b) the height of the ball above the ground 2 seconds after being struck by the golf club.

Q12

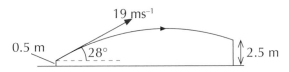

A cricket ball is hit from a point 0.5 m above flat, horizontal ground. The ball's initial speed is 19 ms⁻¹, at an angle of 28° above the horizontal. It is caught on its descent by a fielder when it is 2.5 m above the ground. Find:
a) the length of time that the ball is in the air,
b) the fielder's horizontal distance from the batsman,
c) the speed of the ball at the point where it is caught.

Q13 A body is projected from a point on flat, horizontal ground with speed U ms^{-1} at an angle θ above the horizontal. Show that:

a) the body reaches a maximum height of $\dfrac{U^2 \sin^2 \theta}{2g}$ metres above the ground,

b) the body reaches its maximum height $\dfrac{U \sin \theta}{g}$ seconds after it is projected.

Q14

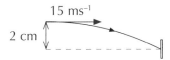

A dart is thrown horizontally towards a dartboard with speed 15 ms^{-1}. It hits the dartboard 2 cm vertically below the level at which it was thrown.

a) Find the horizontal distance from the point the dart is released to the dartboard.

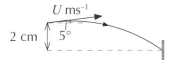

A second dart is thrown from the same point, but at an angle of 5° above the horizontal. It hits the dartboard at the same point as the first dart.

b) Find U, the speed that the second dart is thrown at.

Q15 A projectile is moving relative to the x- and y-coordinate axes. The projectile is fired from the origin with speed 3 ms^{-1}, at an angle α above the x-axis. The particle moves freely under gravity and passes through the point $(3, 1)$ m. Show that:

$$1 = 3 \tan \alpha - \frac{g}{2 \cos^2 \alpha}$$

Q16

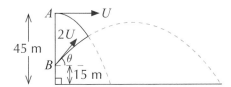

Particle A is projected horizontally from a point 45 m above ground level. At the same time, particle B is projected at an angle θ above the horizontal, from a point 15 m above ground level, directly below the point of projection of particle A.
The particles collide 2 seconds after they are projected.
Given that the speed of projection of B is twice the speed of projection of A, find:

a) the value of θ,

b) the speed of projection of each of the two particles.

i and j vectors

Tip: Remember, **i** and **j** are a pair of perpendicular vectors, each of magnitude one unit. **i** and **j** are directed horizontally and vertically respectively.

You can describe projectile motion in terms of the **unit vectors i** and **j**.

This isn't really all that different to any of the stuff from the last few pages — the **i**-component of the vector describes the **horizontal** motion of the projectile, and the **j**-component of the vector describes the **vertical** motion of the projectile.

When you're using **i** and **j** vectors to describe projectile motion, you can either consider horizontal and vertical motion **separately**, as before, or you can deal with both components in one go using the *uvast* equations in **vector form**:

Tip: $v^2 = u^2 + 2as$ doesn't have a vector equivalent, as you can't really square a vector.

$$\mathbf{v} = \mathbf{u} + \mathbf{a}t \qquad\qquad \mathbf{s} = \mathbf{u}t + \frac{1}{2}\mathbf{a}t^2$$

$$\mathbf{s} = \frac{1}{2}(\mathbf{u} + \mathbf{v})t \qquad\qquad \mathbf{s} = \mathbf{v}t - \frac{1}{2}\mathbf{a}t^2$$

If you're using the *uvast* equations in vector form, then acceleration will always be $\mathbf{a} = -9.8\mathbf{j}$ ms^{-2} — it has no horizontal component as acceleration due to gravity always acts vertically downwards.

Example 1

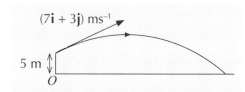

A particle is projected from the point 5**j** m, relative to a fixed origin *O*. The particle's initial velocity is (7**i** + 3**j**) ms^{-1}, and it moves freely under gravity.

a) Find the position vector of the particle 0.8 seconds after it is projected.

- Write down the *uvast* values:
  $$\mathbf{u} = (7\mathbf{i} + 3\mathbf{j}), \qquad \mathbf{a} = -9.8\mathbf{j}, \qquad \mathbf{s} = \mathbf{s}, \qquad t = 0.8$$

- Using $\mathbf{s} = \mathbf{u}t + \frac{1}{2}\mathbf{a}t^2$:
  $$\mathbf{s} = 0.8(7\mathbf{i} + 3\mathbf{j}) - \frac{1}{2} \times (9.8\mathbf{j}) \times 0.8^2$$
  $$= 5.6\mathbf{i} + 2.4\mathbf{j} - 3.136\mathbf{j}$$
  $$= (5.6\mathbf{i} - 0.736\mathbf{j}) \text{ m}$$

- This is the particle's displacement from the point of projection 0.8 seconds after it is projected. Add this to its initial position vector to find its new position vector:
  $$5\mathbf{j} + 5.6\mathbf{i} - 0.736\mathbf{j} = (5.6\mathbf{i} + 4.264\mathbf{j}) \text{ m}$$

b) Find the velocity of the particle at this time.

- Using $\mathbf{v} = \mathbf{u} + \mathbf{a}t$:
  $$\mathbf{v} = (7\mathbf{i} + 3\mathbf{j}) + 0.8(-9.8\mathbf{j})$$
  $$= 7\mathbf{i} + 3\mathbf{j} - 7.84\mathbf{j}$$
  $$= (7\mathbf{i} - 4.84\mathbf{j}) \text{ ms}^{-1}$$

Example 2

A stone is thrown from a point 1.2 metres vertically above the point O, which is on flat, horizontal ground. The stone is thrown with velocity $(2q\mathbf{i} + q\mathbf{j})$ ms⁻¹, where q is a constant. It travels freely under gravity for 4 seconds, before landing on the ground.

a) **Find the value of q and hence the initial speed of the stone.**

- Resolving vertically, taking up as positive:

$$u = q, \quad a = -9.8, \quad s = -1.2, \quad t = 4$$

Using $s = ut + \frac{1}{2}at^2$:

$$-1.2 = 4q + (-4.9 \times 4^2)$$

$$4q = 77.2$$

$$\Rightarrow \boxed{q = 19.3}$$

- So the stone's initial velocity is $(38.6\mathbf{i} + 19.3\mathbf{j})$ ms⁻¹.
  Now you can find its initial speed using Pythagoras' theorem:

$$\text{speed} = \sqrt{38.6^2 + 19.3^2}$$

$$= \boxed{43.2 \text{ ms}^{-1}} \text{ (3 s.f.)}$$

> **Tip:** An initial velocity of $(2q\mathbf{i} + q\mathbf{j})$ ms⁻¹ means that the horizontal component of velocity is $2q$ ms⁻¹ and the vertical component is q ms⁻¹.

b) **Find the horizontal range of the stone.**

- Resolving horizontally, taking right as positive:

$$u = 38.6, \quad a = 0, \quad s = s, \quad t = 4$$

Using $s = ut + \frac{1}{2}at^2$:

$$s = 38.6 \times 4 = \boxed{154.4 \text{ m}}$$

c) **Find the position vector of the stone relative to O when it is at its highest point.**

- First consider only the vertical motion to find the time taken for the stone to reach its maximum height. Resolving vertically, taking up as positive:

$$u = 19.3, \quad v = 0, \quad a = -9.8, \quad t = t$$

Using $v = u + at$:

$$0 = 19.3 - 9.8t$$

$$\Rightarrow t = 1.969... \text{ seconds}$$

- Now consider the horizontal and vertical components of motion together using the *uvast* equations in vector form:

$$\mathbf{u} = (38.6\mathbf{i} + 19.3\mathbf{j}), \quad \mathbf{a} = -9.8\mathbf{j}, \quad \mathbf{s} = \mathbf{s}, \quad t = 1.969...$$

Using $\mathbf{s} = \mathbf{u}t + \frac{1}{2}\mathbf{a}t^2$:

$$\mathbf{s} = (1.969...)(38.6\mathbf{i} + 19.3\mathbf{j}) + (1.969...^2)(-4.9\mathbf{j})$$

$$= 76.01...\mathbf{i} + 38.00...\mathbf{j} - 19.00...\mathbf{j}$$

$$= (76.01...\mathbf{i} + 19.00...\mathbf{j}) \text{ m}$$

> **Tip:** You could just find the stone's horizontal and vertical displacements separately, then write it in vector form at the end.

- This is the stone's displacement from its starting point when it reaches its highest point. Add it to the stone's initial position vector to find its new position vector:

$$1.2\mathbf{j} + 76.01...\mathbf{i} + 19.00...\mathbf{j} = 76.01...\mathbf{i} + 20.20...\mathbf{j}$$

$$= \boxed{(76.0\mathbf{i} + 20.2\mathbf{j}) \text{ m}} \text{ (3 s.f.)}$$

Q1 A particle is projected from a point on flat, horizontal ground with velocity $(12\mathbf{i} + 16\mathbf{j})$ ms^{-1}. Find the particle's velocity:

a) 2 seconds after projection,

b) when it reaches its maximum height,

c) when it hits the ground.

Q2 A projectile is fired from a height of 5 m directly above a fixed point O, which is on flat, horizontal ground. The particle's initial velocity is $(17\mathbf{i} + 10\mathbf{j})$ ms^{-1}. Find:

a) the particle's maximum height above the ground,

b) the speed of the particle as it hits the ground,

c) the direction of motion of the particle when it hits the ground.

Q3 A stone is thrown with velocity $(6\mathbf{i} + 9\mathbf{j})$ ms^{-1} from a window 2.5 m vertically above flat, horizontal ground. It is aimed towards a target on the ground, a horizontal distance of 20 m from the window. Find:

a) the length of time that the stone is at least 6 m above the ground,

b) the distance by which the stone falls short of the target.

Q4 A golf ball is hit off the edge of a 40 m high vertical cliff with velocity $(a\mathbf{i} + b\mathbf{j})$ ms^{-1}, where a and b are constants. It takes 5 seconds to land on the ground below, level with the foot of the cliff, a horizontal distance of 200 m away. Find:

a) the values of a and b,

b) the velocity of the golf ball when it hits the ground.

Q5

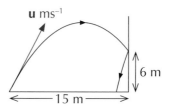

A football is kicked from a point on flat, horizontal ground towards a vertical wall, a horizontal distance of 15 m away. The ball's initial velocity is $\mathbf{u}$ ms^{-1}. The ball hits the wall 6 m above the ground, 3 seconds after being kicked. Find, as vectors in $\mathbf{i} + \mathbf{j}$ notation:

a) the initial velocity of the ball,

b) the velocity of the ball as it hits the wall.

The ball rebounds from the wall and lands on the ground. As a result of the impact with the wall, the horizontal component of the ball's velocity is reversed and halved in magnitude. The vertical component of its velocity is unaffected by the impact.

c) Find the horizontal distance between the wall and the point on the ground where the ball lands.

2. Variable Acceleration in 1 Dimension

Learning Objectives:

- Be able to find a body's displacement at a particular time given an expression for its velocity or acceleration.
- Be able to find a body's velocity at a particular time given an expression for its displacement or acceleration.
- Be able to find a body's acceleration at a particular time given an expression for its velocity or displacement.

As you know, you can use the uvast equations to describe the motion of a body which is moving with constant acceleration.

However, in M2, you'll also need to be able to describe the motion of a body that is moving with acceleration that varies with time.

To do this, you'll need to use calculus — given an expression for the motion of an body in terms of time, t, you can differentiate or integrate the expression to find out more information.

Differentiating to find velocity and acceleration

Differentiating to find velocity

- You should remember from M1 that a body's **velocity** is the **rate of change** of its **displacement** from a particular point with respect to **time**.
- You should also remember from C1 that to find the **rate of change** of one quantity with respect to another, you can use **differentiation**.
- So if you are given an expression for a body's **displacement** from a particular point **as a function of time**, t, you can find an expression for that body's **velocity** by **differentiating** with respect to time.

Differentiating to find acceleration

- Similarly, a body's **acceleration** is the **rate of change** of its **velocity** with respect to **time**.
- Therefore, if you are given an expression for a body's **velocity** in terms of **time**, t, then you can find an expression for its **acceleration** by **differentiating** with respect to time.
- To find an expression for a body's **acceleration** given an expression for its **displacement**, just **differentiate twice** with respect to time.

Tip: You can also think of this graphically — the gradient of a displacement-time graph gives a body's velocity, and the gradient of a velocity-time graph gives a body's acceleration. To find the gradient of a graph at a particular point, you differentiate.

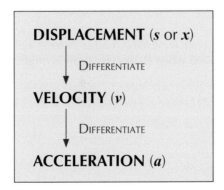

Remember that displacement, velocity and acceleration are **vector quantities**, so the **direction** of motion is important. If the motion is in a straight line, then it's a good idea to choose which direction is **positive**, then any motion in the **opposite direction** will be **negative**.

Tip: You'll often be told that a body is 'moving along the x-axis in the direction of x increasing' — so it makes sense to take this direction as positive.

Example 1

At time $t = 0$, a particle of mass 5 kg leaves the origin and moves along the x-axis in the direction of x increasing. At time t seconds, its displacement from its starting point is given by $x = (7t - 2t^3)$ m.

a) Find the particle's velocity at time $t = 3$ seconds.

- Differentiate the expression for displacement with respect to time:
$$v = \frac{dx}{dt} = (7 - 6t^2) \text{ ms}^{-1}$$

- Substitute $t = 3$ into the expression for velocity:
$$v = 7 - (6 \times 3^2) = -47 \text{ ms}^{-1}$$

Tip: The particle's velocity is negative at time $t = 3$ seconds because it is moving in the negative direction — i.e. in the direction of x decreasing.

b) Find the time after the particle leaves the origin when it is momentarily at rest.

- When the particle is at rest, $v = 0 \text{ ms}^{-1}$:
$$7 - 6t^2 = 0$$
$$t^2 = 7 \div 6 = 1.166...$$
$$\Rightarrow t = 1.08 \text{ s (3 s.f.)}$$

c) Find the resultant force acting on the particle at time $t = 2$ seconds.

- Differentiate the expression for velocity with respect to time:
$$a = \frac{dv}{dt} = -12t \text{ ms}^{-2}$$

Tip: The examiners will assume you remember everything from M1, like Newton's second law: $F_{net} = ma$, which you need to use here.

- Substitute $t = 2$ into the expression for acceleration:
$$a = -12 \times 2 = -24 \text{ ms}^{-2}$$

- Now use $F_{net} = ma$ to find the resultant force acting on the particle:
$$F_{net} = 5 \times -24 = -120 \text{ N}$$

Example 2

At time t seconds, a particle of mass 5 kg is moving at $(-t^2 + 5t - 2)$ ms^{-1}. Find the particle's speed when its acceleration is momentarily zero.

Tip: You can also answer this question graphically. The particle's velocity forms an n-shaped quadratic curve, and acceleration will be zero at the curve's turning point. You can find the location of the turning point by completing the square.

- Differentiate the expression for velocity with respect to time, then make the resulting expression equal to zero:
$$a = \frac{dv}{dt} = (-2t + 5) \text{ ms}^{-2}$$
$$-2t + 5 = 0$$
$$\Rightarrow t = 2.5 \text{ seconds}$$

- So its acceleration is zero at time $t = 2.5$ seconds. Using the expression for velocity, its speed at this time is:
$$-(2.5)^2 + 5(2.5) - 2 = 4.25 \text{ ms}^{-1}$$

Q1 A particle moves in a straight line along the x-axis in the direction of x increasing. At time t seconds, the particle's displacement from the origin is given by $x = (3t^3 + 5t^2)$ m. Find:

a) an expression for the particle's velocity in terms of t,

b) an expression for the particle's acceleration in terms of t,

c) the particle's mass, given that the resultant force acting on the particle is 480 N when $t = 3$.

Q2 A body moves in a straight line in the direction of the positive x-axis. At time t seconds, the body's displacement from the origin is given by $x = (bt^2 + 6t)$ m, where b is a constant. At time $t = 3$ seconds, its velocity is 18 ms^{-1}.

a) Calculate the value of b.

b) Show that the body is moving with constant acceleration.

Q3 An object moves in a straight line. At time t seconds, its displacement from its starting point is given by $s = (2t^3 - 21t^2 + 60t)$ m. Find:

a) an expression for the object's velocity at time t seconds,

b) the times that the object is momentarily at rest,

c) an expression for the object's acceleration at time t seconds,

d) the object's initial acceleration.

Q4 A particle of mass 1.4 kg moves in a straight line along the x-axis. At time t seconds, the x-coordinate of its position is given by $x = 12t^2 + 60t - t^3$. Find:

a) the particle's initial position,

b) the time that the particle is moving with zero acceleration,

c) the resultant force acting on the particle at time $t = 0.5$ seconds,

d) the particle's maximum positive displacement from the origin.

Q4 d) Hint: The particle will stop momentarily when it reaches its maximum positive displacement from the origin (assuming that it does reach a maximum displacement, and doesn't just carry on in that direction forever).

Q5 A vehicle is travelling along a straight track. At time t hours, its displacement from its initial point is given by $s = (12t - 15t^2 + 4t^3)$ km.

a) Find the times that the vehicle is momentarily at rest.

b) Find the distance travelled by the vehicle between these times.

Q6 A train travels along a straight track between two stations. The train is at rest at both of these stations, and is moving at all times on the journey between the stations. At time t hours, the train's distance from the first station is given by $s = (90t^2 - 45t^3)$ km. Find:

a) the time taken to travel between the two stations,

b) the distance between the two stations,

c) the maximum speed the train reaches in travelling between the two stations.

Integrating to find velocity and displacement

Tip: Again, you can think of this graphically. The area under an acceleration-time graph gives a body's velocity, and the area under a velocity-time graph gives a body's displacement from a particular point. To find the area under a graph, you integrate.

To 'go back the other way', you have to **integrate**:

- Given an expression for a body's **acceleration** in terms of t, you can find its **velocity** at time t by **integrating** with respect to time.
- Similarly, given an expression for a body's **velocity**, you can find its **displacement** from a particular point at time t by **integrating** with respect to time.
- To find a body's **displacement** from a particular point given an expression for its **acceleration**, just **integrate twice** with respect to time.
- When you're integrating, don't forget to add a **constant**. Often, you'll be given enough information in the question to find the value of the constant.

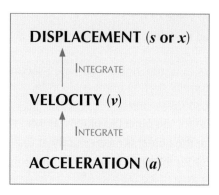

Example 1

A particle is moving in a straight line in the direction of the positive x-axis. At time t seconds, the particle's acceleration is given by $a = (26 - 12t)$ ms^{-2}. At time $t = 4$ seconds, the particle passes through the point where $x = 80$ m with velocity 12 ms^{-1}.

a) Find an expression for the particle's velocity at time t seconds.

Tip: Remember:
$$\int x^n \, dx = \frac{x^{(n+1)}}{n+1} + C$$

- Integrate the expression for acceleration with respect to time to find an expression for the particle's velocity:
$$v = \int a \, dt$$
$$= 26t - 6t^2 + C$$

Tip: Use information given in the question to find the values of the constants.

- When $t = 4$, $v = 12$, so:
$$12 = 26(4) - 6(4)^2 + C$$
$$\Rightarrow C = 4$$

- So the particle's velocity at time t is given by:
$$v = (26t - 6t^2 + 4) \text{ ms}^{-1}.$$

b) Find the particle's displacement from the origin at time $t = 5$ seconds.

- Integrate the expression for velocity with respect to time to find an expression for the particle's displacement:

$$x = \int v \, dt$$
$$= 13t^2 - 2t^3 + 4t + D$$

Tip: You've already used the letter C to represent the constant of integration in part a), so this time use another letter — I've used D.

- When $t = 4$, $x = 80$, so:

$$80 = 13(4)^2 - 2(4)^3 + 4(4) + D$$
$$\Rightarrow D = -16$$

- So the particle's displacement from the origin at time t is given by $x = (13t^2 - 2t^3 + 4t - 16)$ m.

- Therefore, at time $t = 5$ seconds:

$$x = 13(5)^2 - 2(5)^3 + 4(5) - 16$$
$$= \boxed{79 \text{ m}}$$

Example 2

A particle is moving in a straight line along the x-axis. At time $t = 0$, the particle passes through the origin, O. The particle's velocity at time t seconds is given by $v = (12 - t^2)$ ms^{-1}, measured in the direction of x increasing. Find the time taken for the particle to return to O.

- Integrate the expression for velocity with respect to time to find the particle's displacement from O:

$$x = \int v \, dt$$
$$= 12t - \frac{t^3}{3} + C$$

- The particle passes through the origin at $t = 0$, so at $t = 0$, $x = 0$:

$$0 = 12(0) - \frac{0^3}{3} + C$$
$$\Rightarrow C = 0$$

- So the particle's displacement from O at time t is given by:

$$x = (12t - \frac{t^3}{3}) \text{ m}.$$

- When the particle is at O, $x = 0$ m:

$$12t - \frac{t^3}{3} = 0$$
$$36t - t^3 = 0$$
$$t(36 - t^2) = 0$$
$$t(6 - t)(6 + t) = 0$$
$$\Rightarrow t = 0, t = 6 \text{ or } t = -6$$

Tip: $t = 0$ is the time that the particle initially passes through O, and $t = -6$ can be ignored because you're looking for a positive time. So the correct solution must be $t = 6$.

- So the particle takes $\boxed{6 \text{ seconds}}$ to return to O.

Q1 A particle is travelling in a straight line along the x-axis in the direction of x increasing. At time $t = 0$, the particle passes through the origin, O, with a velocity of 10 ms^{-1}. The particle moves with constant acceleration 5 ms^{-2}. Find:

    a) (i)   an expression for the particle's velocity in terms of t,

        (ii) the particle's velocity 6 seconds after it passes through O,

    b) (i)   an expression for the particle's displacement from O in terms of t,

        (ii) the particle's displacement from O 6 seconds after it passes through O.

Q2 An object is travelling in a straight line. At time t seconds, its velocity is given by $v = (3t^2 - 14t + 8)$ ms^{-1}. When $t = 1$, the object's displacement from its initial position is 8 m. Find:

    a) an expression for the object's displacement from its initial position in terms of t,

    b) the times that the object is instantaneously at rest,

    c) the distance between the two points that the object is instantaneously at rest.

Q3 A particle is travelling in a straight line in the direction of the positive x-axis. At time $t = 0$, the particle passes through the origin with velocity 6 ms^{-1}. The particle's acceleration at time t seconds is given by $a = (2t - 6)$ ms^{-2}. Find:

    a) an expression for the particle's velocity at time t seconds,

    b) an expression for the particle's displacement from the origin at time t seconds,

    c) the times that the particle passes through the origin for $t > 0$.

Q4 At time $t = 0$, an object sets off from rest at the origin, O, and travels along the x-axis. At time t seconds, the object is accelerating at a rate of $(2t - 4)$ ms^{-2}. Find:

    a) the object's velocity 5 seconds after it leaves O,

    b) the x-coordinate of the object's position 5 seconds after it leaves O,

    c) the value of t at which the object reverses its direction,

    d) the value of t at which the object returns to O.

Q5 A particle is travelling in a straight line in the direction of the positive x-axis. At time t seconds, the particle's acceleration is given by $a = (k - 18t^2)$ ms^{-2}, where k is a constant. At time $t = 0$, the particle passes through the origin, O, with velocity 7 ms^{-1}. One second later, the particle passes through the point Q with velocity 9 ms^{-1}. Find:

    a) the value of k,

    b) the distance of the point Q from O.

Motion described by multiple expressions

The motion of a body can sometimes be defined by **different expressions** for **different time intervals**.

This means that you'll have to deal with each time interval **separately** when you're differentiating or integrating.

Example 1

A particle sets off from the origin at time $t = 0$ and moves in a straight line along the x-axis in the direction of x increasing. The particle's velocity t seconds after leaving the origin is v ms^{-1}, where v is given by:

$$v = \begin{cases} 2t - \dfrac{t^2}{4} & 0 \leqslant t \leqslant 6 \\[2mm] 21 - 3t & t > 6 \end{cases}$$

a) **Find the particle's displacement from the origin when $t = 6$.**

- Integrate the expression for velocity with respect to time in the time interval $0 \leq t \leq 6$:

$$x = \int v \, dt = \int \left(2t - \frac{t^2}{4} \right) dt$$

$$= t^2 - \frac{t^3}{12} + C \qquad 0 \leq t \leq 6$$

> **Tip:** Make sure you read the question carefully, so you know which time interval to use in your calculations.

- When $t = 0$, the particle is at the origin (i.e. $x = 0$):

$$0 = 0^2 - \frac{0^3}{12} + C$$

$$\Rightarrow C = 0$$

- So the particle's displacement from the origin at time t is given by $x = t^2 - \dfrac{t^3}{12}$ for $0 \leq t \leq 6$. Substituting $t = 6$ into this equation:

$$x = 6^2 - \frac{6^3}{12} = \boxed{18 \text{ m}}$$

b) **Find the particle's maximum speed in the interval $0 \leq t \leq 6$.**

- The equation for the particle's velocity in the interval $0 \leq t \leq 6$ forms an n-shaped quadratic curve.
- The particle's maximum speed in this interval could either be at the curve's turning point (if it is in this interval), or at one of the boundaries of the interval (at $t = 0$ or $t = 6$).
- First check the turning point. This is the point where $a = 0$.

$$a = 2 - \frac{t}{2} \text{ for } 0 \leq t \leq 6$$

$$2 - \frac{t}{2} = 0 \Rightarrow t = 4$$

- So acceleration is zero when $t = 4$. Substitute this into the equation for velocity to find the particle's speed at this time:

$$v = 2(4) - \frac{4^2}{4} = 4 \text{ ms}^{-1}$$

> **Tip:** The quadratic's turning point represents the particle's maximum positive velocity. However, speed is a scalar, so a large negative value of v is a high speed, which means you need to check the boundaries of the interval to see if the magnitude of the largest negative velocity in the given interval is greater than the maximum positive velocity.

- Now check the boundaries:

$$\text{When } t = 0, v = 2(0) - \frac{0^2}{4} = 0 \text{ ms}^{-1}$$

$$\text{When } t = 6, v = 2(6) - \frac{6^2}{4} = 3 \text{ ms}^{-1}$$

- Therefore, the particle's maximum speed in the interval $0 \le t \le 6$ occurs when $t = 4$, and is $\boxed{4 \text{ ms}^{-1}}$.

At some time $t > 6$, the particle reaches A, the point of maximum positive displacement from the origin. From A, the particle begins to move in a straight line along the x-axis back towards the origin.

c) Find the distance of A from the origin.

- Integrate the expression for velocity with respect to time in the time interval $t > 6$:

$$x = \int v \, dt = \int (21 - 3t) \, dt$$

$$= 21t - \frac{3}{2}t^2 + D \qquad t > 6$$

Tip: Use $t = 6$, $x = 18$ as your initial condition to find D — even though 6 isn't in the interval $t > 6$, it is still the lower limit of the interval.

- From part a), when $t = 6$, $x = 18$. So:

$$18 = 21(6) - \frac{3}{2}(6^2) + D \implies D = -54$$

- So the particle's displacement from the origin at time t is given by $x = 21t - \frac{3}{2}t^2 - 54$ for $t > 6$.

Tip: You're told in the question that the particle changes direction at A.

- The particle changes direction at A, so will be momentarily at rest (i.e. v will be 0). The question states that this is when $t > 6$, so:

$$v = 0 = 21 - 3t \implies t = 7 \text{ seconds}$$

- So the distance of A from the origin is the distance the particle has travelled after 7 seconds:

$$x = 21(7) - \frac{3}{2}(7^2) - 54 = \boxed{19.5 \text{ m}}$$

Example 2

A particle is moving in a straight line along the x-axis in the direction of x increasing. At time $t = 0$, the particle passes through the origin, O. The particle's velocity at time t seconds is v ms^{-1}, where v is given by:

$$v = \begin{cases} 6t + 6 & 0 \le t \le 5 \\ \\ 21 + 18t - 3t^2 & t > 5 \end{cases}$$

a) Find the time when the particle is instantaneously at rest.

- When the particle is at rest, velocity will be zero. So, for $0 \le t \le 5$:

$$6t + 6 = 0 \implies t = -1$$

- $t = -1$ isn't in the range $0 \le t \le 5$, so the particle doesn't change direction in the interval $0 \le t \le 5$.

- For $t > 5$:

$$21 + 18t - 3t^2 = 0$$
$$t^2 - 6t - 7 = 0 \longleftarrow \boxed{\text{Dividing throughout by } -3, \text{ and rearranging.}}$$
$$(t - 7)(t + 1) = 0$$
$$\Rightarrow t = 7 \text{ or } t = -1$$

- Again, you can't have a negative time, so the particle changes direction at time $t = 7$ seconds.

b) Find the total distance travelled by the particle at time $t = 10$ seconds.

Tip: You can use the limits $t = 0$ and $t = 5$ to form a definite integral. Or, if you prefer, you could just do an indefinite integral and use the given values to find the constant of integration as usual.

- Consider the motion for $0 \leq t \leq 5$.
  Integrate the expression for velocity with respect to time to find the particle's displacement from O at time $t = 5$ seconds:

$$x = \int_0^5 v \, dt = \int_0^5 (6t + 6) \, dt = [3t^2 + 6t]_0^5$$
$$= [3(5)^2 + 6(5)] - [3(0)^2 + 6(0)] = 105$$

- So the particle's displacement from O at time $t = 5$ seconds is 105 m.

- Now consider the motion for $t > 5$.
  Integrate the expression for velocity with respect to time to find the particle's displacement from O for $t > 5$:

$$x = \int v \, dt = \int (21 + 18t - 3t^2) \, dt$$
$$= 21t + 9t^2 - t^3 + D \qquad t > 5$$

Tip: Even though $t = 10$ is in the time interval $t > 5$, you still need to consider the motion for $0 \leq t \leq 5$ first so you can find the value of x at $t = 5$, which you can then use to find the constant of integration in the next step.

- At time $t = 5$, $x = 105$ m, so:

$$105 = 21(5) + 9(5)^2 - 5^3 + D$$
$$\Rightarrow D = -100$$

- So $x = 21t + 9t^2 - t^3 - 100$ for $t > 5$.

- From part a), the particle changes direction at time $t = 7$ seconds. So consider the particle's displacement from O at time $t = 7$ s and $t = 10$ s separately.

- The particle's displacement from O at time $t = 7$ seconds is:

$$x = 21(7) + 9(7)^2 - 7^3 - 100 = 145 \text{ m}$$

- And its displacement from O at time $t = 10$ seconds is:

$$x = 21(10) + 9(10)^2 - 10^3 - 100 = 10 \text{ m}$$

- So from $t = 0$ seconds to $t = 7$ seconds, the particle travels 145 m. From $t = 7$ seconds to $t = 10$ seconds, the particle travels 145 m – 10 m = 135 m back towards O.

- So the total distance travelled by the particle is:

$$145 \text{ m} + 135 \text{ m} = \boxed{280 \text{ m}}$$

Q1   A particle moves in a straight line along the x-axis.
At time t seconds, the particle's velocity is v ms^{-1}, where v is given by:

$$v = \begin{cases} 6t - 9t^2 & 0 \leq t \leq 5 \\ \dfrac{625}{t^3} - 200 & t > 5 \end{cases}$$

Q1 Hint: Remember:
$$\dfrac{a}{x^b} = ax^{-b}.$$

When $t = 0$, the particle is at the origin. Find:
a) the particle's displacement from the origin when $t = 5$,
b) the particle's displacement from the origin when $t = 10$.

Q2   A body moves in a straight line along the x-axis in the direction
of x increasing. At time $t = 0$, the body is at the origin.
At time t s, the body's acceleration is a ms^{-2}, where a is given by:

$$a = \begin{cases} 4t & 0 \leq t \leq 3 \\ 18 - 2t & t > 3 \end{cases}$$

When $t = 2$, the body's velocity is 8 ms^{-1}.
a) Find the body's velocity:
    (i) when $t = 3$,   (ii) when $t = 5$.
b) Find the maximum speed of the body.
c) Show that the body returns to the origin T seconds after setting off,
    where T is a solution of the equation $T^3 - 27T^2 + 81T - 81 = 0$.

Q3   An object moves in a straight line along the x-axis. At time t seconds,
the object's displacement from the origin is x m, where x is given by:

$$x = \begin{cases} 2t^2 + t + 40 & 0 \leq t \leq 2 \\ t^3 - 12t^2 + 45t & t > 2 \end{cases}$$

a) Find two expressions for the object's velocity in terms of t.
b) Find the distance between the two points
    where the object is momentarily at rest.
c) Find the object's speed when its acceleration
    is instantaneously zero.

Q4   At time $t = 0$, a particle leaves the origin and moves in a straight
line along the x-axis in the direction of x increasing.
Its velocity at time t seconds is v ms^{-1}, where v is given by:

$$v = \begin{cases} 5t - t^2 & 0 \leq t \leq 3 \\ 12 - 2t & t > 3 \end{cases}$$

a) Find the time at which the particle reverses direction.
b) Find the particle's displacement from the origin at time $t = 3$ s.
c) Find the total distance travelled by the particle
    between the times $t = 0$ and $t = 8$ seconds.

3. Variable Acceleration in 2 Dimensions

Using calculus to find expressions describing the motion of a body works pretty much the same when the body is moving in two dimensions. The only difference is that the expressions will be written in vector form, so you'll have to be able to differentiate and integrate vectors.

Using vectors

- When you've got a body moving in **two dimensions** (i.e. in a **plane**), you can describe its **position**, **velocity** and **acceleration** using the **unit vectors i** and **j**.
- The **i**-component describes the body's **horizontal** motion, and the **j**-component usually describes the body's **vertical** motion.
- You've already seen how to use the *uvast* equations in vector form, but, just like in one dimension, if the body is moving with **variable acceleration**, you'll have to use **calculus** instead.
- The relationships between **displacement** (or **position**), **velocity** and **acceleration** are just the same as on pages 15-24:

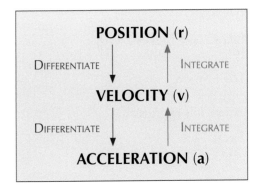

Tip: In two dimensions, it's more usual to refer to a body's <u>position vector</u>. This is just the vector describing the body's displacement from the origin.

- To differentiate or integrate vectors written in **i** and **j** notation, just differentiate or integrate each component **separately**:

Differentiating Vectors

If $\mathbf{r} = x\mathbf{i} + y\mathbf{j}$ is the position vector of a body, then:

the body's velocity, $\mathbf{v} = \dfrac{d\mathbf{r}}{dt} = \dfrac{dx}{dt}\mathbf{i} + \dfrac{dy}{dt}\mathbf{j}$

and the body's acceleration, $\mathbf{a} = \dfrac{d\mathbf{v}}{dt} = \dfrac{d^2\mathbf{r}}{dt^2}$

$$= \dfrac{d^2x}{dt^2}\mathbf{i} + \dfrac{d^2y}{dt^2}\mathbf{j}$$

Tip: The shorthand for $\dfrac{d\mathbf{r}}{dt}$ is $\dot{\mathbf{r}}$ (the single dot means differentiate **r** once with respect to time). The shorthand for $\dfrac{d^2\mathbf{r}}{dt^2}$ is $\ddot{\mathbf{r}}$ (the double dots mean differentiate **r** twice with respect to time).

Integrating Vectors

If $\mathbf{a} = p\mathbf{i} + q\mathbf{j}$ is the acceleration of a body, then:

the body's velocity, $\mathbf{v} = \int \mathbf{a} \, dt = \int (p\mathbf{i} + q\mathbf{j}) \, dt$

$$= \left(\int p \, dt \right)\mathbf{i} + \left(\int q \, dt \right)\mathbf{j}$$

If $\mathbf{v} = w\mathbf{i} + z\mathbf{j}$ is the velocity of a body, then:

the body's position vector, $\mathbf{r} = \int \mathbf{v} \, dt = \int (w\mathbf{i} + z\mathbf{j}) \, dt$

$$= \left(\int w \, dt \right)\mathbf{i} + \left(\int z \, dt \right)\mathbf{j}$$

Tip: When you're integrating, you'll still need to add a constant of integration, **C**, but it will be a vector with **i** and **j** components.

Example 1

A particle is moving in a plane. At time t seconds, its position in the plane is given by r = $[(t^2 - 1)\mathbf{i} + (2 + 5t)\mathbf{j}]$ m relative to a fixed origin O. Find the particle's speed and direction of motion at time t = 7.5 seconds.

- Differentiate the expression for the particle's position vector to find its velocity. Remember to treat the **i** and **j** components separately:

$$\mathbf{v} = \frac{d\mathbf{r}}{dt} = \left[\frac{d}{dt}(t^2 - 1) \right]\mathbf{i} + \left[\frac{d}{dt}(2 + 5t) \right]\mathbf{j}$$

$$= [2t\mathbf{i} + 5\mathbf{j}] \text{ ms}^{-1}$$

- Substitute t = 7.5 into this expression:

$$\mathbf{v} = 2(7.5)\mathbf{i} + 5\mathbf{j}$$

$$= (15\mathbf{i} + 5\mathbf{j}) \text{ m}$$

- Use the **i** and **j** components to draw a right-angled triangle:

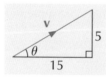

- Now use Pythagoras' theorem to find the particle's speed, and trigonometry to find its direction of motion:

$$\text{speed} = |\mathbf{v}| = \sqrt{15^2 + 5^2}$$

$$= 15.8 \text{ ms}^{-1} \text{ (3 s.f.)}$$

$$\theta = \tan^{-1}\left(\frac{5}{15} \right)$$

$$= 18.4° \text{ (3 s.f.) above } \mathbf{i}$$

Example 2

A particle is moving in a vertical plane so that at time t seconds it has velocity v ms^{-1}, where $v = (8 + 2t)\mathbf{i} + (t^3 - 6t)\mathbf{j}$. When $t = 2$, the particle has position vector $(10\mathbf{i} + 3\mathbf{j})$ m with respect to a fixed origin O.

a) **Find the acceleration of the particle at time t.**

- Differentiate the expression for velocity with respect to time:

$$\mathbf{a} = \frac{d\mathbf{v}}{dt} = \left[\frac{d}{dt}(8 + 2t)\right]\mathbf{i} + \left[\frac{d}{dt}(t^3 - 6t)\right]\mathbf{j}$$

$$= [2\mathbf{i} + (3t^2 - 6)\mathbf{j}]\text{ ms}^{-2}$$

b) **Show that the position vector of the particle when $t = 4$ is $\mathbf{r} = (38\mathbf{i} + 27\mathbf{j})$ m.**

- Integrate the expression for velocity with respect to time:

$$\mathbf{r} = \int \mathbf{v}\, dt = \left(\int (8 + 2t)\, dt\right)\mathbf{i} + \left(\int (t^3 - 6t)\, dt\right)\mathbf{j}$$

$$= (8t + t^2)\mathbf{i} + \left(\frac{t^4}{4} - 3t^2\right)\mathbf{j} + \mathbf{C}$$

- When $t = 2$, $\mathbf{r} = (10\mathbf{i} + 3\mathbf{j})$. Use these values to find $\mathbf{C}$:

$$10\mathbf{i} + 3\mathbf{j} = (8(2) + 2^2)\mathbf{i} + \left(\frac{2^4}{4} - 3(2)^2\right)\mathbf{j} + \mathbf{C}$$

$$10\mathbf{i} + 3\mathbf{j} = 20\mathbf{i} - 8\mathbf{j} + \mathbf{C}$$

$$\Rightarrow \mathbf{C} = (10 - 20)\mathbf{i} + (3 - -8)\mathbf{j}$$

$$= -10\mathbf{i} + 11\mathbf{j}$$

> **Tip:** To find $\mathbf{C}$, collect $\mathbf{i}$ and $\mathbf{j}$ terms, and add or subtract to simplify.

$$\Rightarrow \mathbf{r} = \left[(8t + t^2 - 10)\mathbf{i} + \left(\frac{t^4}{4} - 3t^2 + 11\right)\mathbf{j}\right] \text{m}$$

- Substitute $t = 4$ into the equation:

$$\mathbf{r} = (8(4) + (4)^2 - 10)\mathbf{i} + \left(\frac{4^4}{4} - 3(4)^2 + 11\right)\mathbf{j}$$

$$= (32 + 16 - 10)\mathbf{i} + (64 - 48 + 11)\mathbf{j}$$

$$= (38\mathbf{i} + 27\mathbf{j})\text{ m} \quad \text{— as required.}$$

c) **Find the value of t for which the particle is directly above O.**

- When the particle is directly above O, the $\mathbf{i}$-component of its position vector will be zero:

$$8t + t^2 - 10 = 0$$

- Solve for t using the quadratic formula:

$$t = \frac{-8 \pm \sqrt{8^2 - (4 \times 1 \times -10)}}{2}$$

$$\Rightarrow t = 1.099... \text{ or } t = -9.099...$$

- Check that the $\mathbf{j}$-component of $\mathbf{r}$ is greater than zero for $t = 1.099...$

$$\frac{(1.099...)^4}{4} - 3(1.099...)^2 + 11 = 7.741... > 0$$

- So the particle is directly above O when $t = 1.10$ s (3 s.f.)

> **Tip:** You need to check that the $\mathbf{j}$-component of $\mathbf{r}$ is greater than 0 to make sure that the particle is above O (rather than at it or below it).

Example 3

A body is moving on a plane. At time t seconds, the body's acceleration is given by $a = [(4 - 18t)i + 72tj]$ ms^{-2}, relative to a fixed origin O. When $t = 1$, the body has position vector $r = 2i$ m, relative to O. When $t = 2$, the body is moving with velocity $v = (-20i + 135j)$ ms^{-1}. Find the body's position vector when it is moving parallel to i.

- First, integrate the expression for acceleration with respect to time to find an expression for velocity:
$$v = \int a \, dt = \left(\int (4 - 18t) \, dt \right)i + \left(\int 72t \, dt \right)j$$
$$= (4t - 9t^2)i + 36t^2j + C$$

- When $t = 2$, $v = -20i + 135j$. Use these values to find C:
$$-20i + 135j = (4(2) - 9(2)^2)i + 36(2)^2j + C$$
$$-20i + 135j = -28i + 144j + C$$
$$\Rightarrow C = 8i - 9j$$

- So the particle's velocity at time t is given by:
$$v = [(4t - 9t^2 + 8)i + (36t^2 - 9)j] \text{ ms}^{-1}$$

- When the particle is moving parallel to i, the j-component of its velocity is zero...
$$36t^2 - 9 = 0$$
$$t^2 = 9 \div 36 = 0.25$$
$$\Rightarrow t = 0.5 \text{ seconds}$$

Tip: As always, ignore the negative value of t.

Tip: You need to check that the i component of velocity is non-zero for the value of t you've found. If it was zero, then the particle wouldn't be moving parallel to i at this time — it would be stationary.

- ...and the i-component of its velocity is non-zero:
$$4(0.5) - 9(0.5)^2 + 8 = 7.75 \neq 0$$

- So the particle is moving parallel to i at time $t = 0.5$ seconds. Now integrate the expression for velocity to find an expression for the particle's position vector:
$$r = \int v \, dt = \left(\int (4t - 9t^2 + 8) \, dt \right)i + \left(\int (36t^2 - 9) \, dt \right)j$$
$$= (2t^2 - 3t^3 + 8t)i + (12t^3 - 9t)j + D$$

- When $t = 1$, $r = 2i$. Use these values to find D:
$$2i = (2(1)^2 - 3(1)^3 + 8(1))i + (12(1)^3 - 9(1))j + D$$
$$2i = 7i + 3j + D$$
$$\Rightarrow D = -5i - 3j$$

- So the particle's position vector relative to O at time t is given by:
$$r = [(2t^2 - 3t^3 + 8t - 5)i + (12t^3 - 9t - 3)j] \text{ m}$$

- Substitute $t = 0.5$ into this equation to find the particle's position vector when it is travelling parallel to i:
$$r = (2(0.5)^2 - 3(0.5)^3 + 8(0.5) - 5)i + (12(0.5)^3 - 9(0.5) - 3)j$$
$$= (-0.875i - 6j) \text{ m}$$

Q1 A particle is moving in a plane. At time t seconds, the particle's
    position relative to a fixed origin O is given by
    $\mathbf{r} = [(t^3 - 3t)\mathbf{i} + (t^2 + 2)\mathbf{j}]$ m. Find:
    a) (i)   an expression for the particle's velocity in terms of t,
       (ii) the particle's speed and direction of motion at time $t = 3$ s,
    b) (i)   an expression for the particle's acceleration in terms of t,
       (ii) the magnitude of the particle's acceleration at time $t = 4$ s.

Q2 An object is travelling in a plane. Its velocity at time t seconds is
    given by the expression $\mathbf{v} = [(t^3 - 6t^2 - 36t)\mathbf{i} + 14\mathbf{j}]$ ms^{-1}.
    Find the object's velocity when it is moving with zero acceleration.

Q3 A body is moving in a plane. At time t seconds, the body's
    acceleration is given by $\mathbf{a} = (3t\mathbf{i} + 6\mathbf{j})$ ms^{-2}. At time $t = 2$ seconds, the
    body has position vector $\mathbf{r} = (2\mathbf{i} - 9\mathbf{j})$ m relative to a fixed origin O,
    and is travelling at $(4\mathbf{i} + 6\mathbf{j})$ ms^{-1}. $\mathbf{i}$ and $\mathbf{j}$ are the unit vectors directed
    due east and due north respectively. Find:
    a) an expression for the body's velocity in terms of t,
    b) an expression for the body's position vector in terms of t,
    c) (i)   the value of t for which the body is due east of O,
       (ii) the body's distance from O at this time.

Q4 The velocity of a particle at time t seconds $(t \geq 0)$ is given by
    $\mathbf{v} = [(t^2 - 6t)\mathbf{i} + (4t + 5)\mathbf{j}]$ ms^{-1}. The particle is moving in a plane, and
    at time $t = 0$ the particle passes through the origin, O. Find:
    a) an expression for the particle's acceleration at time t seconds,
    b) an expression for the particle's position vector at time t seconds,
    c) the values of t for which the particle is travelling parallel to $\mathbf{j}$,
    d) the value of b, given that the particle passes through the point
       with position vector $(b\mathbf{i} + 12\mathbf{j})$ m, where b is a constant.

Q5 Particle A is moving in a vertical plane. At time t seconds, the
    particle's position relative to a fixed origin O is given by
    $\mathbf{r}_A = [(t^3 - t^2 - 4t + 3)\mathbf{i} + (t^3 - 2t^2 + 3t - 7)\mathbf{j}]$ m. Find:
    a) the value of t for which the particle's velocity is $(-3\mathbf{i} + 2\mathbf{j})$ ms^{-1},
    b) the value of t for which the direction of motion of the particle is
       45° above $\mathbf{i}$.

    > **Q5 b) Hint:** Think
    > about the relationship
    > between the horizontal
    > and vertical components
    > of the particle's velocity
    > when it is moving in this
    > direction.

    A second particle, B, is moving in the same plane as particle A.
    At time t seconds, the acceleration of B is given by
    $\mathbf{a}_B = (6t\mathbf{i} + 6t\mathbf{j})$ ms^{-2}. At time $t = 1$ second, B passes the point
    $(2\mathbf{i} + 3\mathbf{j})$ m relative to O, with velocity $(4\mathbf{i} - \mathbf{j})$ ms^{-1}. Find:
    c) an expression for the position vector of particle B
       relative to O in terms of t,
    d) an expression for the position vector of particle B
       relative to particle A in terms of t,
    e) the distance between particles A and B at time $t = 4$ seconds.

Forces

Because a **resultant force** causes a body to **accelerate**, you may have to use Newton's second law, $\mathbf{F} = m\mathbf{a}$, as well as calculus, to find expressions describing the motion of a body.

Example 1

A particle P is moving under the action of a single force, F newtons. The position vector, r m, of P after t seconds is given by $\mathbf{r} = (2t^3 - 3)\mathbf{i} + \frac{t^4}{2}\mathbf{j}$.

a) **Find an expression for the acceleration of P at time t seconds.**

- Differentiate the expression for P's position vector to find the expression for velocity:
  $$\mathbf{v} = \dot{\mathbf{r}} = (6t^2\mathbf{i} + 2t^3\mathbf{j}) \text{ ms}^{-1}$$

- Differentiate again to find the expression for acceleration:
  $$\mathbf{a} = \dot{\mathbf{v}} = (12t\mathbf{i} + 6t^2\mathbf{j}) \text{ ms}^{-2}$$

b) **P has mass 6 kg. Find the magnitude of F when $t = 3$.**

- Substitute $t = 3$ into the expression for acceleration:
  $$\mathbf{a} = 12(3)\mathbf{i} + 6(3^2)\mathbf{j}$$
  $$= (36\mathbf{i} + 54\mathbf{j}) \text{ ms}^{-2}$$

- Now use $\mathbf{F} = m\mathbf{a}$, with $m = 6$:
  $$\mathbf{F} = (6 \times 36)\mathbf{i} + (6 \times 54)\mathbf{j}$$
  $$= 216\mathbf{i} + 324\mathbf{j}$$

- Finally, use Pythagoras' theorem to find the magnitude:
  $$|\mathbf{F}| = \sqrt{216^2 + 324^2}$$
  $$= 389 \text{ N (3 s.f.)}$$

Tip: You could find the magnitude of **a** first instead if you wanted, then just multiply by m.

Example 2

A particle of mass 4 kg moves in a plane under the action of a single force, F N, where F is given by $\mathbf{F} = 24t\mathbf{i} - 8\mathbf{j}$. At time $t = 0$, the velocity of the particle is $(7\mathbf{i} + 22\mathbf{j}) \text{ ms}^{-1}$.

a) **The velocity of the particle at time t seconds is v ms⁻¹. Show that $\mathbf{v} = (3t^2 + 7)\mathbf{i} + (22 - 2t)\mathbf{j}$.**

- Use $\mathbf{F} = m\mathbf{a}$ to find an expression for the acceleration of the particle at time t:
  $$24t\mathbf{i} - 8\mathbf{j} = 4\mathbf{a}$$
  $$\Rightarrow \mathbf{a} = (6t\mathbf{i} - 2\mathbf{j}) \text{ ms}^{-2}$$

- Integrate the expression for acceleration to find an expression for velocity:
  $$\mathbf{v} = \int \mathbf{a} \, dt = \int (6t\mathbf{i} - 2\mathbf{j}) \, dt$$
  $$= 3t^2\mathbf{i} - 2t\mathbf{j} + \mathbf{C}$$

- When $t = 0$, $\mathbf{v} = (7\mathbf{i} + 22\mathbf{j})$ ms^{-1}. Use this information to find $\mathbf{C}$:

$$7\mathbf{i} + 22\mathbf{j} = 0\mathbf{i} + 0\mathbf{j} + \mathbf{C}$$
$$\Rightarrow \mathbf{C} = 7\mathbf{i} + 22\mathbf{j}.$$

- So $\mathbf{v}$ is given by:

$$\mathbf{v} = 3t^2\mathbf{i} - 2t\mathbf{j} + 7\mathbf{i} + 22\mathbf{j}$$
$$= (3t^2 + 7)\mathbf{i} + (22 - 2t)\mathbf{j} \text{ — as required.}$$

b) **Find the value of t when the particle is moving parallel to i.**

- When the particle is moving parallel to $\mathbf{i}$, the $\mathbf{j}$ component of $\mathbf{v}$ is 0...

$$22 - 2t = 0$$
$$\Rightarrow t = 11$$

- ...and the $\mathbf{i}$ component is non-zero:

$$3(11)^2 + 7 = 370 \neq 0$$

- So the particle is moving parallel to the vector $\mathbf{i}$ at time $t = 11$ s.

Exercise 3.2

Q1   A body moves in a plane under the action of a single force, $\mathbf{F}$ N.
At time $t = 5$ seconds, $\mathbf{F} = 15\mathbf{i} - 8\mathbf{j}$. The velocity of the body at time
t seconds is given by $\mathbf{v} = [t^3\mathbf{i} + (1 - 4t^2)\mathbf{j}]$ ms^{-1}.
Find the mass of the body.

Q2   An object of mass 1.8 kg moves in a plane under the action of a
single force, $\mathbf{F}$ N. At time t seconds, the object's position vector
relative to a fixed origin, O, is given by $\mathbf{r} = [(-t^2 + 2)\mathbf{i} + (3t^2 + t)\mathbf{j}]$ m.
Show that $\mathbf{F}$ is constant.

Q3   An object of mass 14 kg moves in a plane under the action of a
single force, $\mathbf{F}$ N. At time t seconds, the object's position vector
relative to a fixed origin, O, is given by
$\mathbf{r} = [(t^2 - 4t - 5)\mathbf{i} + (t^2 - 4t + 3)\mathbf{j}]$ m.
Find:
a) the time at which the object is momentarily at rest,
b) the object's distance from O when it is momentarily at rest,
c) an expression for $\mathbf{F}$ in terms of t.

Q4   A particle of mass 3 kg moves in a plane under the action of a single force, **F** N. At time t seconds, the force is given by $\mathbf{F} = 3\mathbf{i} + 6t\mathbf{j}$.
At time $t = 0$, the particle passes through the origin, O, with velocity $\mathbf{v} = (-2\mathbf{i} + 5\mathbf{j})$ ms^{-1}.

Find:

a) the magnitude of the particle's acceleration at time $t = 1$ second,

b) an expression for the particle's velocity in terms of t,

c) the force acting on the particle when it is moving parallel to **j**,

d) an expression for the particle's position vector relative to O in terms of t,

e) the particle's distance from O at time $t = 3$ seconds.

Q5   A particle of mass 0.2 kg moves in a vertical plane under the action of a single force, **F** N. At time t seconds, the particle's velocity is given by $\mathbf{v} = [(5t - 2)\mathbf{i} + 3t^2\mathbf{j}]$ ms^{-1}. At time $t = 1$ second, the particle has position vector $\mathbf{r} = (-16\mathbf{i} - 8\mathbf{j})$ m, relative to a fixed origin, O.

Find:

a) an expression for **F** in terms of t,

b) the magnitude of **F** at time $t = 2$ seconds,

c) an expression for the particle's position vector relative to O in terms of t,

d) the value of t for which the particle is directly above O.

Q6   A particle of mass 0.5 kg moves under the action of a single force, **F** N. At time t seconds, **F** is given by $\mathbf{F} = (3t - 4)\mathbf{i} + (t - 3t^2)\mathbf{j}$.
At time $t = 0$, the particle passes through the origin, O, with velocity $\mathbf{v} = (-3\mathbf{i} + 45\mathbf{j})$ ms^{-1}.

Find:

a) the particle's speed when $t = 3$,

b) the particle's distance from O when $t = 3$.

Q7 Hint: Take a look back at pages 12-14 for a reminder about projectiles in vector form.

Q7   At time $t = 0$, a projectile of mass 2 kg is fired from a point, O, on flat, horizontal ground. It moves in a vertical plane under the action of a single force. At time t seconds, the position vector of the projectile relative to O is given by $\mathbf{r} = [8t\mathbf{i} + (19.6t - 4.9t^2)\mathbf{j}]$ m.

Find:

a) the horizontal range of the projectile,

b) an expression for the projectile's velocity in terms of t,

c) the maximum height reached by the projectile,

d) the force acting on the projectile.

Review Exercise — Chapter 1

Q1   A particle is projected with initial velocity u ms^{-1} at an angle α to the horizontal.
     Write down the horizontal and vertical components of the particle's initial velocity.

Q2

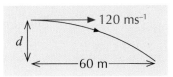

A rifle fires a bullet horizontally at 120 ms^{-1}. The bullet hits a target a horizontal distance of
60 m from the end of the rifle. Find the vertical distance, d, between the target and the rifle.

Q3   A golf ball is hit with a golf club from a point on flat, horizontal ground.
     The ball lands 4 seconds after it is hit. Given that the ball leaves the club
     with a speed of 22 ms^{-1}, at an angle of α to the horizontal, find α.

Q4   A projectile is fired from a point 0.3 m above flat, horizontal ground.
     The projectile's initial speed is 6.5 ms^{-1}, at an angle of 29° above the horizontal. Find:
     a) the horizontal range of the projectile,
     b) the speed of the projectile when it lands.

Q5   A body is projected from a point on flat, horizontal ground with velocity $(2\mathbf{i} + 11\mathbf{j})$ ms^{-1}. Find:
     a) the velocity of the body 0.8 seconds after projection,
     b) the time of flight of the body,
     c) the maximum height reached by the body.

Q6

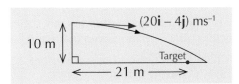

A ball is projected from the top of a building of height 10 m with velocity $(20\mathbf{i} - 4\mathbf{j})$ ms^{-1}.
The ball is aimed towards a target on flat, horizontal ground, 21 m from the foot of the
building. The ball overshoots, and lands beyond the target. Find:
     a) the time taken for the ball to land on the ground,
     b) the horizontal distance by which the ball overshoots the target,
     c) the speed of the ball when it is vertically above the target.

Q7   A particle sets off from the origin at $t = 0$ and moves along the x-axis with velocity
     $v = (8t^2 - 2t)$ ms^{-1}. Find an expression for:
     a) the acceleration of the particle at time t seconds,
     b) the displacement of the particle at time t seconds.

Q8   An object of mass 0.1 kg moves in a straight line along the x-axis.
     At time t seconds, the object's velocity is given by $v = (3t^2 - 9t + 4)$ ms^{-1}. Find:
     a) an expression for the object's acceleration in terms of t,
     b) the resultant force acting on the object when $t = 3$,
     c) the value of t for which the resultant force acting on the object is momentarily zero.

Q9   A particle moves in a straight line along the x-axis.
     At time t seconds, the particle's velocity is v ms^{-1}, where v is given by:

$$v = \begin{cases} t^2 - 3t & 0 \le t \le 2 \\ 2 - t^2 & t > 2 \end{cases}$$

     When $t = 0$, the particle is at the origin. Find:
     a) the particle's maximum speed in the time interval $0 \le t \le 2$,
     b) the particle's displacement from the origin when $t = 2$,
     c) the particle's displacement from the origin when $t = 4$.

Q10 At time $t = 0$, a particle sets off from rest at the origin, O, and moves in a
     plane with velocity $\mathbf{v} = (4t\mathbf{i} + t^2\mathbf{j})$ ms^{-1}, where t is the time in seconds. Find:
     a) the particle's acceleration at time t,
     b) the particle's position vector at time t.

Q11 A particle moves in a vertical plane. At time t seconds, the particle's position vector
     relative to a fixed origin, O, is given by $\mathbf{r} = [(t^2 - 3t + 2)\mathbf{i} + (t^2 - 5)\mathbf{j}]$ m. Find:
     a) the particle's initial position,
     b) the values of t for which the particle is directly below O,
     c) the velocity of the particle when $t = 4$.

Q12 A body is moving in a plane with acceleration $\mathbf{a} = -10\mathbf{j}$ ms^{-2} relative to a fixed origin, O.
     The body's initial velocity is $(15\mathbf{i} + 12\mathbf{j})$ ms^{-1}. At time $t = 1$ second, the body passes through
     the point with position vector $(15\mathbf{i} + 16\mathbf{j})$ m. Given that $\mathbf{i}$ and $\mathbf{j}$ are unit vectors directed
     due east and due north respectively, find:
     a) an expression for the body's velocity at time t seconds,
     b) an expression for the body's position vector at time t seconds,
     c) the body's velocity when it is due east of O.

Q13 A particle of mass 7.5 kg moves under the action of a single force, $\mathbf{F}$ N. At time t seconds,
     the particle has velocity $\mathbf{v}$ ms^{-1}, where $\mathbf{v}$ is given by $\mathbf{v} = (3t^2 - 8t)\mathbf{i} + (6 + 4t)\mathbf{j}$.
     When $t = 3$, the particle has position vector $(-4\mathbf{i} + 32\mathbf{j})$ m, relative to a fixed origin, O.
     Find:
     a) an expression for $\mathbf{F}$ in terms of t,
     b) an expression for the particle's position vector in terms of t.

1

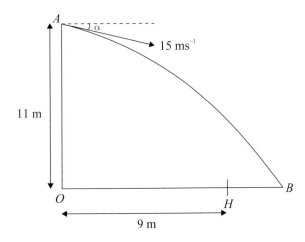

A stone is thrown from point A on the edge of a cliff, towards a point H, which is on horizontal ground. The point O is on the ground, 11 m vertically below the point of projection. The stone is thrown with speed 15 ms⁻¹ at an angle α below the horizontal, where $\tan\alpha = \frac{3}{4}$. The horizontal distance from O to H is 9 m. The stone misses the point H and hits the ground at point B, as shown above. Find:

a) the time taken by the stone to reach the ground,   *(5 marks)*

b) the horizontal distance from H to B,   *(3 marks)*

c) the speed of projection which would have ensured that the stone landed at H.   *(5 marks)*

2   A particle P is moving in a horizontal plane under the action of a single force, $\mathbf{F}$ N. After t seconds, P has position vector:

$$\mathbf{r} = [(2t^3 - 7t^2 + 12)\mathbf{i} + (3t^2 - 4t^3 - 7)\mathbf{j}] \text{ m}$$

where the unit vectors $\mathbf{i}$ and $\mathbf{j}$ are in the directions of east and north respectively. Find:

a) an expression for the velocity of P after t seconds,   *(2 marks)*

b) the speed of P when $t = \frac{1}{2}$, and the direction of motion of P at this time.   *(3 marks)*

At $t = 2$, the magnitude of $\mathbf{F}$ is 170 N. Find:

c) the acceleration of P at $t = 2$,   *(3 marks)*

d) the mass of the particle,   *(3 marks)*

e) the value of t when $\mathbf{F}$ is acting parallel to $\mathbf{j}$.   *(3 marks)*

3   A stationary football is kicked from a point on flat, horizontal ground towards a goal a horizontal distance of 30 m away. The ball is kicked with speed 20 ms^{-1}, at an angle of 30° to the horizontal. The crossbar is 2.5 m above the level ground. Assuming the path of the ball is not impeded, determine whether the ball passes above or below the crossbar. What assumptions does your model make?

(6 marks)

4   A particle sets off from the origin O at $t = 0$ and moves in a straight line along the x-axis. At time t seconds, the velocity of the particle is v ms^{-1} where v is given by:

$$v = \begin{cases} 9t - 3t^2 & 0 \leqslant t \leqslant 4 \\[2mm] \dfrac{-192}{t^2} & t > 4 \end{cases}$$

Find:

a)   the maximum speed of the particle in the interval $0 \leqslant t \leqslant 4$,

(5 marks)

b)   the displacement of the particle from O at:

(i) $t = 4$,

(3 marks)

(ii) $t = 6$.

(4 marks)

5   A golf ball is hit from a tee at point O on the edge of a vertical cliff. Point O is 30 m vertically above A, the base of the cliff. The ball is hit with velocity $(14\mathbf{i} + 35\mathbf{j})$ ms^{-1} towards a hole, H, which lies on flat, horizontal ground below the cliff. At time t seconds, the position of the ball is $(x\mathbf{i} + y\mathbf{j})$ m relative to O.

a)   By writing down expressions for x and y in terms of t, show that

$$y = \frac{5x}{2} - \frac{x^2}{40}$$

(4 marks)

The ball lands on the ground at point B, 7 m beyond H, where AHB is a straight, horizontal line. Find:

b)   the horizontal distance AB,

(3 marks)

c)   the speed of the ball as it passes through a point vertically above H.

(4 marks)

1. Particles

In M1, you used moments to find the location of the centre of mass of a non-uniform rod. In this chapter, you'll use moments to find the centres of mass of groups of particles, laminas and frameworks.

You'll also use centres of mass to solve problems involving laminas in equilibrium.

Learning Objectives:

- Be able to find the centre of mass of a group of particles arranged in a line.
- Be able to find the centre of mass of a group of particles on a plane.

Particles in a line

- The **weight** of an object is considered to act at its **centre of mass** (**COM**).

- It's often convenient to model an object as a **particle** (point mass) — the position of the particle will be the centre of mass of the object.

- A **group of objects** also has a centre of mass — this is the point from which the **total weight** of all the objects can be considered to act.

- In this case, the group of objects is modelled as a **group of particles**.

- The centre of mass of a group of particles **isn't** necessarily in the **same position** as any one of the particles.

- If a group of particles all lie in a **line**, then the centre of mass of the group will lie somewhere **on that line**.

- Just as with rigid bodies, you can find the centre of mass of a group of particles using **moments**.

- The **moment** of a particle's **weight** about a **point** is given by the formula:

$$\text{Moment} = \frac{\text{Weight}}{(W = mg)} \times \frac{\text{Horizontal Distance}}{\text{(from the particle to the point)}}$$

Tip: Remember — a moment is the turning effect a force has about a point. When you're calculating moments, you need to use the perpendicular distance from the line of action of the force to the point. As weight acts vertically downwards, this distance is horizontal.

Particles in a horizontal line

- The expression for the moment of a particle's weight about a point can be written as *mgx*, where x is the horizontal distance from the point to the particle.

- The **moment** of a group of particles in a **horizontal line** about a point on the horizontal line can be found by adding together all the individual moments about the point — $\Sigma\, mgx$.

- This has the same effect as the **combined weight** of the particles ($\Sigma\, mg$) acting at the **centre of mass** of the whole group ($\overline{x}$). i.e. $\Sigma\, mgx = \overline{x}\,\Sigma\, mg$, or, cancelling the g's to simplify:

$$\Sigma\, mx = \overline{x}\,\Sigma\, m$$

Tip: $\overline{x}$ is the horizontal distance from the point you're taking moments about to the centre of mass of the group of particles.

- Use this simplified formula to find the centre of mass, $\overline{x}$, of a group of particles in a horizontal line.

Example

$$3 \text{ kg} \qquad\qquad 1.5 \text{ kg} \quad 0.5 \text{ kg}$$
$$(-2, 0) \qquad 0 \qquad\qquad (3, 0) \qquad (5, 0)$$

Three particles are placed at positions along the *x*-axis, as shown. Find the coordinates of the centre of mass of the group of particles.

- Write down the different values you know:

  $m_1 = 3, x_1 = -2 \qquad m_2 = 1.5, x_2 = 3 \qquad m_3 = 0.5, x_3 = 5$

- Now use the formula $\sum mx = \overline{x} \sum m$:

  $m_1 x_1 + m_2 x_2 + m_3 x_3 = \overline{x}(m_1 + m_2 + m_3)$

  $(3 \times -2) + (1.5 \times 3) + (0.5 \times 5) = \overline{x}(3 + 1.5 + 0.5)$

  $1 = 5\overline{x}$

  $\Rightarrow \overline{x} = 0.2$

- So the centre of mass of the group has coordinates (0.2, 0).

Tip: The *x*-coordinate of each particle gives its distance from the origin (the point about which you're taking moments). Negative coordinates go into the formula as they are (you don't have to change the sign), because weights of particles placed here cause the system to rotate in the opposite direction to those placed at points with positive coordinates.

Particles in a vertical line

Finding the centre of mass of a group of particles arranged in a **vertical line** is pretty much the same — you just need to use the **vertical distance** from the point you're taking moments about to each particle (i.e. just change the *x*'s to *y*'s in the formula):

Tip: $\overline{y}$ is the vertical distance from the point you're taking moments about to the centre of mass of the group of particles.

$$\sum my = \overline{y} \sum m$$

Example

A light, vertical rod, *AB*, has particles attached at various positions, as shown. Find the distance of the centre of mass of the loaded rod from *A*.

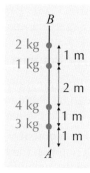

- Write down the values you know — first you'll need to work out the distance of each particle from *A*:

  $m_1 = 3, \ y_1 = 1 \qquad m_2 = 4, \ y_2 = 2$

  $m_3 = 1, \ y_3 = 4 \qquad m_4 = 2, \ y_4 = 5$

- Now use the formula $\sum my = \overline{y} \sum m$:

  $m_1 y_1 + m_2 y_2 + m_3 y_3 + m_4 y_4 = \overline{y}(m_1 + m_2 + m_3 + m_4)$

  $(3 \times 1) + (4 \times 2) + (1 \times 4) + (2 \times 5) = \overline{y}(3 + 4 + 1 + 2)$

  $25 = 10\overline{y}$

  $\Rightarrow \overline{y} = 2.5$

- So the centre of mass of the loaded rod is 2.5 m from *A*.

Tip: Remember — 'light' means the rod has negligible mass, so you only need to worry about the masses of the particles when using the formula.

Q1   Three particles are placed on the x-axis. A particle of mass 4 kg is placed at the point where $x = 3$, a particle of mass 6 kg is placed at the point where $x = 5$, and a particle of mass 10 kg is placed at the point where $x = 7$. Find the centre of mass of the three particles.

Q2   Three particles of mass 8 kg, 4 kg and M kg are placed at the points $(-3, 0)$, $(1, 0)$ and $(13, 0)$ respectively. Given that the centre of mass of the particles is at $(5, 0)$, find the value of M.

Q3   Three objects are attached to a light, horizontal rod, AB. The objects have mass 2 kg, 1 kg and 1.5 kg and are attached at distances of 1 m, 2.5 m and 3 m from A respectively. Find the distance of the centre of mass of the loaded rod from A.

Q4

Three particles are placed in a horizontal line, as shown. Find the distance of the centre of mass of the particles from O.

Q5   Particles of mass 0.8 kg, 1.2 kg, 1.8 kg and 2.1 kg are placed at the points $(0, -2)$, $(0, -2.6)$, $(0, -3.5)$ and $(0, -3.8)$ respectively. Find the coordinates of the centre of mass of the group of particles.

Q6   Particles are placed on the y-axis as follows: 3 kg at $(0, -7)$, 2 kg at $(0, -5)$, 4 kg at $(0, -1)$, 1 kg at $(0, 0)$, 4 kg at $(0, 6)$ and 6 kg at $(0, 8)$. Find the coordinates of the centre of mass of the particles.

Q7   Five particles of mass 1 kg, 2 kg, 3 kg, 4 kg and 5 kg are equally spaced along the x-axis, with the 1 kg particle at the origin and the 5 kg particle at the point $(12, 0)$. Find the coordinates of the centre of mass of the particles.

Q8   Bodies of mass M kg, $2M$ kg and 5 kg are placed at the points $(0, -3)$, $(0, 1)$ and $(0, 2)$ respectively. Given that the centre of mass of the bodies is at the origin, find the value of M.

Q9   Two light, inextensible strings, P and Q, each of length 2 m, are hung vertically from a horizontal ceiling. String P has a particle of mass 5 kg attached at its midpoint and a particle of mass 4 kg attached to its lower end. String Q has a particle of mass 4 kg attached at its midpoint and a particle of mass 5 kg attached to its lower end. Find the vertical distance between the centres of mass of the two strings.

Q10   Four stones are attached to a light rod, AB, of length 1 m. A stone of mass 1.5 kg is attached at A, a stone of mass 0.5 kg is attached at B, and a stone of mass 2 kg is attached at the rod's midpoint. A stone of mass 0.2 kg is attached at the point C. Given that the centre of mass of the loaded rod is at the point C, find the length AC.

Particles in two dimensions

- The same principles from the last few pages apply to finding the centre of mass of a group of particles in a **plane**.

- There are two ways of finding the centre of mass of a group of particles in two dimensions. The first way is to find the values of $\bar{x}$ and $\bar{y}$ **separately** (where $(\bar{x}, \bar{y})$ are the coordinates of the centre of mass of the group).

Tip: A position vector describes the position of a point relative to the origin.

- The second way is to find $\bar{x}$ and $\bar{y}$ at the **same time** using **position vectors**.

- Using position vectors, the formula becomes:

$$\Sigma m\mathbf{r} = \bar{\mathbf{r}}\Sigma m$$

where $\bar{\mathbf{r}}$ is the position vector of the centre of mass of the group of particles.

- The quickest way is to use position vectors, but Example 1 below shows both methods, so you can choose which you prefer.

Example 1

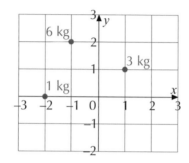

Find the coordinates of the centre of mass of the system of particles shown in the diagram.

THE LONG WAY — finding $\bar{x}$ and $\bar{y}$ separately.

- Write down the values you know:

$$m_1 = 6, x_1 = -1 \qquad m_2 = 3, x_2 = 1 \qquad m_3 = 1, x_3 = -2$$

- Find the x-coordinate of the centre of mass of the group first (pretend the particles are in a horizontal line):

$$\Sigma mx = \bar{x}\Sigma m$$
$$m_1x_1 + m_2x_2 + m_3x_3 = \bar{x}(m_1 + m_2 + m_3)$$
$$(6 \times -1) + (3 \times 1) + (1 \times -2) = \bar{x}(6 + 3 + 1)$$
$$-5 = 10\bar{x}$$
$$\Rightarrow \bar{x} = -0.5$$

- Now find the y-coordinate in the same way:

$$y_1 = 2, \qquad y_2 = 1, \qquad y_3 = 0$$
$$\Sigma my = \bar{y}\Sigma m$$
$$m_1y_1 + m_2y_2 + m_3y_3 = \bar{y}(m_1 + m_2 + m_3)$$
$$(6 \times 2) + (3 \times 1) + (1 \times 0) = \bar{x}(6 + 3 + 1)$$
$$15 = 10\bar{y}$$
$$\Rightarrow \bar{y} = 1.5$$

- So the centre of mass has coordinates $(\bar{x}, \bar{y}) = (-0.5, 1.5)$.

<u>**The Short Way**</u> — using position vectors.

- Write down the mass, m, and position vector, $\mathbf{r}$, for each particle:

$$m_1 = 6, \mathbf{r}_1 = \begin{pmatrix} -1 \\ 2 \end{pmatrix} \qquad m_2 = 3, \mathbf{r}_2 = \begin{pmatrix} 1 \\ 1 \end{pmatrix} \qquad m_3 = 1, \mathbf{r}_3 = \begin{pmatrix} -2 \\ 0 \end{pmatrix}$$

- Use the formula $\sum m\mathbf{r} = \bar{\mathbf{r}}\sum m$:

$$m_1\mathbf{r}_1 + m_2\mathbf{r}_2 + m_3\mathbf{r}_3 = \bar{\mathbf{r}}(m_1 + m_2 + m_3)$$

$$\Rightarrow 6\begin{pmatrix} -1 \\ 2 \end{pmatrix} + 3\begin{pmatrix} 1 \\ 1 \end{pmatrix} + 1\begin{pmatrix} -2 \\ 0 \end{pmatrix} = \bar{\mathbf{r}}(6 + 3 + 1)$$

$$\Rightarrow \begin{pmatrix} -6 \\ 12 \end{pmatrix} + \begin{pmatrix} 3 \\ 3 \end{pmatrix} + \begin{pmatrix} -2 \\ 0 \end{pmatrix} = 10\bar{\mathbf{r}}$$

$$\Rightarrow \begin{pmatrix} -5 \\ 15 \end{pmatrix} = 10\bar{\mathbf{r}}$$

$$\Rightarrow \bar{\mathbf{r}} = \begin{pmatrix} -0.5 \\ 1.5 \end{pmatrix}$$

- So the centre of mass has position vector $\bar{\mathbf{r}} = \begin{pmatrix} -0.5 \\ 1.5 \end{pmatrix}$, and coordinates $(\bar{x}, \bar{y}) = (-0.5, 1.5)$.

Tip: It's easiest to write the particles' positions as column vectors — these are just like coordinates standing upright: $\mathbf{r} = \begin{pmatrix} x \\ y \end{pmatrix}$.
When adding column vectors, add the horizontal and vertical components separately.

Example 2

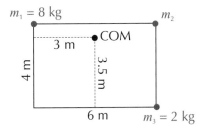

The diagram shows the position of the centre of mass (COM) of a system of three particles attached to the corners of a light, rectangular lamina. Find m_2.

- First of all, pick your origin — the bottom-left corner looks as good as anywhere — and define all your positions from this point:

$$\mathbf{r}_1 = \begin{pmatrix} 0 \\ 4 \end{pmatrix} \qquad \mathbf{r}_2 = \begin{pmatrix} 6 \\ 4 \end{pmatrix} \qquad \mathbf{r}_3 = \begin{pmatrix} 6 \\ 0 \end{pmatrix} \qquad \bar{\mathbf{r}} = \begin{pmatrix} 3 \\ 3.5 \end{pmatrix}$$

- Use the formula $\sum m\mathbf{r} = \bar{\mathbf{r}}\sum m$:

$$m_1\mathbf{r}_1 + m_2\mathbf{r}_2 + m_3\mathbf{r}_3 = \bar{\mathbf{r}}(m_1 + m_2 + m_3)$$

$$\Rightarrow 8\begin{pmatrix} 0 \\ 4 \end{pmatrix} + m_2\begin{pmatrix} 6 \\ 4 \end{pmatrix} + 2\begin{pmatrix} 6 \\ 0 \end{pmatrix} = \begin{pmatrix} 3 \\ 3.5 \end{pmatrix} \times (8 + m_2 + 2)$$

$$\Rightarrow \begin{pmatrix} 0 \\ 32 \end{pmatrix} + \begin{pmatrix} 6m_2 \\ 4m_2 \end{pmatrix} + \begin{pmatrix} 12 \\ 0 \end{pmatrix} = \begin{pmatrix} 3 \\ 3.5 \end{pmatrix} \times (m_2 + 10)$$

$$\Rightarrow \begin{pmatrix} 6m_2 + 12 \\ 4m_2 + 32 \end{pmatrix} = \begin{pmatrix} 3m_2 + 30 \\ 3.5m_2 + 35 \end{pmatrix}$$

- Use the top row to solve for m_2:

$$6m_2 + 12 = 3m_2 + 30$$

$$\Rightarrow m_2 = 6 \text{ kg}$$

Tip: A lamina is a flat body whose thickness can be ignored. This lamina is light, so it also has negligible mass.

Tip: You can check your value of m_2 using the bottom row of the vector equation:
$$4m_2 + 32 = 3.5m_2 + 35$$

Example 3

A particle of mass 0.4 kg is placed at the origin, a particle of mass 0.6 kg is placed at the point (3, −2), and a particle of mass 0.2 kg is placed at the point (1, 5). At what point must a particle of mass 0.8 kg be placed for the centre of mass of the four particles to be at (−0.6, 1.5)?

- Write down the values you know:

$$m_1 = 0.4, \ \mathbf{r}_1 = \begin{pmatrix} 0 \\ 0 \end{pmatrix} \qquad m_2 = 0.6, \ \mathbf{r}_2 = \begin{pmatrix} 3 \\ -2 \end{pmatrix}$$

$$m_3 = 0.2, \ \mathbf{r}_3 = \begin{pmatrix} 1 \\ 5 \end{pmatrix} \qquad m_4 = 0.8, \ \mathbf{r}_4 = \begin{pmatrix} a \\ b \end{pmatrix}$$

$$\bar{\mathbf{r}} = \begin{pmatrix} -0.6 \\ 1.5 \end{pmatrix}$$

a and *b* are constants that you need to find.

- Use the formula $\sum m\mathbf{r} = \bar{\mathbf{r}} \sum m$:

$$m_1\mathbf{r}_1 + m_2\mathbf{r}_2 + m_3\mathbf{r}_3 + m_4\mathbf{r}_4 = \bar{\mathbf{r}}(m_1 + m_2 + m_3 + m_4)$$

$$\Rightarrow 0.4\begin{pmatrix} 0 \\ 0 \end{pmatrix} + 0.6\begin{pmatrix} 3 \\ -2 \end{pmatrix} + 0.2\begin{pmatrix} 1 \\ 5 \end{pmatrix} + 0.8\begin{pmatrix} a \\ b \end{pmatrix}$$

$$= \begin{pmatrix} -0.6 \\ 1.5 \end{pmatrix} \times (0.4 + 0.6 + 0.2 + 0.8)$$

$$\Rightarrow \begin{pmatrix} 0 \\ 0 \end{pmatrix} + \begin{pmatrix} 1.8 \\ -1.2 \end{pmatrix} + \begin{pmatrix} 0.2 \\ 1 \end{pmatrix} + 0.8\begin{pmatrix} a \\ b \end{pmatrix} = \begin{pmatrix} -1.2 \\ 3 \end{pmatrix}$$

$$\Rightarrow 0.8\begin{pmatrix} a \\ b \end{pmatrix} = \begin{pmatrix} -3.2 \\ 3.2 \end{pmatrix}$$

$$\Rightarrow \begin{pmatrix} a \\ b \end{pmatrix} = \begin{pmatrix} -4 \\ 4 \end{pmatrix}$$

- So the particle should be placed at the point (−4, 4).

Exercise 1.2

Q1   Find the coordinates of the centre of mass of the following group of particles: a particle of mass 2 kg at the point (3, 1), a particle of mass 3 kg at the point (2, 4), and a particle of mass 5 kg at the point (5, 2).

Q2

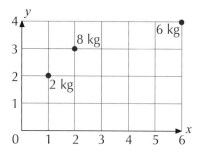

Find the coordinates of the centre of mass of the group of particles shown above.

Q3   A particle of mass 3 kg is placed at (1, 2), a particle of mass 4 kg is placed at (5, 1), a particle of mass 5 kg is placed at (3, 6), and a particle of mass M kg is placed at (0, 1). The centre of mass of the group of particles is at (1.9, 2.4). Find the value of M.

Q4 Four particles are placed on an x- and y-coordinate grid as follows:
3 kg at (2, 1), 4 kg at (4, 0), M_1 kg at (–4, 0), and M_2 kg at (0, –5).
The centre of mass of the particles is at the origin.
a) Find the value of M_1.
b) Find the value of M_2.

Q5 A light rectangular lamina $ABCD$ has lengths $AB = 8$ cm and
$BC = 10$ cm. A stone of mass 200 g is placed at A, a stone of mass
250 g is placed at B, a stone of mass 300 g is placed at C, and a
stone of mass 250 g is placed at D.
Find the distance from the centre of mass of
the loaded lamina to the point A.

Q5 Hint: Don't just find
the position of the COM
— the question asks for
its distance from A.

Q6 Four particles are placed on an x- and y-coordinate grid as follows:
2.5 kg at (–3, 1), 2 kg at (–2, –4), 3 kg at (4, –3), and 1.5 kg at (2, 3).
A fifth particle, of mass 1 kg, is to be placed on the grid so that the
centre of mass of the five particles is at (0.65, –0.8).
Where should this particle be placed?

Q7 A light wire is shaped into a rectangle, $ABCD$, where $AB = 30$ cm and
$BC = 20$ cm. A particle of mass 9 kg is fixed to the rectangle at the
midpoint of side AB, a particle of mass 6 kg is fixed to the midpoint
of BC, a particle of mass 12 kg is fixed to the midpoint of CD and a
particle of mass 3 kg is fixed to the midpoint of AD.
a) Taking A to be (0, 0), D to be on the positive x-axis and B to be on
the positive y-axis, find the coordinates of the centre of mass of
the system.
b) A particle of mass M kg is attached to AB in such a way that the
centre of mass of the system lies on the line EF, where E and F
are the midpoints of AD and BC respectively. Find the value of M.

Q8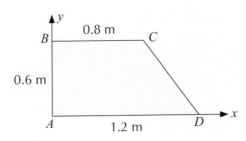

The light trapezium-shaped lamina, $ABCD$, is shown above.
E is the midpoint of AC and F is the midpoint of BD.
a) Taking A as the origin, find the coordinates of E and F.
b) Particles of mass 0.5 kg, 0.75 kg, 0.25 kg and 1 kg
are attached to E, F, C and D respectively.
Find the coordinates of the centre of mass of the loaded lamina.
c) A particle of mass M kg is attached at B in such a way that the
centre of mass of the system lies on AC. Find the value of M.
d) Find the new coordinates of the centre
of mass of the loaded lamina.

Q8 c) Hint: Find the
equation of AC to help
you form a pair of
simultaneous equations.
Then solve to find M.

2. Laminas

Learning Objectives:

- Be able to find the centre of mass of standard shapes such as rectangles, triangles, circles and sectors of circles.

- Be able to find the centre of mass of a composite shape made up of standard shapes.

- Be able to find the centre of mass of a shape with parts removed.

A lamina is a flat body whose thickness can be ignored.
In this section, you'll learn how to find the position of a lamina's centre of mass.

Uniform laminas

- The mass of a **uniform lamina** is **spread out evenly** across the area of the shape.

- The centre of mass of a lamina always lies on the shape's **lines of symmetry** (if it has any).

- For shapes with **more than one** line of symmetry, the centre of mass is where the lines of symmetry **intersect**:

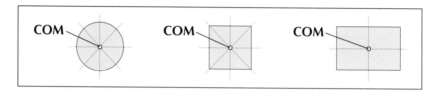

Example

Find the coordinates of the centre of mass of a uniform rectangular lamina with vertices $A(-4, 7)$, $B(2, 7)$, $C(-4, -3)$ and $D(2, -3)$.

- Sketch the lamina:

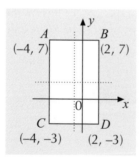

Tip: The dotted lines are the lines of symmetry of the rectangular lamina. The lamina's centre of mass is at the point where the dotted lines intersect.

- Call the coordinates of the centre of mass $(\overline{x}, \overline{y})$.

- $\overline{x}$ is the x-coordinate of the midpoint of AB (or CD):
$$(-4 + 2) \div 2 = -1$$

- $\overline{y}$ is the y-coordinate of the midpoint of AC (or BD):
$$(7 + -3) \div 2 = 2$$

- So the required coordinates are (−1, 2).

Triangles

- In a triangle, the lines from each vertex to the midpoint of the opposite side are called **medians**.
- If you draw in the medians on any triangle, the point where they cross will be **two thirds** of the way up each median from each vertex.
- This point is called the **centroid**, and it's the **centre of mass** in a **uniform triangular lamina**.

Tip: In an equilateral triangle, the medians are lines of symmetry:

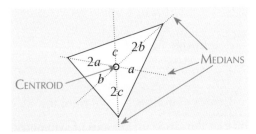

- There's a **formula** for finding the coordinates of the centroid / centre of mass, $(\overline{x}, \overline{y})$:

For a triangle with vertices at (x_1, y_1), (x_2, y_2) and (x_3, y_3):

$$(\overline{x}, \overline{y}) = \left(\frac{x_1 + x_2 + x_3}{3}, \frac{y_1 + y_2 + y_3}{3}\right)$$

(i.e. the mean x-coordinate and mean y-coordinate)

Example

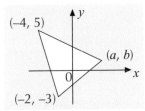

The centre of mass of the triangle shown is at (–1, 1).
Find the values of the constants a and b.

- Use the formula with the values $(x_1, y_1) = (-4, 5)$, $(x_2, y_2) = (-2, -3)$, $(x_3, y_3) = (a, b)$, and $(\overline{x}, \overline{y}) = (-1, 1)$:

$$(\overline{x}, \overline{y}) = \left(\frac{x_1 + x_2 + x_3}{3}, \frac{y_1 + y_2 + y_3}{3}\right)$$

$$(-1, 1) = \left(\frac{-4 - 2 + a}{3}, \frac{5 - 3 + b}{3}\right)$$

- Equating x-coordinates:

$$-1 = \frac{-4 - 2 + a}{3}$$

$$\Rightarrow \; -3 = -6 + a \; \Rightarrow \; \boxed{a = 3}$$

- Equating y-coordinates:

$$1 = \frac{5 - 3 + b}{3}$$

$$\Rightarrow \; 3 = 2 + b \; \Rightarrow \; \boxed{b = 1}$$

Sectors of Circles

Tip: A sector of a circle is a portion of a circle bound by two radii and an arc. You can picture a sector as being a 'slice' of the circle:

There's a formula you can use to find the **centre of mass** of a **sector of a circle**:

For a uniform circle sector, radius r and angle 2α radians:

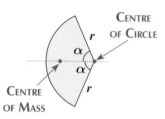

Centre of mass is $\dfrac{2r\sin\alpha}{3\alpha}$ from the centre of the circle on the axis of symmetry.

Example 1

A sector is cut from a uniform circle of radius 3 cm, centre P. The sector is an eighth of the whole circle. How far along the axis of symmetry is the centre of mass of the sector from P?

- The angle of the sector is an eighth of the whole circle, i.e. $\frac{2\pi}{8}$ rads or $\frac{\pi}{4}$ rads:

Tip: Remember — a full circle has angle 2π radians at its centre.

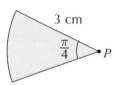

- In the formula for the centre of mass of a sector, this angle is 2α, so $\alpha = \frac{\pi}{8}$.

- Now using the formula with $r = 3$ cm:

Tip: Don't forget to set your calculator to work in radians rather than degrees.

$$\frac{2r\sin\alpha}{3\alpha} = \frac{2 \times 3 \times \sin\frac{\pi}{8}}{\frac{3\pi}{8}}$$

$$= 1.9489...$$

- So the centre of mass of the sector is 1.95 cm (3 s.f.) from P.

Example 2

A semicircle is formed from half a uniform circular lamina of diameter 10 cm and centre P. Find the distance of the centre of mass of the semicircle from P, giving your answer in terms of π.

- The angle of the sector is half of the whole circle, i.e. π rads:

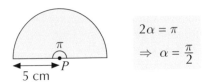

$$2\alpha = \pi$$
$$\Rightarrow \alpha = \frac{\pi}{2}$$

- Using the formula $\frac{2r\sin\alpha}{3\alpha}$ with $r = 5$ cm:

$$\frac{2r\sin\alpha}{3\alpha} = \frac{2 \times 5 \times \sin\frac{\pi}{2}}{\frac{3\pi}{2}}$$

$$= \frac{10}{3\pi/2} = \frac{20}{3\pi}$$

Tip: Remember — $\sin\left(\frac{\pi}{2}\right) = 1$.

- So the centre of mass of the sector is $\frac{20}{3\pi}$ cm from P.

Exercise 2.1

Q1 A uniform square lamina has vertices $A(1, 2)$, $B(1, 5)$, $C(4, 5)$ and $D(4, 2)$. Find the coordinates of the centre of mass of the lamina.

Q2 The vertices of a uniform triangular lamina are $P(-3, -2)$, $Q(-5, -6)$ and $R(-7, -1)$. Find the coordinates of its centre of mass.

Q3

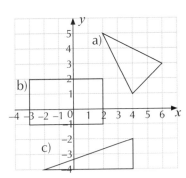

Find the coordinates of the centre of mass of each uniform lamina shown above.

Q4 $A(-5, -5)$ and $B(1, 3)$ are points on a uniform circular lamina such that AB is a diameter of the circle. Find the coordinates of the circle's centre of mass.

Q5   A semicircle is formed from half a uniform circular lamina of radius 16 cm and centre Q. How far along the axis of symmetry from Q is the centre of mass of the semicircle?

Q6 Hint: The diagonals of a parallelogram bisect each other.

Q6   A uniform lamina in the shape of a parallelogram has vertices $E(-2, -1)$, $F(1, 3)$, $G(6, 3)$ and $H(3, -1)$. Find the coordinates of its centre of mass.

Q7   The centre of mass of a uniform triangular lamina is at $(2, 0)$. Given that the triangle's vertices are $X(-2, -3)$, $Y(7, 0)$ and $Z(z_1, z_2)$, find the values of the constants z_1 and z_2.

Q8   A sector is cut from a uniform circular lamina of radius 12 cm. The angle of the sector is $90°$. How far along the axis of symmetry from its vertex is the centre of mass of the sector?

Q9   The centre of mass of a uniform rectangle is 6.5 cm from each vertex. The length of the shorter side of the rectangle is 5 cm. Find the length of the longer side of the rectangle.

Q10 A uniform circular lamina of radius 5 cm and centre Q has a sector of $\frac{\pi}{3}$ radians cut from it.
   a) Find the distance from Q of the centre of mass of the sector.
   b) Find the distance from Q of the centre of mass of the remainder of the circle.

Q11 The centre of mass of a uniform semicircle is 5 cm from the centre of the circle. Find the circle's radius.

Q12 ABC is a uniform lamina in the shape of an isosceles triangle with $AC = BC$. D is the centre of mass of the lamina, and E is the midpoint of AB. Given that $AB = 16$ cm and $DE = 2$ cm, find the distance AC.

Q13

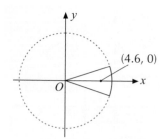

A sector is cut from a uniform circular lamina centred at the origin of a coordinate grid, as shown. The angle at the vertex of the sector is $\frac{\pi}{5}$ radians, and the centre of mass of the sector is at the point $(4.6, 0)$.

Find the coordinates of the point where the arc of the sector crosses the x-axis.

Loaded laminas and composite shapes

Loaded laminas

Tip: You've seen loaded laminas before — e.g. in Example 2, page 41 — but there the lamina was always light. Here, you need to take the lamina's mass into account in your calculations.

- You may be asked to find the centre of mass of a **loaded lamina** — i.e. a lamina with **particles attached** to it.
- To do this, first find the centre of mass of the **lamina**.
- Then model the lamina as being replaced by a **particle** of the same mass, in the position of its centre of mass.
- Then you can use the method for finding the centre of mass of a **group of particles** in a **plane** from page 40.

Example

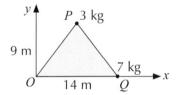

The diagram shows a uniform lamina in the shape of an isosceles triangle, *OPQ*, of height 9 m, base width 14 m and mass 10 kg. Particles of mass 3 kg and 7 kg are attached to the triangle at *P* and *Q* respectively.

Find the coordinates of the centre of mass of the loaded lamina relative to *O*.

- First find the coordinates of the centre of mass of the triangular lamina — use the formula $(\bar{x}, \bar{y}) = \left(\frac{x_1 + x_2 + x_3}{3}, \frac{y_1 + y_2 + y_3}{3}\right)$ with the values $(x_1, y_1) = (0, 0)$, $(x_2, y_2) = (7, 9)$, $(x_3, y_3) = (14, 0)$:

$$(\bar{x}, \bar{y}) = \left(\frac{0 + 7 + 14}{3}, \frac{0 + 9 + 0}{3}\right) = (7, 3)$$

- Now imagine the lamina as a particle of mass 10 kg at (7, 3).

- Combining this with the other two particles — 3 kg at (7, 9) and 7 kg at (14, 0) — and using the formula for the centre of mass of particles in a plane:

$$\sum m\mathbf{r} = \bar{\mathbf{r}} \sum m$$
$$\Rightarrow m_1\mathbf{r}_1 + m_2\mathbf{r}_2 + m_3\mathbf{r}_3 = \bar{\mathbf{r}}(m_1 + m_2 + m_3)$$
$$\Rightarrow 10\binom{7}{3} + 3\binom{7}{9} + 7\binom{14}{0} = \bar{\mathbf{r}}(10 + 3 + 7)$$
$$\Rightarrow \binom{189}{57} = 20\bar{\mathbf{r}}$$
$$\Rightarrow \bar{\mathbf{r}} = \frac{1}{20}\binom{189}{57} = \binom{9.45}{2.85}$$

Tip: This is the formula from page 40.

- So the centre of mass of the loaded lamina is at (9.45, 2.85) m.

Composite shapes

- A **composite shape** is one that can be **broken up into standard parts**, such as triangles, rectangles, circles and sectors of circles.
- To find the **centre of mass** of a composite shape, first break it down into its **individual parts**, and find the centre of mass of each part **individually**.
- Once you've found the individual centres of mass, imagine replacing each part with a **particle** of the same mass in the position of its centre of mass.
- You can then find the **centre of mass** of the **group** of 'particles' — this gives you the centre of mass of the **entire composite shape**.
- If the individual parts are made from the **same uniform material**, then the **mass** of each part will be **in proportion** to its **area**. This means you can use the shapes' **areas** rather than their **masses** in your calculations.

Example 1

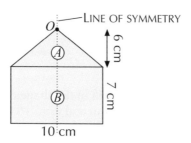

A house-shaped lamina, with dimensions as shown, is cut from a single uniform piece of card. Find the location of the centre of mass of the shape in relation to the point O.

- First, split the shape up into a triangle (A) and rectangle (B).

- As both bits are made of the same material, the masses of A and B are in proportion to their areas, so you can say:

$$m_A = \tfrac{1}{2} \times 10 \times 6 = 30$$
$$m_B = 10 \times 7 = 70$$

These are just the areas, in cm², of A and B respectively.

- The shape has a line of symmetry, so the centre of mass must be on that line, directly below the point O.

- Find the vertical position of the centres of mass of both A and B individually.

- y_A, the position of the centre of mass of A, is $\tfrac{2}{3}$ of the way down from O to the base of A (as the vertical line of symmetry is a median of A):

$$y_A = \tfrac{2}{3} \times 6 \text{ cm}$$
$$= 4 \text{ cm down from } O$$

- y_B, the position of the centre of mass of B, is 'the height of A plus half the height of B' down from O (as B has a horizontal line of symmetry halfway down):

$$y_B = 6 \text{ cm} + (7 \text{ cm} \div 2)$$
$$= 9.5 \text{ cm down from } O$$

Tip: Use symmetry where you can — but make sure you explain what you've done.

- Treat the shapes as two particles positioned at the centres of mass of each shape, and use the formula for the centre of mass of particles in a vertical line:

$$\sum my = \overline{y} \sum m$$
$$\Rightarrow m_A y_A + m_B y_B = \overline{y}(m_A + m_B)$$
$$\Rightarrow (30 \times 4) + (70 \times 9.5) = \overline{y}(30 + 70)$$
$$\Rightarrow 785 = 100\overline{y}$$
$$\Rightarrow \overline{y} = 785 \div 100 = 7.85 \text{ cm}$$

Tip: This is the formula from page 38.

- So the centre of mass of the whole shape is 7.85 cm vertically below O on the line of symmetry.

Example 2

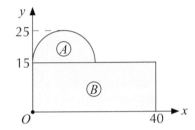

A semicircle and a rectangle are cut from the same uniform lamina. They are fixed together as shown. Find the coordinates of the centre of mass of the composite shape.

- Call the semicircle A and the rectangle B.

- A and B are cut from the same uniform lamina, so the masses of A and B are proportional to their areas:

$$m_A = \frac{1}{2} \times \pi \times 10^2 = 50\pi$$

$$m_B = 15 \times 40 = 600$$

Tip: From the diagram, the radius of the semicircle is 10 units.

- A has a vertical line of symmetry through its centre. The radius of A is 10 units, so the line of symmetry is the line $x = 10$. The centre of mass of A lies on this line, so its x-coordinate is $x_A = 10$.

- Using the expression $\frac{2r\sin\alpha}{3\alpha}$ with $r = 10$ and $\alpha = \frac{\pi}{2}$:

$$\frac{2r\sin\alpha}{3\alpha} = \frac{2 \times 10 \times \sin\frac{\pi}{2}}{\frac{3\pi}{2}} = \frac{40}{3\pi}$$

Tip: Take a look back at page 47 for a reminder of how to find the COM of a semicircle.

- So the y-coordinate of the centre of mass of A is $y_A = 15 + \frac{40}{3\pi}$.

- Therefore, the centre of mass of A is at $\left(10, \ 15 + \frac{40}{3\pi}\right)$.

- B has a horizontal line of symmetry and a vertical line of symmetry which cross at its centre. So the centre of mass of B is at $(20, 7.5)$

- As in the previous example, treat the shapes as two particles positioned at the centres of mass of each shape.
- This time though, use the formula for the centre of mass of particles in a plane:

$$\sum m\mathbf{r} = \bar{\mathbf{r}} \sum m$$

$$\Rightarrow m_A \mathbf{r}_A + m_B \mathbf{r}_B = \bar{\mathbf{r}}(m_A + m_B)$$

$$\Rightarrow 50\pi \begin{pmatrix} 10 \\ 15 + \frac{40}{3\pi} \end{pmatrix} + 600 \begin{pmatrix} 20 \\ 7.5 \end{pmatrix} = \bar{\mathbf{r}}(50\pi + 600)$$

$$\Rightarrow \begin{pmatrix} 13570.79... \\ 7522.86... \end{pmatrix} = \bar{\mathbf{r}}(757.07...)$$

$$\Rightarrow \bar{\mathbf{r}} = \frac{1}{757.07...} \begin{pmatrix} 13570.79... \\ 7522.86... \end{pmatrix} = \begin{pmatrix} 17.925... \\ 9.936... \end{pmatrix}$$

- So the centre of mass of the whole shape is at (17.9, 9.94) (3 s.f.)

The removal method

You may have a shape that looks like a 'standard' shape with other standard shapes '**removed**', rather than stuck to it.

You can find the **centre of mass** of this kind of shape using the '**removal method**' — this is pretty similar to the method used in the previous examples, except the individual centres of mass are **subtracted** rather than added.

Example

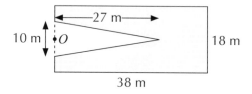

An isosceles triangle of height 27 m and base width 10 m is cut from a uniform 38 m × 18 m rectangular lamina, as shown. The midpoint of the base of the triangle is at the midpoint of the side of the rectangle. This is the point O.

Find the position of the centre of mass of the shape in relation to O.

- Call the rectangle A and the triangle which has been removed B.

- A is uniform, so the masses of A and B are in proportion to their areas:

$$m_A = 38 \times 18 = 684$$

$$m_B = \frac{1}{2} \times 10 \times 27 = 135$$

Tip: With shapes which have a bit removed, the centre of mass of the resulting shape will not necessarily be on the shape itself — it could be in the gap left by the removed bit.

- The shape has a horizontal line of symmetry passing through O. The centre of mass of the shape lies on this line.

- Find the horizontal position of the centre of mass of each shape individually.

- By symmetry, the centre of mass of A is at its centre:
$$x_A = 38 \div 2 = 19 \text{ m}$$

- The line of symmetry of the shape is a median of the triangle, so the centre of mass of B lies on this line, $\frac{2}{3}$ of the way along the median from the triangle's vertex, or $\frac{1}{3}$ of the way along from O:
$$x_B = \frac{1}{3} \times 27 = 9 \text{ m}$$

- Treat A and B as two particles positioned at the centres of mass of each shape, and use the removal method to find $\overline{x}$, the horizontal distance of the centre of mass of the leftover shape from O:
$$m_A x_A - m_B x_B = \overline{x}(m_A - m_B)$$
$$(684 \times 19) - (135 \times 9) = \overline{x}(684 - 135)$$
$$11\,781 = 549\overline{x}$$
$$\Rightarrow \overline{x} = 21.459...$$

Tip: The triangle has been taken away from the rectangle, so subtract $m_B x_B$ from $m_A x_A$, rather than adding it.

- So the centre of mass of the shape is
21.5 m (3 s.f.) horizontally to the right of O, on the line of symmetry.

Exercise 2.2

Q1 A uniform square lamina of mass 4.5 kg has vertices $A(1, 1)$, $B(1, 7)$, $C(7, 7)$ and $D(7, 1)$. Particles of mass 4 kg and 1.5 kg are fixed to the points $(5, 4)$ and $(2, 2)$ respectively.
Find the coordinates of the centre of mass of the loaded lamina.

Q2

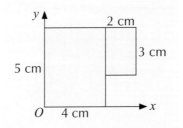

Two rectangles are cut from the same uniform lamina.
The rectangles measure 4 cm × 5 cm and 2 cm × 3 cm,
and are fixed together as shown in the diagram.
Find the coordinates of the centre of mass of
the composite shape relative to O.

Q3 A uniform lamina has vertices $A(1, 2)$, $B(7, 2)$, $C(7, 7)$ and $D(1, 7)$.
A circle of radius 1 unit centred at $(4, 5)$ is cut from the lamina.
Find the coordinates of the centre of mass of the resulting shape.

Q4

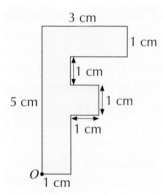

A letter F is cut from a uniform sheet of card, as shown above.
Find the distance of the centre of mass of the letter from the point O.

Q5

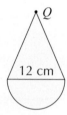

The diagram above shows a 2-dimensional shape consisting of a
semicircular lamina of diameter 12 cm and a lamina in the shape
of an isosceles triangle of base 12 cm, joined as shown. The two
laminas are made of the same uniform material. The shape's centre
of mass lies at the midpoint of the base of the triangle.

a) What is the triangle's height?

b) A particle of mass 1.4 kg is attached to the point Q, shown in
the diagram. Given that the shape's mass before the particle is
attached is 2.6 kg, find the distance of the centre of mass of the
loaded shape from Q.

Q6

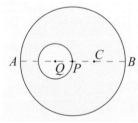

A circular disc of radius 4 cm is removed from a uniform circular
disc of radius 12 cm, as shown above. P is the centre of the
12 cm-radius disc, and Q is the centre of the 4 cm-radius disc.
P lies on the circumference of the 4 cm-radius disc. C is the centre
of mass of the resulting shape. A and B are points on the edge of the
shape such that A, Q, P, C and B all lie on the same horizontal line.
Find the distance AC.

Q7

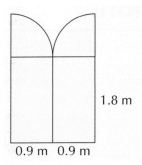

1.8 m

0.9 m   0.9 m

The diagram above shows a pair of swing doors. The doors are made up of two 0.9 m × 1.8 m rectangles and two quarter-circles of radius 0.9 m. By modelling the pair of doors as a uniform lamina, find the vertical distance from the doors' base to the centre of mass of the pair of doors.

Q8

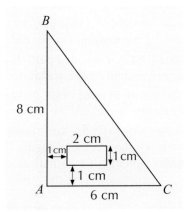

A template is made by removing a 2 cm × 1 cm rectangle from a uniform right-angled triangular lamina of height 8 cm and base width 6 cm, as shown above. Find:

a) the distance of the centre of mass of the template from AB,

b) the distance of the centre of mass of the template from AC.

A particle is attached to the template at C so that the centre of mass of the loaded template is now 3.5 cm from the side AB. Given that the template has a mass of 0.3 kg, find:

c) the mass of the particle,

d) the distance of the centre of mass of the loaded template from the side AC.

3. Frameworks

Learning Objectives:

- Be able to find the centre of mass of a framework.
- Be able to find the centre of mass of an arc.

A framework is made up of rods fixed together or a wire bent into a particular shape. In this section, you'll learn how to find the centre of mass of a framework.

Frameworks

Imagine bending a wire coathanger into something shapely, or fixing a load of rods together. These shapes are called **frameworks**.

In a framework, there's nothing in the middle, so all the mass is within the **wires** or **rods** that make up the shape's edges.

Finding the centre of mass of a framework is similar to finding the centre of mass of a composite shape:

- Imagine each side of the framework as a **separate rod** — even if it's a single wire bent into shape — and find the centre of mass of **each rod individually**.

- If the rods or wires are **straight** and **uniform**, the centre of mass of each one is at the **midpoint** of the rod.

- Next, imagine replacing each rod with a **particle** of the same mass in the position of its centre of mass.

- You can then find the **centre of mass** of the **group** of 'particles' — this gives you the centre of mass of the **framework**.

- If the rods or wires are made from the **same uniform material**, then their **mass** will be in proportion to their **length**. This means you can use the shapes' **lengths** rather than their **masses** in your calculations.

Example 1

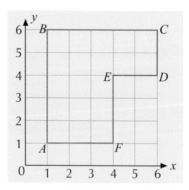

The diagram shows a uniform wire bent into the framework *ABCDEF*.

a) Find the coordinates of the centre of mass of the framework.

- The centre of mass of each side of the framework is at its midpoint.
- Write down the position vector of the centre of mass of each side:

$$\mathbf{r}_{AB} = \begin{pmatrix} 1 \\ 3.5 \end{pmatrix} \qquad \mathbf{r}_{BC} = \begin{pmatrix} 3.5 \\ 6 \end{pmatrix} \qquad \mathbf{r}_{CD} = \begin{pmatrix} 6 \\ 5 \end{pmatrix}$$

$$\mathbf{r}_{DE} = \begin{pmatrix} 5 \\ 4 \end{pmatrix} \qquad \mathbf{r}_{EF} = \begin{pmatrix} 4 \\ 2.5 \end{pmatrix} \qquad \mathbf{r}_{FA} = \begin{pmatrix} 2.5 \\ 1 \end{pmatrix}$$

Tip: You know that the centre of mass of each side is at its midpoint because you're told that the framework is made from a uniform wire, so its mass is spread evenly along its length.

- The mass of each side is proportional to its length:

$$m_{AB} = 5 \qquad m_{BC} = 5 \qquad m_{CD} = 2$$
$$m_{DE} = 2 \qquad m_{EF} = 3 \qquad m_{FA} = 3$$

Tip: You know that the mass of each side is proportional to its length because each side is made from the same uniform wire.

- You've now got the equivalent of a group of 6 particles, so put it all in the formula from page 40:

$$\sum m\mathbf{r} = \bar{\mathbf{r}} \sum m$$

$$m_{AB}\mathbf{r}_{AB} + m_{BC}\mathbf{r}_{BC} + m_{CD}\mathbf{r}_{CD} + m_{DE}\mathbf{r}_{DE} + m_{EF}\mathbf{r}_{EF} + m_{FA}\mathbf{r}_{FA} =$$
$$\bar{\mathbf{r}}(m_{AB} + m_{BC} + m_{CD} + m_{DE} + m_{EF} + m_{FA})$$

$$5\begin{pmatrix}1\\3.5\end{pmatrix} + 5\begin{pmatrix}3.5\\6\end{pmatrix} + 2\begin{pmatrix}6\\5\end{pmatrix} + 2\begin{pmatrix}5\\4\end{pmatrix} + 3\begin{pmatrix}4\\2.5\end{pmatrix} + 3\begin{pmatrix}2.5\\1\end{pmatrix} =$$
$$(5 + 5 + 2 + 2 + 3 + 3)\bar{\mathbf{r}}$$

$$\begin{pmatrix}5 + 17.5 + 12 + 10 + 12 + 7.5\\17.5 + 30 + 10 + 8 + 7.5 + 3\end{pmatrix} = 20\bar{\mathbf{r}}$$

$$\Rightarrow \bar{\mathbf{r}} = \frac{1}{20}\begin{pmatrix}64\\76\end{pmatrix} = \begin{pmatrix}3.2\\3.8\end{pmatrix}$$

- So the coordinates of the centre of mass are (3.2, 3.8).

b) A particle with the same mass as the whole framework is attached to the frame at A. Find the new centre of mass of the system.

- The system consists of the framework with COM at (3.2, 3.8) (from part a)), plus the particle at (1, 1).

- As they're the same mass, you can call each mass '1'.

- Using the formula $\sum m\mathbf{r} = \bar{\mathbf{r}} \sum m$:

$$1\mathbf{r}_{Frame} + 1\mathbf{r}_{Particle} = 2\bar{\mathbf{r}}$$

$$\Rightarrow \begin{pmatrix}3.2\\3.8\end{pmatrix} + \begin{pmatrix}1\\1\end{pmatrix} = 2\bar{\mathbf{r}}$$

$$\Rightarrow \bar{\mathbf{r}} = \frac{1}{2}\begin{pmatrix}4.2\\4.8\end{pmatrix} = \begin{pmatrix}2.1\\2.4\end{pmatrix}$$

Tip: You're only really interested in the masses of each part of the system <u>relative to each other</u>. Calling the equal masses '1' is a good way to simplify the calculation.

- So the coordinates of the new centre of mass are (2.1, 2.4).

Example 2

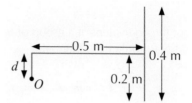

The diagram shows a framework made up of three pieces cut from the same uniform rod. The centre of mass of the framework is a horizontal distance of 0.325 m from O.

a) Find the distance d, shown in the diagram.

- You're given the horizontal position of the framework's centre of mass, so use the formula $\sum mx = \bar{x} \sum m$.

- Let the d m rod be '1', the 0.5 m rod be '2' and the 0.4 m rod be '3'.

Tip: x_1, x_2 and x_3 are the horizontal distances of the COM of each rod from O.

- The centre of mass of each rod is at its midpoint, and the mass of each rod is proportional to its length, so:

$$m_1 = d, \, x_1 = 0 \qquad m_2 = 0.5, \, x_2 = 0.25 \qquad m_3 = 0.4, \, x_3 = 0.5$$

$$\sum mx = \bar{x} \sum m$$

$$m_1 x_1 + m_2 x_2 + m_3 x_3 = \bar{x}(m_1 + m_2 + m_3)$$

$$(d \times 0) + (0.5 \times 0.25) + (0.4 \times 0.5) = 0.325(d + 0.5 + 0.4)$$

$$\Rightarrow 0.325 = 0.325(d + 0.9)$$

$$\Rightarrow 1 = d + 0.9$$

$$\Rightarrow \boxed{d = 0.1 \text{ m}}$$

b) Find the vertical distance of the centre of mass of the framework from O.

- This time, use the formula $\sum my = \bar{y} \sum m$.

$$m_1 = 0.1, \, y_1 = 0.05 \qquad m_2 = 0.5, \, y_2 = 0.1 \qquad m_3 = 0.4, \, y_3 = 0.1$$

Tip: y_1, y_2 and y_3 are the vertical distances of the COM of each rod from O.

$$\sum my = \bar{y} \sum m$$

$$m_1 y_1 + m_2 y_2 + m_3 y_3 = \bar{y}(m_1 + m_2 + m_3)$$

$$(0.1 \times 0.05) + (0.5 \times 0.1) + (0.4 \times 0.1) = \bar{y}(0.1 + 0.5 + 0.4)$$

$$\Rightarrow 0.095 = 1\bar{y}$$

$$\Rightarrow \boxed{\bar{y} = 0.095 \text{ m}}$$

Exercise 3.1

Q1

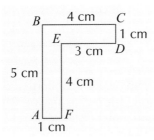

A uniform wire is bent to form the shape *ABCDEF*, as shown. Find:

a) the distance of the centre of mass of the shape from the side *AB*,

b) the distance of the centre of mass of the shape from the side *AF*.

Q2

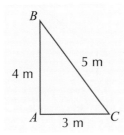

A uniform wire is bent to form the right-angled triangle *ABC*, shown.

a) Find the distance of the centre of mass of *ABC* from *AC*.

A particle of mass M kg is attached to the framework at *B*.
The centre of mass of the loaded framework is 2.4 m from *AC*.
Given that each metre of wire has mass 1 kg, find:

b) the value of M,

c) the distance of the centre of mass of the
loaded framework from *AB*.

Q3 A framework is made up of three uniform rods forming an isosceles
triangle *ABC*. *AC* has length 12 cm and mass 1.5 kg, *AB* has length
10 cm and mass 1 kg and *BC* has length 10 cm and mass 2 kg.
Find the distance of the centre of mass of the framework from *AC*.

> **Q3 Hint:** Don't worry
> that the rods have
> different masses — the
> principle's the same as
> ever: just treat each rod
> as a particle positioned
> at its centre of mass.

Q4

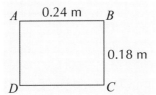

Four uniform rods are fixed together to form the rectangular
framework *ABCD*, as shown. Rod *AB* has mass M kg, rod *BC* has
mass $2M$ kg and rod *CD* has mass $1.5M$ kg.

a) The centre of mass of the framework is 0.15 m from *AD*.
Find the mass of rod *AD*, in terms of M.

b) Find the distance of the centre of mass of the framework from *AB*.

Q5

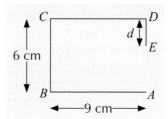

Four pieces cut from the same uniform rod are fixed together to form the framework *ABCDE*, as shown. The centre of mass of the framework is a horizontal distance of 5.4 cm from *A*. Find:

a) the distance *d*, shown in the diagram,

b) the vertical distance of the centre of
   mass of the framework from *A*.

Q6

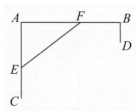

A bracket for a hanging basket is made from four pieces cut from the same uniform iron rod, as shown. You are given that $AB = 20$ cm, $AC = 15$ cm, $BD = 4$ cm, $AE = 9$ cm and $AF = 12$ cm.

a) Find the distance of the centre of mass of the bracket from *A*.

b) A hanging basket of twice the mass of the bracket is attached at *D*. Modelling the hanging basket as a particle positioned at *D*, find the distance of the centre of mass of the loaded bracket from *A*.

Q7

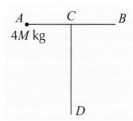

A framework consists of two uniform rods, *AB* and *CD*, each of length 12 cm. *AB* is horizontal, *CD* is vertical, and *C* is fixed to the midpoint of *AB*, as shown. The mass of each rod is *M* kg. A particle, *P*, of mass $4M$ kg, is fixed at *A*.

a) Where on *AB* should you fix a second particle, *Q*, of mass $6M$ kg, so that the centre of mass of the loaded framework lies on *CD*?

b) (i)   Where on *CD* should you fix the particle *Q* so that the centre of mass of the loaded framework is 4 cm vertically below *AB*?

   (ii) With *Q* positioned as in part b), how far from *CD* is the centre of mass of the loaded framework?

Arcs

An **arc** is part of the **edge** of a **circle**. Just like sectors, arcs have their own **formula** to find their centre of mass:

For a uniform arc of a circle of radius r with an angle of 2α **radians** at its centre:

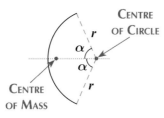

CENTRE OF **C**IRCLE

α

α

r

r

CENTRE OF **M**ASS

Centre of mass is $\frac{r\sin\alpha}{\alpha}$ from the centre of the circle on the axis of symmetry.

Example

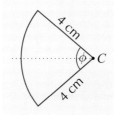

4 cm

4 cm

ϕ C

A uniform wire is bent to form a sector of a circle of radius 4 cm with angle $\phi = \frac{\pi}{3}$ radians at its centre, as shown. Find the horizontal distance of the centre of mass of the framework from the point C.

- The framework is made from the same piece of wire, so the mass of each side of the shape is in proportion to its length.

- First find the length of the arc:

  arc length $= r\phi$

  $$= 4 \times \frac{\pi}{3} = \frac{4\pi}{3} \text{ cm}$$

- Let the arc be '1', the 'upper' radius be '2', and the 'lower' radius be '3'.

- Find x_1, the horizontal distance of the centre of mass of the arc from C:

  $$r = 4 \text{ cm}, \ 2\alpha = \frac{\pi}{3} \ \Rightarrow \ \alpha = \frac{\pi}{6}$$

  $$x_1 = \frac{r\sin\alpha}{\alpha}$$

  $$= \frac{4 \times \sin\frac{\pi}{6}}{\frac{\pi}{6}} = \frac{12}{\pi} \text{ cm}$$

Tip: The COM of the framework lies on the line of symmetry, which passes through C. So you only need to find the horizontal distance of the COM from C.

Tip: Remember — the length of an arc of a circle of radius r with angle θ at its centre is given by: arc length $= r\theta$

- The two straight rods each have their centre of mass 2 cm along their length. x_2 and x_3, the horizontal distance of each centre of mass from C, can be found using trigonometry:

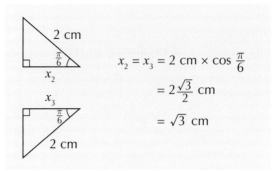

$$x_2 = x_3 = 2 \text{ cm} \times \cos \frac{\pi}{6}$$
$$= 2\frac{\sqrt{3}}{2} \text{ cm}$$
$$= \sqrt{3} \text{ cm}$$

- Now treat the three rods like particles on a horizontal line and use the formula $\sum m\overline{x} = \overline{x} \sum m$:

$$m_1 x_1 + m_2 x_2 + m_3 x_3 = \overline{x}(m_1 + m_2 + m_3)$$
$$\left(\frac{4\pi}{3} \times \frac{12}{\pi}\right) + (4 \times \sqrt{3}) + (4 \times \sqrt{3}) = \overline{x}\left(\frac{4\pi}{3} + 4 + 4\right)$$
$$\Rightarrow 16 + 8\sqrt{3} = \left(8 + \frac{4\pi}{3}\right)\overline{x}$$
$$\Rightarrow \boxed{\overline{x} = 2.45 \text{ cm (3 s.f.)}}$$

Exercise 3.2

Q1

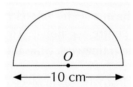

A uniform wire is bent to form a closed semicircular framework of diameter 10 cm, as shown. Find the distance of the centre of mass of the framework from O, the midpoint of the straight section of wire.

Q2

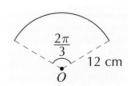

A uniform wire of mass 100 g is bent into an arc of radius 12 cm and angle $\frac{2\pi}{3}$ radians, centred at O.

a) Find the distance of the centre of mass of the arc from O.

b) A particle of mass M is attached to each end of the arc, so that the centre of mass of the loaded arc is 8 cm from O, on the line of symmetry of the shape. Find the value of M.

Q3

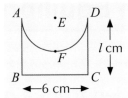

The framework shown above is made up of three straight sides, AB, BC and CD, and a semicircular side centred at E, where E is the midpoint of AD. The sides are all cut from the same piece of uniform wire. The centre of mass of the framework is at F, on the semicircle directly below E. Find the value of l, as shown in the diagram.

Q4

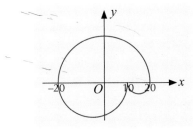

A length of uniform wire is cut into three pieces, which are bent to form semicircles and then fixed together to form a piece of jewellery, as shown. The semicircles have radii of 20 units, 15 units and 5 units respectively, and are centred at $(0, 0)$, $(-5, 0)$ and $(15, 0)$ respectively. Find:

a) the coordinates of the centre of mass of each semicircle,

b) the coordinates of the centre of mass of the piece of jewellery.

Q5

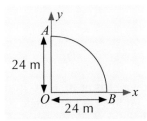

Straight, uniform wires OA and OB are fixed to the uniform wire arc AB, as shown. The wires form a quarter-circle, OAB, of radius 24 m. Arc AB has mass 2 kg and wires OA and OB each have mass 1 kg.

a) Show that the position vector of the centre of mass of OAB is
$$\bar{\mathbf{r}}_1 = \begin{pmatrix} 24/\pi + 3 \\ 24/\pi + 3 \end{pmatrix} \text{ m.}$$

Particles of mass p kg and q kg are fixed to OAB at the points A and B respectively, so that the position vector of the centre of mass of the loaded framework is $\bar{\mathbf{r}}_2 = \begin{pmatrix} 12 \\ 10 \end{pmatrix}$ m.

b) Find the values of p and q.

4. Laminas in Equilibrium

Finding the centre of mass of a lamina helps you work out what will happen when the lamina is tilted or suspended from a point.

Laminas suspended from a point

When you **suspend** a shape, either from a point on its edge or from a **pivot point** within the shape, it will hang in **equilibrium** so that the **centre of mass** is **vertically below** the **suspension point**.

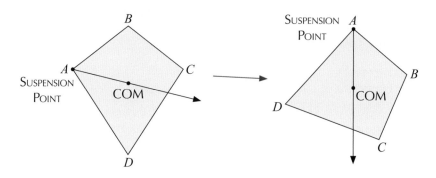

Knowing the position of the centre of mass of the shape will let you work out the **angle** that the shape hangs at.

Example 1

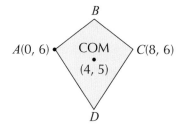

In the shape $ABCD$, shown, A is at $(0, 6)$, C is at $(8, 6)$, and the centre of mass is at $(4, 5)$. Find the angle AC makes with the vertical when the shape is freely suspended from A.

- When the shape is suspended from A, it will hang with its centre of mass vertically below A.

- Draw in the line representing the vertical from A to the centre of mass and label the angle you need to find α. You can then use this to form a right-angled triangle:

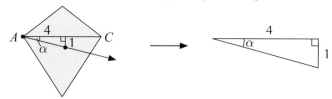

- You can now find the angle using trigonometry:

$$\alpha = \tan^{-1}\left(\tfrac{1}{4}\right) = \boxed{14.0° \text{ (3 s.f.)}}$$

Example 2

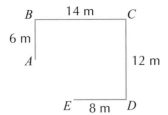

The diagram shows a uniform wire bent to form the framework *ABCDE*. Find the angle that *BC* makes with the vertical when the framework is freely suspended from *B*.

Tip: Don't worry that this is asking about a framework rather than a lamina — the principle's the same.

- First find the centre of mass of the framework — it's being suspended from *B*, so you might as well find the position of the centre of mass relative to that point.

- The sides are made of the same uniform material, so the mass of each side is proportional to its length, and, by symmetry, the centre of mass of each side is at its midpoint.

- Write down the individual masses and centres of mass of each side of the framework relative to *B*:

$$m_{AB} = 6, \ \mathbf{r}_{AB} = \begin{pmatrix} 0 \\ -3 \end{pmatrix} \qquad m_{BC} = 14, \ \mathbf{r}_{BC} = \begin{pmatrix} 7 \\ 0 \end{pmatrix}$$

$$m_{CD} = 12, \ \mathbf{r}_{CD} = \begin{pmatrix} 14 \\ -6 \end{pmatrix} \qquad m_{DE} = 8, \ \mathbf{r}_{DE} = \begin{pmatrix} 10 \\ -12 \end{pmatrix}$$

- Now, using the formula $\sum m\mathbf{r} = \bar{\mathbf{r}} \sum m$:

$$m_{AB}\mathbf{r}_{AB} + m_{BC}\mathbf{r}_{BC} + m_{CD}\mathbf{r}_{CD} + m_{DE}\mathbf{r}_{DE} = \bar{\mathbf{r}}(m_{AB} + m_{BC} + m_{CD} + m_{DE})$$

$$6\begin{pmatrix} 0 \\ -3 \end{pmatrix} + 14\begin{pmatrix} 7 \\ 0 \end{pmatrix} + 12\begin{pmatrix} 14 \\ -6 \end{pmatrix} + 8\begin{pmatrix} 10 \\ -12 \end{pmatrix} = \bar{\mathbf{r}}(6 + 14 + 12 + 8)$$

$$\begin{pmatrix} 346 \\ -186 \end{pmatrix} = 40\bar{\mathbf{r}}$$

$$\Rightarrow \bar{\mathbf{r}} = \begin{pmatrix} 8.65 \\ -4.65 \end{pmatrix}$$

- When the framework is suspended from *B*, it will hang with its centre of mass vertically below *B*.

- Draw in the line from *B* to the centre of mass, and form a right-angled triangle:

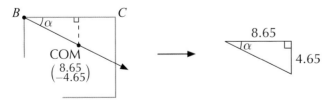

- You can now find the angle using trigonometry:

$$\alpha = \tan^{-1}\left(\frac{4.65}{8.65}\right) = 28.3° \text{ (3 s.f.)}$$

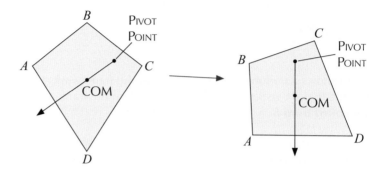

In some cases, a lamina will be 'free to rotate about a fixed horizontal axis'. This just means that the lamina is **pivoted** about a point somewhere **on the shape**, rather than being suspended from one of its vertices.

Again, the lamina will hang in **equilibrium** with its **centre of mass** directly **below** the pivot.

Tip: The 'horizontal axis' bit just means that the lamina is free to rotate about an axis (line) which passes through the pivot point, perpendicular to the lamina.

Example

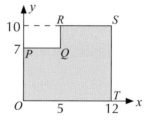

A uniform rectangular lamina has a smaller rectangle cut from it, as shown in the diagram. The leftover shape, *OPQRST*, is pivoted at (10, 8), and allowed to freely rotate about this point.

a) **Find the angle that *ST* makes with the vertical.**

- First you need to find the centre of mass of the shape.
- Let *A* be the larger rectangle and *B* be the smaller rectangle which is removed.
- *A* is uniform, so the masses of *A* and *B* are proportional to their areas:

$$m_A = 12 \times 10 = 120 \qquad m_B = 5 \times 3 = 15$$

- By symmetry, the centre of mass of each of *A* and *B* are at their centres, so:

$$\mathbf{r}_A = \begin{pmatrix} 6 \\ 5 \end{pmatrix} \qquad \mathbf{r}_B = \begin{pmatrix} 2.5 \\ 8.5 \end{pmatrix}$$

- Using the removal method to find the centre of mass of the whole shape:

$$m_A\mathbf{r}_A - m_B\mathbf{r}_B = \bar{\mathbf{r}}(m_A - m_B)$$
$$120\begin{pmatrix} 6 \\ 5 \end{pmatrix} - 15\begin{pmatrix} 2.5 \\ 8.5 \end{pmatrix} = \bar{\mathbf{r}}(120 - 15)$$
$$\begin{pmatrix} 682.5 \\ 472.5 \end{pmatrix} = 105\bar{\mathbf{r}}$$
$$\Rightarrow \bar{\mathbf{r}} = \begin{pmatrix} 6.5 \\ 4.5 \end{pmatrix}$$

- Draw a diagram to show the line from the pivot point to the centre of mass, and draw a right-angled triangle to help you find α, the angle ST makes with the vertical:

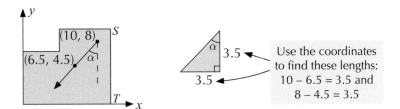

Tip: The dotted line is parallel to ST, so the angle between the vertical and the dotted line is the same as the angle between the vertical and ST.

Use the coordinates to find these lengths:
$10 - 6.5 = 3.5$ and
$8 - 4.5 = 3.5$

- Finally, using trigonometry:

$$\alpha = \tan^{-1}\left(\frac{3.5}{3.5}\right)$$

$$= 45°$$

b) **The mass of the shape is 3 kg. A particle of mass M kg is fixed to the shape at the midpoint of ST, such that the shape hangs in equilibrium with ST vertical. Find the value of M.**

- Draw a diagram to show what's going on:

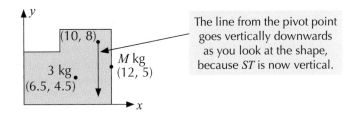

The line from the pivot point goes vertically downwards as you look at the shape, because ST is now vertical.

- From M1, you should remember that, for a rigid body in equilibrium, 'clockwise moments = anticlockwise moments'.
- The pivot point is $(10, 8)$, so you want to take moments about this point.
- When taking moments, you need to use the **perpendicular distance** from the line of action of each force to the pivot.
- The weights of the shape and the particle both act **vertically downwards**, so you need to use the **horizontal** distance from the **position of the particle** to the **pivot**, and the **horizontal** distance from the **centre of mass of the lamina** to the **pivot**:

Moments clockwise = Moments anticlockwise

$Mg \times (12 - 10) = 3g \times (10 - 6.5)$

$\Rightarrow M = 10.5g \div 2g$

$= 5.25$ kg

Tip: Another way to answer this question would be to first find the COM of the loaded lamina in terms of M. Then, for the loaded lamina to hang with ST vertical, the x-coordinate of its COM must be 10. You can use this to find the value of M.

Tip: Use the x-coordinates of the position of the particle, the COM of the lamina and the pivot point to find the horizontal distances you need for the formula.

Q1

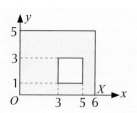

A square is cut from a uniform rectangular lamina, as shown.

a) Find the coordinates of the centre of mass of the resulting shape.

b) The shape is freely suspended from O. Find the angle that OX makes with the vertical, where X is the point $(6, 0)$.

Q2

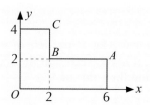

A uniform wire is bent to form the framework shown above.

a) Find the coordinates of the centre of mass of the framework.

b) The framework is freely suspended from $A(6, 2)$. Find the angle that AB makes with the vertical, where B is the point $(2, 2)$.

A particle of mass 2.5 kg is fixed to the framework at $C(2, 4)$, such that, when the framework is suspended from A, AB is vertical.

c) Find the mass of the framework.

Q3 The uniform rectangular lamina $ABCD$ has vertices $A(0, 0)$, $B(12, 0)$, $C(12, 8)$ and $D(0, 8)$. A circle of radius 2 units centred at $(9, 3)$ is cut from the rectangle. The remaining shape is freely pivoted at the point $(1, 1)$. Find the angle that AB makes with the vertical.

Q4

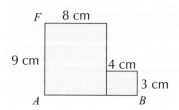

A composite shape consists of two uniform rectangular laminas of the same material, as shown.

a) Find the distance of the centre of mass of the shape from AF.

b) Find the distance of the centre of mass of the shape from AB.

c) The shape is freely suspended from A.
Find the angle that AF makes with the vertical.

d) The shape is now freely suspended from F.
Find the angle that AF now makes with the vertical.

Q5

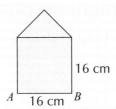

16 cm

A 16 cm B

The diagram shows a composite lamina consisting of a square and an isosceles triangle made from the same uniform material. When the shape is freely suspended from A, AB makes an angle of θ with the vertical, where $\tan\theta = 1.25$. Find the height of the triangle.

Q6

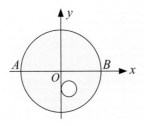

A uniform circular lamina of radius 10 units is centred at O. A circle of radius 2 units centred at $(2, -4)$ is cut from the lamina, as shown. The resulting shape is freely pivoted about an axis perpendicular to the lamina at O.

a) Find the angle that AB makes with the vertical.

A particle of mass 0.9 kg is fixed to the shape at B.

b) Given that the unloaded shape has mass 0.7 kg, find the angle that AB makes with the vertical when the loaded shape is freely pivoted at O.

Q6 b) Hint: First find the centre of mass of the loaded shape.

Q7

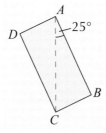

A uniform rectangular lamina, $ABCD$, of mass 0.5 kg, is freely suspended from A. The lamina hangs in equilibrium with AC vertical. The length of AB is 50 cm, and it makes an angle of 25° with the vertical, as shown.

A particle of mass 0.2 kg is fixed to the lamina at D. Find the angle that AB makes with the vertical in the new position of equilibrium.

Laminas on an inclined plane

Tilting a shape placed on an **inclined plane** will make it **topple** over eventually (assuming there's enough friction to stop it sliding).

To make the shape fall over, you need to incline the plane above an angle, α, where the shape's **centre of mass** is **vertically above** the **bottom corner** or **edge** of the shape.

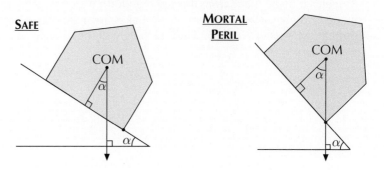

SAFE

MORTAL PERIL

Example

The house-shaped composite lamina from page 50 is in equilibrium on a plane inclined at an angle α to the horizontal.
Find the value of α at the point where the shape is about to topple.

- Sketch the shape to show what's going on — draw in a line between the COM and the corner point (T) of the shape — this line will be vertical at the tipping point.

Tip: The COM of this composite shape was found on pages 50–51 — it's 7.85 cm down from the vertex of the triangular part, on the line of symmetry of the shape. Take a look back for a reminder.

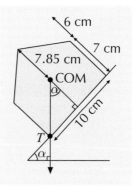

- Use your diagram to draw a right-angled triangle, then use trigonometry to find α:

Tip: The triangle's side lengths are calculated from the dimensions in the original diagram:
$6 + 7 - 7.85 = 5.15$ cm
$10 \div 2 = 5$ cm

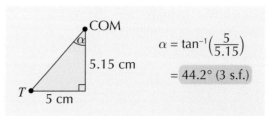

$$\alpha = \tan^{-1}\left(\frac{5}{5.15}\right)$$
$$= 44.2° \text{ (3 s.f.)}$$

Q1 Diagrams a) and b), below, show a uniform rectangular lamina
and a uniform lamina in the shape of an isosceles triangle.
Each shape is placed on a plane inclined at an angle α to the
horizontal. In each case, find the value of α for which the
lamina is on the point of toppling.

a)

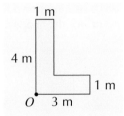

b)

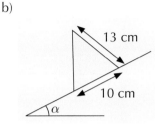

Q2

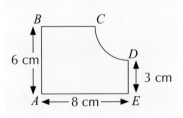

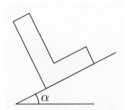

The first diagram above shows a uniform L-shaped lamina.

a) Find the position vector of the centre of mass of the lamina
relative to O.

The lamina is placed on a plane inclined at an angle α to the
horizontal, as shown in the second diagram.

b) Find the value of α for which the lamina is about to topple.

Q3

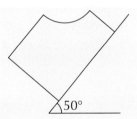

A uniform rectangular lamina has a quarter circle cut from it to give
the shape $ABCDE$, shown in the first diagram. Find:

a) (i) the distance of the centre of mass of the shape from AB,

   (ii) the distance of the centre of mass of the shape from AE.

The shape is placed on a plane inclined at an angle of 50° to the
horizontal, as shown in the second diagram.

b) Determine whether or not the shape will topple.

Q4   A uniform square lamina, $ABCD$, has vertices $A(0, 0)$,
     $B(0, 6)$, $C(6, 6)$ and $D(6, 0)$, relative to A.
     A circle of radius 1 unit centred at $(4, 2)$ is removed.

a) Find the coordinates of the centre of mass
   of the resultant shape relative to A.

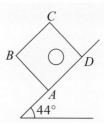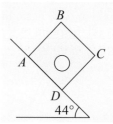

b) The shape is placed on a plane inclined at an angle of 44° to
   the horizontal, with D uppermost, as shown in the first diagram.
   Determine whether or not the shape will topple.

c) The shape is now placed on a plane inclined at an angle of 44°
   to the horizontal, with A uppermost, as shown in the second
   diagram. Determine whether or not the shape will topple.

Q5

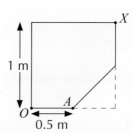

Q5 Hint: This question's
a bit different in that
the shape isn't on an
inclined plane. The
idea's the same though
— the shape will be on
the point of toppling
when its COM is directly
above A.

An isosceles triangle is cut from a uniform square lamina, as shown.
The resulting shape has mass 2 kg.

a) Find the position of the centre of mass of the resulting shape
   relative to O.

A particle of mass M kg is fixed to the shape at X, such that
the loaded shape is on the point of toppling about A.

b) Find the value of M.

Q6

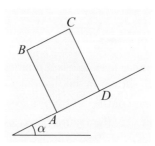

A uniform rectangular lamina, $ABCD$, is placed on a plane inclined
at an angle α to the horizontal, such that AD is in contact with
the plane, as shown. When $\alpha = 35°$, the lamina is on the point of
toppling. The lamina is now placed on the plane such that CD is in
contact with the plane. Find the value of α for which the lamina is
on the point of toppling in this case.

Review Exercise — Chapter 2

Q1 Three particles have mass $m_1 = 1$ kg, $m_2 = 2$ kg and $m_3 = 3$ kg.
Find the centre of mass of the system of particles if their coordinates are, respectively:

a) $(1, 0)$, $(2, 0)$, $(3, 0)$ b) $(0, 3)$, $(0, 2)$, $(0, 1)$ c) $(3, 4)$, $(3, 1)$, $(1, 0)$

Q2 A system of particles located at coordinates $A(0, 0)$, $B(0, 4)$, $C(5, 4)$ and $D(5, 0)$ have masses m kg, $2m$ kg, $3m$ kg and 12 kg respectively. The centre of mass of the system is at $(3.5, 2)$. Find the value of m.

Q3 Find the coordinates of the centre of mass of each of the uniform laminas shown below.

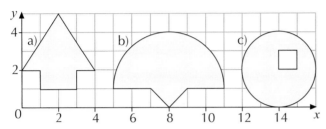

Q4 A square uniform lamina of width 10 cm has a smaller square of width 2 cm cut from its top left corner. Find the distance of the centre of mass of the remaining shape from its top edge.

Q5

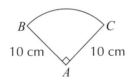

A uniform wire of mass 0.1 kg is bent to form the quarter circle ABC, of radius 10 cm, as shown.

a) Find the distance of the centre of mass of the framework from A.

Particles of mass 0.3 kg and 0.4 kg are fixed to the framework at B and C respectively.

b) Find the distance of the centre of mass of the loaded framework from A.

Q6

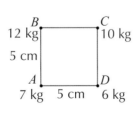 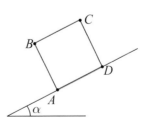

A light square framework has side lengths of 5 cm.
Particles are attached to the corners of the square, as shown in the first diagram.

a) Find the distance of the centre of mass of the loaded framework from:

    (i) AD (ii) AB

b) The loaded framework is placed on a plane inclined at an angle α to the horizontal, as shown in the second diagram. Find the value of α for which the framework is on the point of toppling.

Q7 A wire arc and a straight wire are fixed together to form a semicircle of radius 5 cm. The arc and the straight wire are made from the same kind of uniform wire.

a) Find the distance of the centre of mass from the straight edge.

The frame is suspended from one of its corners and hangs in equilibrium.

b) Find the angle the straight edge makes with the vertical.

Q8 *ABCD* is a loaded rectangular lamina with dimensions $AB = 60$ cm and $AD = 70$ cm. When *ABCD* is freely suspended from *A*, *AD* makes an angle of 45° with the vertical. When *ABCD* is freely suspended from *D*, *AD* makes an angle of 60° with the vertical.

a) (i) Find the distance of the centre of mass of *ABCD* from *AD*.

(ii) Find the distance of the centre of mass of *ABCD* from *AB*.

b) Find the angle that *BC* makes with the vertical when *ABCD* is freely suspended from *B*.

Q9

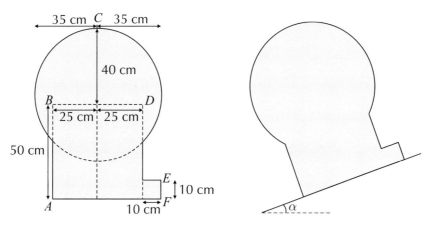

A cardboard advertising sign is modelled as two uniform square laminas with a uniform circular lamina attached, as shown in the first diagram. The masses of the small and large squares are 1 kg and 4 kg respectively. The mass of the circle is 5 kg.

a) Show that the centre of mass of the sign is 28 cm from *AB* and 38 cm from *AF*.

The sign is placed on a plane inclined at an angle α to the horizontal, as shown in the second diagram. The value of α is slowly increased.

b) Find the value of α for which the sign is on the point of toppling about *A*.

Q10

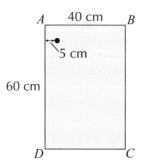

A uniform rectangular lamina, *ABCD*, has dimensions $AB = 40$ cm and $AD = 60$ cm. The lamina is freely pivoted at a point 5 cm from *AD*, as shown. The lamina hangs in equilibrium with *AD* at an angle of 35° to the vertical. Find the distance of the pivot from *AB*.

1　The diagram below shows three particles attached to a light rectangular lamina at coordinates $A(1, 3)$, $B(5, 1)$ and $C(4, y)$.

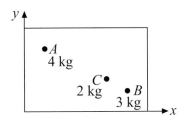

The centre of mass of the system is at $(\overline{x}, 2)$. Show that:

a)　$y = 1.5$,

(3 marks)

b)　$\overline{x} = 3$.

(3 marks)

The light lamina is replaced with a uniform rectangle $PQRS$, of mass 6 kg and with vertices at $P(0, 0)$, $Q(0, 5)$, $R(7, 5)$ and $S(7, 0)$. Particles A, B and C remain at their existing coordinates.

c)　Find the coordinates of the new centre of mass of the whole system.

(6 marks)

2　A wire sculpture is modelled as a framework made from two uniform rods; a straight rod AB, of mass $2m$ kg, and a semicircular arc of mass πm kg. Particles of mass $3m$ kg and $4m$ kg are attached to the points A and B, as shown.

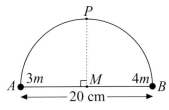

M is the midpoint of the rod AB, and P is the point on the arc directly above M.

a)　Find, in cm to 4 decimal places, the distance of the centre of mass of the loaded framework from:

　　(i)　MP,

(3 marks)

　　(ii)　AB.

(3 marks)

The sculpture is freely suspended from the point P, and hangs in equilibrium.

b)　Find the angle MP makes with the vertical.

(3 marks)

3

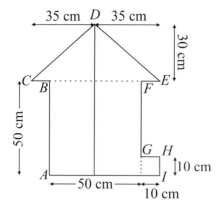

A cardboard 'For Sale' sign is modelled as a uniform lamina consisting of two squares and an isosceles triangle. The line of symmetry through the triangle coincides with that of the larger square, as shown.

a)   Show that the centre of mass of the sign, to 3 significant figures,
     is 25.8 cm from AB and 34.5 cm from AI.

(6 marks)

The sign has mass 1 kg. A particle is attached at A, such that, when the sign is freely suspended from D, it hangs in equilibrium with AI horizontal.

b)   Find the mass of the particle needed to make the sign hang in this way.

(3 marks)

4

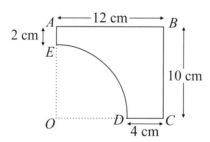

The stencil shown above is made by removing a quarter circle centred at O from a uniform sheet of metal.

a)   Taking OC as being the positive x-axis and OA as being the positive y-axis, find the coordinates of the centre of mass of the stencil.

(7 marks)

Particles are attached to the stencil so that the centre of mass is now at $(9, 6)$ cm relative to O. The stencil rests in equilibrium on a rough inclined plane, as shown on the right. The angle of incline is increased until the shape is on the point of toppling about D.

b)   Find the angle of incline above which the shape will topple.

(3 marks)

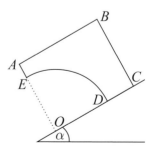

1. Work Done

Some of this chapter may seem familiar to you from GCSE science — it's all about the transfer of energy when things move due to the action of a force.

Work done

- Mechanical '**work**' is done by a **force** when the force **moves** an object through a **distance**.
- The '**work done**' by the force is equivalent to the **energy transferred** in moving the object, so work done is a measure of energy.
- You can calculate the work done by **any force** acting on an object using the following **formula**:

> **Work done = force (F) ×** **distance moved in the direction of that force (s)**

- Or: **Work done = Fs**.
- The values for distance and force used in the formula must be in the **same direction**. This means you will often have to **resolve forces** to find the component of the force in the direction of motion.

Learning Objectives:

- Be able to calculate the work done by or against a force acting on a moving object.
- Be able to find the work done on a moving object.

Tip: For an object moving with constant velocity, work is done **by** or **against** the forces which act on it. For an accelerating object, work is also done **on** the object itself, by those forces which are acting to change the velocity of the object.

Example 1

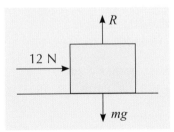

An object is accelerated a distance of 4 m across a horizontal floor by a horizontal force of magnitude 12 N.
Find the work done by the 12 N force.

- The object moves in the same direction as the force (horizontally), so just put the values in the formula:

    Work done = force × distance moved in the direction of the force

    $= 12 \times 4 = \boxed{48 \text{ J}}$

Tip: mg and R act perpendicular to the direction of motion, so they do no work on the object.

Tip: For a force in newtons, and a distance in metres, the unit of work done is the joule, J.

Example 2

A rock is pulled across a smooth horizontal surface by a rope attached at an angle of 25° above the horizontal.
Given that the work done by the tension in the rope is 470 J and the tension in the rope is 120 N, find the distance the rock is moved.

- Resolving horizontally and using the formula 'Work done = Fs':

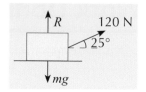

$$470 = 120\cos 25° \times s$$
$$\Rightarrow s = 470 \div 120\cos 25°$$
$$= 4.32 \text{ m (3 s.f.)}$$

Tip: The block moves horizontally, so you need the horizontal component of the tension.

- If a **resistive force** acts on a body to oppose motion, then work is done **against** the resistive force.

- You may also see this referred to as the work done **by** the resistive force. In this case, if the direction of motion is taken as positive, then the work done by the resistive force will be **negative** — because the resistive force acts in the **opposite** direction to motion.

Tip: It may seem odd for work done to be negative — but remember that work done is a transfer of energy. So, if the work done on the body is negative, then the body experiences a loss of energy.

Example 3

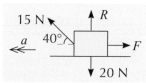

A block of weight 20 N is pulled 1.4 m across a rough horizontal floor by a rope. The tension in the rope is 15 N, acting at 40° above the horizontal. The coefficient of friction between the floor and the block is 0.3.

a) **Find the work done against friction.**

- There is no vertical motion, so, resolving vertically:
$$R + 15\sin 40° = 20$$
$$\Rightarrow R = 20 - 15\sin 40° = 10.358... \text{ N}$$

- Friction is limiting, so, using $F = \mu R$:
$$F = 0.3 \times 10.358... = 3.107... \text{ N}$$

- Now, using 'Work done = Fs':
$$\text{Work done against friction} = 3.107... \times 1.4$$
$$= 4.35 \text{ J (3 s.f.)}$$

b) **Find the work done on the block as it moves this distance.**

- In part a), you were only interested in the work done against friction. Now, you're looking for the work done **on the block**.
- This is equal to the product of the **resultant force** acting on the block and the **distance** through which the block is moved.
- Resolving horizontally, taking the direction of motion (left) as positive, and using the formula for work done:
$$\text{Work done} = (15\cos 40° - 3.107...) \times 1.4$$
$$= 11.7 \text{ J (3 s.f.)}$$

Tip: Remember — for a body moving across a rough surface, the frictional force, F, between the two is given by $F = \mu R$.

Tip: You're asked for the work done against friction, so don't worry about the tension in the rope just yet.

Tip: You can think of the work done on the block as being the work done by the resultant force.

Example 4

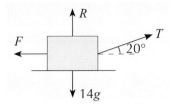

A body of mass 14 kg is pulled across a rough, horizontal plane by a rope inclined at an angle of 20° above the horizontal. The body moves 4 m at a constant speed. The work done against friction is 96 J.

a) **Find the magnitude of the tension in the rope.**

- Work done against friction is 96 J, so:

$$\text{Work done} = Fs$$
$$96 = F \times 4$$
$$\Rightarrow F = 24 \text{ N}$$

- The body is moving at a constant speed (i.e. acceleration is zero), so resolving horizontally and using $F_{net} = ma$:

$$T\cos 20° - 24 = 14 \times 0$$
$$\Rightarrow T = 24 \div \cos 20° = 25.540...$$
$$= 25.5 \text{ N (3 s.f.)}$$

b) **Find the coefficient of friction between the plane and the block.**

- Resolving vertically:

$$R + (25.540...)\sin 20° = 14g$$
$$\Rightarrow R = 128.464... \text{ N}$$

- Now, using $F = \mu R$:

$$24 = \mu \times 128.464...$$
$$\Rightarrow \mu = 0.19 \text{ (2 d.p.)}$$

Exercise 1.1

Q1 A train travels 0.3 km along a horizontal stretch of track. The resistance to motion is modelled as a constant horizontal force of magnitude 500 N. Find the work done against this resistive force.

Q2 A toy car travels 1.6 m along a smooth horizontal floor. It is powered by a horizontal driving force, P. If the work done is 8 J, find P.

Q3 A dart is thrown at a board, strikes it horizontally, and penetrates to a distance of d metres. The resistance to motion caused by the board is 84 N. If the work done against this resistive force is 0.428 J, find d.

Q4

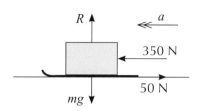

A package is placed on a sledge at rest on rough horizontal ground. A horizontal force of magnitude 350 N is applied to the sledge, which then moves a distance of 0.7 m. A frictional force of magnitude 50 N acts between the ground and the sledge. Find:

a) the work done against friction,

b) the work done on the sledge as it moves along the ground.

Q5 An object is pulled 1150 m along smooth horizontal ground by a rope. The rope is attached at an angle of 18° above the horizontal, and the tension in the rope is 2000 N.
Find the work done by the tension in the rope.

Q6 A particle is pushed 25 m across a rough, horizontal plane by a force, P, applied to the particle at an angle of 30° above the horizontal. The particle moves at constant speed. Given that the work done against friction is 55 J, find the magnitude of P.

Q7 A body of mass 0.15 kg is accelerated 6 m along rough, horizontal ground by a wire. The wire is attached to the body at an angle of 24° above the horizontal, and the tension in the wire is 2.2 N.
The coefficient of friction between the ground and the body is 0.14.

a) Find the work done against friction.

b) Find the work done on the body as it moves along the ground.

Q8 A box of mass 12 kg is pulled with increasing speed along rough, horizontal ground by a light, inextensible string. The string is attached to the box at an angle of 15° above the horizontal, and the magnitude of the tension in the string is 32 N. The coefficient of friction between the ground and the box is 0.18.

a) Given that the work done against friction is 45 J, find the distance the box moves.

b) Hence find the work done on the box as it moves this distance.

Q9

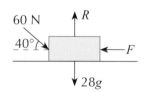

A parcel of mass 28 kg is pushed 3.5 m across a rough, horizontal floor by a pushing force of magnitude 60 N, applied to the parcel at an angle of 40° to the horizontal, as shown above.
The work done on the parcel as it moves this distance is 28 J.
Find the coefficient of friction between the parcel and the floor.

Gravity

- When a body **falls freely under gravity**, **work is done** by **gravity**.
- The force that causes the body to fall is the body's **weight**: $W = mg$.
- So for a body which falls through a height h:

> Work done by gravity = Weight × Height
> $$= mgh$$

- A force **lifting** a body vertically does work **against gravity**.
- The work done by a force **against** gravity is also given by mgh:

A body of mass m kg is attached to a vertical rope and raised h m at a **constant speed**. The tension in the rope is T.

Resolving vertically, taking up as positive, and using $F_{net} = ma$:

$$F_{net} = ma$$
$$T - mg = m \times 0$$
$$\Rightarrow T = mg$$

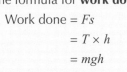

Tip: $a = 0$ because the body is moving at a constant speed.

Using the formula for **work done**:

Work done $= Fs$
$$= T \times h$$
$$= mgh$$

So the **work done against gravity** for an object moving **vertically upwards** is given by:

Work done $= mgh$

- For a body being lifted vertically, mgh only gives you the work done **against gravity**. If the body is moving at **constant speed**, there will be **no resultant force** on the body, and the tension in the rope (or whatever force is doing the lifting) will be **equal** to the body's weight. So the **work done by the tension** in the rope will be equal to the **work done against gravity**.

Tip: For a body moving at a constant speed, the work done **on the body** is zero.

- However, if the body is **accelerating**, then there **will** be a **resultant force**, and the work done by the tension in the rope and the work done against gravity **won't** be equal. Some of the work done overcomes the **resistance** of gravity, and the rest of the work is done **on the body** and causes it to **accelerate**.

Example 1

A 20 kg sack of flour is raised vertically by a light rope at a constant speed. The work done is 1400 J. Find the distance, d, the sack is raised.

- The sack is being lifted vertically at a constant speed, so:

Work done $= mgh$
$$1400 = 20 \times 9.8 \times d$$
$$\Rightarrow d = 1400 \div 196$$
$$= 7.14 \text{ m (3 s.f.)}$$

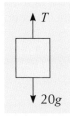

Tip: The sack is moving at constant speed, so the work done in lifting it is just the work done against gravity.

Example 2

A particle of mass 1.8 kg is lifted vertically upwards by a light, inextensible string. The particle accelerates uniformly from rest to a speed of 6 ms^{-1} in 4 seconds.

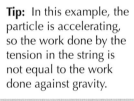

a) **Find the work done against gravity.**

- First, find the distance the particle travels.
  Taking up as positive:

  $$u = 0, \quad v = 6, \quad s = s, \quad t = 4$$

  $$s = \left(\frac{u + v}{2}\right)t$$

  $$s = \left(\frac{0 + 6}{2}\right) \times 4 = 12 \text{ m}$$

- Now, using the formula for work done against gravity:

  $$\text{Work done} = mgh$$

  $$= 1.8 \times 9.8 \times 12$$

  $$= \boxed{211.68 \text{ J}}$$

b) **Find the work done on the particle.**

Tip: In this example, the particle is accelerating, so the work done by the tension in the string is not equal to the work done against gravity.

- First, find the particle's acceleration.
  Taking up as positive:

  $$u = 0, \quad v = 6, \quad a = a, \quad t = 4$$

  $$v = u + at$$

  $$6 = 0 + 4a$$

  $$\Rightarrow a = 1.5 \text{ ms}^{-2}$$

- Now, resolving vertically, taking up as positive, and using $F_{net} = ma$:

  $$F_{net} = 1.8 \times 1.5$$

  $$= 2.7 \text{ N}$$

- Finally, using the formula for work done:

  $$\text{Work done} = F_{net} \times s$$

  $$= 2.7 \times 12$$

  $$= \boxed{32.4 \text{ J}}$$

Exercise 1.2

Q1   A pebble of mass 1.3 g is dropped a distance of 37 m. Find the work done by gravity in the pebble's fall.

Q2   A person of mass 57 kg is lifted by a rescue helicopter. If 16 367 J of work is done against gravity, calculate the vertical height through which the person is raised.

Q3   A car is lifted through a vertical distance of 2.7 m at constant speed.
      The work done in lifting the car is 22 491 J. Find the car's mass.

Q4
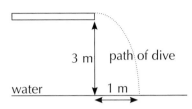

A diver of mass 48 kg dives from a height of 3 m.
The path of the dive is shown below. How much work is done by
gravity on the diver before she hits the water?

Q4 Hint: The path of
the dive doesn't matter
— it's only the vertical
height that you're
interested in.

Q5   A light, inextensible wire raises a bucket of water, with a
      total mass of 3 kg, from the bottom to the top of a well.
      The depth of the well is 9.5 m.
      a) Assuming that the bucket is raised at a constant speed, find:
          (i)   the tension in the wire,
          (ii)   the work done by the tension in the wire.
      b) Now assume that the bucket is raised with a constant
          acceleration of 1.5 ms^{-2}. Find:
          (i)   the tension in the wire,
          (ii)   the work done on the bucket as it is raised
                 to the top of the well.

Q6   A stone of mass 2 kg is dropped from the top of a cliff.
      It falls freely under gravity and lands in the sea below after 3 s.
      a) Calculate the height of the cliff.
      b) Find the work done by gravity on the stone.
      c) List any assumptions you have made.

Q7   A particle is lifted 9 m vertically upwards by a light, inextensible
      string. The tension in the string has magnitude 44 N.
      Given that the particle accelerates at a rate of 0.16 ms^{-2}, find:
      a) the mass of the particle,
      b) the work done on the particle.

Q8   An object of mass 25 kg is lifted vertically upwards by a light,
      inextensible wire. The object accelerates uniformly from rest
      to a speed of 4.2 ms^{-1} in 10 seconds. Find:
      a) the work done against gravity,
      b) the magnitude of the tension in the wire,
      c) the work done by the tension in the wire.

Friction and gravity

- If a body slides **down a rough slope**, work will be done **by gravity**. Some of this work will be done **against friction** between the body and the slope.
- If a force moves a body **up a rough slope** then work will be done **by that force**, **against friction** and **against gravity**.
- To find the work done by or against each force, you need to **resolve forces** to find the **component** of each force in the **direction of motion**.
- Then the formula '**Work done = *Fs***' can be used as normal.

Example 1

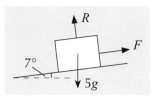

A block of mass 5 kg slides 0.5 m down a rough plane inclined at an angle of 7° to the horizontal. The coefficient of friction between the block and the plane is 0.12.

a) Find the work done by gravity in moving the block.

- The block moves 0.5 m down the plane.
- Resolving vertically, taking down as positive, the block moves through a vertical distance of $0.5 \sin 7°$ m.
- Using the formula for work done by gravity:

$$\text{Work done by gravity} = mgh$$
$$= 5 \times 9.8 \times 0.5 \sin 7°$$
$$= 2.99 \text{ J (3 s.f.)}$$

b) Find the work done against friction as the block slides.

- Resolving perpendicular to the plane:

$$R = 5g \cos 7°$$

- Now, using $F = \mu R$:

$$F = 0.12 \times 5g \cos 7°$$
$$= 5.836... \text{ N}$$

- Now, using the formula for work done:

$$\text{Work done against friction} = \text{Force} \times \text{distance}$$
$$= F \times 0.5$$
$$= 5.836... \times 0.5$$
$$= 2.92 \text{ J (3 s.f.)}$$

Tip: Instead of finding the vertical distance, you could resolve the block's weight to find its component parallel to the plane, then use Work done = *Fs* $= 5g \sin 7° \times 0.5$

Example 2

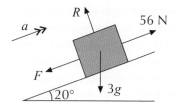

A block of mass 3 kg accelerates 9 m up a rough plane inclined at an angle of 20° to the horizontal. The block is pulled by a rope which is parallel to the plane. The tension in the rope has magnitude 56 N. The coefficient of friction between the block and the plane is 0.36.

Find the work done on the block as it is pulled up the plane.

- First find the frictional force, F, between the plane and the block.
- Resolving perpendicular to the plane:

   $R = 3g\cos 20° \text{ N}$

- Now, using $F = \mu R$:

   $F = 0.36 \times 3g\cos 20° = 9.945... \text{ N}$

- Now, resolving parallel to the plane, taking up the plane as positive, and using the formula for work done:

   Work done $= (56 - 9.945... - 3g\sin 20°) \times 9$

   $= \boxed{324 \text{ N (3 s.f.)}}$

Tip: The block is accelerating, so there is a resultant force acting on it. It's this resultant force that you want to use to find the overall work done on the block.

Exercise 1.3

Q1   A body of mass 90 kg slides 1.4 m down a smooth plane inclined at an angle of 70° to the horizontal. Find the work done by gravity.

Q2

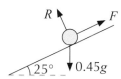

A particle of mass 0.45 kg slides 2 m down a rough plane inclined at an angle of 25° to the horizontal. The coefficient of friction between the plane and the particle is 0.37. Find:
a) the work done by gravity,
b) the work done against friction.

Q3 A package of mass 8 kg is pulled 1.5 m up a rough plane by a light, inextensible rope which is parallel to the plane. The plane is inclined at an angle of 22° to the horizontal, and the coefficient of friction between the package and the plane is 0.55.

a) Find the work done against gravity.

b) Find the work done against friction.

Q4

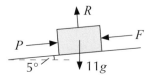

A rock of mass 11 kg is pushed up a rough plane by a force P, applied to the rock in a direction parallel to the plane. The plane is inclined at an angle of 5° to the horizontal, and the rock moves at a constant speed. Given that the coefficient of friction between the plane and the rock is 0.08, find the work done by P in pushing the rock 16 m up the plane.

Q5

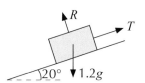

A light, inextensible string pulls a particle of mass 1.2 kg a distance of 4.5 m up a smooth ramp inclined at an angle of 20° to the horizontal. The particle is initially at rest, and it accelerates uniformly to a final speed of 5 ms^{-1}. The string is parallel to the ramp. Find the work done on the particle as it is pulled up the ramp.

Q6

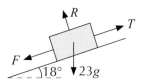

A light, inextensible rope pulls a block of mass 23 kg a distance of 0.75 m up a rough plane inclined at an angle of 18° to the horizontal. The rope is parallel to the plane and the block accelerates up the plane at a rate of 0.95 ms^{-2}. The coefficient of friction between the block and the plane is 0.36. Find:

a) the magnitude of the tension in the rope,

b) the work done on the block as it is pulled up the plane.

2. Kinetic and Potential Energy

In mechanics, the two types of energy you have to deal with most are kinetic energy and potential energy. A body could experience a change in either of these if the body moves and work is done.

The big thing to remember about energy is that it's always conserved — you can't lose or gain energy, it just gets converted between forms.

Kinetic energy

- Any body that is **moving** has **kinetic energy** (K.E.).
- You can find the kinetic energy of a particle using the formula:

$$\text{Kinetic Energy} = \frac{1}{2} \times \text{mass} \times \text{velocity}^2$$
$$\text{or } \mathbf{K.E.} = \frac{1}{2}mv^2$$

- If mass, m, is measured in kg, and velocity, v, in ms^{-1}, then kinetic energy will be measured in joules, J.

Learning Objectives:
- Be able to find the kinetic energy of a moving body.
- Be able to find the work done by a force in changing the velocity of a body.
- Be able to find the potential energy of a body.

Example

An ice skater of mass 60 kg is moving at a constant velocity of 8 ms^{-1}. Find the ice skater's kinetic energy.

Just put the values for mass and velocity straight in the formula:

Kinetic energy $= \frac{1}{2}mv^2 = \frac{1}{2} \times 60 \times 8^2 = $ 1920 J

Exercise 2.1

Q1 A golf ball has a mass of 45 g. In flight it has a velocity of 20 ms^{-1}. Find the kinetic energy of the golf ball.

Q2 At a point on her fall, a skydiver of mass 60 kg has kinetic energy 94 080 J. Find her speed at this point.

Q3 A plane has mass 11 249 kg and is flying at 1462 kmh^{-1}. Find the kinetic energy of the plane.

Q4 An alpha particle has a mass of 6.64×10^{-27} kg and is moving at 1.5×10^6 ms^{-1}. What is its kinetic energy?

Q5 A particle travels 14 m in 3.5 seconds at a constant speed. Its kinetic energy is 22 J. Find the particle's mass.

Q6 Two cars, A and B, have the same mass, but A is travelling at twice the speed of B. Find the ratio of the kinetic energy of A to the kinetic energy of B.

Kinetic energy and work done

- Remember, **work done** is a **transfer of energy**.
- The **work done** by a **resultant force** on a body moving **horizontally** is equal to the change in that body's **kinetic energy**:

Tip: You need to remember to find the work done by the **resultant** force, rather than any individual force. If there's no resultant force, there'll be no change in speed, and hence no change in kinetic energy.

Consider a **resultant force**, F_{net}, acting horizontally on a particle of mass m kg, causing it to **accelerate** horizontally from u ms^{-1} to v ms^{-1}.

The force is given by Newton's second law: $F_{net} = ma$

The particle's acceleration can be found using a **constant acceleration equation**:

$$v^2 = u^2 + 2as$$

$$\Rightarrow a = \frac{v^2 - u^2}{2s}$$

So, $F_{net} = m\left(\dfrac{v^2 - u^2}{2s}\right)$

The work done by this force can then be found using the formula '**Work done = Force × Distance**':

$$\text{Work done} = Fs$$

$$= m\left(\frac{v^2 - u^2}{2s}\right) \times s$$

$$= \tfrac{1}{2}mv^2 - \tfrac{1}{2}mu^2$$

Therefore, **Work done = change in kinetic energy**

Example 1

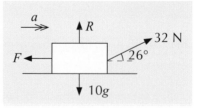

A body of mass 10 kg is pulled along a rough horizontal plane by a rope inclined at an angle of 26° above the horizontal. The magnitude of the tension in the rope is 32 N. The body starts from rest, and accelerates to a speed of 8 ms^{-1} over a distance of 14 m.

a) Find the work done on the body as it is pulled along the plane.

- The work done on the body is equal to the body's change in kinetic energy:

$$\text{Work done} = \tfrac{1}{2}mv^2 - \tfrac{1}{2}mu^2$$

$$= \tfrac{1}{2} \times 10 \times 8^2 - \tfrac{1}{2} \times 10 \times 0^2$$

$$= 320 \text{ J}$$

b) Find the coefficient of friction between the plane and the body.

- Resolving horizontally, the resultant force, F_{net}, acting on the body is:

$$F_{net} = 32\cos 26° - F$$

- Using the formula 'Work done = Force × distance':

$$320 = (32\cos 26° - F) \times 14$$
$$22.857... = 32\cos 26° - F$$
$$\Rightarrow F = 5.904... \text{ N}$$

- Now, resolving vertically:

$$R + 32\sin 26° = 10g$$
$$\Rightarrow R = 83.972... \text{ N}$$

- So, using $F = \mu R$:

$$5.904... = \mu \times 83.972...$$
$$\Rightarrow \boxed{\mu = 0.07 \text{ (2 d.p.)}}$$

Example 2

A particle of mass 6 kg is pulled along a rough horizontal plane by a horizontal force of magnitude 40 N. The particle travels 4 m in a straight line between two points on the plane, A and B. The particle passes B with speed 8 ms⁻¹. Given that the coefficient of friction between the particle and the plane is 0.35, find the particle's speed as it passed A.

- Draw a diagram to show what's going on:

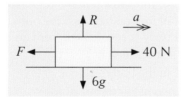

- First, you need to find the magnitude of the frictional force, F, between the particle and the plane.

- Resolving vertically:

$$R = 6g$$

- Now, using $F = \mu R$:

$$F = 0.35 \times 6g = 20.58 \text{ N}$$

- So, the resultant force, F_{net}, acting on the particle is:

$$F_{net} = 40 - 20.58 = 19.42 \text{ N}$$

- Now, using Work done = Force × distance:

$$\text{Work done by resultant force} = 19.42 \times 4$$
$$= 77.68 \text{ J}$$

- The work done by this force is equal to the change in the particle's kinetic energy, so:

$$77.68 = \frac{1}{2}mv^2 - \frac{1}{2}mu^2$$

$$77.68 = \frac{1}{2} \times 6 \times 8^2 - \frac{1}{2} \times 6 \times u^2$$

$$\Rightarrow u^2 = 38.106...$$

$$\Rightarrow u = 6.17 \text{ ms}^{-1} \text{ (3 s.f.)}$$

Exercise 2.2

Exam Hint: Drawing a diagram can help you picture what's going on in these questions.

Q1 A particle is pulled across a rough, horizontal surface by a horizontal wire. The tension in the wire has magnitude 0.6 N, and resistance to motion is modelled as a constant horizontal force of magnitude 0.0147 N.

a) If the particle's kinetic energy increases by 3.62×10^{-3} J, calculate the distance, s, it has travelled.

b) Calculate the particle's mass, given that its initial speed was 0.210 ms^{-1} and its final speed is 1.222 ms^{-1}.

Q2 Hint: Don't confuse the resistance to motion, R, with the normal reaction force, which is also often denoted R.

Q2 A lorry of mass 1800 kg is driven along a straight horizontal road. It undergoes a constant horizontal resistance to motion of magnitude R. At the point where the speed of the lorry is 11 ms^{-1}, the engine is switched off and the lorry coasts to a stop over a distance of 96 m. Find R.

Q3 A body of mass 3 kg is pulled along a rough, horizontal surface by a horizontal rope. The tension in the rope has magnitude 15.88 N and the coefficient of friction between the body and the surface is 0.2. Given that the body is accelerated from an initial speed of 3 ms^{-1} to a final speed of 7 ms^{-1}, find:

a) the change in the body's kinetic energy,

b) the magnitude of the frictional force between the body and the surface,

c) the distance travelled by the body.

Q4 A dart of mass 22 g is thrown towards a vertical dartboard. It hits the board horizontally at a speed of 8 ms^{-1} and its point enters to a depth of 0.5 cm. Find:

a) the kinetic energy of the dart as it strikes the board,

b) the work done on the dart,

c) the magnitude of the constant resultant force experienced by the dart.

Q5 A body of mass 11 kg is pulled along a rough, horizontal plane by a rope inclined at an angle of 15° above the horizontal. The tension in the rope has magnitude 65 N. The coefficient of friction between the body and the plane is 0.19. Find the distance the body travels as it accelerates from a speed of 2 ms^{-1} to a speed of 14 ms^{-1}.

Potential energy

- The **gravitational potential energy** (P.E.) of a particle is the energy it has due to its **height**. The greater the height of a particle above some 'base level', the greater that particle's gravitational potential energy.

- Potential energy can be calculated using the following formula:

$$\text{Potential Energy} = \text{mass} \times g \times \text{vertical height above base level}$$
$$\text{or } \textbf{P.E.} = \textbf{\textit{mgh}}$$

Tip: This formula should be familiar to you — it's the same as the formula for the work done by or against gravity when a body moves vertically.

- If mass, m, is in kg, acceleration due to gravity, g, is in ms^{-2}, and the vertical height above the base level, h, is in m, then P.E. is measured in joules, J.

Example 1

A lift has a total mass of 750 kg. The lift moves vertically from the 1st floor of a building, 6.1 m above the ground, to the 17th floor, 64.9 m above the ground.

Find the gravitational potential energy gained by the lift in travelling between the two floors.

- You want the potential energy gained by the lift in moving between the two floors, so use the formula P.E. = mgh, where h is the vertical distance between the two floors:

  P.E. gained = $750 \times 9.8 \times (64.9 - 6.1)$

  $= \boxed{432\,000 \text{ J}}$ (3 s.f.) or $\boxed{432 \text{ kJ}}$ (3 s.f.)

Tip: Here, the 'base level' is the 1st floor, not the ground. So h is the difference in height between the two floors, not the height of the 17th floor.

- When you're working out the potential energy of a particle, the value of h you use should always be the **vertical** height above the 'base level'.

- So, for a particle moving on a **slope**, you'll have to use **trigonometry** to find the vertical distance travelled.

Example 2

A skateboarder and her board have a combined mass of 65 kg. She starts from rest and freewheels down a slope inclined at 15° to the horizontal. She travels 40 m down the line of greatest slope.

a) Find the gravitational potential energy lost by the skateboarder.

- You need to find h, the vertical distance she travels:

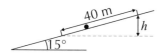

- Using trigonometry:

  $h = 40\sin 15°$

- So, using P.E. = mgh:

  P.E. lost = $65 \times 9.8 \times 40\sin 15°$

  $= \boxed{6590 \text{ J}}$ (3 s.f.) or $\boxed{6.59 \text{ kJ}}$ (3 s.f.)

b) She reaches the bottom of the incline and starts to freewheel up a different slope, inclined at an angle θ to the horizontal. After travelling 5 m up the slope she has gained 2 kJ of P.E. Find θ.

Tip: Don't forget to change the energy in kJ to J first.

- Using P.E. = mgh:

$$2000 = 65 \times 9.8 \times 5\sin\theta$$

$$\sin\theta = 0.627...$$

$$\Rightarrow \theta = \boxed{38.9° \text{ (3 s.f.)}}$$

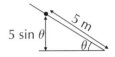

Exercise 2.3

Q1 A cat of mass 3.7 kg jumps onto a chair of height 41 cm and from there onto a table of height 73 cm. Find the potential energy gained by the cat in jumping from the chair to the table.

Q2 A fly loses 7.2×10^{-5} J of potential energy dropping from a height of 1.63 m to a height of 1.02 m. Find the mass of the fly.

Q3 A rocket of mass 3039 tonnes leaves the ground and travels vertically upwards. At its highest point, it has 5×10^{12} J of potential energy. Find, to the nearest km, the maximum height reached by the rocket. You may assume that the mass of the rocket remains constant, and that the value of g remains constant at 9.8 ms^{-2}.

Q4 A postman pushes a trolley of mass 20 kg a distance of 3.7 m up a slope inclined at an angle θ to the horizontal, where $\theta = \arcsin\left(\frac{1}{8}\right)$. Find the potential energy gained by the trolley.

Q5

A cable car travels 240 m, at an angle of 13° below the horizontal. It loses 1 MJ of potential energy. Find the cable car's mass.

Q6 A lump of snow of mass 0.6 kg slides 3 m down a roof inclined at an angle θ to the horizontal. It loses 6.032 J of potential energy. Find θ.

Q7

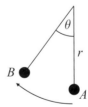

Q7 Hint: Use trigonometry to find the change in height of the particle.

A particle of mass m kg is fixed to the end of a light, inextensible string of length r, the other end of which is fixed in position. As part of its movement, it swings from its lowest point, A, through an angle θ, to the point B. Find an expression for the particle's gain in potential energy in moving from A to B.

3. The Work-Energy Principle

In the last section you saw how the kinetic and potential energies of a body can change as it moves. The mechanical energy of a body is the sum of its kinetic and potential energies.

As work done is a transfer of energy, you'll see in this section the effect that doing work on a body can have on its mechanical energy.

The principle of conservation of mechanical energy

Mechanical energy

The **mechanical energy** of a body is the sum of its **kinetic** and **potential** energies:

> Total Mechanical Energy =
> Kinetic Energy + Gravitational Potential Energy

Learning Objectives:

- Be able to find a body's mechanical energy.
- Be able to solve problems using the principle of conservation of mechanical energy.
- Be able to solve problems using the work-energy principle.

Tip: Strictly speaking, mechanical energy also includes elastic potential energy, but you don't need to know about that in M2.

Example

A paper plane weighs 20 g. At the highest point in its flight it has a mechanical energy of 0.6 J and is 2.8 m above the ground. Find its speed at this point in the flight.

- Mechanical energy = Kinetic energy + Potential energy

$$= \frac{1}{2}mv^2 + mgh$$

- Substituting in the values from the question:

$$0.6 = (\frac{1}{2} \times 0.02 \times v^2) + (0.02 \times 9.8 \times 2.8)$$

$$0.6 = 0.01v^2 + 0.5488$$

$$v^2 = 5.12$$

$$\Rightarrow v = 2.26 \text{ ms}^{-1} \text{ (3 s.f.)}$$

The principle of conservation of mechanical energy

- The principle of conservation of mechanical energy says that:

> If there are **no external forces** doing work on an object, the **total** mechanical energy of the object will remain **constant**.

An **external force** is any force other than the **weight** of the object. So this includes things like friction, air resistance, tension in a rope, etc.

- This means that the **sum** of a body's potential and kinetic energies **remains the same** throughout the body's motion.

- So a **decrease** in **potential energy** will mean an **increase** in **kinetic energy** of the **same amount**.

Example 1

A BASE jumper of mass 88 kg jumps from a ledge on a building and falls vertically downwards. When he is 150 m above the ground, his velocity is 6 ms⁻¹. When he is 60 m above the ground, he releases his parachute.

a) Find the kinetic energy of the jumper when he is 150 m above the ground.

Initial K.E. $= \frac{1}{2}mu^2$

$= \frac{1}{2} \times 88 \times 6^2 = \boxed{1584 \text{ J}}$

b) Use the principle of conservation of mechanical energy to find the jumper's kinetic energy and speed at the point where he releases his parachute.

- Applying the principle of conservation of mechanical energy:
  Increase in K.E. = Decrease in P.E.

  Decrease in P.E. $= mgh$
  $= 88 \times 9.8 \times (150 - 60)$
  $= \boxed{77\ 616 \text{ J}}$

- So, at the point where he opens his parachute, he has 77 616 J more K.E. than he had at a height of 150 m. So:

  K.E. when parachute released = K.E. at 150 m + Decrease in P.E.
  $= 1584 + 77\ 616 = 79\ 200 \text{ J} = \boxed{79.2 \text{ kJ}}$

- Using K.E. $= \frac{1}{2}mv^2$ to find the speed at this point:

  $79\ 200 = \frac{1}{2} \times 88 \times v^2$

  $v = \sqrt{\dfrac{79\ 200}{\frac{1}{2} \times 88}} = \boxed{42.4 \text{ ms}^{-1} \text{ (3 s.f.)}}$

c) State one assumption you have made in modelling this situation.

The only force acting on the jumper is his weight (i.e. there's no air resistance or any other external forces).

Tip: The principle states that the total mechanical energy is conserved, so any loss in potential energy must result in an equal gain in kinetic energy.

Tip: if you don't make this assumption, then you can't use the principle of conservation of mechanical energy.

Example 2

A package is projected up a smooth plane inclined at an angle of 4° to the horizontal. At the bottom of the incline it has a speed of 5 ms⁻¹. How far up the plane will it travel before instantaneously coming to rest?

- When the package comes to rest, it will have no kinetic energy.
- By the principle of conservation of mechanical energy, assuming that there are no external forces acting on the package, all of the package's kinetic energy at the bottom of the incline will have been converted to potential energy at the point where it comes to rest.

  i.e. Initial K.E. = Final P.E.

  $\Rightarrow \frac{1}{2}mu^2 = mgh$

- Cancelling m from both sides and substituting in the values from the question:

$$\frac{1}{2} \times 5^2 = 9.8 \times h$$
$$12.5 = 9.8h$$
$$\Rightarrow h = 1.275... \text{ m}$$

- h is the vertical height travelled, but you need to find the distance travelled **up the slope**. Call this x.

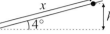

- Using trigonometry:

$$\sin 4° = \frac{h}{x}$$
$$\Rightarrow x = 1.275... \div \sin 4° = 18.3 \text{ m (3 s.f.)}$$

Exercise 3.1

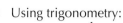

Q1 At its highest point, a carriage of a roller coaster has 70 560 J of mechanical energy. At its lowest point, it has 52 920 J of kinetic energy. Find the carriage's potential energy at its lowest point.

> **Exam Hint:** Throughout this exercise, you may assume that there are no external forces acting.

Q2 A tennis ball of mass 57 g is dropped from a height of 1.13 m. Find:
   a) the total mechanical energy of the ball immediately before it is dropped,
   b) the ball's speed at the instant it hits the ground.

Q3 An object is dropped and falls freely under gravity. It hits the ground with speed 11 ms⁻¹. Find the height from which the object is dropped.

Q4

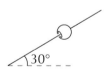

A bead is threaded on a smooth, straight wire. The wire is held at an angle of 30° above the horizontal, as shown. The bead is flicked upwards. It travels a distance of 6 cm along the wire and loses 1.47 mJ of kinetic energy. Find the mass of the bead.

> **Q4 Hint:** Watch out for units here:
> 1 J = 1000 mJ.

Q5 A projectile of mass 50 g is launched vertically upwards from ground level and moves freely under gravity. When it is 52 m above the ground, the projectile is moving upwards at a speed of 10.1 ms⁻¹. Find:
   a) the total mechanical energy of the projectile at this point,
   b) the maximum height the projectile reaches,
   c) the speed of projection of the projectile.

Q6

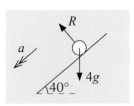

A particle of mass 4 kg slides 7 m down a smooth plane inclined at an angle of 40° to the horizontal. Its initial velocity is 3 ms⁻¹. Find:

a) the change in the particle's potential energy,

b) the particle's final velocity.

Q7   A body is released from rest at the top of a smooth ramp inclined at an angle of 19° to the horizontal. It slides down the ramp and reaches the bottom with speed 4.5 ms⁻¹.

Find the length of the sloped surface of the ramp.

Q8   A particle of mass 13 kg is fired up a smooth plane inclined at 25° to the horizontal. Its initial speed is 16 ms⁻¹. Find:

a) the distance the particle travels up the plane before it first comes to rest,

b) the distance the particle has travelled up the plane when it is travelling with speed 10 ms⁻¹.

The work-energy principle

- As you saw on pages 93-95, if there are **no external forces doing work** on a body, then the **total mechanical energy** of the body remains **constant**.

- However, if there **is an external force doing work** on a body, then the total mechanical energy of the body will **change**.

- This is the **work-energy principle**:

> The **work done** on a body by external forces is equal to the **change** in the **total mechanical energy** of that body.

Tip: Doing work on a body will always cause a change in the body's kinetic energy — no matter the direction of movement. If some (or all) of the work is done in moving the body vertically (i.e. if work is done by or against gravity), then there will also be a change in the body's potential energy.

- In M2, the 'external force' will usually be a **resistive force**, such as **friction**. Remember — talking about a resistive force doing work **on** a body is really just another way of saying that work is being done **against** the resistive force.

- If the **only** external forces acting on the body are **resistive forces**, then **doing work against** these resistive forces will cause the overall mechanical energy of the body to **decrease**.

- In this case, the best way to think of the work-energy principle is:

Initial Mechanical Energy of a body	−	Final Mechanical Energy of the body	=	Work Done against resistive forces

Example 1

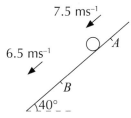

7.5 ms⁻¹

6.5 ms⁻¹

A

B

40°

A particle of mass 1.5 kg slides down a rough plane inclined at an angle of 40° to the horizontal. The particle passes through point A with speed 7.5 ms⁻¹ and point B with speed 6.5 ms⁻¹. The distance AB is 6.8 m.
Find the coefficient of friction between the plane and the particle.

- Take B as the 'base level' — i.e. the point where the particle's height is measured from.

Tip: The 'base level' is the point where the particle has no potential energy.

- First, you need to find the particle's initial mechanical energy — i.e. its mechanical energy at A:

    Initial Mechanical Energy = Initial K.E. + Initial P.E.

    $= \frac{1}{2}mu^2 + mgh_{\text{initial}}$

    $= (\frac{1}{2} \times 1.5 \times 7.5^2) + (1.5 \times 9.8 \times 6.8\sin 40°)$

    $= 106.440...$ J

- Next, find the particle's final mechanical energy — i.e. its mechanical energy at B:

    Final Mechanical Energy = Final K.E. + Final P.E.

    $= \frac{1}{2}mv^2 + mgh_{\text{final}}$

    $= (\frac{1}{2} \times 1.5 \times 6.5^2) + (1.5 \times 9.8 \times 0)$

    $= 31.6875$ J

- Now, using the work-energy principle:

    Initial Mechanical Energy − Final Mechanical Energy = Work done against friction

    $\Rightarrow 106.440... - 31.6875 = 74.753...$ J

Tip: The only external force doing work on the particle is the frictional force.

- So the work done against friction is 74.753... J.

- Now, using 'Work done = Fs' to find the magnitude of F, the frictional force acting on the particle:

    $74.753... = F \times 6.8$

    $\Rightarrow F = 10.993...$ N

- Finally, resolving perpendicular to the plane and using $F = \mu R$:

    $10.993... = \mu \times 1.5g\cos 40°$

    $\Rightarrow \mu = 0.98 \text{ (2 d.p.)}$

Example 2

A particle of mass 3 kg is projected up a rough plane inclined at an angle θ to the horizontal, where $\tan\theta = \frac{5}{12}$. The particle moves through point A with speed 11 ms⁻¹. The particle continues to move up the line of greatest slope and comes to rest at point B before sliding back down the plane. The coefficient of friction between the particle and the slope is $\frac{1}{3}$.

a) Use the work-energy principle to find the distance AB.

Tip: You're told that $\tan\theta = \frac{5}{12}$, so using Pythagoras' theorem and trigonometry you can work out that $\sin\theta = \frac{5}{13}$ and $\cos\theta = \frac{12}{13}$.

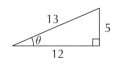

- Take A as the base level. Let the distance AB be x.

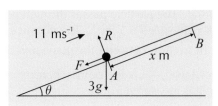

- First find the particle's initial mechanical energy — i.e. its mechanical energy at A:

    Initial Mechanical Energy = Initial K.E. + Initial P.E.

    $= \frac{1}{2}mu^2 + mgh_{\text{initial}}$

    $= (\frac{1}{2} \times 3 \times 11^2) + (3 \times g \times 0) = \boxed{181.5 \text{ J}}$

- Next, find the particle's final mechanical energy — i.e. its mechanical energy at B:

    Final Mechanical Energy = Final K.E. + Final P.E.

    $= \frac{1}{2}mv^2 + mgh_{\text{final}}$

    $= (\frac{1}{2} \times 3 \times 0^2) + (3 \times g \times x\sin\theta)$

    $= 3gx \times \frac{5}{13} = \boxed{\frac{15gx}{13} \text{ J}}$

Tip: $v = 0$ as the particle is at rest at B.
$h_{\text{final}} = x\sin 40°$ comes from using trigonometry to find the vertical distance travelled when moving from A to B.

- Now, using the work-energy principle:

$$\begin{array}{ccc} \text{Initial Mechanical} \\ \text{Energy} \end{array} - \begin{array}{c} \text{Final Mechanical} \\ \text{Energy} \end{array} = \begin{array}{c} \text{Work done} \\ \text{against friction} \end{array}$$

$$\Rightarrow \boxed{181.5 - \frac{15gx}{13} = \begin{array}{c}\text{Work done} \\ \text{against friction}\end{array}} \text{ — call this equation 1}$$

- To find x, you need to find the work done against friction.

- Resolving perpendicular to the plane:

$$R = 3g\cos\theta = 3g \times \frac{12}{13} = \boxed{\frac{36g}{13} \text{ N}}$$

- So, using $F = \mu R$:

$$F = \frac{1}{3} \times \frac{36g}{13} = \boxed{\frac{12g}{13} \text{ N}}$$

- Now, using 'Work done = Fs':

$$\text{Work done against friction} = \frac{12g}{13} \times x = \frac{12gx}{13} \text{ J} \quad \text{— call this } \textbf{equation 2}$$

- So, using the work-energy principle, substitute **equation 2** into **equation 1**:

$$181.5 - \frac{15gx}{13} = \frac{12gx}{13}$$

$$181.5 = \frac{27gx}{13}$$

$$\Rightarrow x = \frac{181.5 \times 13}{27g} = 8.917...$$

$$= 8.92 \text{ m (3 s.f.)}$$

b) **Find the speed of the particle when it returns to A.**

- From part a), the particle's initial mechanical energy (i.e. its mechanical energy the first time it's at A) is 181.5 J.

- The particle's final mechanical energy (i.e. its mechanical energy the second time it's at A) is given by:

$$\text{Final Mechanical Energy = Final K.E. + Final P.E.}$$

$$= \frac{1}{2}mv^2 + mgh_{\text{final}}$$

$$= \left(\frac{1}{2} \times 3 \times v^2\right) + (3 \times g \times 0)$$

$$= \frac{3v^2}{2} \text{ J}$$

- The work done against friction as the particle moves from A to B and back to A again is given by:

$$\text{Work done} = Fs$$

$$= \frac{12g}{13} \times 2x$$

$$= \frac{12g}{13} \times 2(8.917...)$$

$$= 161.333... \text{ J}$$

> **Tip:** s, the distance travelled by the particle, is $2x$ m, because it moves x m from A to B, then x m back to A again, and friction always acts in the same direction relative to motion (i.e. to oppose motion or likely motion).

- So, using the work-energy principle:

$$\text{Initial Mechanical Energy} - \text{Final Mechanical Energy} = \text{Work done against friction}$$

$$\Rightarrow 181.5 - \frac{3v^2}{2} = 161.333...$$

$$\frac{3v^2}{2} = 20.166...$$

$$v^2 = 13.444...$$

$$\Rightarrow v = 3.67 \text{ ms}^{-1} \text{ (3 s.f.)}$$

Q1

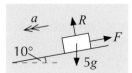

A block of mass 5 kg is released from rest and slides down a rough ramp inclined at an angle of 10° to the horizontal. After sliding 12 m down the ramp, the block has speed 3.5 ms⁻¹. Find the work done against friction as the block slides down the ramp.

Q2

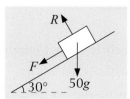

A body of mass 50 kg is projected up a rough slope inclined at an angle of 30° to the horizontal. The body's initial speed is 8 ms⁻¹. After travelling 3.4 m up the slope, the body's speed is 1.5 ms⁻¹.

a) Find the work done against friction during this time.

b) Find the magnitude of the frictional force between the body and the slope.

Q3 A body of mass 7.9 kg is released from rest at the top of a slide inclined at an angle of 45° to the horizontal. The body accelerates down the rough surface of the slide, reaching a speed of 6 ms⁻¹ after it has travelled a distance of 5 m. Find:

a) the work done against friction during this time,

b) the coefficient of friction between the body and the slide's surface.

Q4

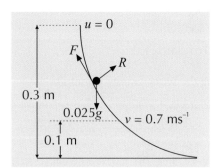

An object of mass 25 g is placed on a curved surface. It starts from rest a height of 0.3 m above the ground and slides down a rough track which follows an arc of a circle. When the object is a height of 0.1 m above the ground, its speed is 0.7 ms⁻¹.

Find the work done against friction during this time.

Q5 A particle of mass 9 kg is projected vertically upwards from ground level with speed 14 ms⁻¹. The particle reaches a maximum height of 9 m above the ground, then begins to fall back down again. Throughout its motion, the particle experiences a constant resistive force, F, acting in the opposite direction to the particle's motion.

a) Find the work done by the resistive force from the time that the particle is projected to the time that it reaches its maximum height.

b) Find the particle's speed as it lands back on the ground.

Q5 Hint: Don't worry that this one is a bit different — the maths is just the same. Find the change in total mechanical energy and use the work-energy principle as usual.

Q6 An object of mass 5.5 kg is projected with speed 6.25 ms⁻¹ up a rough plane inclined at an angle of 17° to the horizontal. The coefficient of friction between the object and the plane is 0.22.

a) Find the distance that the object travels up the plane before it comes to rest.

b) The object then slides down the plane. Find the object's speed as it passes back through its initial point of projection.

Q7

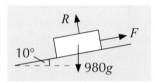

A vehicle of mass 980 kg is travelling down a rough road inclined at an angle of 10° to the horizontal. The driver stops accelerating, so that the only external force acting on the vehicle is the frictional force between the vehicle and the road. The vehicle passes through point A with speed U ms⁻¹, and then through point B with speed 10 ms⁻¹. The coefficient of friction between the vehicle and the road is 0.32, and the distance between the points A and B is 65 m.

Find the value of U.

Q8

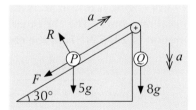

Two particles, P and Q, are fixed to either end of a light, inextensible string which passes over a fixed, smooth pulley. P has mass 5 kg and is at rest on a rough plane inclined at an angle of 30° to the horizontal. Q has mass 8 kg and hangs at rest below the pulley. P and Q are level. The system is released from rest so that the particles each accelerate to a speed of 4 ms⁻¹ over a distance of 2.5 m. Assuming that P does not hit the pulley and Q does not hit the ground, find:

a) the mechanical energy lost from the system after the particles have reached a speed of 4 ms⁻¹,

b) the coefficient of friction between P and the plane.

Q8 Hint: This question is a bit more tricky, as you've got two particles to worry about. Just find the change in mechanical energy of each particle, then combine to find the change in mechanical energy of the whole system.

4. Power

So far in this chapter, you've learnt all about work done and how it relates to the transfer of energy from one form to another. This section is about the rate at which all this happens.

Power

- **Power** is a measure of the **rate** at which a force does **work** on a body:

$$\text{Power} = \frac{\text{Work Done}}{\text{Time}}$$

The unit for power is the watt (W), where 1 watt = 1 joule per second.

Using the formula 'Work Done = Force × Distance', this becomes

$\text{Power} = \frac{\text{Force} \times \text{Distance}}{\text{Time}}$, but as $\frac{\text{Distance}}{\text{Time}}$ is speed, you can then derive:

$$\text{Power} = \text{Force} \times \text{Speed}$$

- So for an engine generating a **driving force** of magnitude F N, moving a vehicle at a **speed** v ms^{-1}, the power of the engine in watts is given by $P = Fv$.

This is the version of the formula you'll end up using most of the time. But don't forget what power **means** — it's the **rate of doing work**.

Examples

a) **A motor boat moves horizontally through water with speed 12 ms^{-1}. The driving force of the engine is 4250 N. Find the engine's power.**

Power $= Fv = 4250 \times 12$

$\qquad = 51\,000$ W $=$ **51 kW**

b) **A car with a 95 kW engine is driven at its maximum speed on a straight horizontal race track. The car experiences a constant resistance to motion of 2375 N. Find the car's maximum speed.**

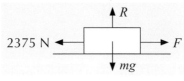

- The car is driven at its maximum speed, so there is no acceleration. So, resolving horizontally in the direction of motion gives:

$$F_{net} = ma$$
$$F - 2375 = m \times 0$$
$$\Rightarrow F = 2375 \text{ N}$$

- Now, using the formula for power:

$$\text{Power} = Fv$$
$$95\,000 = 2375 \times v_{max}$$
$$\Rightarrow v_{max} = 40 \text{ ms}^{-1}$$

You can apply the same principles to situations where an object is moving on an **inclined plane**.

Example

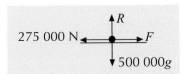

A train of mass 500 tonnes is travelling along a straight horizontal track with a constant speed of 20 ms⁻¹. The train experiences a constant resistance to motion of magnitude 275 000 N.

a) **Find the rate at which the train's engine is working. Give your answer in kW.**

- Resolving horizontally:

$F - 275\,000 = m \times 0$

$\Rightarrow F = 275\,000$ N

- Power $= Fv$

$= 275\,000 \times 20$

$= 5\,500\,000$ W $= \boxed{5500 \text{ kW}}$

Tip: The speed is constant, so $a = 0$ ms⁻².

b) **The train now moves up a hill inclined at 2° to the horizontal. If the engine continues to work at the same rate and the magnitude of the non-gravitational resistance to motion remains the same, find the new constant speed of the train.**

- Draw a diagram to show what's going on:

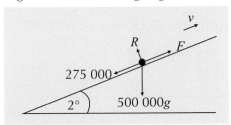

- Resolving parallel to the slope (taking up the slope as positive):

$F - 275\,000 - (500\,000 \times 9.8 \times \sin 2°) = m \times 0$

$\Rightarrow F = 275\,000 + (500\,000 \times 9.8 \times \sin 2°)$

$= 446\,007.5...$ N

- Now using Power $= Fv$:

$5\,500\,000 = 446\,007.5... \times v$

$\Rightarrow v = 5\,500\,000 \div 446\,007.5...$

$= \boxed{12.3 \text{ ms}^{-1} \text{ (3 s.f.)}}$

Tip: The driving force and non-gravitational resistance to motion stay the same as in part a), but now you have to think about the effect of the train's weight.

If an object is moving with **constant acceleration**, you'll have to resolve in the direction of motion to find the **resultant force** acting on it, then use $F_{net} = ma$.

Because the velocity of the object will be **constantly changing**, you can only use the formula $P = Fv$ if you consider the object's motion at a particular **instant**, rather than considering its entire motion.

Tip: N has been used to denote the normal reaction force of the slope on the tractor, as R has been used to denote the resistance to motion.

Example

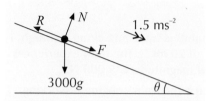

A tractor of mass 3000 kg is moving down a hill inclined at an angle of θ to the horizontal, where $\sin\theta = \frac{1}{24}$.

When the tractor is travelling at a speed of 8 ms⁻¹, its acceleration is 1.5 ms⁻², and its engine is working at a constant rate of 30 kW.

Find the magnitude of the resistance to motion, R, at the instant when the tractor is travelling at a speed of 8 ms⁻¹.

▪ First, use $P = Fv$ to find the driving force, F:

$$30\,000 = F \times 8$$
$$\Rightarrow F = 3750 \text{ N}$$

▪ Now, resolving parallel to the slope, taking down the slope as positive, and using $F_{net} = ma$:

$$F + 3000g\sin\theta - R = 3000 \times 1.5$$
$$3750 + (3000 \times 9.8 \times \frac{1}{24}) - R = 4500$$
$$\Rightarrow R = 3750 + 1225 - 4500$$
$$= \boxed{475 \text{ N}}$$

Exercise 4.1

Q1 A train travels along a straight horizontal track at a constant velocity of 144 kmh⁻¹. Its engine generates a driving force of 65 000 N. Find the power of the train's engine, giving your answer in kW.

Q2 A model boat has a maximum speed of 1.8 ms⁻¹ when moving horizontally through the water against a resistance to motion of magnitude 85 N. Find the power of its engine.

Q3 A vehicle is driven at a constant speed of 19 ms⁻¹ along a level road. Its engine works at a rate of 130 kW. Find the driving force of the vehicle's engine.

Q4

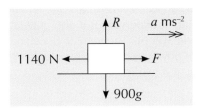

A car of mass 900 kg is driven along a straight horizontal road.
It undergoes a constant acceleration and experiences a constant
horizontal resistance to motion of magnitude 1140 N.
The power generated by the engine when the car moves at a speed
of 11 ms^{-1} is 23.1 kW. Find the car's acceleration.

Q5 a) A motorbike and its rider have a combined mass of 250 kg.
It travels along a straight, flat road at a constant speed of 32 ms^{-1},
with its engine working at a rate of 96 kW. Find R, the constant
resistance to motion experienced by the motorbike.

b) The motorbike moves onto a section of road that slopes upwards
at an angle θ to the horizontal. The engine's power and the
constant resistance to motion remain unchanged. The motorbike
climbs the hill at a constant speed of 28 ms^{-1}. Find θ.

Q6 A man uses a rope to lift an object of weight 52 N through a vertical
distance of 2.4 m in 11 s. The object moves at constant speed and
experiences a constant resistance to motion of 4.2 N.
Find the rate at which the man does work as he lifts the object.

Q7

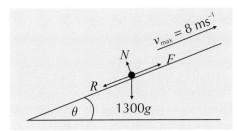

A car of mass 1300 kg travels in a straight line up a slope inclined
at an angle θ to the horizontal, where $\tan\theta = \left(\frac{1}{2\sqrt{6}}\right)$.
The maximum speed of the car up this slope is 8 ms^{-1}.
At this speed the engine is working at a power of 29 kW.
Find the non-gravitational resistance to motion, R, that the car
experiences as it climbs the slope.

Q8 A vehicle of mass 660 kg travels up a ramp inclined at an angle of
17° to the horizontal. Its engine is working at 16 kW. The vehicle
experiences a constant non-gravitational resistance to motion of
magnitude 140 N.

a) Find the vehicle's maximum speed up the ramp.

b) When the vehicle is travelling at its maximum speed, its engine
cuts out. Assuming that the resistance to motion is unchanged,
find the distance the vehicle will travel before first coming to rest.

Q8 b) Hint: When its
engine cuts out, the
only forces experienced
by the vehicle will
be its weight and the
resistance to motion.

Q9 A vehicle of mass 1230 kg travels up a slope inclined at an angle of 25° to the horizontal. It experiences a non-gravitational resistance to motion of magnitude 305 N. The vehicle decelerates at a rate of 0.28 ms⁻². Find the power output of the vehicle's engine when the vehicle is travelling at 8 ms⁻¹.

Q10

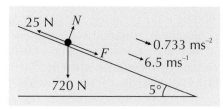

25 N N
$\rightarrow$ 0.733 ms⁻²
F
$\rightarrow$ 6.5 ms⁻¹
720 N
5°

A cyclist and her cycle have a combined weight of 720 N. As she rides down a hill with a slope of 5° to the horizontal, her acceleration is 0.733 ms⁻². She experiences a constant resistance to motion of 25 N. Find her power when her speed is 6.5 ms⁻¹.

Q11 A car of mass 860 kg accelerates up a ramp inclined at an angle of 3° to the horizontal at a rate of 0.65 ms⁻². It experiences a non-gravitational resistance to motion of magnitude 175 N. It reaches the top of the ramp with speed 16 ms⁻¹.

a) Find the power generated by the car's engine as the car reaches the top of the ramp.

When the car reaches the top of the ramp, it begins to travel along a straight, horizontal track. The non-gravitational resistance to motion remains unchanged.

b) Find the car's instantaneous acceleration as it begins to travel along the track.

Q12 A van of mass 1050 kg drives up a ramp inclined at an angle of 15° to the horizontal at a constant speed of 8 ms⁻¹. It experiences a non-gravitational resistance to motion of magnitude 204 N.

a) Find the power output of the van's engine.

When the van reaches the top of the ramp, it begins to travel down another ramp inclined at an angle of 12° to the horizontal. The non-gravitational resistance to motion remains unchanged.

b) Find the van's instantaneous acceleration as it begins to travel down the ramp.

Q13 A vehicle of mass m_1 tows a trailer of mass m_2 at a constant velocity, v, along a road sloping upwards at an angle of $\arcsin\left(\frac{1}{25}\right)$ to the horizontal. The vehicle and trailer are connected by a light and inextensible rope. The power output of the towing vehicle's engine is P. The constant non-gravitational resistance to motion of the towing vehicle is R_1 and the constant non-gravitational resistance to motion of the trailer is R_2.

Show that $P = v\left(R_1 + R_2 + \dfrac{(m_1 + m_2)g}{25}\right)$.

Review Exercise — Chapter 3

Q1   A crate is pushed across a smooth horizontal floor by a force of magnitude 250 N, acting in the direction of motion. Find the work done in pushing the crate a distance of 3 m.

Q2

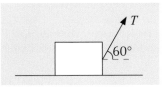

A roll-along cart is pulled along the ground a distance of 0.4 m by a cord with a tension force, T, acting at 60° to the horizontal. If the work done by the tension is 1.3 J, find T.

Q3   A fighter plane flies horizontally for 40 s at a speed of 363 ms⁻¹.
The thrust exerted by the engines is 105 000 N. Find the work done by the thrust.

Q4   A crane lifts a concrete block 12 m vertically at constant speed. If the crane does 34 kJ of work against gravity, find the mass of the concrete block.

Q5   On the moon, an astronaut lifts a mass of 3 kg through a vertical height of 0.6 m, doing 2.92 J of work against gravity. Find an estimate of the acceleration due to gravity on the moon, g_{moon}. Give your answer correct to 3 significant figures.

Q6

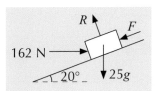

A 25 kg flight case is pushed 10 m up a ramp at an angle of 20° to the horizontal, by a force of magnitude 162 N acting horizontally. The coefficient of friction between the ramp and the case is 0.19. Find the work done on the case as it is pushed up the ramp.

Q7   A horse of mass 450 kg is galloping at a speed of 13 ms⁻¹. Find the horse's kinetic energy.

Q8   An ice skater of mass 65 kg sets off from rest. After travelling 40 m in a straight line across smooth horizontal ice, she has done 800 J of work. Find her speed at this point.

Q9   A supercar of mass 1000 kg moves along a straight horizontal test track. The resistance to motion has a constant magnitude of 590 N. To test the brakes, the driver accelerates to 100 ms⁻¹ and then applies a constant braking force of 8500 N.
     a) Find the work done by the braking force in bringing the car to a stop.
     b) Find the work done by the resistance to motion in bringing the car to a stop.
     c) Show that the work done by the resultant force equals the change in kinetic energy.

Q10   A particle of mass 0.5 kg is projected upwards from ground level and reaches a maximum height of 150 m above the ground. Find the increase in its gravitational potential energy.

Q11

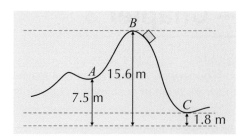

A car in a roller coaster follows the path shown. The mass of the car is 680 kg.
Describe the changes in potential energy it undergoes between *A*, *B* and *C*.

Q12 A jubilant cowboy throws his hat vertically upwards with a velocity of 5 ms⁻¹.
Use the principle of conservation of mechanical energy to find the maximum height the hat
reaches above the point of release.

Q13 A boy tries to score a goal in football. Unfortunately, when he shoots, the ball just passes
over the top of the goal. The height of the goal is 1.94 m and the ball's mass is 0.4 kg.
The boy's kick gives the ball an initial kinetic energy of 39.2 J. By modelling the ball as a
particle, find its kinetic energy at the instant it passes over the top of the goal.

Q14 A particle of mass 15 kg is released from rest and slides down from the top of a rough ramp
of length 9 m, inclined at an angle of 11° to the horizontal. It reaches the bottom of the ramp
with speed 4.2 ms⁻¹. Find the work done against friction as the particle slides down the ramp.

Q15

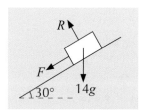

A body of mass 14 kg is projected up a rough slope inclined at an angle of 30° to the
horizontal. The body's initial speed is 5.5 ms⁻¹.
After travelling 2.5 m up the slope, the body's speed is 0.4 ms⁻¹.
a) Find the work done against friction during this time.
b) Find the coefficient of friction between the body and the slope.

Q16 A car's engine is working at a rate of 350 kW. The car moves with speed 22 ms⁻¹.
Find the driving force of the engine.

Q17 A vehicle of mass 820 kg drives down a slope inclined at an angle of 5° to the horizontal.
It accelerates at a rate of 0.75 ms⁻² and experiences a constant resistance to motion of
magnitude 188 N. Find the power output of the vehicle's engine when its speed is 10 ms⁻¹.

Q18 A motorbike and its rider, of combined mass 725 kg, travel up a ramp inclined at an angle of
8° to the horizontal. The motorbike's engine works at a rate of 25 kW. The motorbike and
rider experience a constant non-gravitational resistance to motion of magnitude 128 N.
Find the motorbike's maximum speed up the ramp.

1

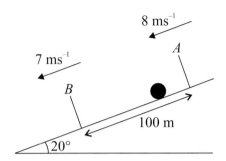

A man skis down a rough plane inclined at an angle of 20° to the horizontal.
The man and his skis have a combined mass of 90 kg. He passes through two gates,
A and B, which are 100 m apart. His speed at gate A is 8 ms⁻¹. At gate B, his speed
has decreased to 7 ms⁻¹. Find:

a)   the decrease in the skier's total mechanical energy as he moves from
     gate A to gate B,

     (3 marks)

b)   the coefficient of friction between the man's skis and the plane.
     You may assume that air resistance is negligible.

     (5 marks)

2   A stone of mass 0.3 kg is dropped down a well.
     The stone hits the surface of the water in the well with a speed of 20 ms⁻¹.

a)   Calculate the kinetic energy of the stone as it hits the water.

     (2 marks)

b)   By modelling the stone as a particle and using conservation of energy, find
     the height above the surface of the water from which the stone was dropped.

     (3 marks)

When the stone hits the water, it begins to sink vertically and experiences a constant
resistive force of 23 N.

c)   Use the work-energy principle to find the depth the stone has sunk to when
     the speed of the stone has been reduced to 1 ms⁻¹.

     (5 marks)

3   A van of mass 2700 kg is travelling at a constant speed of 16 ms⁻¹ up a road inclined at an angle of 12° to the horizontal. The non-gravitational resistance to motion is modelled as a single force of magnitude of 800 N.

   a)   Find the rate of work of the engine.

   (4 marks)

   When the van passes a point A, still travelling at 16 ms⁻¹, the engine is switched off and the van comes to rest without braking, a distance x m from A. If all resistance to motion remains constant, find:

   b)   the distance x,

   (5 marks)

   c)   the time taken for the van to come to rest.

   (4 marks)

4

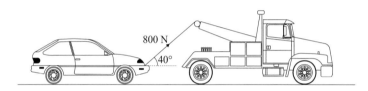

   A car of mass 1500 kg is towed 320 m along a straight horizontal road by a rope attached to a pick-up truck. The rope is attached to the car at an angle of 40° to the horizontal and the tension in the rope is 800 N.

   The car experiences a constant resistance to motion from friction.

   a)   Find the work done by the towing force.

   (3 marks)

   b)   Over the 320 m, the car increases in speed from 11 ms⁻¹ to 16 ms⁻¹.
        Assuming that the magnitude of the towing force remains constant at 800 N, find the coefficient of friction between the car and the road.

   (4 marks)

5   A cyclist is riding up a road at a constant speed of 4 ms⁻¹. The road is inclined at an angle α to the horizontal. The cyclist is working at a rate of 250 W and experiences a constant non-gravitational resistance to motion of magnitude 35 N. The cyclist and his bike have a combined mass of 88 kg.

   a)   Find the angle of the slope, α.

   (4 marks)

   b)   The cyclist now increases his work rate to 370 W. If all resistances to motion remain unchanged, find the cyclist's acceleration when his speed is 4 ms⁻¹.

   (4 marks)

1. Momentum and Impulse

You should already be familiar with momentum and impulse in one dimension from M1. In M2, you need to be able to use the impulse-momentum principle and the conservation of linear momentum for particles moving in two dimensions, and use the formulas with velocities in vector notation.

Impulse

- All moving objects have **momentum**, which can be found by multiplying the **mass** of an object by its **velocity**.

$$\text{Momentum} = \text{mass} \times \text{velocity}$$
$$= mv$$

- If an object receives an **impulse** (I — measured in Newton seconds, or Ns) its **momentum will change**. The size of the change is the size of the impulse. This is called the **impulse-momentum principle**:

$$\text{Impulse} = \text{final momentum} - \text{initial momentum}$$
$$I = mv - mu$$

Tip: u is the object's initial velocity and v is its final velocity.

- Velocity is a **vector quantity**, so both **momentum** and **impulse** are also vector quantities. This means that you can use velocities written in **vector notation** in the formulas.

$$\text{Momentum} = m\mathbf{v} \qquad \text{Impulse } (\mathbf{I}) = m\mathbf{v} - m\mathbf{u}$$

Tip: In M2, you'll only need to use vectors written in $\mathbf{i}$ and $\mathbf{j}$ notation for $\mathbf{u}$, $\mathbf{v}$ and $\mathbf{I}$ — but they could be written using any notation, e.g. as column vectors.

Example 1

A ball of mass 0.1 kg travelling with velocity $(5\mathbf{i} + 12\mathbf{j})$ ms^{-1} receives an impulse of I Ns. If the ball's new velocity is $(15\mathbf{i} + 22\mathbf{j})$ ms^{-1}, find I.

$(15\mathbf{i} + 22\mathbf{j})$ ms^{-1}

0.1 kg

I Ns

$(5\mathbf{i} + 12\mathbf{j})$ ms^{-1}

- Don't be put off by the vector notation. Plug the info in the formula like in M1:

$$\mathbf{I} = m\mathbf{v} - m\mathbf{u}$$
$$= 0.1(15\mathbf{i} + 22\mathbf{j}) - 0.1(5\mathbf{i} + 12\mathbf{j})$$
$$= 1.5\mathbf{i} + 2.2\mathbf{j} - 0.5\mathbf{i} - 1.2\mathbf{j}$$
$$= 1\mathbf{i} + 1\mathbf{j}$$

- So the ball receives an impulse of $\mathbf{I} = (\mathbf{i} + \mathbf{j})$ Ns.

Tip: $m = 0.1$, $\mathbf{v} = 15\mathbf{i} + 22\mathbf{j}$ and $\mathbf{u} = 5\mathbf{i} + 12\mathbf{j}$.

Tip: Remember to add and subtract the $\mathbf{i}$- and $\mathbf{j}$-components separately.

Example 2

A particle of mass 0.6 kg receives an impulse of (9i + 12j) Ns, which causes it to move with velocity (15i − 8j) ms⁻¹.
Find the velocity of the particle prior to it receiving the impulse.

- Use the impulse-momentum principle:

$$\mathbf{I} = m\mathbf{v} - m\mathbf{u}$$
$$= m(\mathbf{v} - \mathbf{u})$$

Tip: To divide a vector in **i** and **j** notation by a scalar, just divide each component by the scalar separately.

- Now substitute in the values of **I**, m and **v** given in the question, and solve to find **u**:

$$9\mathbf{i} + 12\mathbf{j} = 0.6[(15\mathbf{i} - 8\mathbf{j}) - \mathbf{u}]$$
$$15\mathbf{i} + 20\mathbf{j} = (15\mathbf{i} - 8\mathbf{j}) - \mathbf{u}$$
$$\mathbf{u} = (15\mathbf{i} - 8\mathbf{j}) - (15\mathbf{i} + 20\mathbf{j})$$
$$= -28\mathbf{j} \text{ ms}^{-1}$$

- Remember, with vectors you can use the horizontal **i**-component and the vertical **j**-component to form a **right-angled triangle**.
- Then you can use basic **trigonometry** and **Pythagoras' theorem** to find the **direction** and **magnitude** (size) of impulses or velocities.

Example 3

A badminton player smashes a shuttlecock (m = 0.005 kg) with an impulse of (0.035i − 0.065j) Ns. Given that the shuttlecock was initially travelling at (−3i + j) ms⁻¹, find its speed and the angle between its direction of motion and i following the smash.

- First, find the final velocity as a vector, using the impulse-momentum principle:

$$\mathbf{I} = m\mathbf{v} - m\mathbf{u}$$
$$0.035\mathbf{i} - 0.065\mathbf{j} = 0.005\mathbf{v} - 0.005(-3\mathbf{i} + \mathbf{j})$$
$$0.035\mathbf{i} - 0.065\mathbf{j} = 0.005\mathbf{v} + 0.015\mathbf{i} - 0.005\mathbf{j}$$
$$0.005\mathbf{v} = 0.02\mathbf{i} - 0.06\mathbf{j}$$
$$\mathbf{v} = (4\mathbf{i} - 12\mathbf{j}) \text{ ms}^{-1}.$$

- Now draw a right-angled triangle showing the velocity vector, **v**.

Tip: Finding the magnitude of a vector this way should be familiar to you from M1.

- Use Pythagoras' theorem to find the speed (the magnitude of the velocity):

$$|\mathbf{v}| = \sqrt{4^2 + 12^2}$$
$$= 12.6 \text{ ms}^{-1} \text{ (3 s.f.)}$$

Tip: You might see $|\mathbf{v}|$ written as v.

- Use trigonometry to find the angle of the direction of motion with **i**:

$$\theta = \tan^{-1}\left(\frac{12}{4}\right) = 71.6° \text{ (3 s.f.) below } \mathbf{i}$$

Example 4

A ball of mass 0.4 kg is released from rest and falls freely under gravity. After it has fallen 1.5 m, the ball is struck by a bat and receives an impulse of Q Ns. Immediately after being struck, the velocity of the ball is (3i + 4j) ms⁻¹.

Find the magnitude of Q and the angle between Q and i.

- First, find the velocity of the ball after it has fallen 1.5 m using $v^2 = u^2 + 2as$, where $u = 0$, $a = 9.8$ ms⁻² and $s = 1.5$ m (taking vertically downwards as positive):

$$v^2 = u^2 + 2as$$
$$= 2 \times 9.8 \times 1.5$$
$$v = 5.422... \text{ ms}^{-1}$$

- You need to write this velocity in vector form.

- The ball is falling vertically downwards, so its velocity has no horizontal component and the vertical component will be negative. So the velocity of the ball before being struck is (–5.422...j) ms⁻¹.

- Now use the impulse-momentum principle to find **Q**:

$$\mathbf{Q} = m(\mathbf{v} - \mathbf{u})$$
$$= 0.4[(3\mathbf{i} + 4\mathbf{j}) - (-5.422...\mathbf{j})]$$
$$= (1.2\mathbf{i} + 3.768...\mathbf{j}) \text{ Ns}$$

- Finally, find the magnitude of **Q**...

$$|\mathbf{Q}| = \sqrt{1.2^2 + 3.768...^2}$$
$$= 3.96 \text{ Ns (3 s.f.)}$$

- ...and the angle between **Q** and **i**:

$$\theta = \tan^{-1}\left(\frac{3.768...}{1.2}\right) = 72.3° \text{ (3 s.f.) above } \mathbf{i}.$$

Tip: The vertical component of velocity is negative because **j** is defined as the unit vector in the positive y-direction (i.e. vertically upwards), and the ball is falling vertically downwards.

This is separate from the direction which was taken as positive when calculating v.

Exercise 1.1

Q1 A ball of mass 50 g is rolling with velocity (2i – 3j) ms⁻¹ when it is given an impulse which alters its velocity to (5i + 3j) ms⁻¹. Find the impulse given to the ball in Ns.

Q2 A smooth stone of mass 12 kg is sliding on ice with velocity (–4i + 7j) ms⁻¹ when it receives an impulse of 60j Ns. Find its new velocity.

Q3 A particle of mass 9 kg moving with velocity (3i + 4j) ms⁻¹ is given an impulse, **Q**. As a result, the particle's velocity changes to (–7i – j) ms⁻¹. Find **Q**.

Q4 A boy intercepts a ball of mass 300 g travelling at (3i + 4j) ms⁻¹, and kicks it away with velocity (–5i – 2j) ms⁻¹. Find the impulse given to the ball by the boy.

Q5 A ball of mass 200 g is rolling across a smooth surface when it receives an impulse of $(4\mathbf{i} - 6\mathbf{j})$ Ns which changes its velocity to $(-10\mathbf{i} + 20\mathbf{j})$ ms^{-1}. Find the velocity of the ball prior to receiving the impulse.

Q6 A stone sliding across an icy pond is given an impulse of $(9\mathbf{i} + 6\mathbf{j})$ Ns. As a result, its velocity changes from $(3\mathbf{i} - 4\mathbf{j})$ ms^{-1} to $(6\mathbf{i} - 2\mathbf{j})$ms^{-1}. Find the mass of the stone.

Q7 A ball in a pinball machine rolls down onto a spring-loaded cue with a velocity of $-0.2\mathbf{j}$ ms^{-1}. The cue pushes it back up with a velocity of $2\mathbf{j}$ ms^{-1}. Calculate the magnitude of the impulse given to the ball, given that the ball has mass 15 g.

Q8 A puck of mass 200 g is sliding across a smooth surface with velocity $(-9\mathbf{i} + 4\mathbf{j})$ ms^{-1}. An impulse, $\mathbf{Q}$, is given to the puck, changing its velocity to $(3\mathbf{i} - 4\mathbf{j})$ ms^{-1}. Calculate the magnitude of $\mathbf{Q}$ and the angle between $\mathbf{Q}$ and $\mathbf{i}$.

Q9 A particle is moving when it is given an impulse of $(45\mathbf{i} - 30\mathbf{j})$ Ns, resulting in a change of velocity to $(4\mathbf{i} - 6\mathbf{j})$ ms^{-1}. Given that the mass of the particle is 7.5 kg, find the magnitude of its initial velocity and its initial direction of motion.

Q10 A cricket ball of mass 160 g approaches a batsman with velocity $50\mathbf{i}$ ms^{-1}. The batsman hits the ball, which moves away with velocity $(-30\mathbf{i} - 40\mathbf{j})$ ms^{-1}. Find:

a) the magnitude of the impulse given to the ball by the bat,

b) the angle between the ball's path before and after being hit.

Q11 A particle of mass 0.5 kg travels with constant velocity from the point with position vector $(4\mathbf{i} - 7\mathbf{j})$ m, relative to a fixed origin, to the point $(12\mathbf{i} + 5\mathbf{j})$ m in 4 seconds.

It then receives an impulse which moves it to the point $(2\mathbf{i} - 10\mathbf{j})$ m in 5 seconds, again travelling with constant velocity.

a) Calculate the magnitude of the impulse the particle receives.

b) Find the change in direction of the particle.

Q11 Hint: First, find the velocities before and after the particle receives the impulse using $\mathbf{v} = \frac{\mathbf{s}}{t}$.

Q12 An ice hockey player intercepts a puck of mass 170 g travelling at $(7\mathbf{i} - 8\mathbf{j})$ ms^{-1} and hits it, providing an impulse of $(-3\mathbf{i} + 4\mathbf{j})$ Ns.

Find the change in direction of the puck following the impact.

Q13 A tennis player throws a ball vertically upwards into the air and hits it as it is falling back down. The ball has mass 60 g and has fallen 1 m from its highest point when the player hits it. The velocity of the ball immediately after being hit is $(40\mathbf{i} + 16\mathbf{j})$ ms^{-1}.

Calculate the magnitude of $\mathbf{Q}$, the impulse given to the ball by the tennis racket, and the angle between $\mathbf{Q}$ and $\mathbf{i}$.

Conservation of momentum

- When two objects that are **free to move** around collide, they exert an **equal and opposite** impulse on each other — these impulses 'cancel out', so there is no overall impulse for the system as a whole.

- No impulse means **no change in momentum**.

- This is known as the **principle of conservation of momentum**, and you should be familiar with it from M1:

> momentum before collision = momentum after collision
>
> $$m_A u_A + m_B u_B = m_A v_A + m_B v_B$$

Tip: m_A, u_A, v_A, m_B, u_B and v_B refer to the mass, initial velocity and final velocity of objects A and B respectively.

- In M1, you only looked at collisions between two objects moving along the same straight line, but you can also use the principle of conservation of momentum for collisions between objects moving in **two dimensions** along **any intersecting straight lines**.

  Just like the formulas on page 111, you can use the above formula with velocities written in **vector notation**:

  $$m_A \mathbf{u}_A + m_B \mathbf{u}_B = m_A \mathbf{v}_A + m_B \mathbf{v}_B$$

- If the objects **coalesce** (stick together) as a result of the collision, they'll move off together with the **same velocity**, **v**. So the formula becomes:

  $$m_A \mathbf{u}_A + m_B \mathbf{u}_B = (m_A + m_B)\mathbf{v}$$

Example

Particles A (mass 5 kg) and B (mass 3 kg) are moving with velocity $(4\mathbf{i} + 3\mathbf{j})$ ms^{-1} and $(-2\mathbf{i} + 7\mathbf{j})$ ms^{-1} respectively when they collide.

a) **Given that, as a result of the collision, the velocity of A is $-2\mathbf{i}$ ms^{-1} and the two particles move separately at different velocities, find B's velocity immediately following the collision.**

- It's often a good idea to do a quick sketch of the particles to help you work out what's going where:

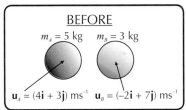
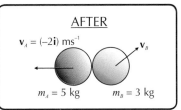

- Then plug the values into the formula:

$$m_A \mathbf{u}_A + m_B \mathbf{u}_B = m_A \mathbf{v}_A + m_B \mathbf{v}_B$$
$$5(4\mathbf{i} + 3\mathbf{j}) + 3(-2\mathbf{i} + 7\mathbf{j}) = 5(-2\mathbf{i}) + 3\mathbf{v}_B$$
$$20\mathbf{i} + 15\mathbf{j} - 6\mathbf{i} + 21\mathbf{j} = -10\mathbf{i} + 3\mathbf{v}_B$$
$$3\mathbf{v}_B = 24\mathbf{i} + 36\mathbf{j}$$
$$\boxed{\mathbf{v}_B = (8\mathbf{i} + 12\mathbf{j}) \text{ ms}^{-1}}$$

b) If, instead, the two particles coalesce as a result of the collision, find the speed and direction of motion of the combined particle immediately following the collision.

- Again, make a sketch of the particles. The 'before' sketch is the same as in part a).

  The combined particle will have mass 8 kg and velocity **v** ms^{-1}.

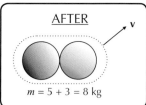
AFTER

$m = 5 + 3 = 8$ kg

- Now use the formula for conservation of momentum, adjusted for coalesced particles, and plug in the values you know:

  $$m_A\mathbf{u}_A + m_B\mathbf{u}_B = (m_A + m_B)\mathbf{v}$$
  $$5(4\mathbf{i} + 3\mathbf{j}) + 3(-2\mathbf{i} + 7\mathbf{j}) = (5 + 3)\mathbf{v}$$
  $$20\mathbf{i} + 15\mathbf{j} - 6\mathbf{i} + 21\mathbf{j} = 8\mathbf{v}$$
  $$8\mathbf{v} = 14\mathbf{i} + 36\mathbf{j}$$
  $$\mathbf{v} = (1.75\mathbf{i} + 4.5)\mathbf{j} \text{ ms}^{-1}$$

Tip: If you need to, draw the vector as a right-angled triangle before finding the magnitude and angle. For **v**, the triangle looks like:

v 4.5

θ

1.75

- Use Pythagoras' theorem to find the magnitude of the velocity vector (i.e. the speed):

  $$|\mathbf{v}| = \sqrt{1.75^2 + 4.5^2} = 4.83 \text{ ms}^{-1} \text{ (to 3 s.f.)}$$

- And use trigonometry to find the direction of motion:

  $$\theta = \tan^{-1}\left(\frac{4.5}{1.75}\right) = 68.7° \text{ (to 3 s.f.) above } \mathbf{i}.$$

Exercise 1.2

Q1   Each diagram below represents a collision between two particles moving in straight lines. Find the missing mass or velocity in each case, given that all masses are in kg and all velocities in ms^{-1}.

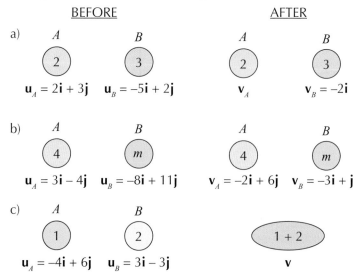

BEFORE   AFTER

a)   A   B   A   B

      2   3   2   3

   $\mathbf{u}_A = 2\mathbf{i} + 3\mathbf{j}$ $\mathbf{u}_B = -5\mathbf{i} + 2\mathbf{j}$ $\mathbf{v}_A$ $\mathbf{v}_B = -2\mathbf{i}$

b)   A   B   A   B

      4   m   4   m

   $\mathbf{u}_A = 3\mathbf{i} - 4\mathbf{j}$ $\mathbf{u}_B = -8\mathbf{i} + 11\mathbf{j}$ $\mathbf{v}_A = -2\mathbf{i} + 6\mathbf{j}$ $\mathbf{v}_B = -3\mathbf{i} + \mathbf{j}$

c)   A   B

      1   2   1 + 2

   $\mathbf{u}_A = -4\mathbf{i} + 6\mathbf{j}$ $\mathbf{u}_B = 3\mathbf{i} - 3\mathbf{j}$ $\mathbf{v}$

Q2 Two particles, A (mass $3m$) and B (mass $2m$), travelling with initial velocity $(3\mathbf{i} - \mathbf{j})$ ms^{-1} and $\mathbf{u}_B$ respectively, collide and coalesce, moving off with velocity $(-\mathbf{i} + \mathbf{j})$ ms^{-1}. Calculate $\mathbf{u}_B$.

Q3 A particle travelling with velocity $(5\mathbf{i} - 3\mathbf{j})$ ms^{-1} collides with a stationary particle of equal mass. As a result, the two particles coalesce and move off together. Calculate the velocity of the combined particle following the collision.

Q4 Two particles, A (mass 10 kg) and B (mass m kg) are moving with velocity $(7\mathbf{i} - 10\mathbf{j})$ ms^{-1} and $(-5\mathbf{i} + 8\mathbf{j})$ ms^{-1} respectively when they collide. As a result of the collision, A moves with velocity $(2\mathbf{i} - 5\mathbf{j})$ ms^{-1} and B with velocity $(5\mathbf{i} - 2\mathbf{j})$ ms^{-1}. Find m.

Q5 Particle A, of mass 600 g, moves with velocity $(6\mathbf{i} - 2\mathbf{j})$ ms^{-1}. It collides with particle B, of mass 400 g. Given that both particles are brought to rest by the collision, find the velocity of B prior to the collision.

Q6 Two identical snooker balls, A and B, collide and move apart with velocity $(3\mathbf{i} - 8\mathbf{j})$ ms^{-1} and $(-5\mathbf{i} + 7\mathbf{j})$ ms^{-1} respectively. Given that A has velocity $(4\mathbf{i} - 6\mathbf{j})$ ms^{-1} before the collision, calculate the speed of B before the collision.

Q7 A curling stone of mass 20 kg travelling at $5\mathbf{j}$ ms^{-1} hits a stationary curling stone of mass 24 kg. As a result of the collision, the velocity of the 20 kg stone changes to $(0.2\mathbf{i} + 2\mathbf{j})$ ms^{-1}. Find the speed of the 24 kg stone and the direction of its motion following the collision.

Q8 At time t s, two identical particles, A and B, are moving with velocity $\mathbf{u}_A$ ms^{-1} and $\mathbf{u}_B$ ms^{-1} respectively, where $\mathbf{u}_A = [(t - 8)\mathbf{i} + 2t\mathbf{j}]$ and $\mathbf{u}_B = [(3t + 2)\mathbf{i} - t^2\mathbf{j}]$. The particles collide, and following the collision A has velocity $(12\mathbf{i} + 2\mathbf{j})$ ms^{-1} and B has velocity $(-6\mathbf{i} - 5\mathbf{j})$ ms^{-1}. Find the value of t for which they collide.

Q9 A pinball accelerates from rest at 2 ms^{-2} for 0.4 seconds in a direction parallel to the positive y-axis. It then collides with a stationary ball of the same mass. This second ball moves off at a speed of 0.5 ms^{-1} on a path which is at an angle of 60° clockwise from the positive y-axis.

Calculate the velocity of the first ball following the collision, giving your answer as a vector in terms of $\mathbf{i}$ and $\mathbf{j}$.

Q10 A snooker player attempts to pot a red ball in a pocket. He gives the stationary white ball (mass 160 g) an impulse of $(0.25\mathbf{i} - 0.125\mathbf{j})$ Ns with his cue. The white ball collides with a stationary red ball of equal mass, and rebounds at a velocity of $(0.3\mathbf{i} - 0.4\mathbf{j})$ ms^{-1}.

a) What is the velocity of the red ball following the collision?

b) In order to go into the pocket, the path of the red ball must deviate by no more than 5° from the original path of the white ball. Does the ball go into the pocket?

2. Collisions

Sometimes you won't know anything about the mass of colliding objects. For problems like this, knowing something about the way the objects collide can help you work out any missing velocities.

Newton's law of restitution

When two objects collide in a **direct impact** (i.e. when they're moving in the **same straight line**), the speeds they bounce away at depend on the **coefficient of restitution**, e, between the two objects. This is known as **Newton's law of restitution**, and looks like this:

$$e = \frac{\text{speed of separation of objects}}{\text{speed of approach of objects}}$$

$$e = \frac{v_B - v_A}{u_A - u_B}$$

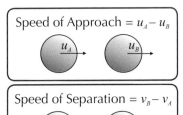

Speed of Approach = $u_A - u_B$

Speed of Separation = $v_B - v_A$

Tip: Just like the coefficient of friction, e has no units.

- e always lies between **0 and 1**.
- When $e = 0$ the collision is called '**perfectly inelastic**', and the objects will **coalesce**.
- When $e = 1$ the collision is '**perfectly elastic**', and the objects will bounce apart with no loss of speed (i.e. speed of separation = speed of approach).
- The value of e depends on the **material** that the objects are made of: balls of modelling clay would be near the $e = 0$ end of the scale, while ping pong balls are nearer to $e = 1$.

Example 1

Two particles collide directly with speeds as shown below. Find the coefficient of restitution between the particles.

BEFORE

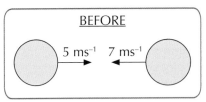

5 ms⁻¹   7 ms⁻¹

AFTER

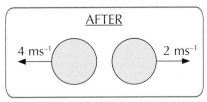

4 ms⁻¹   2 ms⁻¹

Tip: Think of 'left to right' as positive, so particles travelling 'right to left' will have a negative velocity.

- Firstly, work out the speeds of approach and separation, taking care with positives and negatives:
Speed of approach = $u_A - u_B = 5 - (-7) = 12$ ms⁻¹.
Speed of separation = $v_B - v_A = 2 - (-4) = 6$ ms⁻¹.

- Use $e = \dfrac{\text{speed of separation of particles}}{\text{speed of approach of particles}}$:

$$e = \frac{6}{12} = 0.5.$$

- So the coefficient of restitution is 0.5.

Example 2

Two particles collide directly with velocities as shown below.
The coefficient of restitution between the two particles is $e = 0.24$.
Find the missing velocity, v_B.

Tip: Example 1 gives speeds in the question, but Example 2 gives velocities. You could be given either in a question, so make sure you read the question properly and use the correct positive/ negative values in your calculations.

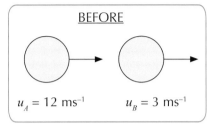
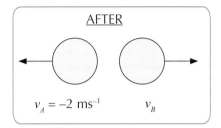

BEFORE

$u_A = 12$ ms^{-1} $u_B = 3$ ms^{-1}

AFTER

$v_A = -2$ ms^{-1} v_B

- Again, begin by working out the speeds of approach and separation:
  Speed of approach $= u_A - u_B = 12 - 3 = 9$ ms^{-1}.
  Speed of separation $= v_B - v_A = v_B - (-2) = (v_B + 2)$ ms^{-1}.

- Use $e = \dfrac{\text{speed of separation of particles}}{\text{speed of approach of particles}}$:

  $$0.24 = \frac{v_B + 2}{9}$$
  $$v_B + 2 = 2.16$$
  $$v_B = 0.16 \text{ ms}^{-1}$$

Exercise 2.1

Q1 Each diagram below represents a collision between two particles moving along the same straight line with velocities as shown. Find the coefficient of restitution in each case.

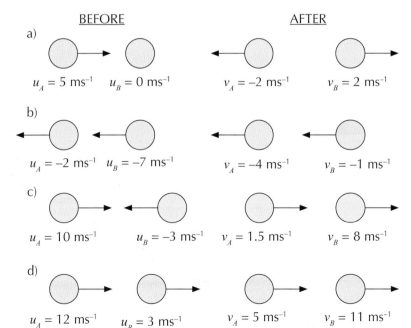

BEFORE   AFTER

a)

$u_A = 5$ ms^{-1} $u_B = 0$ ms^{-1} $v_A = -2$ ms^{-1} $v_B = 2$ ms^{-1}

b)

$u_A = -2$ ms^{-1} $u_B = -7$ ms^{-1} $v_A = -4$ ms^{-1} $v_B = -1$ ms^{-1}

c)

$u_A = 10$ ms^{-1} $u_B = -3$ ms^{-1} $v_A = 1.5$ ms^{-1} $v_B = 8$ ms^{-1}

d)

$u_A = 12$ ms^{-1} $u_B = 3$ ms^{-1} $v_A = 5$ ms^{-1} $v_B = 11$ ms^{-1}

Q2 Each diagram below represents a collision between two particles moving along the same straight line with velocities as shown. The coefficient of restitution, e, for each collision is given. Find the missing velocity in each case.

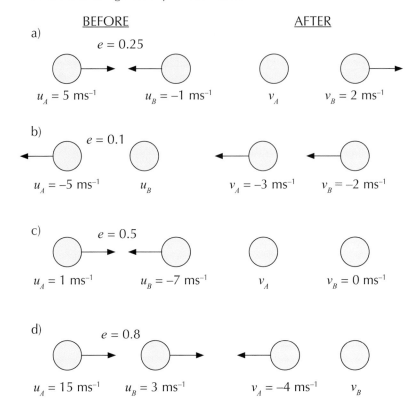

Q2 Hint: It's best to always assume that an object is travelling in the positive direction (here, left to right), then if your answer is negative you'll know that it's travelling in the opposite direction.

BEFORE   AFTER

a)
$e = 0.25$
$u_A = 5$ ms^{-1} $u_B = -1$ ms^{-1} v_A $v_B = 2$ ms^{-1}

b)
$e = 0.1$
$u_A = -5$ ms^{-1} u_B $v_A = -3$ ms^{-1} $v_B = -2$ ms^{-1}

c)
$e = 0.5$
$u_A = 1$ ms^{-1} $u_B = -7$ ms^{-1} v_A $v_B = 0$ ms^{-1}

d)
$e = 0.8$
$u_A = 15$ ms^{-1} $u_B = 3$ ms^{-1} $v_A = -4$ ms^{-1} v_B

Finding velocities

Often you'll be given the value of e and asked to find the velocities of **both objects** either before or after impact. As there are **two unknowns**, you'll need to use the formula for **conservation of momentum** (on page 115) along with the **law of restitution** to form a pair of **simultaneous equations**.

Example 1

Two particles, A and B, are moving in opposite directions along the same straight line when they collide, as shown below.

If $e = \frac{1}{3}$ for the collision, find the velocities of both particles after impact.

$m_A = 4$ kg $m_B = 12$ kg

$u_A = 10$ ms^{-1} $u_B = -2$ ms^{-1}

- Use $e = \frac{v_B - v_A}{u_A - u_B}$ to get the first equation:

$$\frac{1}{3} = \frac{v_B - v_A}{10 - (-2)} \Rightarrow v_B - v_A = 4 \quad \text{Call this equation 1.}$$

- Use $m_A u_A + m_B u_B = m_A v_A + m_B v_B$ to get the second equation:

$(4 \times 10) + (12 \times -2) = 4v_A + 12v_B$

$\Rightarrow 16 = 4v_A + 12v_B \Rightarrow v_A + 3v_B = 4 \quad \text{Call this equation 2.}$

- Now solve the simultaneous equations:
equation 1 + **equation 2** gives $4v_B = 8$,
so $v_B = 2 \text{ ms}^{-1}$ (i.e. 2 ms^{-1} going left to right).

- Substituting in **equation 1** gives:
$2 - v_A = 4$, so $v_A = -2 \text{ ms}^{-1}$ (i.e. 2 ms^{-1} going right to left).

Tip: Remember — velocity is a vector so the direction of motion is important.

Example 2

A particle, A, of mass m is travelling in a straight line with speed u ms^{-1}. It collides directly with B, a stationary particle of mass $2m$. As a result of the collision, the direction of motion of A is reversed and B moves in the opposite direction from A along the same straight line. Given that the coefficient of restitution between A and B is e, find expressions for the speed of A and B following the collision.

- It's often useful to draw a quick sketch of the situation, if you're not given one in the question.

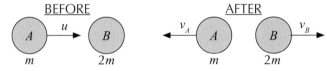

- Again, use $e = \frac{v_B - v_A}{u_A - u_B}$ to get the first equation:

$e = \frac{v_B - -v_A}{u} \Rightarrow v_B + v_A = eu. \quad \text{Call this equation 1.}$

- Use $m_A u_A + m_B u_B = m_A v_A + m_B v_B$ to get the second equation:
$(m \times u) + (2m \times 0) = -mv_A + 2mv_B$
$\Rightarrow 2v_B - v_A = u. \quad \text{Call this equation 2.}$

- Now solve the simultaneous equations:
equation 1 + **equation 2** gives $3v_B = eu + u$,

So $v_B = \left(\frac{e + 1}{3}\right)u \text{ ms}^{-1}$

- Substituting in **equation 1** gives:

$v_A = eu - \left(\frac{e + 1}{3}\right)u$

$= \left(\frac{2e - 1}{3}\right)u \text{ ms}^{-1}$

Q1   Find the missing velocities in each collision below:

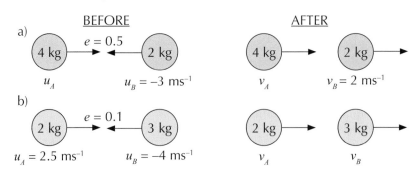

Q2   A white snooker ball collides directly with a blue snooker ball of the same mass. The blue ball is initially stationary and following the collision, both balls move in the direction of the white ball prior to the collision. Given that the initial velocity of the white ball is 1.5 ms^{-1} and the coefficient of restitution for the collision is 0.8, find the velocity of both balls after the impact.

Q3   A railway truck of mass 3000 kg collides directly with a stationary truck of mass 4000 kg, which moves off at 6 ms^{-1}. Given that the 3000 kg truck does not change direction as a result of the collision and the coefficient of restitution between the trucks is 0.6, find the initial and final speeds of the 3000 kg truck.

Q4   Particle A, of mass 45 kg, is travelling at 50 ms^{-1} when it collides with particle B, of mass 60 kg, travelling at 30 ms^{-1} in the opposite direction along the same straight line.
      Find the velocity of both particles following the collision if the coefficient of restitution between the particles is:
      a) 0.05
      b) 0.95

Q5   In a game, a marble of mass 40 g collides directly with a second, stationary, marble of mass 20 g. If the velocity of the first marble just before impact is 1.5 ms^{-1} and the coefficient of restitution between the marbles is 0.9, find the velocity of each marble after the impact.

Q6   A particle, A, of mass 5 kg, moving with speed 16 ms^{-1}, collides with particle B, mass 3 kg, moving with speed 10 ms^{-1}. The coefficient of restitution between the particles is 0.8.
      Find the final velocity of both particles if:
      a) both particles are travelling in the same direction when they collide,
      b) the particles are travelling in opposite directions when they collide.

Q7 Two particles, A and B, collide directly. They are initially moving at the same speed, u, but in opposite directions.
The coefficient of restitution between the particles is 0.4.
Find the final velocity of both A and B in terms of u if:
a) the mass of A is 4 times the mass of B,
b) the mass of B is 9 times the mass of A.

Q8 A ball, A, of mass m, is moving across a smooth horizontal surface in a straight line with speed $4u$. A second ball, B, of mass $3m$, is moving along the same straight line in the opposite direction with speed u. The balls collide directly, and as a result the direction of motion of each ball is reversed. The coefficient of restitution between the two balls is e. Find an expression for the speed of each ball immediately following the collision.

Q9 Two particles, P and Q, of mass $5m$ and m respectively, lie on a smooth horizontal surface. Q is initially at rest when P collides directly with it. As a result of the collision, both P and Q move in the same direction and P has speed v. The coefficient of restitution between the particles is e.
a) Show that the speed of P before the collision is given by $\dfrac{6v}{5-e}$.
b) Find an expression for the speed of Q following the collision in terms of v and e.

Collisions with smooth planes

Objects don't just collide with each other. They can collide with a **fixed flat surface** — such as when a ball is kicked against a **vertical wall**, or dropped onto a **horizontal floor**.

As long as the surface can be modelled as **smooth** (i.e. no friction) and **perpendicular** to the motion of the object, the law of restitution can be simplified to:

$$e = \frac{\text{speed of rebound of object}}{\text{speed of approach of object}} = \frac{v}{u}$$

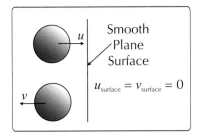

Smooth Plane Surface

$u_{surface} = v_{surface} = 0$

Tip: Momentum is not conserved in collisions with a fixed surface — only for collisions between things that are free to move.

Because a fixed surface is assumed not to move, the speeds of approach and rebound are just the **speed of the object** before and after the collision.

So for these types of collisions v and u are often used to represent an object's **speed**, rather than its velocity.

Example 1

An object sliding along a smooth horizontal floor at 6 ms^{-1} hits a smooth vertical wall, with coefficient of restitution $e = 0.65$.
Find the speed of the object as it rebounds.

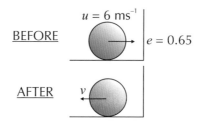

- Using $e = \frac{v}{u}$:
  $$0.65 = \frac{v}{6} \Rightarrow v = 0.65 \times 6 = 3.9 \text{ ms}^{-1}.$$

- So the object rebounds at a speed of 3.9 ms^{-1}.

Things get a tiny bit trickier when an object is dropped onto a horizontal surface because **acceleration** under **gravity** comes into play. It means that you might have to use one of the **constant acceleration equations** as well as the formula above.

Example 2

A basketball is dropped vertically from rest at a height of 1.4 m above a horizontal floor. It rebounds to a height of 0.9 m.
Find e, the coefficient of restitution between the ball and the floor.

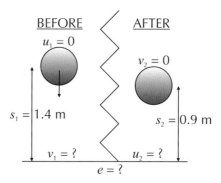

Tip: You should be familiar with using the constant acceleration equations in situations like this from M1.

- Assuming the ball is a particle, and the floor is smooth, use $e = \frac{v}{u}$.
  For the diagram shown, this would be $e = \frac{u_2}{v_1}$, as you need the velocity just before the impact (v_1) and the velocity just after (u_2).

- Using $v^2 = u^2 + 2as$ **before** the impact with the floor, taking down as positive:
  $$v_1^2 = 0 + 2 \times 9.8 \times 1.4 = 27.44$$
  $$\Rightarrow v_1 = 5.238... \text{ ms}^{-1}$$

- Using $v^2 = u^2 + 2as$ **after** the impact with the floor, taking up as positive:

$$0 = u_2^2 + 2 \times -9.8 \times 0.9$$
$$\Rightarrow u_2 = 4.2 \text{ ms}^{-1}$$

- Finally, find e: $e = \dfrac{u_2}{v_1} = \dfrac{4.2}{5.238...} = 0.802$ (to 3 s.f.)

Example 3

A particle of mass 600 g is projected from a point X across a smooth horizontal surface with constant velocity 8 ms⁻¹. When the particle has travelled 12 m, it collides directly with a smooth vertical wall and rebounds along the same straight line. The coefficient of restitution between the particle and the wall is $e = 0.7$.

a) **Find the time between the particle's projection and it returning to point X.**

- Use $e = \dfrac{v}{u}$ to find the speed of the particle after it rebounds:

$$e = \frac{v}{u}$$
$$0.7 = \frac{v}{8}$$
$$v = 5.6 \text{ ms}^{-1}$$

- Now work out the time taken for each part of the particle's motion: First, from point X to the wall:

$$t_1 = \frac{12}{u} = \frac{12}{8}$$
$$= 1.5 \text{ s}$$

Tip: The particle is moving with constant speed, so use $t = \frac{s}{v}$ to find times.

- And then from the wall back to point X:

$$t_2 = \frac{12}{v} = \frac{12}{5.6}$$
$$= 2.142... \text{ s}$$

- So the total time taken is:

$$t = t_1 + t_2$$
$$= 1.5 + 2.142...$$
$$= 3.64 \text{ s (to 3 s.f.)}$$

b) **Calculate the magnitude of the impulse given to the particle by the wall.**

- The impulse given to the particle is equal to the change in the particle's momentum:

$$\text{Change in momentum} = mv - mu$$
$$= (0.6 \times -5.6) - (0.6 \times 8)$$
$$= -8.16 \text{ Ns}$$

- So the magnitude of the impulse given to the particle is 8.16 Ns.

Tip: Impulse is a **vector quantity** (i.e. it has direction as well as magnitude), so in part b) you have to use **velocities** rather than **speeds** in the calculation.

The particle is travelling in different directions before and after hitting the wall — and that means that one of v or u must be **negative**. Here, the direction the particle is moving before the impact is taken as positive.

Q1 For the following direct collisions between a particle and a smooth vertical wall, find the missing speed or coefficient of restitution. All speeds are given in ms⁻¹.

a)
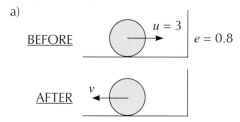

b)
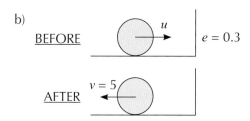

c)
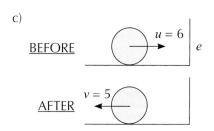

Q2 A particle is fired directly at a smooth vertical wall. The speed of the particle just before the impact is 50 ms⁻¹ and the speed just after is 5 ms⁻¹. Find the coefficient of restitution between the wall and the particle.

Q3 A football is kicked directly against a smooth vertical wall. When the speed of approach is 10 ms⁻¹, the speed of rebound is 8 ms⁻¹. Find the speed of rebound when the speed of approach is 12 ms⁻¹.

Q4 A ball of mass 3 kg collides directly with a smooth vertical wall. Given that the coefficient of restitution between the ball and the wall is 0.6, and the ball rebounds with speed 1.5 ms⁻¹, find the magnitude of the impulse given to the ball by the wall.

Q5 A ball is projected from rest across a smooth horizontal floor. It moves with acceleration 0.4 ms⁻² for 8 m before colliding directly with a smooth vertical wall. As a result of the collision, the ball rebounds and moves along the same straight line with constant speed and returns to its starting point 4.5 s after hitting the wall. Find the coefficient of restitution between the ball and the wall.

Q5 Hint: Start by finding the speeds of approach and rebound of the ball.

Q6

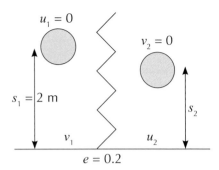

$u_1 = 0$

$v_2 = 0$

$s_1 = 2$ m

s_2

v_1

u_2

$e = 0.2$

A ball is dropped from a height of 2 m onto a smooth horizontal floor, as shown above. The coefficient of restitution between the ball and the floor is 0.2. Find:

a) v_1 and u_2, the speeds of approach and rebound of the ball,

b) s_2, the height the ball rebounds to.

Q7

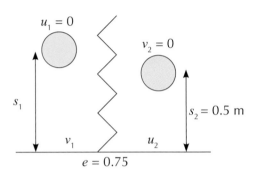

$u_1 = 0$

$v_2 = 0$

s_1

$s_2 = 0.5$ m

v_1

u_2

$e = 0.75$

A ball is dropped onto a smooth horizontal floor, as shown above. The coefficient of restitution between the ball and the floor is 0.75, and the ball rebounds to a height of 0.5 m. Find:

a) v_1 and u_2, the speeds of approach and rebound of the ball,

b) s_1, the height the ball was dropped from.

Q8 A ball is dropped from a height of 3 m onto a smooth horizontal floor. It rebounds to a height of 1 m.

What is the coefficient of restitution between the ball and the floor?

Q9 A toy car falls vertically from the edge of a table to the floor below and rebounds. The car takes 1.5 seconds to hit the floor, and the coefficient of restitution between the car and the floor is 0.05.

a) How high will the car rebound?

b) List three assumptions that have been used in this model.

3. Complex Collisions

Learning Objectives:

- Be able to solve problems involving the successive impact of up to three objects.
- Be able to solve problems involving the successive impact of up to two objects and a plane surface.

So far, all the collisions have been restricted to a single impact between two objects or one object and a plane surface. Now it's time to look at some more tricky collisions — ones involving more than two objects, or successive collisions with a plane surface.

Successive collisions

Think of this as a multi-object **pile-up**. One object collides with another, which then shoots off to collide with a third.

There's no extra maths required to solve problems like this, but quite a bit of **extra thinking**. The best thing to do is treat **each collision separately**.

Example 1

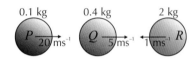

0.1 kg   0.4 kg   2 kg

Particles *P*, *Q* and *R* are travelling at different speeds along the same smooth straight line, as shown above. Particles *P* and *Q* collide first (*e* = 0.6), then *Q* goes on to collide with *R* (*e* = 0.2).

a) **What are the velocities of *P*, *Q* and *R* after the second collision?**

- Take things step by step. Forget about *R* for the moment and concentrate on the first collision — the one between *P* and *Q*:

Use $e = \dfrac{v_{Q1} - v_{P1}}{u_{P1} - u_{Q1}}$ first:

$$0.6 = \frac{v_{Q1} - v_{P1}}{20 - 5} \Rightarrow v_{Q1} - v_{P1} = 9 \text{ (equation 1).}$$

Then use $m_P u_{P1} + m_Q u_{Q1} = m_P v_{P1} + m_Q v_{Q1}$:

$$(0.1 \times 20) + (0.4 \times 5) = 0.1 v_{P1} + 0.4 v_{Q1}$$
$$\Rightarrow 4 = 0.1 v_{P1} + 0.4 v_{Q1} \quad \Rightarrow \quad v_{P1} + 4 v_{Q1} = 40 \text{ (equation 2).}$$

equation 1 + **equation 2** gives:
$$5 v_{Q1} = 49 \quad \Rightarrow \quad \boxed{v_{Q1} = 9.8 \text{ ms}^{-1}.}$$

Substituting in **equation 1** gives:
$$9.8 - v_{P1} = 9 \quad \Rightarrow \quad v_{P1} = 9.8 - 9 = \boxed{0.8 \text{ ms}^{-1}.}$$

- So, for the first collision:

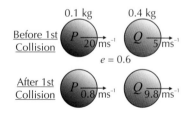

0.1 kg   0.4 kg

Before 1st Collision   *P* 20 ms⁻¹   *Q* 5 ms⁻¹

e = 0.6

After 1st Collision   *P* 0.8 ms⁻¹   *Q* 9.8 ms⁻¹

Tip: There are lots of velocities to find here, so label them clearly — e.g. v_{Q1} is the final velocity of *Q* after collision 1, etc.

- For the second collision, which is between Q and R: $e = \frac{v_{R2} - v_{Q2}}{u_{Q2} - u_{R2}}$.

  $u_{Q2} = v_{Q1}$ — it's the same as the velocity of Q after the first collision
  — you found this above (9.8 ms⁻¹), so:

  $$0.2 = \frac{v_{R2} - v_{Q2}}{9.8 - (-1)} \quad \Rightarrow \quad v_{R2} - v_{Q2} = 2.16 \quad \textbf{(equation 3)}.$$

  Then $m_Q u_{Q2} + m_R u_{R2} = m_Q v_{Q2} + m_R v_{R2}$:
  $$(0.4 \times 9.8) + (2 \times -1) = 0.4 v_{Q2} + 2 v_{R2}$$
  $$\Rightarrow 1.92 = 0.4 v_{Q2} + 2 v_{R2} \quad \Rightarrow \quad 0.2 v_{Q2} + v_{R2} = 0.96 \quad \textbf{(equation 4)}.$$

  equation 4 – **equation 3** gives:
  $$1.2 v_{Q2} = -1.2 \quad \Rightarrow \quad \boxed{v_{Q2} = -1 \text{ ms}^{-1}.}$$

  Substituting in **equation 3** gives:
  $$v_{R2} - (-1) = 2.16 \quad \Rightarrow \quad v_{R2} = 2.16 - 1 = \boxed{1.16 \text{ ms}^{-1}.}$$

- So, for the second collision:

- Velocities after both collisions are:
  $P = 0.8$ ms⁻¹, $Q = -1$ ms⁻¹ and $R = 1.16$ ms⁻¹.

b) **Following the second collision, P is removed and R hits a smooth vertical wall at a right angle. How big would e have to be for this impact to allow R to collide again with Q, assuming Q is moving with velocity –1 ms⁻¹?**

- Think things through carefully. Q is going at 1 ms⁻¹ in the opposite direction to R. To hit Q again, R needs to bounce off the wall with a rebound speed higher than 1 ms⁻¹, so it can 'catch up'.
  So speed of rebound of R, $v > 1$.

- For the impact with the wall,
  $$e = \frac{v}{u} \quad \Rightarrow \quad v = eu, \text{ and so } eu > 1.$$

- From part a), $u = v_{R2} = 1.16$ ms⁻¹, so:
  $$1.16e > 1 \quad \Rightarrow \quad e > \frac{1}{1.16} \quad \Rightarrow \quad e > 0.8620...$$

- So, R colliding again with Q requires $e > 0.862$ (3 s.f.)

Example 2

A particle, A, of mass 1.5 kg, moving in a straight line with speed 6 ms⁻¹ across a smooth horizontal floor, collides directly with a smooth vertical wall. The impulse given to A by the wall has magnitude 15 Ns.

a) **Show that the coefficient of restitution between A and the wall is $e = \frac{2}{3}$.**

> **Tip:** As ever, you need to decide on a positive direction. In a), the initial direction of motion of A has been taken as positive, so the impulse and v_{A1} will both be negative.

- Start by using the impulse-momentum principle to find the rebound speed of A:

  Impulse = Change in momentum
  $$-15 = 1.5(v_{A1} - 6)$$
  $$-10 = v_{A1} - 6$$
  $v_{A1} = -4$ ms⁻¹. So rebound speed is 4 ms⁻¹.

- Use this to find the coefficient of restitution between A and the wall:
  $$e = \frac{\text{Speed of rebound}}{\text{Speed of approach}}$$
  $$= \frac{4}{6} = \frac{2}{3} \text{ — as required.}$$

After rebounding from the wall, A collides directly with a second particle, B, of mass 4 kg, which is moving towards A with speed 2 ms⁻¹.

b) **Given that the coefficient of restitution between A and B is $\frac{5}{6}$, show that A will collide with the wall a second time.**

- Draw a sketch showing particles A and B.
  For this collision, $u_{A2} = v_{A1} = -4$ ms⁻¹, from part a).

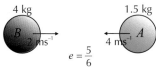

- Use $e = \frac{v_{A2} - v_{B2}}{u_{B2} - u_{A2}}$:
  $$\frac{5}{6} = \frac{v_{A2} - v_{B2}}{2 - (-4)} \Rightarrow 5 = v_{A2} - v_{B2} \text{ — call this \textbf{equation 1}.}$$

- Now use $m_A u_{A2} + m_B u_{B2} = m_A v_{A2} + m_B v_{B2}$:
  $$(1.5 \times -4) + (4 \times 2) = 1.5v_{A2} + 4v_{B2}$$
  $$2 = 1.5v_{A2} + 4v_{B2} \text{ — call this \textbf{equation 2}.}$$

- Now solve the simultaneous equations:
  equation 2 + (4 × **equation 1**) gives
  $$2 + 20 = 1.5v_{A2} + 4v_{B2} + 4v_{A2} - 4v_{B2}$$
  $$22 = 5.5v_{A2} \Rightarrow v_{A2} = 4 \text{ ms}^{-1}$$

  Substituting in **equation 1** gives:
  $$4 - v_{B2} = 5 \Rightarrow v_{B2} = -1 \text{ ms}^{-1}$$

- Particle A is now moving in the same direction as it was before collision 1 (as v_{A2} is positive), so it is moving back towards the wall. Particle B is moving in the opposite direction (as v_{B2} is negative), so will not prevent A from colliding with the wall a second time.

The first collision between A and B occurs d metres from the wall.
The particles collide again at point X, after A has collided a second time with the wall.

c) **Find, in terms of d, the distance of point X from the wall.**

- Following the collision with B, A travels for d metres with speed 4 ms^{-1} and collides with the wall. So:

$$\text{Time} = \frac{d}{4} \text{ seconds}$$

> **Tip:** There's lots of use of speed $= \frac{\text{distance}}{\text{time}}$ in this example.

- In this time, B will have travelled $1 \times \frac{d}{4} = \frac{d}{4}$ metres further away from the wall (as B has speed 1 ms^{-1} after it collides with A). So when A hits the wall, B is $d + \frac{d}{4} = \frac{5d}{4}$ m from the wall.

- Use $e = \frac{v}{u}$ to find the speed with which A rebounds from the wall:

$$\frac{2}{3} = \frac{v}{4} \Rightarrow v = \frac{8}{3} \text{ ms}^{-1}$$

- Let x be the distance from the wall to point X and find the time each particle takes to get to point X, from the time that A hits the wall:

$$T_A = x \div \frac{8}{3} = \frac{3}{8}x \text{ seconds}$$
$$T_B = \left(x - \frac{5d}{4}\right) \div 1 = \left(x - \frac{5d}{4}\right) \text{ seconds}$$

> **Tip:** B has to travel $x - \frac{5d}{4}$ m to get to point X, as it's already $\frac{5d}{4}$ m from the wall when A collides with the wall.

- When A and B collide, $T_A = T_B$, so:

$$\frac{3}{8}x = x - \frac{5d}{4}$$
$$\frac{-5x}{8} = \frac{-5d}{4} \Rightarrow x = 2d \text{ m}$$

- So point X is **$2d$ m** from the wall.

Exercise 3.1

Q1

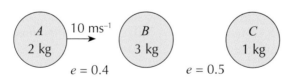

A 2 kg $\quad$ 10 ms^{-1} $\quad$ B 3 kg $\quad$ C 1 kg

$e = 0.4$ $\qquad$ $e = 0.5$

Particles A, B and C, of mass 2 kg, 3 kg and 1 kg respectively, lie at rest on the same straight line on a smooth horizontal plane.
A is projected towards B with speed 10 ms^{-1} and collides directly with B. As a result of this collision, B goes on to collide directly with C. The coefficient of restitution between A and B is 0.4 and between B and C is 0.5.

Find the speed of C following the second collision.

Q2 Particle *A*, of mass 60 kg, is moving in a straight line across a smooth horizontal surface with speed 4 ms^{-1} when it collides directly with a stationary particle, *B*, of mass 20 kg. As a result of this collision, Particle *B* goes on to collide directly with a smooth vertical wall.

Find the speed at which *B* rebounds from the wall, given that the coefficient of restitution between the two particles is 0.3 and the coefficient of restitution between *B* and the wall is 0.7.

Q3 A snooker player hits the white ball into a stationary red ball of the same mass. The balls collide directly and the red ball then collides with the vertical side cushion of the table at right angles and rebounds with speed 1.2 ms^{-1}. If the coefficient of restitution between the balls is 0.8 and the coefficient of restitution between any ball and the side cushion is 0.5, find the initial speed of the white ball. You may assume that the surface of the table is smooth.

Q4

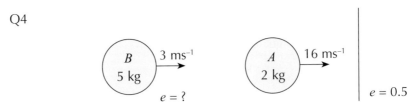

Particle *A*, of mass 2 kg, and moving in a straight line along a smooth surface at 16 ms^{-1}, collides directly with a smooth vertical wall and rebounds. It then collides directly with particle *B*, of mass 5 kg, which is moving along the same surface towards the wall in a straight line at a speed of 3 ms^{-1}. The coefficient of restitution between particle *A* and the wall is 0.5. If particle *A* is brought to rest as a result of the collision with particle *B*, find the coefficient of restitution between the two particles.

Q5

Particle *A*, of mass 6 kg, and travelling along a smooth surface at 3 ms^{-1}, collides directly with a stationary particle, *B*, of mass 5 kg. As a result, *B* moves along the surface and collides directly with a second stationary particle, *C*, of mass 2 kg.

Given that the coefficient of restitution for the first collision is *e* and for the second collision is 0.75, and that the speed of *C* is 3 ms^{-1} following the second collision, find the speed of particles *A* and *B* after the second collision, and the value of *e*.

Q6

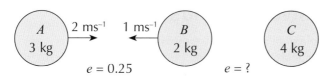

Particle A, of mass 3 kg, and travelling in a straight line on a smooth surface with speed 2 ms^{-1}, collides directly with particle B, of mass 2 kg, which is travelling with speed 1 ms^{-1} along the same straight line but in the opposite direction. Particle C, of mass 4 kg, is at rest on the same surface, positioned on the same straight line as A and B, such that B and C will collide directly if the direction of motion of B is reversed. The coefficient of restitution between A and B is 0.25.

a) Show that there will be a collision between B and C.

b) Find the range of values of e which would cause B to change direction as a result of colliding directly with C.

Q6 Hint: Think about the direction of motion of B after each collision.

Q7   Two balls, A and B, of mass 6 kg and 4 kg respectively, are moving on a smooth horizontal plane. A is travelling with speed 2 ms^{-1} and B is travelling in the opposite direction along the same straight line with speed 4 ms^{-1}. The two balls collide directly, and, as a result, the direction of motion of B is reversed. B then goes on to collide directly with a smooth, fixed vertical wall.

a) Show that there will be a second collision between A and B, given that the coefficient of restitution between A and B is 0.9 and between B and the wall is 0.95.

b) The first collision between A and B occurs 5.68 m from the wall. Show that A is 10.8 m from the wall when B collides with the wall.

Q8

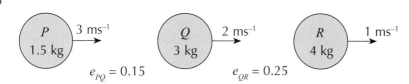

Three particles, P, Q and R, are moving along the same smooth straight line with velocities and coefficients of restitution as shown above. P collides directly with Q, which goes on to collide directly with R. Find the speed of each particle following the collision between Q and R.

Q9   Two particles, A and B, are at rest on a smooth horizontal surface. A has mass m and B has mass $3m$. A is projected towards B with speed 5 ms^{-1} and the two particles collide directly. The coefficient of restitution between the two particles is e. B then goes on to collide directly with a smooth vertical wall and rebounds. The coefficient of restitution for this collision is 0.85. Given that B collides with A a second time, find the range of values for e, to 3 significant figures.

Successive rebounds

Not all complex collisions involve multiple objects.
One object **repeatedly rebounding** from a smooth surface can be a complex situation to model. As with the previous collisions, you can tackle **successive rebound** problems by treating each collision **separately**.

Example 1

A ball falls from a height of 10 m and rebounds several times from the ground, where $e = 0.8$ for each impact.

Find the height the ball reaches after each of the first three bounces, stating any assumptions you have made.

- First list some assumptions: the ball is a particle, air resistance can be ignored, the ball is initially at rest and falls vertically onto a horizontal, smooth, plane surface, under a constant acceleration downwards of $g = 9.8$ ms^{-2}.

- For each bounce use $v^2 = u^2 + 2as$ to find the approach speed to the ground and the law of restitution, $e = \frac{v}{u}$, to find the rebound speed. Then use $v^2 = u^2 + 2as$ again to find the height the ball reaches (s) after the bounce.

BOUNCE 1

Falling: (Taking down as positive)

$v^2 = u^2 + 2as$ where $u = 0$, $a = 9.8$ and $s = 10$:

$$v^2 = 0 + (2 \times 9.8 \times 10) \quad \Rightarrow \quad v = \sqrt{2 \times 9.8 \times 10} = 14 \text{ ms}^{-1}.$$

Colliding:

$e = \frac{v}{u} \quad \Rightarrow \quad v = eu$, where v is the velocity just after the impact, $e = 0.8$ and u is the velocity just before the impact (i.e. 14 ms^{-1}).

$$\Rightarrow v = 0.8 \times 14 = 11.2 \text{ ms}^{-1}.$$

Rebounding: (Taking up as positive)
$v^2 = u^2 + 2as$, where $v = 0$, $a = -9.8$,
and u is the velocity just after the impact (i.e. 11.2 ms^{-1}).

$$0 = 11.2^2 + (2 \times -9.8)s$$

$$\Rightarrow \text{Height of Rebound 1} = s = \frac{11.2^2}{2 \times 9.8} = \boxed{6.4 \text{ m.}}$$

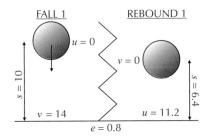

Tip: Set v to zero here because you want to know how far it will travel upwards (with an acceleration of $-g$) before it stops and begins to fall back down.

BOUNCE 2

Falling:
The motion as the ball rises then falls is <u>symmetrical</u> — it covers the same distance under the same magnitude of acceleration on the second fall as it did on the first rebound. So it hits the floor the second time with the same speed it left it at — 11.2 ms^{-1}.

Tip: If you're not convinced, put the numbers in the equation of motion again to see for yourself.

Colliding:
Again, $v = eu$, where v is the velocity after the second impact, $e = 0.8$ and $u = 11.2$ ms^{-1} (velocity just before impact).

$$v = 0.8 \times 11.2 = 8.96 \text{ ms}^{-1}.$$

Rebounding: (Taking up as positive)
$v^2 = u^2 + 2as$, where $v = 0$, $a = -9.8$ and $u = 8.96$ (velocity after impact):

$$0 = 8.96^2 + (2 \times -9.8)s$$

$$\Rightarrow \text{Height of Rebound 2} = s = \frac{8.96^2}{2 \times 9.8} = \boxed{4.096 \text{ m}}$$

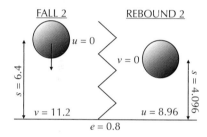

BOUNCE 3

Falling:
Again, using the symmetry of the vertical motion, velocity just before third impact = velocity after second impact = 8.96 ms^{-1}.

Colliding:
$v = eu$, where v is the velocity after the third impact, $e = 0.8$ and $u = 8.96$ ms^{-1}.

$$v = 0.8 \times 8.96 = 7.168 \text{ ms}^{-1}.$$

Rebounding:
$v^2 = u^2 + 2as$, where $v = 0$, $u = 7.168$ and $a = -9.8$:

$$0 = 7.168^2 + (2 \times -9.8)s$$

$$\Rightarrow \text{Height of Rebound 3} = s = \frac{7.168^2}{2 \times 9.8} = \boxed{2.62 \text{ m (3 s.f.)}}$$

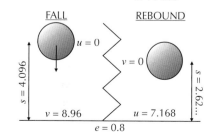

- The **height** of each bounce of a rebounding object will be a **multiple** of the height of the **previous bounce**, and that multiple is the **same** for each successive bounce.

- This means that the heights that the object reaches on successive bounces will form a **converging geometric progression**.

- Once you know what the **common ratio** of the progression is, you can find the **height of the nth bounce** using the formula for the nth term of a geometric progression: $u_n = ar^{n-1}$

- You can use the formula for the **sum to infinity** of a geometric progression ($s_\infty = \frac{a}{1-r}$) to find the **total distance** the object bounces before stopping.

Example 2

A ball is dropped from a height of 10 m and hits a smooth, horizontal floor at right angles. The coefficient of restitution between the ball and the floor is 0.5. Model the ball as a particle falling freely under gravity.

a) Find the height the ball rebounds to after each of the first two bounces.

- Work out the rebound heights the same way as in Example 1:

BOUNCE 1

Falling: (Taking down as positive)

$v^2 = u^2 + 2as$ where $u = 0$, $a = 9.8$ and $s = 10$:

$$v^2 = 0 + (2 \times 9.8 \times 10) \quad \Rightarrow \quad v = \sqrt{2 \times 9.8 \times 10} = 14 \text{ ms}^{-1}$$

Colliding:

$e = \frac{v}{u} \quad \Rightarrow \quad v = eu \quad \Rightarrow \quad v = 0.5 \times 14 = 7 \text{ ms}^{-1}.$

Rebounding: (Taking up as positive)
$v^2 = u^2 + 2as$, where $v = 0$, $a = -9.8$,
and u is the velocity just after the impact (i.e. 7 ms^{-1}).

$$0 = 7^2 + (2 \times -9.8)s$$
$$\Rightarrow \text{Height of Rebound 1} = s = \frac{7^2}{2 \times 9.8} = 2.5 \text{ m}$$

BOUNCE 2

Falling:
The motion as the ball rises then falls is <u>symmetrical</u> — it covers the same distance under the same magnitude of acceleration on the second fall as it did on the first rebound. So it hits the floor the second time with the same speed it left it at — 7 ms^{-1}.

Colliding:
Again, $v = eu$, where v is the velocity after the second impact, $e = 0.5$ and $u = 7$ ms^{-1}.

$$v = 0.5 \times 7 = 3.5 \text{ ms}^{-1}.$$

Rebounding: (Taking up as positive)
$v^2 = u^2 + 2as$, where $v = 0$, $a = -9.8$ and $u = 3.5$:

$$0 = 3.5^2 + (2 \times -9.8)s$$
$$\Rightarrow \text{Height of Rebound 2} = s = \frac{3.5^2}{2 \times 9.8} = 0.625 \text{ m}$$

---

b) Find the height the ball rebounds to after the sixth bounce.

- Height of Rebound 1 $= s_1 = 2.5$ m
  Height of Rebound 2 $= s_2 = 0.625$ m
  $$\frac{s_2}{s_1} = \frac{1}{4} \implies s_2 = \frac{1}{4}s_1$$

- The height of Rebound 3 will be $\frac{1}{4}$ of the height of Rebound 2, and so on. The heights of successive rebounds form a geometric progression, with common ratio $\frac{1}{4}$.

- The first term in the sequence is the height of Rebound 1 ($= 2.5$), so use the formula for finding the nth term of a geometric progression:
  $$u_n = ar^{n-1}$$

- The height of the sixth bounce will be the sixth term in the progression:
  $$u_6 = 2.5\left(\frac{1}{4}\right)^5 = 0.002441... \text{ m} = \boxed{2.44 \text{ mm (3 s.f.)}}$$

Tip: You could work out the rebound heights of some more bounces using the method in part a) if you want to double check that they are multiplied by ¼ each time.

Tip: a is the first term of the sequence and r is the common ratio. You should remember this formula from Core 2.

c) Find the total distance the ball travels before coming to rest.

- The ball is dropped from a height of 10 m, so it initially travels 10 m before the first bounce, then bounces to a height of 2.5 m and falls 2.5 m to the ground, and continues to rise and fall following each bounce.

- So, write out the distances travelled as a sum:
  $$\text{Total distance} = 10 + 2.5 + 2.5 + 0.625 + 0.625 + ...$$
  $$= 10 + 2(2.5 + 0.625 + ...)$$

- From part b), this can be rewritten as:
  $$\text{Total distance} = 10 + 2[2.5 + 2.5\left(\frac{1}{4}\right) + 2.5\left(\frac{1}{4}\right)^2 + ...]$$

- The terms in the square brackets form a convergent series, so use the formula for the sum to infinity of a geometric series:
  $$\text{Total distance} = 10 + 2\left(\frac{2.5}{1 - \frac{1}{4}}\right) = \boxed{16.7 \text{ m (3 s.f.)}}$$

Exercise 3.2

Q1 A ball is dropped from 20 m above a smooth horizontal surface and falls freely under gravity. The ball collides at right angles with the surface and rebounds, and the coefficient of restitution for the collision is $e = 0.75$. Find:

a) the height the ball rebounds to after the first bounce,

b) the speed of the ball immediately after the second bounce,

c) the height the ball rebounds to after the second bounce.

Q2 A ball falls 3 m under gravity and collides with a smooth horizontal floor at right angles. It rebounds to a height of 2 m.

a) Find the coefficient of restitution between the ball and the floor.

b) Calculate the height reached by the ball after the second bounce.

Q3 A particle is dropped onto a smooth horizontal surface from a height of 10 m. Given that the coefficient of restitution between the particle and the surface is 0.6, after how many bounces is the rebound height less than 1 m?

Q4 A particle is dropped onto a smooth horizontal surface and rebounds after colliding with the surface at right angles. The speed of the particle just before it collides with the surface is u and the coefficient of restitution between the particle and the surface is e.

Q4 Hint: In part a), start by finding expressions for v_1 and v_2 in terms of e and u.

a) Show that the speed of the particle immediately following the nth bounce is:
$$v_n = ue^n$$

b) Given that the particle is initially dropped from height H above the surface, show that the height the particle rebounds to after the nth bounce is:
$$h_n = He^{2n}$$

Q5 A ball is dropped from a height H and falls under gravity until it collides at right angles with a smooth horizontal floor.
The coefficient of restitution for the collision is $e = 0.3$.
The ball rebounds repeatedly, reaching a height of 0.2 cm after the third bounce. Find H.

Q6 Find an expression for the total distance travelled by a particle which is released from rest at height H above a smooth horizontal plane and rebounds from the surface repeatedly until coming to rest. Let the coefficient of restitution between the particle and the surface be e.

You may use the fact that the sum to infinity of a converging geometric series is given by $\frac{a}{1-r}$, where a is the first term in the series, and r is the common ratio.

Q7 A ball is dropped onto a smooth horizontal surface from a height of 2.5 m. The ball collides with the surface at right angles and rebounds. Given that the ball travels a total distance of 3 m in coming to rest, find the coefficient of restitution between the ball and the surface to 2 decimal places.

Q8 A small marble falls freely under gravity and collides at right angles with a smooth horizontal floor and then rebounds repeatedly until it comes to rest. The speed of the marble immediately following the second bounce is $v_2 = 5.5$ ms^{-1}. Given that the coefficient of restitution between the marble and the floor is $e = 0.8$, find the total distance travelled by the marble before it comes to rest.

4. Collisions and Energy

Any object that is moving has kinetic energy. If a moving object collides with another object, then the kinetic energy of the object will usually change. Working out the change in kinetic energy is fairly straightforward once you know how to deal with collisions.

Kinetic energy and collisions

For any collision where $e < 1$, some **kinetic energy** will be **lost** (it changes into things like heat and sound).

Kinetic energy is only conserved in **perfectly elastic** collisions — where $e = 1$.

The formula for working out **how much** kinetic energy has been lost is fairly straightforward:

> Loss of K.E. on Impact = Total K.E. before – Total K.E. after
> $$= (\tfrac{1}{2}m_A u_A^2 + \tfrac{1}{2}m_B u_B^2) - (\tfrac{1}{2}m_A v_A^2 + \tfrac{1}{2}m_B v_B^2)$$

The tricky bit is finding the u's and v's to put in the formula...

Example 1

A particle, P, of mass m kg, is moving across a smooth horizontal plane with velocity $(6i + 8j)$ ms^{-1}. It collides at right angles with a fixed, smooth vertical wall, and rebounds.

Given that the coefficient of restitution between the particle and the wall is $\frac{2}{5}$ and the kinetic energy lost as a result of the collision is 37.8 J, find the value of m.

- First find the speed of P (i.e. the magnitude of its velocity) before it collides with the wall:

$$u = \sqrt{6^2 + 8^2} = 10 \text{ ms}^{-1}$$

- Now use $e = \frac{v}{u}$ to find the rebound speed of P following the collision with the wall:

$$e = \frac{v}{u}$$
$$\frac{2}{5} = \frac{v}{10} \Rightarrow v = 4 \text{ ms}^{-1}$$

- Next, use the formula for change in kinetic energy. The kinetic energy of the wall can't change as the wall is fixed, so the only change in kinetic energy will be as a result of the changing speed of A, so:

$$\text{Loss of K.E.} = \tfrac{1}{2}mu^2 - \tfrac{1}{2}mv^2$$
$$37.8 = \tfrac{1}{2}m(10^2 - 4^2)$$
$$37.8 = 42m$$
$$\boxed{m = 0.9 \text{ kg}}$$

Learning Objectives:

- Be able to calculate the kinetic energy lost as a result of an inelastic collision.
- Be able to find the change in kinetic energy resulting from the impulse of a force acting on an object.

Tip: Remember — Kinetic energy = $\frac{1}{2} \times$ mass $\times v^2$ (where v is the magnitude of velocity) See page 87 for more about kinetic energy.

Tip: There could also be a gain in K.E. (e.g. when a particle is given an impulse). To find how much K.E. has been gained, use the same formula as for a loss of K.E. but switch the 'before' and 'after' terms.

Tip: You can't use velocities in vector form in $e = \frac{v}{u}$ or K.E. $= \frac{1}{2}mv^2$, so you have to find the magnitude of the velocity first.

Example 2

$$m_C = 0.05 \text{ kg} \qquad m_A = m_B = 0.001 \text{ kg}$$

A tiny cannon fires a ball in a straight line across a smooth horizontal table, as shown. The ball collides directly with another, stationary, ball and following the collision continues in the same straight line with speed 7.5 ms^{-1}. The coefficient of restitution for the collision is $e = 0.7$.

a) **Find the loss of kinetic energy when the balls collide.**

- First find u_A (the initial speed of A) and v_B (the final speed of B).
- Use conservation of momentum and the law of restitution, where $e = 0.7$, $v_A = 7.5$, and $u_B = 0$:

$$e = \frac{v_B - v_A}{u_A - u_B} \Rightarrow 0.7 = \frac{v_B - 7.5}{u_A - 0} \Rightarrow v_B - 0.7u_A = 7.5 \quad \textbf{— eqn 1}$$

$$m_A u_A + m_B u_B = m_A v_A + m_B v_B \text{ and since } m_A = m_B:$$

$$u_A + 0 = 7.5 + v_B \Rightarrow u_A - v_B = 7.5 \quad \textbf{— eqn 2}$$

eqn 1 + **eqn 2**: $\quad 0.3u_A = 15 \Rightarrow u_A = \boxed{50 \text{ ms}^{-1}}$

Sub in **eqn 2**: $\quad 50 - v_B = 7.5 \Rightarrow v_B = 50 - 7.5 = \boxed{42.5 \text{ ms}^{-1}}$

- Finally, put all the values in the kinetic energy formula:

$$\text{Loss of K.E.} = \left(\tfrac{1}{2}m_A u_A^2 + \tfrac{1}{2}m_B u_B^2\right) - \left(\tfrac{1}{2}m_A v_A^2 + \tfrac{1}{2}m_B v_B^2\right)$$

$$= \tfrac{1}{2}m[(u_A^2 + u_B^2) - (v_A^2 + v_B^2)]$$

$$= \tfrac{1}{2} \times 0.001 \times [(50^2 + 0^2) - (7.5^2 + 42.5^2)]$$

$$= \boxed{0.31875 \text{ J}}$$

> **Tip:** For mass in kg and speed in ms^{-1}, the units of kinetic energy are joules (J).

b) **Find the kinetic energy gained by firing the cannon.**

- Since both the cannon and ball A are stationary before firing, there is no initial kinetic energy.
- The gain in K.E. is simply $\tfrac{1}{2}m_C v_C^2 + \tfrac{1}{2}m_A v_A^2$, where v_A is the speed of the ball after firing (i.e. 50 ms^{-1}).
- So, first work out the velocity of the cannon after it has been fired (v_C).
- Momentum is conserved, so:

$$m_C u_C + m_A u_A = m_C v_C + m_A v_A$$

$$\Rightarrow 0 + 0 = 0.05v_C + (0.001 \times 50)$$

$$\Rightarrow v_C = -(0.001 \times 50) \div 0.05 = \boxed{-1 \text{ ms}^{-1}}$$

$$\text{(i.e. the cannon moves backwards at 1 ms}^{-1}\text{).}$$

> **Tip:** Remember — use the magnitude of velocity in the formula for kinetic energy.

- Gain in K.E. $= \tfrac{1}{2}m_C v_C^2 + \tfrac{1}{2}m_A v_A^2$

$$= \left(\tfrac{1}{2} \times 0.05 \times 1^2\right) + \left(\tfrac{1}{2} \times 0.001 \times 50^2\right)$$

$$= \boxed{1.275 \text{ J}}$$

Q1   A particle of mass 10 kg is travelling in a straight line with speed
     12 ms^{-1} when it collides directly with a second, stationary particle
     of mass 15 kg. Following the collision, the two particles move in
     the same direction along the same straight line. The coefficient of
     restitution for the collision is $e = 0.2$. Find the kinetic energy lost in
     this collision.

Q2

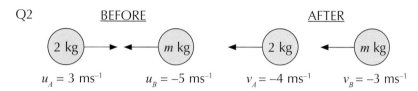

BEFORE   AFTER

$u_A = 3$ ms^{-1} $u_B = -5$ ms^{-1} $v_A = -4$ ms^{-1} $v_B = -3$ ms^{-1}

Particle A, of mass 2 kg, is travelling in a straight line with speed
3 ms^{-1}. It collides directly with particle B, of mass m kg, which is
travelling in the opposite direction along the same straight line with
speed 5 ms^{-1}. As a result of the collision, the direction of motion of
A is reversed and A and B move in the same direction with speed
4 ms^{-1} and 3 ms^{-1} respectively.

a) Find m.

b) Find the kinetic energy lost in this collision.

Q3   Particle A, of mass 5 kg, travels in a straight line with speed 4 ms^{-1}
     and collides directly with particle B, of mass 3 kg, which is travelling
     in the opposite direction along the same straight line with speed
     2 ms^{-1}. Given that the particles coalesce as a result of the collision,
     find the kinetic energy lost.

Q4   Particle A, of mass 2 kg, is travelling with velocity $(6\mathbf{i} + 2\mathbf{j})$ ms^{-1}
     when it collides with a stationary particle, B, of mass 3 kg.
     Immediately following the impact, the velocity of A is $(3\mathbf{i} + 1\mathbf{j})$ ms^{-1}.

     Calculate the kinetic energy lost in the collision.

Q4 Hint: A and B are
travelling along the
same straight line, as
their velocity vectors
are proportional to each
other.

Q5   A stone of mass 5 kg is sliding in a straight line across smooth ice
     with velocity $(4\mathbf{i} - 2\mathbf{j})$ ms^{-1} when it collides with a stone of mass
     3 kg which is moving with velocity $(-3\mathbf{i} + 4\mathbf{j})$ ms^{-1}. As a result of
     the collision, the velocity of the 5 kg stone changes to $(2\mathbf{i} + \mathbf{j})$ ms^{-1}.
     Calculate the kinetic energy lost in the collision.

Q6   An engine of mass 10 tonnes collides directly with a stationary truck
     of mass 2 tonnes. As a result of the collision, the truck moves with
     speed 5 ms^{-1}. Given that 2×10^4 J of kinetic energy is lost in the
     collision, find:

a) the initial and final speeds of the engine,

b) the coefficient of restitution between the engine and truck.

Q7 Ball A, of mass 3 kg, is moving in a straight line with speed 6 ms⁻¹ when it collides directly with ball B, of mass 4 kg, travelling in the opposite direction along the same straight line with speed 4 ms⁻¹. The balls collide with coefficient of restitution $e = 0.4$.
Find the percentage of the initial kinetic energy which is lost as a result of the collision.

Q8 Particles P and Q, of mass m and $2m$ respectively, are moving towards each other along the same straight line. P has speed 6 ms⁻¹ and Q has speed 2 ms⁻¹. The two particles collide directly. As a result, 48 J of kinetic energy is lost, reducing the total kinetic energy of the system to 18 J.
Find all possible values for the velocities of P and Q following the collision. Explain your answer.

Q9 Particle P, of mass $3m$ kg, is travelling with constant velocity across a smooth horizontal surface. Four seconds after leaving the origin, P reaches the point with position vector $(20\mathbf{i} + 8\mathbf{j})$, where it collides with particle Q, of mass m kg, travelling with velocity $(-4\mathbf{i} + \mathbf{j})$ ms⁻¹. As a result of the collision, the velocity of P changes to $(4\mathbf{i} + 3\mathbf{j})$ ms⁻¹.
Given that the kinetic energy lost in the impact is 42 J, find m.

Q10 Two identical particles, A and B, each of mass m, are at rest on a smooth horizontal plane. Particle A is fired towards B with velocity $2u$ and the two particles collide directly.
Given that the coefficient of restitution between the particles is $\frac{1}{4}$, show that the kinetic energy lost as a result of the collision is $\frac{15}{16}mu^2$.

Q11

A snooker player sets up a trick shot as shown in the diagram above, with a white ball (A), a red ball (B) and a model car (C) arranged along the same straight line on a smooth table. The two balls each have mass 160 g and the car has mass 30 g.

The white ball collides directly with the stationary red ball, which then goes on to collide directly with the stationary car. The car must be travelling at exactly 1.6 ms⁻¹ if it is to fall into the pocket. The coefficient of restitution between the two balls is $e_{AB} = 0.4$ and the coefficient of restitution between the red ball and the car is $e_{BC} = 0.8$.

What must the initial kinetic energy of the white ball be to ensure that the car falls into the pocket?

Kinetic energy and impulse

An **impulse** will cause a change in an object's **momentum**.
This can cause the **speed** of the object to **increase** or **decrease**,
meaning an increase or decrease in **kinetic energy**.

Example 1

A fly of mass 0.002 kg is moving at a velocity of $(2\mathbf{i} - \mathbf{j})$ ms^{-1} when it is swatted with an impulse of $(0.01\mathbf{i} - 0.06\mathbf{j})$ Ns. How much kinetic energy is gained by the fly following the impulse?

- Using the impulse-momentum principle:

$$\mathbf{I} = m\mathbf{v} - m\mathbf{u}$$
$$0.01\mathbf{i} - 0.06\mathbf{j} = 0.002\mathbf{v} - 0.002(2\mathbf{i} - \mathbf{j})$$
$$\Rightarrow 0.002\mathbf{v} = 0.01\mathbf{i} - 0.06\mathbf{j} + 0.004\mathbf{i} - 0.002\mathbf{j}$$
$$= 0.014\mathbf{i} - 0.062\mathbf{j}$$
$$\Rightarrow \mathbf{v} = (0.014\mathbf{i} - 0.062\mathbf{j}) \div 0.002$$
$$= (7\mathbf{i} - 31\mathbf{j}) \text{ ms}^{-1}.$$

- The initial speed of the fly: $u = |\mathbf{u}| = \sqrt{2^2 + 1^2} = \sqrt{5}$.
  After the impulse this becomes: $v = |\mathbf{v}| = \sqrt{7^2 + 31^2} = \sqrt{1010}$.

- Increase in K.E. $= \frac{1}{2}mv^2 - \frac{1}{2}mu^2$
$$= (\tfrac{1}{2} \times 0.002 \times 1010) - (\tfrac{1}{2} \times 0.002 \times 5)$$
$$= \boxed{1.005 \text{ J}}$$

Example 2

A particle of mass 2 kg is moving with velocity $(6\mathbf{i} + 8\mathbf{j})$ ms^{-1} when it receives an impulse, I, resulting in a loss of 36 J of kinetic energy. Given that the direction of motion of the particle following the impact is at an angle of θ above the negative horizontal (where $\cos\theta = \frac{4}{5}$), find I.

- The initial speed of the particle: $u = |\mathbf{u}| = \sqrt{6^2 + 8^2} = \sqrt{100}$.

- Use the formula for change in K.E. to find the particle's speed after receiving the impulse.

$$\text{Loss in K.E.} = \tfrac{1}{2}mu^2 - \tfrac{1}{2}mv^2$$
$$36 = (\tfrac{1}{2} \times 2 \times 100) - (\tfrac{1}{2} \times 2 \times v^2)$$
$$v^2 = 64 \Rightarrow v = 8 \text{ ms}^{-1}$$

- Use this to find the horizontal and vertical components of **v**, the particle's velocity after it receives the impulse:

$$\text{Horizontal component} = -8\cos\theta = -\frac{32}{5}$$
$$\text{Vertical component} = 8\sin\theta = \frac{24}{5}$$
$$\Rightarrow \boxed{\mathbf{v} = -\frac{32}{5}\mathbf{i} + \frac{24}{5}\mathbf{j}}$$

- Now, using the impulse-momentum principle:

$$\mathbf{I} = m\mathbf{v} - m\mathbf{u}$$
$$= 2[(-\tfrac{32}{5}\mathbf{i} + \tfrac{24}{5}\mathbf{j}) - (6\mathbf{i} + 8\mathbf{j})] = \boxed{-\frac{124}{5}\mathbf{i} - \frac{32}{5}\mathbf{j}} \text{ Ns} = (-24.8\mathbf{i} - 6.4\mathbf{j}) \text{ Ns}$$

Tip: $\cos\theta = \frac{4}{5}$ means that $\sin\theta = \frac{3}{5}$, because the right-angled triangle will look like this:

Tip: The question tells you that the direction of motion makes an angle of θ above the negative horizontal (i.e. $-\mathbf{i}$), so the horizontal component of the velocity will be negative.

Q1   A marble with mass 30 g is rolling across a smooth horizontal surface with velocity $(2\mathbf{i} + 5\mathbf{j})$ ms^{-1} when it is given an impulse of $(0.06\mathbf{i} + 0.09\mathbf{j})$ Ns. Find the resulting increase in the marble's kinetic energy.

Q2   A skater of mass 50 kg is moving with velocity $(8\mathbf{i} + 6\mathbf{j})$ ms^{-1} when she is given an impulse of $(75\mathbf{i} - 100\mathbf{j})$ Ns. Find the resulting change in her kinetic energy.

Q3   A rocket of mass 5 tonnes is travelling with constant velocity $(500\mathbf{i} + 200\mathbf{j})$ ms^{-1} when it burns a load of fuel, giving the rocket an impulse of $(10^5\mathbf{i} + 3 \times 10^4\mathbf{j})$ Ns. Assuming that burning the fuel causes no significant change in the mass of the rocket, find the new kinetic energy of the rocket.

Q4   In a game of badminton, a shuttlecock of mass 20 g is given an impulse of $(0.1\mathbf{i} - 0.15\mathbf{j})$ Ns, causing it to move with velocity $(3\mathbf{i} - 5\mathbf{j})$ ms^{-1}. Calculate the increase in the shuttlecock's kinetic energy as a result of it receiving the impulse.

Q5 Hint: Find the vector form of the ball's velocity immediately before it's hit.

Q5   A tennis player serves a ball of mass 60 g by throwing it upwards and hitting it as it falls. The ball falls 2.5 m vertically from its highest point before being hit by the racquet, which gives it an impulse of $(3\mathbf{i} + 0.6\mathbf{j})$ Ns. Find the increase in the ball's kinetic energy as a result of the collision.

Q6   A ball of mass 5 kg is moving with velocity $(\sqrt{3}\,\mathbf{i} + 6\mathbf{j})$ ms^{-1} when it receives an impulse, **I**. As a result, its kinetic energy increases to 160 J. Given that the direction of motion of the ball following the impulse is at an angle of $30°$ above $\mathbf{i}$, find **I**.

Review Exercise — Chapter 4

Q1   Find the velocity of a particle of mass 0.1 kg, initially travelling at $(\mathbf{i} + \mathbf{j})$ ms^{-1}, after receiving an impulse of:

a) $(2\mathbf{i} + 5\mathbf{j})$ Ns

b) $(-3\mathbf{i} + \mathbf{j})$ Ns

c) $(-\mathbf{i} - 6\mathbf{j})$ Ns

d) $4\mathbf{i}$ Ns.

Q2   A 2 kg particle, travelling at $(4\mathbf{i} - \mathbf{j})$ ms^{-1}, receives an impulse, $\mathbf{Q}$, changing its velocity to $(-2\mathbf{i} + \mathbf{j})$ ms^{-1}. Find:

a) $\mathbf{Q}$,

b) $|\mathbf{Q}|$, in Ns to 3 significant figures,

c) the angle $\mathbf{Q}$ makes with $\mathbf{i}$, in degrees to 3 significant figures.

Q3   Two particles, A and B, collide, where $m_A = 0.5$ kg and $m_B = 0.4$ kg.
Their initial velocities are $\mathbf{u}_A = (2\mathbf{i} + \mathbf{j})$ ms^{-1} and $\mathbf{u}_B = (-\mathbf{i} - 4\mathbf{j})$ ms^{-1}. Find, to 3 s.f.:

a) the speed of B after impact if A moves away from the collision at a velocity of $(-\mathbf{i} - 2\mathbf{j})$ ms^{-1},

b) their combined speed after the impact if they coalesce instead.

Q4   Two particles travelling directly towards each other at the same speed collide.
The impact causes one particle to stop, and the other to go in the opposite direction at half its original speed. Find the value of e, the coefficient of restitution for the collision.

Q5   A particle of mass 1 kg travelling at 10 ms^{-1} on a horizontal plane has a collision, where $e = 0.4$. Find the particle's rebound speed if it collides head-on with:

a) a smooth vertical wall,

b) a particle of mass 2 kg travelling towards it at 12 ms^{-1}.

Q6   Particles A (mass 1 kg), B (4 kg) and C (5 kg) travel in the same smooth straight line at velocities of $3u$, $2u$ and u, respectively. If A collides with B first ($e = \frac{1}{4}$), then B with C ($e = \frac{1}{3}$), determine whether A and B will collide again.

Q7   An initially stationary particle drops vertically from a height of 1 m and rebounds from a smooth horizontal plane with $e = 0.5$. Find the height that it reaches after its first, second and third bounces.

Q8   Find the loss in kinetic energy when a particle of mass 2 kg travelling at 3 ms^{-1} collides directly with a stationary particle of mass 3 kg on a smooth horizontal plane surface, where $e = 0.3$.

Q9   A cricketer has a ball of mass 100 g bowled to him. The velocity of the ball immediately before he hits it is $(30\mathbf{i} + 10\mathbf{j})$ms^{-1}. The cricketer hits the ball, giving it an impulse of $(-6\mathbf{i} - 2.5\mathbf{j})$ Ns. Find the change in the ball's kinetic energy as a result of being hit.

1   A particle of mass 0.4 kg receives an impulse of $(3\mathbf{i} - 8\mathbf{j})$ Ns.
    The velocity of the particle just before the impulse is $(-6\mathbf{i} + \mathbf{j})$ ms^{-1}.

   a)   Find the speed of the particle immediately after the impulse.
        Give your answer in ms^{-1} to 3 significant figures.

        (5 marks)

   b)   Find the angle between the motion of the particle and $\mathbf{i}$ following the impulse.
        Give your answer in degrees to 3 significant figures.

        (2 marks)

2   A marble of mass 0.02 kg, travelling at 2 ms^{-1}, collides directly with another, stationary,
    marble of mass 0.06 kg. Both can be modelled as smooth spheres on a smooth horizontal
    plane. If the collision is perfectly elastic, find the speed of each marble immediately after
    the collision.

        (4 marks)

3   Particles P (of mass $2m$) and Q (of mass m), travelling in a straight line towards each
    other at the same speed (u) on a smooth horizontal plane surface, collide directly with a
    coefficient of restitution of $\frac{3}{4}$.

   a)   Show that the collision reverses the direction of both particles,
        with Q having eight times the rebound speed of P.

        (6 marks)

   Following the collision, Q goes on to collide with a smooth vertical wall,
   perpendicular to its path. The coefficient of restitution for the impact with the wall is e_{wall}.
   Q goes on to collide with P again on the rebound from the wall.

   b)   Show that $e_{\text{wall}} > \frac{1}{8}$.

        (3 marks)

   c)   Suppose that $e_{\text{wall}} = \frac{3}{5}$. If after the second collision with P, Q
        continues to move away from the wall, but with a speed of 0.22 ms^{-1},
        find the value of u, the initial speed of both particles, in ms^{-1}.

        (7 marks)

4   A particle of mass $2m$ kg, travelling at a speed of $3u$ ms^{-1} on a smooth horizontal plane, collides directly with a particle of mass $3m$ kg travelling at $2u$ ms^{-1} in the same direction. The coefficient of restitution is $\frac{1}{4}$.

Show that the kinetic energy lost in the collision is $\frac{9mu^2}{16}$ J.

(8 marks)

5   Particles A (mass m), B (mass $2m$) and C (mass $4m$) lie on a straight line, as shown:

B and C are initially stationary when A collides directly with B at a speed of $4u$ ($u > 0$), causing B to collide directly with C.
The coefficient of restitution between B and C is $2e$, where e is the coefficient of restitution between A and B.

a)   Show that the collision between A and B does not reverse the direction of A.

(7 marks)

By the time B and C collide, A has travelled a distance of $\frac{d}{4}$ since the first collision.

b)   Show that $e = \frac{1}{3}$.

(3 marks)

c)   Hence find, in terms of u, the speed of C following its collision with B.

(5 marks)

1. Moments and Equilibrium

This chapter is all about solving problems involving rigid bodies in equilibrium. A lot of the stuff should be familiar to you from M1 — things like moments and friction — but you have to be able to apply what you know to different situations.

Moments

A 'moment' is the **turning effect** a **force** has about a **point**.
It is found using the formula:

$$\text{Moment} = \frac{\text{Magnitude}}{\text{of Force}} \times \frac{\text{Perpendicular distance from the line}}{\text{of action of the force to the point}}$$

The **larger** the magnitude of the **force**, and the **greater** the perpendicular **distance** from the line of action of the force to the point, then the **greater** the **moment**.

If the force is measured in newtons, N, and the distance in metres, m, then the units of moments are **newton metres, Nm**.

Often you'll be given a distance between a point and a force, but this distance won't be perpendicular to the force's 'line of action'. You'll need to **resolve** to find the perpendicular distance.

Tip: Remember — a rod is a long, thin, straight body. 'Light' means that the rod has negligible mass.

Tip: Rather than resolving the 5 N force, you could find the perpendicular distance between its line of action and *A*:

$d = 2\sin 60°$
moment $= 5 \times 2\sin 60°$
$= 10\sin 60° = 5\sqrt{3}$ Nm.

Example 1

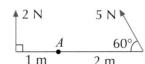

The diagram shows two forces acting on a light rod.
Find the sum of the moments of the forces about the point *A*.

- Calculate the moment of each individual force, then find their sum. Take clockwise as positive, then any anticlockwise moments will be negative:

$$\text{Sum of moments} = (2 \times 1) - (5\sin 60° \times 2)$$
$$= 2 - 5\sqrt{3}$$
$$= -6.660... \text{ Nm}$$

Resolve the 5 N force to find its component perpendicular to the rod.

- So the sum of the moments is 6.66 Nm (3 s.f.) anticlockwise.

Moments are either clockwise or anticlockwise — so remember to give a direction with your answer.

If a rigid body has mass (i.e. is not light) then you'll also need to consider the moment of its **weight**.

A body's weight is considered to act at its **centre of mass**. In the case of a **uniform rod**, this will be at its **midpoint**.

Tip: Take a look at Chapter 2 for more about centres of mass.

Example 2

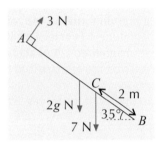

The diagram shows a uniform rod, *AB*, of mass 2 kg and length 6 m. A force of magnitude 3 N is applied to the rod at *A*, perpendicular to the rod, as shown. A second force of magnitude 7 N is applied vertically downwards at the point *C*, 2 m from *B*.

Find the sum of the moments of the forces acting on the rod about *B*.

- Don't worry that the rod is at an angle — just resolve forces to find their components perpendicular to the rod.

- Taking clockwise as positive:

    Sum of moments = $(3 \times 6) - (2g\cos35° \times 3) - (7\cos35° \times 2)$

    $= -41.634...$ Nm

- So the sum of the moments is $\boxed{41.6 \text{ Nm (3 s.f.) anticlockwise.}}$

Tip: Again, rather than resolving forces, you could use trigonometry to find the perpendicular distance from the line of action of each force to the pivot.

Tip: This time, you have to take the rod's weight into account. The rod is uniform, so its weight acts at the midpoint — 3 m from *B*.

Exercise 1.1

Q1

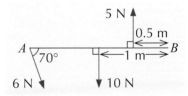

A light rod, *AB*, has length 4 m. A force of magnitude 5 N is applied to *A* at an angle of 40° above the rod, as shown. A second force of magnitude 3 N is applied vertically upwards at the rod's midpoint. Find the sum of the moments of the forces acting on the rod about *B*.

Q2

A uniform rod, *AB*, has length 2 m and weight 10 N. Forces of magnitude 6 N and 5 N act on the rod as shown in the diagram. Find the sum of the moments of the forces acting on the rod about *B*.

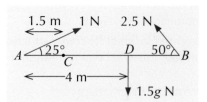

The diagram shows a non-uniform rod, AB, of length 6 m and mass 1.5 kg. A force of magnitude 1 N acts at A, at an angle of 25° above the rod, and a force of magnitude 2.5 N acts at B, at an angle of 50° above the rod. The rod's centre of mass is at the point D, where the length AD is 4 m.
Find the sum of the moments of the forces acting on the rod about point C, where the length AC is 1.5 m.

Q4

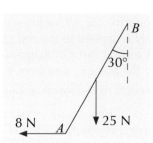

Q4 Hint: Remember — weight always acts vertically downwards.

A uniform rod, AB, of weight 25 N and length 22 m, is inclined at an angle of 30° to the vertical. A horizontal force of magnitude 8 N is applied to the rod at A, as shown.
Find the sum of the moments of the forces acting on the rod about B.

Q5

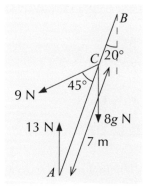

The diagram shows a non-uniform rod, AB, of mass 8 kg and length 12 m. The rod is inclined at an angle of 20° to the vertical.
A vertical force of magnitude 13 N is applied to the rod at A, and a force of magnitude 9 N is applied to the rod at its centre of mass, C, at an angle of 45° to the rod. Given that the length AC is 7 m, find the sum of the moments of the forces acting on the rod about B.

Equilibrium

- A rigid body which is in **static equilibrium** will **not move**.
- This means that there is **no resultant force** in **any direction** — any forces acting on the body will cancel each other out.
- It also means that the **sum of the moments** on the body **about any point** is **zero**.
- So for a body in equilibrium:

Tip: You should recognise this from M1.

> Total Clockwise Moment = Total Anticlockwise Moment

- By **resolving forces** and **equating clockwise and anticlockwise moments**, you can solve problems involving bodies in equilibrium.

Example 1

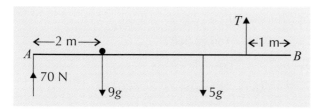

A non-uniform plank, AB, of mass 5 kg and length 7 m, is supported horizontally in equilibrium by a vertical string attached 1 m from B, as shown. One end of the plank, A, rests upon a vertical pole. The tension in the string is T and the normal reaction at the pole is 70 N. A particle of mass 9 kg rests on the plank, 2 m from A, as shown. Find T and the distance of the centre of mass of the plank from A.

- Resolving vertically:

    upward forces = downward forces

    $T + 70 = 9g + 5g$

    $\Rightarrow T = 137.2 - 70$

    $= \boxed{67.2 \text{ N}}$

- Let x be the distance of the centre of mass of the plank from A. Taking moments about A:

    moments clockwise = moments anticlockwise

    $(9g \times 2) + (5g \times x) = 67.2 \times (7 - 1)$

    $49x = 403.2 - 176.4$

    $x = 226.8 \div 49$

    $= \boxed{4.63 \text{ m (3 s.f.)}}$

Tip: You can take moments about any point — pick whichever you think makes the calculation easiest.

Example 2

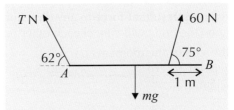

A uniform rod, _AB_, is suspended in equilibrium in a horizontal position by two light, inextensible wires. One wire is attached at _A_, at an angle of 62° to the horizontal, and has tension of magnitude _T_ N.
The other wire is attached 1 m from _B_, at an angle of 75° to the rod, and has tension of magnitude 60 N, as shown.
Find the tension in the wire at _A_, and the mass and length of the rod.

- Resolving horizontally:

    forces 'right' = forces 'left'

    $60\cos 75° = T\cos 62°$

    $\Rightarrow T = 60\cos 75° \div \cos 62° = 33.077...$

    $= 33.1\text{ N (3 s.f.)}$

Tip: The rod's weight acts vertically downwards, so it has no horizontal component.

- Resolving vertically:

    upward forces = downward forces

    $(33.077...)\sin 62° + 60\sin 75° = mg$

    $\Rightarrow m = 87.161... \div 9.8$

    $= 8.89\text{ kg (3 s.f.)}$

- Let _l_ be the rod's length. Taking moments about the rod's midpoint:

    moments clockwise = moments anticlockwise

    $(33.077...)\sin 62° \times \dfrac{l}{2} = 60\sin 75° \times \left(\dfrac{l}{2} - 1\right)$

    $\dfrac{l}{2}(33.077...)\sin 62° = \dfrac{l}{2}60\sin 75° - 60\sin 75°$

    $60\sin 75° = \dfrac{l}{2}(60\sin 75° - (33.077...)\sin 62°)$

    $\dfrac{l}{2} = \dfrac{60\sin 75°}{60\sin 75° - (33.077...)\sin 62°} = 2.015...$

    $\Rightarrow l = 4.03\text{ m (3 s.f.)}$

Tip: The rod is uniform, so its weight acts at its midpoint, $\dfrac{l}{2}$ m from each end.

Example 3

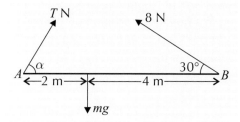

A non-uniform rod, *AB*, of length 6 m and mass *m* kg, is held in equilibrium by two strings, as shown. One string is attached at *A*, at an angle α to the rod, and has a tension of magnitude *T* N. The other string is attached at *B*, at an angle of 30° to the rod, and has a tension of magnitude 8 N.

Find the values of *m*, α and *T*.

- Taking moments about *A*:

  moments clockwise = moments anticlockwise

  $mg \times 2 = 8\sin 30° \times 6$

  $mg = 12$

  $\Rightarrow\ m = 1.224... =$ 1.22 kg (3 s.f.)

- Resolving vertically:

  upward forces = downward forces

  $T\sin \alpha + 8\sin 30° = mg$

  $\Rightarrow\ T\sin \alpha = 12 - 8\sin 30°$

  $\Rightarrow\ T\sin \alpha = 8$ — call this equation ①

- Resolving horizontally:

  forces 'right' = forces 'left'

  $T\cos \alpha = 8\cos 30°$ — call this equation ②

- Dividing equation ① by equation ②:

  $$\frac{T\sin \alpha}{T\cos \alpha} = \frac{8}{8\cos 30°}$$

  $$\tan \alpha = \frac{1}{\cos 30°} = 1.154...$$

  $\Rightarrow\ \alpha = 49.106...° =$ 49.1° (3 s.f.)

- Now using equation ①:

  $$T = \frac{8}{\sin(49.106...°)} =\ \boxed{10.6 \text{ N (3 s.f.)}}$$

Tip: Taking moments about *A* means you don't need to worry about the unknown tension *T* and angle α.

Tip: You could take moments about two different points to find *T* and α, rather than resolving forces, but the calculations are simpler this way.

Q1 A uniform rod, AB, of length 4 m, has weight 4 N. It rests in equilibrium in a horizontal position on vertical supports at C and D, where $AC = 1$ m and $AD = 3.5$ m. Find:

a) the magnitude of the reaction force at C,

b) the magnitude of the reaction force at D.

Q2 A non-uniform beam, AB, of mass 3 kg and length 1.6 m, rests horizontally in equilibrium on vertical supports at A and B. The normal reaction at A is 12 N. Find:

a) the magnitude of the normal reaction at B,

b) the distance of the centre of mass of the beam from A.

Q3 A uniform rod, AB, of mass 8 kg and length 14 m, rests horizontally in equilibrium on vertical supports at C and D. Given that C is 2.5 m from A and D is 1.5 m from B, find the magnitudes of the reaction forces at C and D.

Q4 A non-uniform rod, AB, has length 4.8 m and mass 500 g. It rests horizontally in equilibrium on vertical supports at C and D, where $AC = 1.6$ m and $AD = 4.2$ m, and is held by a light, inextensible, vertical string attached at A. The normal reaction at D is twice that at C, and the tension in the string is 1 N. Find:

a) the magnitudes of the normal reactions at C and D,

b) the distance of the centre of mass of the rod from A.

Q5

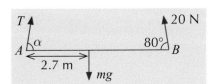

A non-uniform rod, AB, of length 6 m, is held horizontally in equilibrium by two light, inextensible strings, as shown in the diagram. The centre of mass of the rod is 2.7 m from A. Find:

a) the mass of the rod,

b) the value of α,

c) the magnitude of the tension in the string at A.

Q6

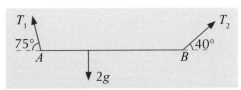

A non-uniform rod, AB, of mass 2 kg and length 2.4 m, is held horizontally in equilibrium by two light, inextensible strings, as shown in the diagram. Find:

a) the tension in each string,

b) the distance of the centre of mass of the rod from A.

Q7

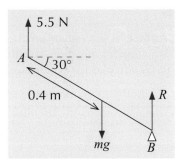

A non-uniform rod, AB, of length 0.65 m, is held in equilibrium by a vertical string at A and a vertical support at B. The rod makes an angle of 30° with the horizontal, as shown. The centre of mass of the rod is 0.4 m from A. Find:

a) the magnitude of R, the reaction force at B,

b) the mass of the rod.

Q8

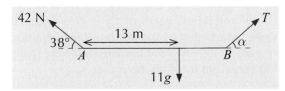

A non-uniform rod, AB, of mass 11 kg, is held horizontally in equilibrium by two light, inextensible strings. The strings are attached to the rod at A and B, where the string attached at B makes an angle α with the horizontal, as shown.
The centre of mass of the rod is 13 m from A. Find:

a) the length of the rod,

b) the value of α,

c) the magnitude of T, the tension in the string attached at B.

Q9

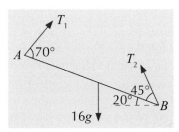

A non-uniform rod, AB, of mass 16 kg and length 10 m, is held in equilibrium by wires attached at A and B. The rod makes an angle of 20° with the horizontal, and the wires at A and B make angles of 70° and 45° with the rod respectively, as shown.
Find:

a) the magnitude of the tension in each wire,

b) the distance of the centre of mass of the rod from A.

Reaction forces

Tip: When a body
is freely hinged, the
reaction force is the
force in the hinge that
helps keep the body
in equilibrium. It's
not the same as the
normal reaction, which
acts when a body
is in contact with a
surface, and always acts
perpendicular to the
surface.

If a **rigid body** is fixed to a **surface** by a **hinge** or **pivot**, you can deal with
the reaction force on the body from the hinge by **splitting it up** into two
components, **parallel** and **perpendicular** to the **surface**.

Example 1

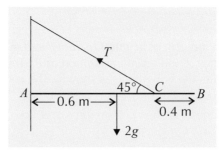

A uniform rod, AB, of mass 2 kg and length 1.2 m, is freely hinged on
a vertical wall. The rod is held horizontally in equilibrium by a light,
inextensible string attached at C, 0.4 m from B, which makes an angle
of 45° with the rod, as shown. Find the tension in the string and the
magnitude of the reaction force on the rod at A.

Tip: Taking moments
about A means you don't
have to worry about
the reaction force when
finding T.

- Taking moments about A:

$$T\sin 45° \times (1.2 - 0.4) = 2g \times 0.6$$
$$T\sin 45° = 14.7$$
$$\Rightarrow \ T = 20.788... = 20.8 \text{ N (3 s.f.)}$$

- Split the reaction into horizontal and vertical
  components, R_H and R_V, and draw a diagram.
- When you're drawing your diagram, you can work out in which
  directions the components act by considering the other forces —
  because the rod is in equilibrium, the horizontal components and
  vertical components of all the forces acting on the rod must sum to zero.

Tip: Don't worry if you
draw the components
acting in the wrong
direction — the numbers
in your calculations will
just come out negative.

- The horizontal component of the tension in the string acts
  on the rod to the left, so the horizontal component of the
  reaction will act to the **right** to balance this out.
- The downward force of the rod's weight ($2g = 19.6$ N) is greater
  than the upward vertical component of the tension in the string
  ($T\sin 45° = 14.7$ N), so the reaction will act **upwards** to balance this out:

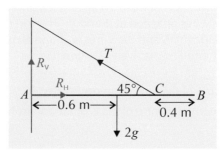

- Resolving horizontally:

$$R_H = T\cos 45° = (20.788...)\cos 45°$$

$$R_H = 14.7 \text{ N}$$

- Resolving vertically:

$$R_V + T\sin 45° = 2g$$

$$R_V = 4.9 \text{ N}$$

- Now use Pythagoras' theorem to find R, the magnitude of the reaction at A:

$$|R| = \sqrt{R_H^2 + R_V^2} = \sqrt{14.7^2 + 4.9^2}$$

$$= 15.5 \text{ N (3 s.f.)}$$

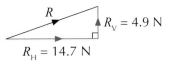

Tip: The rod is in equilibrium, so: 'forces left' = 'forces right' and 'forces up' = 'forces down'.

Example 2

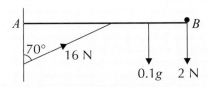

A non-uniform rod, AB, of length 6 m and mass 0.1 kg, is freely hinged on a vertical wall. The rod is supported by a light strut at an angle of 70° to the wall, as shown. The strut exerts a thrust of 16 N at the midpoint of the rod. A particle of weight 2 N rests at B, and the rod is horizontal and in equilibrium.

Find the distance of the centre of mass of the rod from A, and the magnitude and direction of the reaction force on the rod at A.

- Let x be the distance of the centre of mass of the rod from A. Taking moments about A:

$$(0.1g \times x) + (2 \times 6) = 16\cos 70° \times 3$$

$$0.1gx = 4.416...$$

$$\Rightarrow x = 4.507... = 4.51 \text{ m (3 s.f.)}$$

- As in the previous example, split the reaction into its horizontal and vertical components, R_H and R_V, and draw a diagram.

- The horizontal component of the thrust in the strut acts on the rod to the right, so the horizontal component of the reaction will act to the **left** to balance this out.

- The upward vertical component of the thrust in the strut ($16\cos 70° = 5.472...$ N) is greater than the downward force of the two weights ($0.1g + 2 = 2.98$ N), so the reaction will act **downwards** to balance this out.

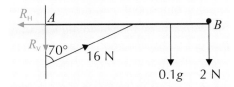

Tip: Taking moments about A means you don't have to worry about the reaction force when finding x.

Tip: The strut supports the rod at the rod's midpoint — so the vertical component of the thrust acts 3 m from A.

Tip: Remember — the reaction force is in the hinge, not the wall, so that's why R can act to the left.

- Resolving horizontally:
$$R_H = 16\sin 70° = 15.035... \text{ N}$$

- Resolving vertically:
$$R_V + 0.1g + 2 = 16\cos 70°$$
$$\Rightarrow R_V = 2.492... \text{ N}$$

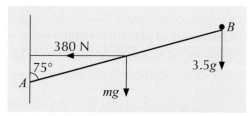

R θ $R_V = 2.492...$ N

$R_H = 15.035...$ N

- Using Pythagoras' theorem to find the magnitude:
$$|R| = \sqrt{R_H^2 + R_V^2} = \sqrt{(15.035...)^2 + (2.492...)^2}$$
$$= 15.2 \text{ N (3 s.f.)}$$

- And using trigonometry to find the direction:
$$\theta = \tan^{-1}\left(\frac{15.035...}{2.492...}\right)$$
$$= 80.6° \text{ (3 s.f.) measured clockwise from the downwards vertical.}$$

Tip: Always specify the line that the angles are measured from.

Example 3

380 N
75°
A
mg
B
3.5*g*

A uniform plank, *AB*, of length 9 m, is freely hinged on a vertical wall. A particle of mass 3.5 kg is placed on the plank at *B*. A light, horizontal wire, fixed at one end to the midpoint of the plank and at the other end to the wall, holds the plank in equilibrium, at an angle of 75° to the wall, as shown. The tension in the wire has magnitude 380 N.
Find the mass of the plank and the magnitude and direction of the reaction force acting on the plank at *A*.

- Taking moments about *A*:
$$(mg \times 4.5\sin 75°) + (3.5g \times 9\sin 75°) = 380 \times 4.5\cos 75°$$
$$\Rightarrow m = 144.399... \div 42.597... = 3.389...$$
$$= 3.39 \text{ kg (3 s.f.)}$$

- Split the reaction into components and draw a diagram.
- The tension in the wire acts on the rod to the left, so the horizontal component of the reaction will act to the **right**.
- The weights act downwards on the rod, so the vertical component of the reaction will act **upwards** on the rod.

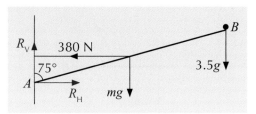

- Resolving horizontally:

    $R_H = 380$ N

- Resolving vertically:

    $R_V = (3.389...)g + 3.5g = 67.520...$ N

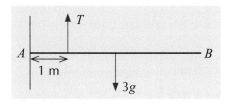

- Using Pythagoras' theorem to find the magnitude:

    $$|R| = \sqrt{R_H^2 + R_V^2} = \sqrt{380^2 + (67.520...)^2}$$
    $$= 386 \text{ N (3 s.f.)}$$

- And using trigonometry to find the direction:

    $$\theta = \tan^{-1}\left(\frac{380}{67.520...}\right)$$
    $$= 79.9° \text{ (3 s.f.) measured clockwise from the upwards vertical.}$$

Exercise 1.3

Q1

A uniform rod, AB, of mass 3 kg and length 4 m, is freely hinged to a vertical wall at A. The rod is held horizontal in equilibrium by a light vertical wire attached to the rod 1 m from A, as shown.
The reaction force, R, at the hinge, acts vertically downwards. Find:

a) the magnitude of the tension in the wire,

b) the magnitude of the reaction force, R, acting on the rod at A.

Q1 Hint: The only other forces acting on the rod are vertical, so R must also be vertical.

Q2

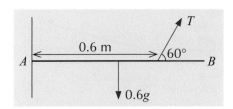

A uniform rod, *AB*, of mass 0.6 kg and length 0.8 m, is freely hinged to a vertical wall at *A*. The rod is held horizontally and in equilibrium by a light wire attached to the rod 0.6 m from *A*. The wire makes an angle of 60° with the rod, as shown. Find:

a) the magnitude of the tension in the wire,

b) the magnitude and direction of the reaction force acting on the rod at *A*.

Q3

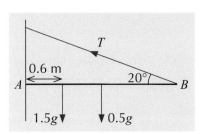

A non-uniform beam, *AB*, of mass 1.5 kg and length 2.4 m, is freely hinged to a vertical wall at *A*. The centre of mass of the beam is 0.6 m from *A*. One end of a light, inextensible string is attached to *B*, and the other end is fixed to the wall, directly above *A*, as shown. The string makes an angle of 20° with the beam. A body of mass 0.5 kg is placed at the beam's midpoint. The beam is horizontal and in equilibrium. Find:

a) the tension in the string,

b) the magnitude and direction of the reaction force acting on the beam at *A*.

Q4

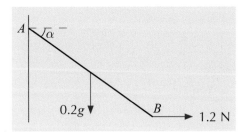

A uniform plank, *AB*, of mass 0.2 kg and length 0.2 m is freely hinged to a vertical wall at *A*. A horizontal light, inextensible string fixed at *B* holds the plank in equilibrium, at an angle α below the horizontal, as shown. The tension in the string is 1.2 N. Find:

a) the value of α,

b) the magnitude and direction of the reaction force acting on the plank at *A*.

Q5

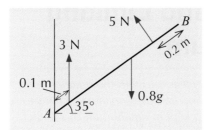

A non-uniform beam, *AB*, of mass 0.8 kg and length 0.9 m, is freely hinged to a vertical wall at *A*. The beam is held in equilibrium, at an angle of 35° above the horizontal, by a vertical wire 0.1 m from *A* and a wire perpendicular to the beam 0.2 m from *B*, as shown. The tensions in the two wires are 3 N and 5 N respectively. Find:

a) the distance of the centre of mass of the beam from *A*,

b) the magnitude and direction of the reaction force acting on the beam at *A*.

Q6

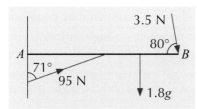

A non-uniform rod, *AB*, of mass 1.8 kg and length 7 m, is freely hinged to a vertical wall at *A*. A light strut, fixed to the wall, supports the rod at its midpoint, so the rod is kept horizontal and in equilibrium. The strut makes an angle of 71° with the wall, and the thrust in the strut has magnitude 95 N. A force of magnitude 3.5 N is applied to the rod at *B*, at an angle of 80° to the rod, as shown. Find:

a) the distance of the centre of mass of the rod from *A*,

b) the magnitude and direction of the reaction force acting on the rod at *A*.

Q7

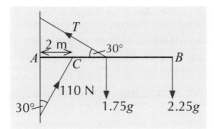

A uniform plank, *AB*, of mass 1.75 kg and length 8 m, is freely hinged to a vertical wall at *A*. An object of mass 2.25 kg is placed on the plank at *B*. The plank is kept horizontal and in equilibrium by a light wire fixed at its midpoint, at an angle of 30° above the plank, and a light strut fixed at *C*, 2 m along the plank from *A*, at an angle of 30° to the wall, as shown. The thrust in the strut has magnitude 110 N. Find:

a) *T*, the magnitude of the tension in the wire,

b) the magnitude and direction of the reaction force acting on the plank at *A*.

2. Friction and Limiting Equilibrium

Learning Objective:

- Be able to solve problems involving rigid bodies in equilibrium under the influence of a frictional force.

In the previous section, you learnt to find the reaction force in a hinge fixing a rigid body to a surface. You can use similar principles to solve problems involving rigid bodies being kept in equilibrium by contact with rough surfaces.

Friction

- You should remember from M1 that if a body is in contact with a **rough** surface, then a **frictional force** will act between the body and the surface to oppose motion.

- The frictional force can take a range of values — when the body is **on the point of moving**, the frictional force will reach its **maximum value**. This value is given by $F = \mu R$, where F is the frictional force, μ is the coefficient of friction between the body and the surface, and R is the normal reaction of the surface on the body. At this point, the object is said to be in '**limiting equilibrium**'.

- If a **rigid body** rests in contact with a **rough surface**, then a **frictional force** will act between them, **parallel** to the surface, in the opposite direction to any potential motion.

- A **normal reaction** force will also act on the body, **perpendicular** to the surface.

Example

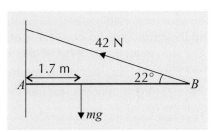

42 N

1.7 m

22°

A B

mg

A non-uniform rod, AB, rests against a rough vertical wall at A. The rod is held in limiting equilibrium perpendicular to the wall by a light, inextensible string attached at B at an angle of 22° above the rod. The tension in the string is 42 N, the length of the rod is 5.5 m and the centre of mass of the rod is 1.7 m from A.

Find the mass of the rod, m, and the coefficient of friction, μ, between the wall and the rod.

- Taking moments about A:

$$mg \times 1.7 = 42\sin 22° \times 5.5$$
$$\Rightarrow m = 86.534... \div 16.66 = 5.194...$$
$$= \boxed{5.19 \text{ kg (3 s.f.)}}$$

- Now draw a diagram showing the forces at A.
- The normal reaction of the wall on the rod acts **perpendicular** to the wall.
- The frictional force acts **parallel** to the wall, in the opposite direction to potential motion at the wall.

- The weight of the rod ($mg = 50.902...$ N) is greater than the upwards vertical component of the tension in the string ($42\sin 22° = 15.733...$ N), so potential movement is downwards at A.

- This means that the frictional force at A acts **upwards**.

- So the diagram looks like:

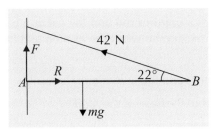

Tip: R is the normal reaction of the wall on the rod — don't confuse it with the reaction in the hinge in the examples in the previous section. There's no hinge here — it's friction which keeps the rod from slipping on the wall.

- Resolving horizontally:
$$R = 42\cos 22° = 38.941... \text{ N}$$

- Resolving vertically:
$$F + 42\sin 22° = mg$$
$$\Rightarrow F = 50.902... - 15.733...$$
$$= 35.168... \text{ N}$$

Tip: You could also take moments about B (or another point) to find F.

- The rod is in limiting equilibrium, so friction is at its maximum:
$$F = \mu R$$
$$35.168... = \mu \times 38.941...$$
$$\Rightarrow \mu = 0.90 \text{ (2 d.p.)}$$

'Ladder' questions

'**Ladder**' questions, where a rigid body rests at an angle against the ground and a wall, are common in M2.

In these questions, you'll need to consider the **normal reaction** of the **ground**, the **normal reaction** of the **wall**, and any **frictional forces** which may be acting.

The question will tell you whether the ground and wall are **rough** or **smooth** — this lets you know whether you need to take friction into account in your calculations.

There are four possible combinations of surfaces for ladder questions:

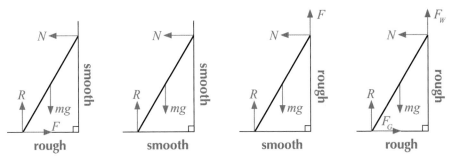

Tip: Friction acts to prevent motion. In each case, think about which way the ladder would slip — the frictional force will act in the opposite direction.

The most common of these scenarios is **rough ground** and a **smooth wall**, but you should be familiar with all the situations.

Example 1

A ladder rests against a smooth vertical wall at an angle of 65° to rough horizontal ground. The ladder has mass 4.5 kg and length $5x$ m. A cat of mass 1.3 kg sits on the ladder at C, $4x$ m from the base. The ladder is in limiting equilibrium.

Modelling the ladder as a uniform rod and the cat as a particle, find the coefficient of friction between the ground and the ladder.

Tip: N is the normal reaction at the wall, R is the normal reaction at the ground. The wall is smooth, so there is no frictional force. The ground is rough, so there is a frictional force between it and the ladder.

- Draw a diagram to show the forces acting between the ladder and the ground, and the ladder and the wall:

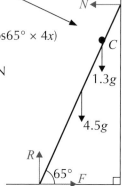

- Taking moments about the base of the ladder:

$N\sin 65° \times 5x = (4.5g\cos 65° \times 2.5x) + (1.3g\cos 65° \times 4x)$

$(4.531...)xN = (46.593..)x + (21.536...)x$

$\Rightarrow N = (68.130...)x \div (4.531...)x = 15.034...$ N

- Resolving vertically:

$R = 1.3g + 4.5g = 56.84$ N

- Resolving horizontally:

$F = N$

- The ladder is in limiting equilibrium, so $F = \mu R$:

$F = \mu R$

$\Rightarrow N = \mu R$

$15.034... = \mu \times 56.84$

$\Rightarrow \mu = 15.034... \div 56.84 = \boxed{0.26 \text{ (2 d.p.)}}$

Example 2

A uniform ladder of mass 11 kg and length 3.8 m rests against a smooth vertical wall, at an angle of 58° to rough horizontal ground. The coefficient of friction between the ladder and the ground is 0.45. A painter of mass 83 kg begins to climb the ladder. He stops when the ladder is on the point of slipping. How far up the ladder is he at this point?

- Draw a diagram to show what's going on:

- Resolving vertically:

$R = 11g + 83g = 921.2$ N

- Resolving horizontally:

$F = N$

Tip: The painter stops when the ladder is on the point of slipping — i.e. when it is in limiting equilibrium.

- The ladder is in limiting equilibrium, so $F = \mu R$:

$F = \mu R$

$\Rightarrow N = \mu R$

$N = 0.45 \times 921.2 = 414.54$ N

- Let x be the painter's distance from the base of the ladder.
  Taking moments about the base of the ladder:

$$N\sin 58° \times 3.8 = (11g\cos 58° \times 1.9) + (83g\cos 58° \times x)$$

$$414.54\sin 58° \times 3.8 = 108.538... + (431.036...)x$$

$$\Rightarrow x = 1227.351... \div 431.036...$$

$$= \boxed{2.85 \text{ m (3 s.f.)}}$$

Example 3

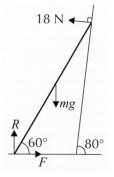

A uniform ladder of length 3 m rests in limiting equilibrium against a smooth wall slanted at 10° to the vertical, as shown. The ladder is at an angle of 60° to rough horizontal ground. The magnitude of the normal reaction of the wall on the ladder is 18 N. Find the mass of the ladder.

> **Tip:** Remember — the normal reaction always acts perpendicular to the surface.

- Split the diagram up into different triangles to help work out the different angles you'll have to use when resolving.

- If the wall was vertical then the angles shown in red below would be equal, as both the wall and the line of action of the ladder's weight would be perpendicular to the ground.

- However, the reaction at the wall is perpendicular to the wall, so you need to calculate the size of the angle between the ladder and the line of action of the reaction at the wall: $180° - 90° - 20° = 70°$

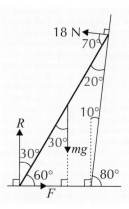

- Taking moments about the base of the ladder:

$$mg\sin 30° \times 1.5 = 18\sin 70° \times 3$$

$$\Rightarrow \boxed{m = 6.90 \text{ kg (3 s.f.)}}$$

Bodies supported along their lengths

Rather than leaning against a wall, a rigid body may be held in equilibrium by resting on **supports** at points along its length. You can solve problems like this just as before, by **resolving forces** and **taking moments**.

You need to know whether the **ground** and **supports** are **rough** or **smooth**, and you should also remember that the **normal reaction** at a **support** will always act **perpendicular** to the body.

Example

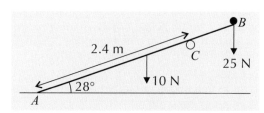

A uniform rod, *AB*, of length 3.3 m and weight 10 N, rests with *A* on rough horizontal ground. The rod is supported by a smooth peg at *C*, where *AC* = 2.4 m, in such a way that the rod makes an angle of 28° with the ground. A particle of weight 25 N is placed at *B*.

Given that the rod is in limiting equilibrium, find the magnitude of the normal reaction, *N*, at the peg and the magnitude of the frictional force, *F*, between the rod and the ground.

- Draw a diagram to show the forces acting on the rod:

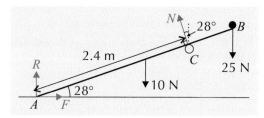

- Taking moments about *A*:

$$2.4N = (10\cos 28° \times 1.65) + (25\cos 28° \times 3.3)$$
$$\Rightarrow N = 36.421...$$
$$= 36.4 \text{ N (3 s.f.)}$$

> The rod's weight acts at its midpoint, 1.65 m from *A*.

- Resolving horizontally:

$$F = N\sin 28° = (36.421...)\sin 28°$$
$$= 17.1 \text{ N (3 s.f.)}$$

Tip: The peg is smooth, so there is no frictional force at *C*. The normal reaction at *C*, *N*, acts perpendicular to the rod. The rod is on the point of slipping to the left, as viewed in the diagram, so the frictional force at *A* acts to the right.

Q1

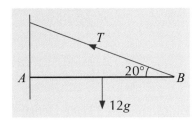

A uniform rod, *AB*, of mass 12 kg and length 16 m, rests against a rough, vertical wall at *A*. The rod is held horizontally in limiting equilibrium by a light wire attached at *B*, at an angle of 20° to the rod, as shown. Find:

a) the magnitude of the tension in the wire,

b) the coefficient of friction between the wall and the rod.

Q2 A uniform ladder of mass 11 kg and length 7 m rests against a rough vertical wall, at an angle of 60° to smooth, horizontal ground, as shown. A horizontal force of magnitude 35 N is applied to the base of the ladder, keeping it in limiting equilibrium, with the ladder on the point of sliding up the wall. Find:

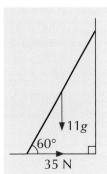

a) the magnitude of the normal reaction of the wall on the ladder,

b) the frictional force between the wall and the ladder,

c) the coefficient of friction between the wall and the ladder.

Q3

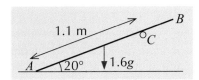

A uniform beam, *AB*, of mass 1.6 kg and length 1.5 m, rests with *A* on rough, horizontal ground. The beam is supported by a smooth peg at *C*, where *AC* = 1.1 m, so that it makes an angle of 20° with the horizontal, as shown. The beam is on the point of slipping. Find:

a) the magnitude of the normal reaction of the peg on the beam,

b) the magnitude of the normal reaction of the ground on the beam,

c) the magnitude of the frictional force between the ground and the beam,

d) the coefficient of friction between the ground and the beam.

Q4 A uniform ladder of mass 10 kg and length 6 m rests with one end on rough, horizontal ground and the other end against a smooth, vertical wall. The coefficient of friction between the ground and the ladder is 0.3, and the ladder makes an angle of 65° with the ground. A girl of mass 50 kg begins to climb the ladder. How far up the ladder can she climb before the ladder slips?

Q5

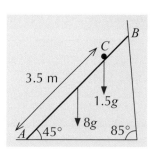

A uniform ladder, AB, of mass 8 kg and length 4 m, rests with A on rough, horizontal ground and B against a smooth wall angled at 5° to the vertical. A body of mass 1.5 kg is placed on the ladder at C, where $AC = 3.5$ m, as shown. The ladder is in limiting equilibrium and makes an angle of 45° with the horizontal. Find:

a) the magnitude of the normal reaction of the wall on the ladder,

b) the coefficient of friction between the ground and the ladder.

Q6   A uniform ladder of mass 9 kg and length 4.8 m rests in limiting equilibrium with one end on rough, horizontal ground and the other end against a rough, vertical wall. The normal reactions at the wall and the ground have magnitude 22 N and 75 N respectively. Find:

a) the angle that the ladder makes with the ground,

b) the coefficient of friction between the wall and the ladder,

c) the coefficient of friction between the ground and the ladder.

Q7

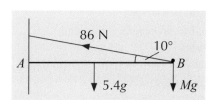

A non-uniform plank, AB, of mass 5.4 kg and length 11 m, rests with A against a rough, vertical wall. A wire with tension of magnitude 86 N is fixed to B, at an angle of 10° to the plank, keeping the plank horizontal. A particle of mass M kg rests on the plank at B, as shown. The plank is in limiting equilibrium. Given that the coefficient of friction between the wall and the plank is 0.55, find:

a) the value of M,

b) the distance of the centre of mass of the plank from A.

Q8

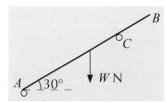

Q8 Hint: You're told that the reaction forces at A and C both act perpendicular to the beam. So it's a good idea to resolve forces parallel and perpendicular to the beam, rather than horizontally and vertically.

A uniform beam, AB, of weight W N rests in limiting equilibrium at an angle of 30° to the horizontal on a rough peg at A and a smooth peg at C, where $AC = 0.75AB$. The reaction forces at A and C are both perpendicular to the beam. Find the coefficient of friction between the peg and the beam at A.

Non-limiting equilibrium problems

If a **rigid body** rests against a **rough surface** and you **don't know** whether the body is on the point of moving along the surface or not, then you don't know if the friction is limiting.

This means that you can't say whether the frictional force is at its maximum. In this case, you need to use $F \leq \mu R$.

Tip: Remember — in limiting equilibrium (i.e. when a body is on the point of moving along a surface), the frictional force between the surface and the object is at its maximum: $F = \mu R$.

Example

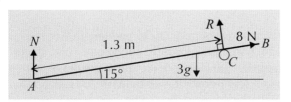

A non-uniform rod, AB, of mass 3 kg and length 1.5 m, rests with A on smooth, horizontal ground. The rod is supported on a rough peg at C, 1.3 m along the rod from A. The centre of mass of the rod is 1.2 m along the rod from A. The rod is in equilibrium at an angle of 15° to the horizontal plane. Given that the frictional force between the peg and the rod has magnitude 8 N, show that $\mu \geq 0.31$ (2 d.p.), where μ is the coefficient of friction between the rod and the peg at C.

- Taking moments about A:

$$R \times 1.3 = 3g\cos 15° \times 1.2$$
$$\Rightarrow R = 26.213... \text{ N}$$

- The rod is in equilibrium, but you don't know if it's on the point of moving, so, using $F \leq \mu R$:

$$8 \leq \mu \times 26.213...$$
$$\Rightarrow \mu \geq 0.31 \text{ (2 d.p.)}$$

Exercise 2.2

Q1

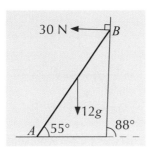

A non-uniform rod, AB, of mass 12 kg and length 2.5 m, rests in equilibrium with A on rough, horizontal ground and B against a smooth wall which is angled at 2° to the vertical. The rod makes an angle of 55° with the horizontal, as shown, and the magnitude of the reaction of the wall on the rod is 30 N. Find:

a) the distance of the centre of mass of the rod from A,

b) the range of possible values of the coefficient of friction between the ground and the rod.

Q2

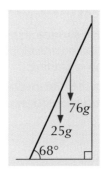

A uniform ladder of mass 25 kg and length 9 m rests with one end on rough, horizontal ground and the other end against a smooth, vertical wall. The ladder makes an angle of 68° with the horizontal, as shown. A window cleaner of mass 76 kg stands two-thirds of the way up the ladder, and the ladder is in equilibrium.

Find the range of possible values of the coefficient of friction between the ground and the ladder.

Q3

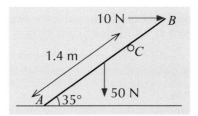

A uniform beam, AB, of weight 50 N and length 2 m, rests with A on rough, horizontal ground, as shown. The beam is supported at an angle of 35° to the ground by a smooth peg at C, where $AC = 1.4$ m. A horizontal force of magnitude 10 N is applied to the beam at B.

Find the range of values of the coefficient of friction between the ground and the beam for which the beam will remain in equilibrium.

Q4

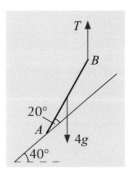

Q4 Hint: You can answer this question by resolving horizontally and vertically, parallel and perpendicular to the plane, or parallel and perpendicular to the pole.

A uniform pole, AB, of mass 4 kg, rests with A on a rough plane inclined at an angle of 40° to the horizontal.
The pole is held in equilibrium at an angle of 20° to the plane by a light vertical wire attached at B, as shown.
The coefficient of friction between the plane and the pole is μ.

a) Find the magnitude of the tension in the wire.

b) Show that $\mu \geq \tan 40°$.

Review Exercise — Chapter 5

Q1 A uniform rod, *AB*, has mass 4.7 kg and length 6.8 m. The rod is pivoted at *A* and a particle of mass 0.75 kg is placed on the rod 1.1 m from *B*. Find the sum of the moments about *A* of the forces acting on the rod when the rod is horizontal.

Q2

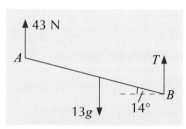

A non-uniform rod, *AB*, of mass 13 kg and length 16 m, is held in equilibrium by light vertical wires attached at *A* and *B*. The magnitude of the tension in the wire at *A* is 43 N. The rod makes an angle of 14° with the horizontal, as shown. Find:
a) the magnitude of the tension in the wire at *B*,
b) the distance of the centre of mass of the rod from *A*.

Q3

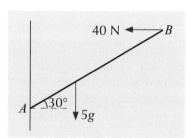

A non-uniform beam, *AB*, of mass 5 kg and length *b* m, is freely hinged to a vertical wall at *A*. The beam is held in equilibrium at an angle of 30° to the horizontal by a force of magnitude 40 N, applied horizontally at *B*, as shown.
Find the distance of the centre of mass of the beam from *A*. Give your answer in terms of *b*.

Q4

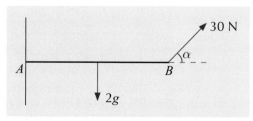

A uniform beam, *AB*, of mass 2 kg and length 1.6 m, is freely hinged to a vertical wall at *A*. The beam is held horizontally in equilibrium by a force of magnitude 30 N applied at *B*, at an angle α to the horizontal, as shown. Find:
a) the value of α,
b) the magnitude and direction of the reaction force in the hinge at *A*.

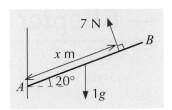

A uniform plank, AB, of mass 1 kg and length 0.8 m, is freely hinged to a vertical wall at A. The plank is held in equilibrium, at an angle of 20° to the horizontal, by a string fixed x m along the plank from A, as shown. The string is perpendicular to the plank, and the tension in the string has magnitude 7 N. Find:

a) the value of x,

b) the magnitude and direction of the reaction force in the hinge at A.

Q6

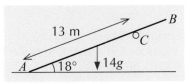

A uniform beam, AB, of mass 14 kg and length 15 m, rests with A on rough, horizontal ground. The beam is supported by a smooth peg at C, where $AC = 13$ m, so that it makes an angle of 18° with the horizontal, as shown. The beam is on the point of slipping.

Find the coefficient of friction between the ground and the beam at A.

Q7 A uniform ladder of mass 20 kg rests with one end on rough, horizontal ground, and the other end against a smooth, vertical wall. The ladder makes an angle of 60° with the horizontal, and is on the point of slipping.

a) Show that the coefficient of friction between the ladder and the ground is $\frac{\sqrt{3}}{6}$.

b) A person of mass 60 kg stands three-quarters of the way up the ladder.
   Find the magnitude of the minimum horizontal force which must be applied to the base of the ladder to keep it in limiting equilibrium.

Q8

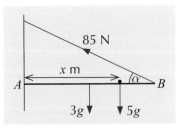

A uniform rod, AB, of mass 3 kg and length 1.2 m, rests horizontally in equilibrium with A against a rough, vertical wall. A wire is attached to the rod at B. The other end of the wire is attached to the wall, 0.9 m directly above A. A particle of mass 5 kg rests on the rod, x m from A, as shown, and the tension in the wire has magnitude 85 N. Find:

a) the value of x,

b) the range of possible values for the coefficient of friction between the wall and the rod at A.

1 A uniform ladder, AB, is positioned against a smooth vertical wall and rests upon rough horizontal ground at an angle θ to the horizontal, as shown. Clive stands on the ladder at point C, two-thirds of the way along the ladder's length from A. The ladder is 4.2 m long and weighs 180 N. The normal reaction at A is 490 N.

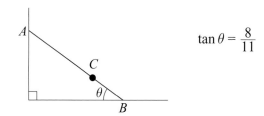

$$\tan \theta = \frac{8}{11}$$

The ladder rests in limiting equilibrium. Modelling Clive as a particle, find:

a) Clive's mass, m, to the nearest kg,

(3 marks)

b) the coefficient of friction, μ, between the ground and the ladder.

(5 marks)

2 A non-uniform rod, AB, is freely hinged to a vertical wall. It is held horizontally in equilibrium by a strut which makes an angle of 55° with the vertical. The strut is attached to the rod at B and to the wall at C, as shown. The thrust in the strut has magnitude 30 N. The mass of the rod is 2 kg, and its centre of mass is 0.4 m from A. The total length of the rod is x m.

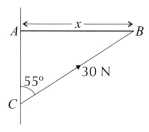

Find:

a) the value of x,

(3 marks)

b) the magnitude and direction of the reaction in the hinge at A.

(5 marks)

3   A uniform rod of mass m kg rests in equilibrium on rough horizontal ground at point A
    and a smooth peg at point B, making an angle of θ with the ground, as shown.
    The rod is l m long and B is $0.75l$ from A.

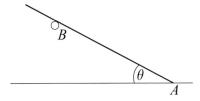

a)   Show that the normal reaction at the peg, $P = \frac{2}{3}mg\cos\theta$ N.

(3 marks)

b)   Given that $\sin\theta = \frac{3}{5}$, find the range of possible values of the coefficient of
     friction between the rod and the ground.

(6 marks)

4   A uniform rod, AB, is held in limiting horizontal equilibrium against a rough wall by a light,
    inextensible string connected to the rod at point C and the wall at point D, as shown.
    A particle of mass m kg rests at point B. The magnitude of the normal reaction of the wall
    on the rod at A is 72.5 N. The mass of the rod is 3 kg.

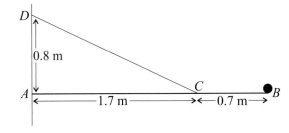

Find:

a)   the magnitude of the tension in the string,

(4 marks)

b)   the value of m,

(3 marks)

c)   the magnitude of the frictional force between the wall and the rod.

(3 marks)

Answers

Chapter 1: Kinematics

1. Projectiles

Exercise 1.1 — The two components of velocity

Q1 a) Horizontal component:
$10\cos20° = 9.40$ ms^{-1} (3 s.f.)
Vertical component:
$10\sin20° = 3.42$ ms^{-1} (3 s.f.)

b) Horizontal component:
$18\cos65° = 7.61$ ms^{-1} (3 s.f.)
Vertical component:
$18\sin65° = 16.3$ ms^{-1} (3 s.f.)

c) Horizontal component:
$-6.8\cos21.6° = -6.32$ ms^{-1} (3 s.f.)
Vertical component:
$6.8\sin21.6° = 2.50$ ms^{-1} (3 s.f.)

d) Horizontal component:
$9.7\cos19.7° = 9.13$ ms^{-1} (3 s.f.)
Vertical component:
$-9.7\sin19.7° = -3.27$ ms^{-1} (3 s.f.)

e) Horizontal component:
$-24\cos84° = -2.51$ ms^{-1} (3 s.f.)
Vertical component:
$-24\sin84° = -23.9$ ms^{-1} (3 s.f.)

f) Horizontal component:
$16\cos123° = -8.71$ ms^{-1} (3 s.f.)
Vertical component:
$16\sin123° = 13.4$ ms^{-1} (3 s.f.)

Q2 Horizontal component:
$8\cos35° = 6.55$ ms^{-1} (3 s.f.)
Vertical component:
$8\sin35° = 4.59$ ms^{-1} (3 s.f.)

Q3 Horizontal component $= 0$ ms^{-1}
Vertical component $= 45$ ms^{-1}

Q4 $(22 \times 1000) \div 60^2 = 6.11$ ms^{-1} (3 s.f.)
Horizontal component $= 6.11\cos\alpha$ ms^{-1}
Vertical component $= 6.11\sin\alpha$ ms^{-1}

Q5 speed $= \sqrt{6^2 + 8^2} = 10$ ms^{-1}
$\theta = \tan^{-1}\left(\frac{8}{6}\right) = 53.1°$ (3 s.f.) above the horizontal

Q6 speed $= \sqrt{17^2 + (-2.5)^2} = 17.2$ ms^{-1} (3 s.f.)
$\theta = \tan^{-1}\left(\frac{-2.5}{17}\right) = -8.37°$ (3 s.f.)
i.e. 8.37° below the horizontal

Exercise 1.2 — The constant acceleration equations

Q1 a) Resolving vertically, taking up as positive:
$u = 15\sin50°$, $v = 0$, $a = -9.8$, $t = t$
$v = u + at$
$0 = 15\sin50° - 9.8t$
$t = 15\sin50° \div 9.8 = 1.17$ s (3 s.f.)

b) Resolving vertically, taking up as positive:
$u = 15\sin50°$, $v = 0$, $a = -9.8$, $s = s$
$v^2 = u^2 + 2as$
$0 = (15\sin50°)^2 - 19.6s$
$s = (15\sin50°)^2 \div 19.6 = 6.74$ m (3 s.f.)

Q2 a) Resolving horizontally, taking right as positive:
$u = 12\cos37°$, $a = 0$, $s = s$, $t = 0.5$
$s = ut + \frac{1}{2}at^2$
$s = 12\cos37° \times 0.5 = 4.791...$
$= 4.79$ m (3 s.f.)

b) Resolving vertically, taking up as positive:
$u = 12\sin37°$, $a = -9.8$, $s = s$, $t = 0.5$
$s = ut + \frac{1}{2}at^2$
$s = (12\sin37° \times 0.5) + (\frac{1}{2} \times -9.8 \times 0.5^2) = 2.385...$
$= 2.39$ m (3 s.f.)

c) $\sqrt{(4.791...)^2 + (2.385...)^2} = 5.35$ m (3 s.f.)

Q3 a) Resolving vertically, taking up as positive:
$u = 8\sin59°$, $a = -9.8$, $s = 0$, $t = t$
$s = ut + \frac{1}{2}at^2$
$0 = 8\sin59°t - 4.9t^2$
$0 = t(8\sin59° - 4.9t)$
$\Rightarrow t = 0$ or $(8\sin59° - 4.9t) = 0$
$8\sin59° - 4.9t = 0$
$\Rightarrow t = 8\sin59° \div 4.9 = 1.399...$
$= 1.40$ s (3 s.f.)

b) Resolving horizontally, taking right as positive:
$u = 8\cos59°$, $a = 0$, $s = s$, $t = 1.399...$
$s = ut + \frac{1}{2}at^2$
$s = 8\cos59° \times 1.399... = 5.77$ m (3 s.f.)

Q4 a) $\tan\theta = \frac{\text{opp.}}{\text{adj.}}$, so draw a right-angled triangle with $\sqrt{3}$ as the 'opposite' side and 1 as the 'adjacent' side. Using Pythagoras' theorem, the hypotenuse will be 2:

So, $\sin\theta = \frac{\sqrt{3}}{2}$ and $\cos\theta = \frac{1}{2}$
Resolving vertically, taking up as positive:
$u = 18\sin\theta = 9\sqrt{3}$, $v = v$, $a = -9.8$, $t = 2$
$v = u + at$
$v = 9\sqrt{3} - 19.6 = -4.011...$
Resolving horizontally, taking right as positive:
$v = u = 18\cos\theta = 9$
So speed $= \sqrt{(-4.011...)^2 + 9^2} = 9.85$ ms^{-1} (3 s.f.)

b) $\alpha = \tan^{-1}\left(\frac{-4.011...}{9}\right) = -24.0°$ (3 s.f.)

i.e. 24.0° below the horizontal.

Q5 a) Resolving vertically, taking down as positive:

$u = 0$, $a = 9.8$, $s = 40$, $t = t$

$s = ut + \frac{1}{2}at^2$

$40 = 4.9t^2$

$t^2 = 8.163...$

$t = 2.857... = 2.86$ s (3 s.f.)

b) Resolving horizontally, taking right as positive:

$u = 80$, $a = 0$, $s = s$, $t = 2.857...$

$s = ut + \frac{1}{2}at^2$

$s = 80 \times 2.857... = 229$ m (3 s.f.)

Q6 Resolving vertically, taking up as positive:

$u = 20\sin45°$, $a = -9.8$, $s = 11 - 4 = 7$, $t = t$

$s = ut + \frac{1}{2}at^2$

$7 = 20\sin45°t - 4.9t^2$

$4.9t^2 - 20\sin45°t + 7 = 0$

Using the quadratic formula:

$t = \dfrac{20\sin45° \pm \sqrt{(-20\sin45°)^2 - (4 \times 4.9 \times 7)}}{9.8}$

$\Rightarrow t = 2.251...$ or $t = 0.634...$

So the object is higher than 11 m above the ground for $2.251... - 0.634... = 1.62$ s (3 s.f.)

Q7 First find the ball's vertical displacement from its starting point when it passes through the first target. Resolving vertically, taking up as positive:

$u = 24\sin70°$, $a = -9.8$, $s = s_1$, $t = 3$

$s = ut + \frac{1}{2}at^2$

$s_1 = (24\sin70° \times 3) + (\frac{1}{2} \times -9.8 \times 3^2)$

$s_1 = 23.557...$ m

Now find the ball's vertical displacement from its starting point when it passes through the second target.

Resolving vertically, taking up as positive:

$u = 24\sin70°$, $a = -9.8$, $s = s_2$, $t = 4$

$s = ut + \frac{1}{2}at^2$

$s_2 = (24\sin70° \times 4) + (\frac{1}{2} \times -9.8 \times 4^2)$

$s_2 = 11.810...$ m

So $h = 23.557... - 11.810... = 11.7$ m (3 s.f.)

Q8 First find the value of α by considering the particle's motion from its point of projection to its maximum height. Resolving vertically, taking up as positive:

$u = 7.5\sin\alpha$, $v = 0$, $a = -9.8$, $s = 2.8 - 0.6 = 2.2$

$v^2 = u^2 + 2as$

$0 = (7.5\sin\alpha)^2 + (2 \times -9.8 \times 2.2)$

$\sin\alpha = 0.875...$

$\Rightarrow \alpha = 61.109...°$

Now resolving horizontally, taking right as positive:

$u = 7.5\cos(61.109...°) = 3.623...$, $a = 0$, $s = s$, $t = 1.2$

$s = ut + \frac{1}{2}at^2$

$s = 3.623... \times 1.2 = 4.35$ m (3 s.f.)

Q9 First find an expression for the ball's time of flight. Resolving horizontally, taking right as positive:

$u = V\cos56°$, $a = 0$, $s = 50$, $t = t$

$s = ut + \frac{1}{2}at^2$

$50 = V\cos56° \times t$

$\Rightarrow t = \dfrac{50}{V\cos 56°}$

Now resolving vertically, taking up as positive:

$u = V\sin56°$, $a = -9.8$, $s = 0$, $t = \dfrac{50}{V\cos 56°}$

$s = ut + \frac{1}{2}at^2$

$0 = \dfrac{50V\sin 56°}{V\cos 56°} - 4.9\left(\dfrac{50}{V\cos 56°}\right)^2$

$50\tan56° = \dfrac{12\,250}{V^2\cos^2 56°}$

$V^2 = \dfrac{12\,250}{\cos^2 56° \times 50\tan 56°}$

$\Rightarrow V = 23.0$ ms^{-1} (3 s.f.)

Q10 a) Resolving vertically, taking down as positive:

$u = 3\sin7°$, $a = 9.8$, $s = 16$, $t = t$

$s = ut + \frac{1}{2}at^2$

$16 = 3\sin7°t + 4.9t^2$

$4.9t^2 + 3\sin7°t - 16 = 0$

Using the quadratic formula:

$t = \dfrac{-3\sin 7° \pm \sqrt{(3\sin 7°)^2 - (4 \times 4.9 \times -16)}}{9.8}$

$\Rightarrow t = 1.770...$ or $t = -1.844...$

So the particle's time of flight is $t = 1.770...$ s

Resolving horizontally, taking right as positive:

$u = 3\cos7°$, $a = 0$, $s = s$, $t = 1.770...$

$s = ut + \frac{1}{2}at^2$

$s = 3\cos7° \times 1.770... = 5.27$ m (3 s.f.)

b) Resolving vertically, taking down as positive:

$u = 3\sin7°$, $v = v_y$, $a = 9.8$, $s = 16$

$v^2 = u^2 + 2as$

$v_y^2 = (3\sin7°)^2 + (2 \times 9.8 \times 16) = 313.733...$

$\Rightarrow v_y = 17.712...$ ms^{-1}

Horizontally, $v_x = u_x = 3\cos7°$ ms^{-1}

$3\cos7°$

Using Pythagoras' theorem:

speed $= \sqrt{(3\cos 7°)^2 + (17.712...)^2}$

$= 18.0$ ms^{-1} (3 s.f.)

Using trigonometry:

$\theta = \tan^{-1}\left(\dfrac{17.712...}{3\cos 7°}\right)$

$= 80.5°$ (3 s.f.) below the horizontal

Q11 a) Resolving horizontally, taking right as positive:

$u = U\cos40°$, $v = V\cos10°$, $a = 0$, $t = 2$

There is no acceleration horizontally, so $u = v$:

$U\cos40° = V\cos10°$

$\Rightarrow V = \dfrac{U\cos 40°}{\cos 10°}$

Resolving vertically, taking upwards as positive:

$u = U\sin40°$, $v = V\sin10°$, $a = -9.8$, $t = 2$

$v = u + at$

$V\sin10° = U\sin40° - 19.6$

Substituting $V = \dfrac{U\cos 40°}{\cos 10°}$ into this equation:

$\dfrac{U\cos 40^\circ}{\cos 10^\circ} \times \sin 10^\circ = U\sin 40^\circ - 19.6$

$U(\cos 40^\circ \tan 10^\circ - \sin 40^\circ) = -19.6$

$\Rightarrow U = 38.604... = 38.6 \text{ ms}^{-1}$ (3 s.f.)

b) Resolving vertically, taking up as positive:
$u = (38.604...)\sin 40^\circ = 24.814...,$
$a = -9.8, s = s, t = 2$
$s = ut + \frac{1}{2}at^2$
$s = (24.814... \times 2) + (\frac{1}{2} \times -9.8 \times 2^2)$
$s = 30.0 \text{ m}$ (3 s.f.)

Q12 a) Resolving vertically, taking up as positive:
$u = 19\sin 28^\circ, a = -9.8, s = 2.5 - 0.5 = 2, t = t$
$s = ut + \frac{1}{2}at^2$
$2 = 19\sin 28^\circ t - 4.9t^2$
$4.9t^2 - 19\sin 28^\circ t + 2 = 0$
Using the quadratic formula:
$t = \dfrac{19\sin 28^\circ \pm \sqrt{(-19\sin 28^\circ)^2 - (4 \times 4.9 \times 2)}}{9.8}$
$\Rightarrow t = 0.261...$ or $t = 1.558...$
So the ball is 2.5 m above the ground 0.261... s after being hit (when it is rising) and 1.558... s after being hit (when it is on its descent).
It is caught when it is on its descent, so it is in the air for 1.558... s = 1.56 s (3 s.f.)

b) Resolving horizontally, taking right as positive:
$u = 19\cos 28^\circ, a = 0, s = s, t = 1.558...$
$s = ut + \frac{1}{2}at^2$
$s = 19\cos 28^\circ \times 1.558... = 26.1 \text{ m}$ (3 s.f.)

c) Resolving vertically, taking up as positive:
$u = 19\sin 28^\circ, v = v_y, a = -9.8, s = 2$
$v^2 = u^2 + 2as$
$v_y^2 = (19\sin 28^\circ)^2 + (2 \times -9.8 \times 2) = 40.365...$
$\Rightarrow v_y = 6.353... \text{ ms}^{-1}$
Horizontally, $v_x = u_x = 19\cos 28^\circ$
Using Pythagoras' theorem:
speed $= \sqrt{(19\cos 28^\circ)^2 + (6.353...)^2}$
$= 17.9 \text{ ms}^{-1}$ (3 s.f.)

Q13 a) Resolving vertically, taking up as positive:
$u = U\sin \theta, v = 0, a = -g, s = s$
$v^2 = u^2 + 2as$
$0 = U^2\sin^2 \theta - 2gs$
$\Rightarrow s = \dfrac{U^2 \sin^2 \theta}{2g} \text{ m}$

b) Resolving vertically, taking up as positive:
$u = U\sin \theta, v = 0, a = -g, t = t$
$v = u + at$
$0 = U\sin \theta - gt$
$\Rightarrow t = \dfrac{U\sin \theta}{g} \text{ s}$

Q14 a) Resolving vertically, taking down as positive:
$u = 0, a = 9.8, s = 0.02, t = t$
$s = ut + \frac{1}{2}at^2$
$0.02 = 4.9t^2$
$\Rightarrow t = 0.063... \text{ s}$
Resolving horizontally, taking right as positive:
$u = 15, a = 0, s = s, t = 0.063...$
$s = ut + \frac{1}{2}at^2$
$s = 15 \times 0.063... = 0.958... = 0.958 \text{ m}$ (3 s.f.)

b) Resolving horizontally, taking right as positive:
$u = U\cos 5^\circ, a = 0, s = 0.958..., t = t$
$s = ut + \frac{1}{2}at^2$
$0.958... = U\cos 5^\circ \times t$
$\Rightarrow t = \dfrac{0.958...}{U\cos 5^\circ}$
Resolving vertically, taking up as positive:
$u = U\sin 5^\circ, a = -9.8, s = -0.02, t = \dfrac{0.958...}{U\cos 5^\circ}$
$s = ut + \frac{1}{2}at^2$
$-0.02 = U\sin 5^\circ \dfrac{0.958...}{U\cos 5^\circ} - 4.9\left(\dfrac{0.958...}{U\cos 5^\circ}\right)^2$
$4.9\left(\dfrac{0.958...}{U\cos 5^\circ}\right)^2 = (0.958... \times \tan 5^\circ) + 0.02$
$U^2 = \dfrac{4.9 \times (0.958...)^2}{(\cos 5^\circ)^2 \times ((0.958...)\tan 5^\circ + 0.02)} = 43.666...$
$\Rightarrow U = 6.61 \text{ ms}^{-1}$ (3 s.f.)

Q15 The coordinates (3, 1) give you the components of the projectile's displacement — when it passes through this point, its horizontal displacement is 3 m and its vertical displacement is 1 m.
Resolving horizontally, taking right as positive:
$u = 3\cos \alpha, a = 0, s = 3, t = t$
$s = ut + \frac{1}{2}at^2$
$3 = 3\cos \alpha \times t$
$\Rightarrow t = \dfrac{1}{\cos \alpha}$
Resolving vertically, taking up as positive:
$u = 3\sin \alpha, a = -g, s = 1, t = \dfrac{1}{\cos \alpha}$
$s = ut + \frac{1}{2}at^2$
$1 = \left(3\sin \alpha \times \dfrac{1}{\cos \alpha}\right) + \left(\dfrac{1}{2} \times -g \times \left(\dfrac{1}{\cos \alpha}\right)^2\right)$
$\Rightarrow 1 = 3\tan \alpha - \dfrac{g}{2\cos^2 \alpha}$, as required

Q16 a) Resolving horizontally for particle A, taking right as positive:
$u = U, a = 0, s = s, t = 2$
$s = ut + \frac{1}{2}at^2$
$\Rightarrow s = 2U$
Resolving horizontally for particle B, taking right as positive:
$u = 2U\cos \theta, a = 0, s = s, t = 2$
$s = ut + \frac{1}{2}at^2$
$\Rightarrow s = 4U\cos \theta$
When the particles collide, their horizontal displacements will be the same:
$2U = 4U\cos \theta$
$\cos \theta = \frac{1}{2}$
$\Rightarrow \theta = 60^\circ$

b) Resolving vertically for particle A, taking down as positive:
$u = 0$, $a = 9.8$, $s = s$, $t = 2$
$s = ut + \frac{1}{2}at^2$
$s = \frac{1}{2} \times 9.8 \times 2^2 = 19.6$ m
So, when the particles collide, A has fallen 19.6 m vertically downwards from a height of 45 m above the ground. Therefore, the particles collide at a height of 25.4 m above the ground.
Resolving vertically for particle B, taking up as positive:
$u = 2U\sin60° = \sqrt{3}\,U$, $a = -9.8$, $s = s$, $t = 2$
$s = ut + \frac{1}{2}at^2$
$s = 2\sqrt{3}\,U + (\frac{1}{2} \times -9.8 \times 2^2) = 2\sqrt{3}\,U - 19.6$
So, when the particles collide (at a height of 25.4 m above the ground), B has travelled $(2\sqrt{3}\,U - 19.6)$ m vertically upwards from a height of 15 m above the ground. So:
$15 + (2\sqrt{3}\,U - 19.6) = 25.4$
$2\sqrt{3}\,U = 30$
$\Rightarrow U = \frac{15}{\sqrt{3}} = 8.6602...$
So, the speed of projection of A is 8.66 ms⁻¹ (3 s.f.), and the speed of projection of B is 17.3 ms⁻¹ (3 s.f.).

Exercise 1.3 — i and j vectors

Q1 a) $\mathbf{u} = (12\mathbf{i} + 16\mathbf{j})$, $\mathbf{v} = \mathbf{v}$, $\mathbf{a} = -9.8\mathbf{j}$, $t = 2$
$\mathbf{v} = \mathbf{u} + \mathbf{a}t$
$\mathbf{v} = (12\mathbf{i} + 16\mathbf{j}) - 19.6\mathbf{j}$
$\mathbf{v} = (12\mathbf{i} - 3.6\mathbf{j})$ ms⁻¹

b) When the particle reaches its maximum height, the vertical component of its velocity will be zero, and the horizontal component of its velocity will be the same as when the particle was projected (as there is no horizontal acceleration).
i.e. its velocity will be $12\mathbf{i}$ ms⁻¹.

c) The particle follows a symmetric curved path, so when it hits the ground, the vertical component of its velocity will have the same magnitude as when it was projected, but in the opposite direction. Again, the horizontal component of velocity remains constant. So the particle's velocity will be $(12\mathbf{i} - 16\mathbf{j})$ ms⁻¹.
You could answer this question by resolving horizontally and vertically and using the uvast equations to find each component if you wanted.

Q2 a) Resolving vertically, taking up as positive:
$u = 10$, $v = 0$, $a = -9.8$, $s = s$
$v^2 = u^2 + 2as$
$0 = 100 - 19.6s$
$s = 5.102...$
So the projectile reaches a maximum height of $5 + 5.102... = 10.1$ m (3 s.f.) above the ground.

b) Resolving vertically, taking up as positive:
$u = 10$, $v = v_y$, $a = -9.8$, $s = -5$
$v^2 = u^2 + 2as$
$v_y^2 = 100 + (2 \times -9.8 \times -5) = 198$

$v_y = -14.071...$ ms⁻¹
v_y *is negative because the projectile is travelling downwards when it hits the ground.*
Horizontally, $v_x = u_x = 17$ ms⁻¹
Using Pythagoras' theorem:
speed $= \sqrt{17^2 + 198} = 22.1$ ms⁻¹ (3 s.f.)

c) Using trigonometry:
$\tan\theta = \left(\frac{-14.071...}{17}\right)$
$\Rightarrow \theta = -39.615...°$
i.e. 39.6° (3 s.f.) below the horizontal.

Q3 a) The stone is thrown from a point 2.5 m above the ground, so when it is at least 6 m above the ground, it is at least $6 - 2.5 = 3.5$ m above its point of projection.
Resolving vertically, taking up as positive:
$u = 9$, $a = -9.8$, $s = 3.5$, $t = t$
$s = ut + \frac{1}{2}at^2$
$3.5 = 9t - 4.9t^2$
$4.9t^2 - 9t + 3.5 = 0$
Using the quadratic formula:
$t = \dfrac{9 \pm \sqrt{(-9)^2 - (4 \times 4.9 \times 3.5)}}{9.8}$
$\Rightarrow t = 0.559...$ or $t = 1.277...$
$1.277... - 0.559... = 0.7186...$
So the stone is at least 6 m above the ground for 0.719 s (3 s.f.)

b) Resolving vertically, taking up as positive:
$u = 9$, $a = -9.8$, $s = -2.5$, $t = t$
$s = ut + \frac{1}{2}at^2$
$-2.5 = 9t - 4.9t^2$
$4.9t^2 - 9t - 2.5 = 0$
Using the quadratic formula:
$t = \dfrac{9 \pm \sqrt{(-9)^2 - (4 \times 4.9 \times -2.5)}}{9.8}$
$\Rightarrow t = 2.081...$ or $t = -0.245...$
Resolving horizontally, taking right as positive:
$u = 6$, $a = 0$, $s = s$, $t = 2.081...$
$s = ut + \frac{1}{2}at^2$
$s = 6 \times 2.081... = 12.490...$ m
$20 - 12.490... = 7.509...$ m
So it falls short of the target by 7.51 m (3 s.f.)

Q4 a) $\mathbf{u} = (a\mathbf{i} + b\mathbf{j})$, $\mathbf{a} = -9.8\mathbf{j}$, $\mathbf{s} = (200\mathbf{i} - 40\mathbf{j})$, $t = 5$
$\mathbf{s} = \mathbf{u}t + \frac{1}{2}\mathbf{a}t^2$
$(200\mathbf{i} - 40\mathbf{j}) = 5(a\mathbf{i} + b\mathbf{j}) + (\frac{1}{2} \times -9.8\mathbf{j} \times 5^2)$
$5(a\mathbf{i} + b\mathbf{j}) = (200\mathbf{i} + 82.5\mathbf{j})$
$(a\mathbf{i} + b\mathbf{j}) = (40\mathbf{i} + 16.5\mathbf{j})$
$\Rightarrow a = 40$ and $b = 16.5$
You could also have answered this by considering the horizontal and vertical components separately, and using the uvast equations as usual.

b) The horizontal component of velocity remains constant at 40 ms⁻¹. So you only need to consider the vertical component.
$u = 16.5$, $v = v$, $a = -9.8$, $t = 5$
$v = u + at$
$v = 16.5 + (-9.8 \times 5) = -32.5$
$\Rightarrow \mathbf{v} = (40\mathbf{i} - 32.5\mathbf{j})$ ms⁻¹

Q5 **a)** $\mathbf{u} = \mathbf{u}$, $\mathbf{a} = -9.8\mathbf{j}$, $\mathbf{s} = (15\mathbf{i} + 6\mathbf{j})$, $t = 3$

$\mathbf{s} = \mathbf{u}t + \frac{1}{2}\mathbf{a}t^2$

$(15\mathbf{i} + 6\mathbf{j}) = 3\mathbf{u} + (\frac{1}{2} \times -9.8\mathbf{j} \times 3^2)$

$3\mathbf{u} = (15\mathbf{i} + 6\mathbf{j}) + 44.1\mathbf{j}$

$\Rightarrow \mathbf{u} = (5\mathbf{i} + 16.7\mathbf{j})$ ms^{-1}

b) $\mathbf{u} = (5\mathbf{i} + 16.7\mathbf{j})$, $\mathbf{v} = \mathbf{v}$, $\mathbf{a} = -9.8\mathbf{j}$, $t = 3$

$\mathbf{v} = \mathbf{u} + \mathbf{a}t$

$\mathbf{v} = (5\mathbf{i} + 16.7\mathbf{j}) + (-9.8\mathbf{j} \times 3)$

$\Rightarrow \mathbf{v} = (5\mathbf{i} - 12.7\mathbf{j})$ ms^{-1}

c) Velocity immediately following impact with wall is $(-2.5\mathbf{i} - 12.7\mathbf{j})$ ms^{-1}.

Resolving vertically, taking down as positive:

$u = 12.7$, $a = 9.8$, $s = 6$, $t = t$

$s = ut + \frac{1}{2}at^2$

$6 = 12.7t + 4.9t^2$

$4.9t^2 + 12.7t - 6 = 0$

Using the quadratic formula:

$t = \dfrac{-12.7 \pm \sqrt{12.7^2 - (4 \times 4.9 \times -6)}}{9.8}$

$\Rightarrow t = 0.4081...$ or $t = -3$

Resolving horizontally, taking left as positive:

$u = 2.5$, $a = 0$, $s = s$, $t = 0.4081...$

$s = ut + \frac{1}{2}at^2$

$s = 2.5 \times 0.4081... = 1.02$ m (3 s.f.)

2. Variable Acceleration in 1 Dimension

Exercise 2.1 — Differentiating to find velocity and acceleration

Q1 **a)** $v = \dfrac{dx}{dt} = (9t^2 + 10t)$ ms^{-1}

b) $a = \dfrac{dv}{dt} = (18t + 10)$ ms^{-2}

c) When $t = 3$, $a = 18(3) + 10 = 64$ ms^{-2}

Using $F = ma$:

$480 = 64m$

$\Rightarrow m = 480 \div 64 = 7.5$ kg

Q2 **a)** $v = \dfrac{dx}{dt} = (2bt + 6)$ ms^{-1}

When $t = 3$, $v = 18$, so:

$18 = 6b + 6$

$\Rightarrow b = 2$

b) $a = \dfrac{dv}{dt} = \dfrac{d}{dt}(4t + 6) = 4$ ms^{-2}, i.e. constant

Q3 **a)** $v = \dfrac{ds}{dt} = (6t^2 - 42t + 60)$ ms^{-1}

b) When the object is at rest, $v = 0$:

$6t^2 - 42t + 60 = 0$

$t^2 - 7t + 10 = 0$

$(t - 2)(t - 5) = 0$

$\Rightarrow t = 2$ s and $t = 5$ s

c) $a = \dfrac{dv}{dt} = (12t - 42)$ ms^{-2}

d) When $t = 0$, $a = 12(0) - 42 = -42$ ms^{-2}

Q4 **a)** When $t = 0$, $x = 12(0)^2 + 60(0) - (0)^3 = 0$ m
i.e. the particle is initially at the origin.

b) $a = \dfrac{d^2x}{dt^2} = \dfrac{d}{dt}(24t + 60 - 3t^2) = (24 - 6t)$ ms^{-2}

$24 - 6t = 0$

$\Rightarrow t = 4$ s

c) When $t = 0.5$, $a = 24 - 6(0.5) = 21$ ms^{-2}

Using $F = ma$:

$F = 1.4 \times 21 = 29.4$ N

d) When the particle reaches its maximum displacement from the origin, $v = 0$:

$24t + 60 - 3t^2 = 0$

$t^2 - 8t - 20 = 0$

$(t - 10)(t + 2) = 0$

$\Rightarrow t = 10$ or $t = -2$

You can't have a negative time, so ignore $t = -2$.

When $t = 10$, $x = 12(10)^2 + 60(10) - (10)^3$

$= 800$ m

Q5 **a)** $v = \dfrac{ds}{dt} = (12 - 30t + 12t^2)$ kmh^{-1}

$12 - 30t + 12t^2 = 0$

$2t^2 - 5t + 2 = 0$

$(2t - 1)(t - 2) = 0$

$\Rightarrow t = 0.5$ h and $t = 2$ h

b) When $t = 0.5$:

$s = 12(0.5) - 15(0.5)^2 + 4(0.5)^3 = 2.75$ km

When $t = 2$:

$s = 12(2) - 15(2)^2 + 4(2)^3 = -4$ km

So the vehicle travels 2.75 km − −4 km = 6.75 km between these two times.

The negative displacement means the particle is 4 km from its starting point, but in the negative direction (i.e. when $t = 2$, the particle is on the 'other side' of its starting point to when $t = 0.5$).

Q6 **a)** Find the times that the train is at rest:

$v = \dfrac{ds}{dt} = (180t - 135t^2)$ ms^{-1}

$180t - 135t^2 = 0$

$4t - 3t^2 = 0$

$t(4 - 3t) = 0$

$\Rightarrow t = 0$ h and $t = \dfrac{4}{3}$ h

So the time taken to travel between the two stations is $\dfrac{4}{3}$ hours, or 1 hour and 20 minutes.

b) When $t = 0$, $s = 90(0)^2 - 45(0)^3 = 0$ km

and when $t = \dfrac{4}{3}$, $s = 90\left(\dfrac{4}{3}\right)^2 - 45\left(\dfrac{4}{3}\right)^3 = 53\dfrac{1}{3}$ km

So the distance between the two stations is 53.3 km (3 s.f.)

c) $a = \dfrac{dv}{dt} = (180 - 270t)$ ms^{-2}

When train reaches its maximum speed, its acceleration will be zero:

$180 - 270t = 0$

$\Rightarrow t = \dfrac{2}{3}$ h

When $t = \dfrac{2}{3}$, $v = 180\left(\dfrac{2}{3}\right) - 135\left(\dfrac{2}{3}\right)^2 = 60$ kmh^{-1}

Exercise 2.2 — Integrating to find velocity and displacement

Q1 **a)** **(i)** $v = \int a\, dt = \int 5\, dt = 5t + C$

When $t = 0$, $v = 10$, so:

$10 = 5(0) + C$

$\Rightarrow C = 10$

So $v = (5t + 10)$ ms^{-1}

(ii) When $t = 6$, $v = 5(6) + 10 = 40$ ms^{-1}

b) (i) $x = \int v \, dt = \int (5t + 10) \, dt = \frac{5}{2}t^2 + 10t + D$
When $t = 0$, $x = 0$, so:
$0 = \frac{5}{2}(0)2 + 10(0) + D$
$\Rightarrow D = 0$
So $x = (\frac{5}{2}t^2 + 10t)$ m

(ii) When $t = 6$, $x = \frac{5}{2}(6)^2 + 10(6) = 150$ m

Q2 a) $x = \int v \, dt = \int (3t^2 - 14t + 8) \, dt$
$= t^3 - 7t^2 + 8t + C$
When $t = 1$, $x = 8$, so:
$8 = (1)^3 - 7(1)^2 + 8(1) + C$
$\Rightarrow C = 6$
So $x = (t^3 - 7t^2 + 8t + 6)$ m

b) The object is at rest when $v = 0$:
$3t^2 - 14t + 8 = 0$
$(3t - 2)(t - 4) = 0$
$\Rightarrow t = \frac{2}{3}$ or $t = 4$
So the object is at rest when $t = 0.667$ s (3 s.f.)
and when $t = 4$ s.

c) When $t = \frac{2}{3}$, $x = \left(\frac{2}{3}\right)^3 - 7\left(\frac{2}{3}\right)^2 + 8\left(\frac{2}{3}\right) + 6$
$= 8.518...$ m
and when $t = 4$, $x = 4^3 - 7(4)^2 + 8(4) + 6$
$= -10$ m
So the distance between the two points is
$8.518... - -10 = 18.5$ m (3 s.f.)

Q3 a) $v = \int a \, dt = \int (2t - 6) \, dt = t^2 - 6t + C$
When $t = 0$, $v = 6$, so:
$6 = (0)^2 - 6(0) + C$
$\Rightarrow C = 6$
So $v = (t^2 - 6t + 6)$ ms^{-1}

b) $x = \int v \, dt = \int (t^2 - 6t + 6) \, dt$
$= \frac{1}{3}t^3 - 3t^2 + 6t + D$
When $t = 0$, $x = 0$, so:
$0 = \frac{1}{3}(0)^3 - 3(0)^2 + 6(0) + D$
$\Rightarrow D = 0$
So $x = (\frac{1}{3}t^3 - 3t^2 + 6t)$ m

c) The particle passes through the origin when $x = 0$:
$\frac{1}{3}t^3 - 3t^2 + 6t = 0$
$t^3 - 9t^2 + 18t = 0$
$t(t^2 - 9t + 18) = 0$
$\Rightarrow t = 0$ and $t^2 - 9t + 18 = 0$
$t^2 - 9t + 18 = 0$
$(t - 3)(t - 6) = 0$
So the particle passes through the origin when
$t = 3$ s and $t = 6$ s.

Q4 a) $v = \int a \, dt = \int (2t - 4) \, dt = t^2 - 4t + C$
When $t = 0$, $v = 0$, so:
$0 = 0^2 - 4(0) + C$
$\Rightarrow C = 0$
So $v = (t^2 - 4t)$ ms^{-1}
When $t = 5$, $v = 5^2 - 4(5) = 5$ ms^{-1}

b) $x = \int v \, dt = \int (t^2 - 4t) \, dt = \frac{1}{3}t^3 - 2t^2 + D$
When $t = 0$, $x = 0$, so:
$0 = \frac{1}{3}(0)^3 - 2(0)^2 + D$
$\Rightarrow D = 0$
So $x = (\frac{1}{3}t^3 - 2t^2)$ m
When $t = 5$, $x = \frac{1}{3}(5)^3 - 2(5)^2 = -\frac{25}{3}$
$= -8.33$ m (3 s.f.)

c) When the object reverses its direction, it will stop momentarily (i.e. $v = 0$):
$t^2 - 4t = 0$
$t(t - 4) = 0$
$\Rightarrow t = 0$ and $t = 4$
So the object reverses its direction at $t = 4$ s.

d) The object returns to O when $x = 0$:
$\frac{1}{3}t^3 - 2t^2 = 0$
$t^3 - 6t^2 = 0$
$t^2(t - 6) = 0$
$\Rightarrow t = 0$ and $t = 6$
So the object returns to O at $t = 6$ s.

Q5 a) $v = \int a \, dt = \int (k - 18t^2) \, dt = kt - 6t^3 + C$
When $t = 0$, $v = 7$, so:
$7 = k(0) - 6(0)^3 + C$
$\Rightarrow C = 7$
So $v = (kt - 6t^3 + 7)$ ms^{-1}
When $t = 1$, $v = 9$, so:
$9 = k(1) - 6(1)^3 + 7$
$\Rightarrow k = 8$

b) $x = \int v \, dt = \int (8t - 6t^3 + 7) \, dt$
$= 4t^2 - \frac{3}{2}t^4 + 7t + D$
When $t = 0$, $x = 0$, so:
$0 = 4(0)^2 - \frac{3}{2}(0)^4 + 7(0) + D$
$\Rightarrow D = 0$
So $x = (4t^2 - \frac{3}{2}t^4 + 7t)$ m
When $t = 1$, $x = 4(1)^2 - \frac{3}{2}(1)^4 + 7(1) = 9.5$ m
So Q is 9.5 m from O.

Exercise 2.3 — Motion described by multiple expressions

Q1 a) For $0 \leq t \leq 5$, $x = \int (6t - 9t^2) \, dt = 3t^2 - 3t^3 + C$
When $t = 0$, $x = 0$, so:
$0 = 3(0)^2 - 3(0)^3 + C \Rightarrow C = 0$
So $x = (3t^2 - 3t^3)$ m $\qquad 0 \leq t \leq 5$
When $t = 5$, $x = 3(5)^2 - 3(5)^3 = -300$ m

b) For $t > 5$, $x = \int (625t^{-3} - 200) \, dt$
$= -312.5t^{-2} - 200t + D$
From part a), when $t = 5$, $x = -300$.
Using this to find the constant of integration:
$-300 = -312.5(5)^{-2} - 200(5) + D$
$\Rightarrow D = 712.5$
So $x = \left(-\dfrac{312.5}{t^2} - 200t + 712.5\right)$ m $\qquad t > 5$
When $t = 10$, $x = \left(-\dfrac{312.5}{10^2} - 200(10) + 712.5\right)$
$= -1290.625$ m

Q2 a) (i) For $0 \leq t \leq 3$, $v = \int 4t \, dt = 2t^2 + C$
When $t = 2$, $v = 8$, so:
$8 = 2(2)^2 + C$
$\Rightarrow C = 0$
So $v = 2t^2$ ms^{-1} $\qquad 0 \leq t \leq 3$
When $t = 3$, $v = 2(3)^2 = 18$ ms^{-1}

(ii) For $t > 3$, $v = \int (18 - 2t) \, dt = 18t - t^2 + D$
From part (i), when $t = 3$, $v = 18$.
Using this to find the constant of integration:
$18 = 18(3) - (3)^2 + D$
$\Rightarrow D = -27$
So $v = (18t - t^2 - 27)$ ms^{-1} $\qquad t > 3$
When $t = 5$, $v = 18(5) - (5)^2 - 27 = 38$ ms^{-1}

b) Maximum speed occurs when $a = 0$.

For $0 \leq t \leq 3$: $0 = 4t$

$\Rightarrow t = 0$

When $t = 0$, $v = 2(0)^2 = 0$ ms^{-1}

For $t > 3$: $0 = 18 - 2t$

$\Rightarrow t = 9$

When $t = 9$, $v = 18(9) - (9)^2 - 27 = 54$ ms^{-1}

So the body's maximum speed is 54 ms^{-1}

c) For $0 \leq t \leq 3$, $x = \int 2t^2 \, dt = \frac{2}{3}t^3 + E$

When $t = 0$, $x = 0$, so:

$0 = \frac{2}{3}(0)^3 + E$

$\Rightarrow E = 0$

So $x = \frac{2}{3}t^3$ m $0 \leq t \leq 3$

For $t > 3$, $x = \int (18t - t^2 - 27) \, dt$

$= 9t^2 - \frac{1}{3}t^3 - 27t + F$

Using $x = \frac{2}{3}t^3$ m, when $t = 3$, $x = \frac{2}{3}(3)^3 = 18$.

Use this to find the constant of integration:

$18 = 9(3)^2 - \frac{1}{3}(3)^3 - 27(3) + F$

$\Rightarrow F = 27$

So $x = (9t^2 - \frac{1}{3}t^3 - 27t + 27)$ m $t > 3$

The body is at the origin at $t = 0$, and returns there when $x = 0$ again (at time $t = T$):

$9T^2 - \frac{1}{3}T^3 - 27T + 27 = 0$

Multiplying throughout by -3 and rearranging:

$T^3 - 27T^2 + 81T - 81 = 0$, as required.

Q3 a) For $0 \leq t \leq 2$:

$v = \frac{d}{dt}(2t^2 + t + 40) = (4t + 1)$ ms^{-1}

For $t > 2$:

$v = \frac{d}{dt}(t^3 - 12t^2 + 45t) = (3t^2 - 24t + 45)$ ms^{-1}

b) For $0 \leq t \leq 2$:

$4t + 1 = 0 \Rightarrow t = -0.25$

This is outside the range $0 \leq t \leq 2$, so ignore this solution.

For $t > 2$:

$3t^2 - 24t + 45 = 0$

$t^2 - 8t + 15 = 0$

$(t - 3)(t - 5) = 0$

$\Rightarrow t = 3$ and $t = 5$

When $t = 3$, $x = (3)^3 - 12(3)^2 + 45(3) = 54$ m

When $t = 5$, $x = (5)^3 - 12(5)^2 + 45(5) = 50$ m

So the distance between the two points where the object is at rest is 54 m − 50 m = 4 m.

Make sure you use the right expression for x in this part — the two times that the object is at rest are in the interval t > 2, so you should be using the equation x = t³ − 12t² + 45t.

c) For $0 \leq t \leq 2$:

$a = \frac{d}{dt}(4t + 1) = 4$ ms^{-2}

So acceleration is constant (and positive) in the interval $0 \leq t \leq 2$, i.e. the object won't move with constant velocity in this time interval.

For $t > 2$:

$a = \frac{d}{dt}(3t^2 - 24t + 45) = (6t - 24)$ ms^{-2}

$6t - 24 = 0 \Rightarrow t = 4$ s

When $t = 4$, $v = 3(4)^2 - 24(4) + 45 = -3$ ms^{-1}

So the object's speed is 3 ms^{-1}.

Q4 a) When the particle changes direction, it will be instantaneously at rest.

For $0 \leq t \leq 3$:

$5t - t^2 = 0$

$t(5 - t) = 0$

$\Rightarrow t = 0$ and $t = 5$

$t = 0$ is when the particle first sets off (i.e. the particle doesn't change direction at this time) and $t = 5$ isn't in the interval $0 \leq t \leq 3$, so the solution can be ignored.

For $t > 3$:

$12 - 2t = 0$

$\Rightarrow t = 6$

So the particle changes direction at time $t = 6$ seconds.

b) For $0 \leq t \leq 3$, $x = \int (5t - t^2) \, dt = \frac{5}{2}t^2 - \frac{1}{3}t^3 + C$

When $t = 0$, $x = 0$, so:

$0 = \frac{5}{2}(0)^2 - \frac{1}{3}(0)^3 + C$

$\Rightarrow C = 0$

So $x = (\frac{5}{2}t^2 - \frac{1}{3}t^3)$ m $0 \leq t \leq 3$

When $t = 3$, $x = \frac{5}{2}(3)^2 - \frac{1}{3}(3)^3 = 13.5$ m

c) For $t > 3$, $x = \int (12 - 2t) \, dt = 12t - t^2 + D$

When $t = 3$, $x = 13.5$, so:

$13.5 = 12(3) - 3^2 + D$

$\Rightarrow D = -13.5$

So $x = (12t - t^2 - 13.5)$ m $t > 3$

From part a), the particle changes direction at time $t = 6$ seconds, so consider the particle's displacement when $t = 6$ and when $t = 8$ separately.

When $t = 6$, $x = 12(6) - 6^2 - 13.5 = 22.5$ m

When $t = 8$, $x = 12(8) - 8^2 - 13.5 = 18.5$ m

So from time $t = 0$ s to $t = 6$ s, the particle travels 22.5 m, and from $t = 6$ s to $t = 8$ s, the particle travels 22.5 m − 18.5 m = 4 m.

Therefore, the total distance travelled is 22.5 m + 4 m = 26.5 m

3. Variable Acceleration in 2 Dimensions

Exercise 3.1 — Using vectors

Q1 a) (i) $\mathbf{v} = \dot{\mathbf{r}} = [(3t^2 - 3)\mathbf{i} + 2t\mathbf{j}]$ ms^{-1}

(ii) When $t = 3$, $\mathbf{v} = (3(3)^2 - 3)\mathbf{i} + 2(3)\mathbf{j}$

$= (24\mathbf{i} + 6\mathbf{j})$ ms^{-1}

Using Pythagoras' theorem:

speed $= \sqrt{24^2 + 6^2} = 24.7$ ms^{-1} (3 s.f.)

Using trigonometry:

$\theta = \tan^{-1}\left(\frac{6}{24}\right)$

$= 14.0°$ (3 s.f.) above $\mathbf{i}$.

b) (i) $\mathbf{a} = \dot{\mathbf{v}} = (6t\mathbf{i} + 2\mathbf{j})$ ms^{-2}

(ii) When $t = 4$, $\mathbf{a} = 6(4)\mathbf{i} + 2\mathbf{j} = (24\mathbf{i} + 2\mathbf{j})$ ms^{-2}

Using Pythagoras' theorem:

magnitude $= \sqrt{24^2 + 2^2} = 24.1$ ms^{-2} (3 s.f.)

Q2 $\mathbf{a} = \dot{\mathbf{v}} = (3t^2 - 12t - 36)\mathbf{i}$ ms^{-2}
$3t^2 - 12t - 36 = 0$
$t^2 - 4t - 12 = 0$
$(t + 2)(t - 6) = 0$
$\Rightarrow t = -2$ and $t = 6$
Ignore the negative time.
When $t = 6$, $\mathbf{v} = [(6)^3 - 6(6)^2 - 36(6)]\mathbf{i} + 14\mathbf{j}$
$= (-216\mathbf{i} + 14\mathbf{j})$ ms^{-1}

Q3 a) $\mathbf{v} = \int \mathbf{a}\,dt = \int (3t\mathbf{i} + 6\mathbf{j})\,dt$
$= \frac{3}{2}t^2\mathbf{i} + 6t\mathbf{j} + \mathbf{C}$
When $t = 2$, $\mathbf{v} = (4\mathbf{i} + 6\mathbf{j})$, so:
$4\mathbf{i} + 6\mathbf{j} = \frac{3}{2}(2)^2\mathbf{i} + 6(2)\mathbf{j} + \mathbf{C}$
$4\mathbf{i} + 6\mathbf{j} = 6\mathbf{i} + 12\mathbf{j} + \mathbf{C}$
$\Rightarrow \mathbf{C} = -2\mathbf{i} - 6\mathbf{j}$
So $\mathbf{v} = [(\frac{3}{2}t^2 - 2)\mathbf{i} + (6t - 6)\mathbf{j}]$ ms^{-1}

b) $\mathbf{r} = \int \mathbf{v}\,dt = \int [(\frac{3}{2}t^2 - 2)\mathbf{i} + (6t - 6)\mathbf{j}]\,dt$
$= (\frac{1}{2}t^3 - 2t)\mathbf{i} + (3t^2 - 6t)\mathbf{j} + \mathbf{D}$
When $t = 2$, $\mathbf{r} = (2\mathbf{i} - 9\mathbf{j})$, so:
$2\mathbf{i} - 9\mathbf{j} = (\frac{1}{2}(2)^3 - 2(2))\mathbf{i} + (3(2)^2 - 6(2))\mathbf{j} + \mathbf{D}$
$2\mathbf{i} - 9\mathbf{j} = 0\mathbf{i} + 0\mathbf{j} + \mathbf{D}$
$\Rightarrow \mathbf{D} = 2\mathbf{i} - 9\mathbf{j}$
So $\mathbf{r} = [(\frac{1}{2}t^3 - 2t + 2)\mathbf{i} + (3t^2 - 6t - 9)\mathbf{j}]$ m

c) (i) When the body is due east of O, the j-component of its position vector is zero:
$3t^2 - 6t - 9 = 0$
$t^2 - 2t - 3 = 0$
$(t + 1)(t - 3) = 0$
$\Rightarrow t = -1$ and $t = 3$
When $t = 3$, the i-component of $\mathbf{r}$ is:
$\frac{1}{2}(3)^3 - 2(3) + 2 = 9.5 > 0$
So the body is due east of O at time $t = 3$ s.
*Remember to check that the i-component of **r** is greater than zero, otherwise you can't be sure that the body isn't at O or due west of O.*

(ii) From c)(i), the i-component of $\mathbf{r}$ at this time is 9.5, so the body's distance from O is 9.5 m.

Q4 a) $\mathbf{a} = \dot{\mathbf{v}} = [(2t - 6)\mathbf{i} + 4\mathbf{j}]$ ms^{-2}

b) $\mathbf{r} = \int \mathbf{v}\,dt = \int [(t^2 - 6t)\mathbf{i} + (4t + 5)\mathbf{j}]\,dt$
$= (\frac{1}{3}t^3 - 3t^2)\mathbf{i} + (2t^2 + 5t)\mathbf{j} + \mathbf{C}$
When $t = 0$, $\mathbf{r} = \mathbf{0}$, so:
$\mathbf{0} = (\frac{1}{3}(0)^3 - 3(0)^2)\mathbf{i} + (2(0)^2 + 5(0))\mathbf{j} + \mathbf{C}$
$\Rightarrow \mathbf{C} = \mathbf{0}$
So $\mathbf{r} = [(\frac{1}{3}t^3 - 3t^2)\mathbf{i} + (2t^2 + 5t)\mathbf{j}]$ m

c) When the particle is travelling parallel to j, the i-component of its velocity is zero:
$t^2 - 6t = 0$
$t(t - 6) = 0$
$\Rightarrow t = 0$ and $t = 6$
When $t = 0$, the j-component of $\mathbf{v}$ is:
$(4(0) + 5) = 5 \neq 0$
and when $t = 6$, the j-component of $\mathbf{v}$ is:
$(4(6) + 5) = 29 \neq 0$
So the particle is travelling parallel to j at time $t = 0$ s and time $t = 6$ s.
Remember to check that the j-component of velocity is non-zero for the values of t you've found — otherwise you can't be sure the particle isn't stationary.

d) $(\frac{1}{3}t^3 - 3t^2)\mathbf{i} + (2t^2 + 5t)\mathbf{j} = b\mathbf{i} + 12\mathbf{j}$
Equating j-components:
$2t^2 + 5t = 12$
$2t^2 + 5t - 12 = 0$
$(2t - 3)(t + 4) = 0$
$\Rightarrow t = 1.5$ and $t = -4$
The time can't be negative, so the particle passes through the point $(b\mathbf{i} + 12\mathbf{j})$ m at time $t = 1.5$ s.
Equating i-components and substituting $t = 1.5$:
$\frac{1}{3}t^3 - 3t^2 = b$
$\frac{1}{3}(1.5)^3 - 3(1.5)^2 = b$
$\Rightarrow b = -5.625$

Q5 a) $\mathbf{v}_A = \dot{\mathbf{r}}_A = [(3t^2 - 2t - 4)\mathbf{i} + (3t^2 - 4t + 3)\mathbf{j}]$ ms^{-1}
$(3t^2 - 2t - 4)\mathbf{i} + (3t^2 - 4t + 3)\mathbf{j} = -3\mathbf{i} + 2\mathbf{j}$
Equating i-components:
$3t^2 - 2t - 4 = -3$
$3t^2 - 2t - 1 = 0$
$(3t + 1)(t - 1) = 0$
$\Rightarrow t = -\frac{1}{3}$ and $t = 1$
When $t = 1$, the j-component of $\mathbf{v}_A$ is:
$3(1)^2 - 4(1) + 3 = 2$
So the particle's velocity is $(-3\mathbf{i} + 2\mathbf{j})$ ms^{-1} at time $t = 1$ second.

b) When the particle's direction of motion is 45° above i, the horizontal and vertical components of the particle's velocity will be equal.
A good way to picture this is that if the particle was moving relative to a pair of coordinate axes, it would be moving along the line y = x (for positive x and y).
$3t^2 - 2t - 4 = 3t^2 - 4t + 3$
$2t = 7 \Rightarrow t = 3.5$ s
This is the value of t for which the horizontal and vertical components of velocity are equal.
You need to check that the particle is moving at 45° above i, not 45° below −i at this time.
(The components will also be equal if the particle is moving along a path 45° below −i.)
From part a),
$\mathbf{v}_A = [(3t^2 - 2t - 4)\mathbf{i} + (3t^2 - 4t + 3)\mathbf{j}]$ ms^{-1}.
When $t = 3.5$, $\mathbf{v}_A = [(3(3.5)^2 - 2(3.5) - 4)\mathbf{i} + (3(3.5)^2 - 4(3.5) + 3)\mathbf{j}]$
$= (25.75\mathbf{i} + 25.75\mathbf{j})$ ms^{-1}
Both components are positive, so the particle is moving along a path 45° above i when $t = 3.5$ s.
You don't actually need to check that both components are positive — if one is, the other one will be too.

c) $\mathbf{v}_B = \int \mathbf{a}_B\,dt = \int (6t\mathbf{i} + 6t\mathbf{j})\,dt$
$= 3t^2\mathbf{i} + 3t^2\mathbf{j} + \mathbf{C}$
When $t = 1$, $\mathbf{v}_B = (4\mathbf{i} - \mathbf{j})$, so:
$4\mathbf{i} - \mathbf{j} = 3(1)^2\mathbf{i} + 3(1)^2\mathbf{j} + \mathbf{C}$
$4\mathbf{i} - \mathbf{j} = 3\mathbf{i} + 3\mathbf{j} + \mathbf{C}$
$\Rightarrow \mathbf{C} = \mathbf{i} - 4\mathbf{j}$
So $\mathbf{v}_B = [(3t^2 + 1)\mathbf{i} + (3t^2 - 4)\mathbf{j}]$ ms^{-1}
$\mathbf{r}_B = \int \mathbf{v}_B\,dt = \int [(3t^2 + 1)\mathbf{i} + (3t^2 - 4)\mathbf{j}]\,dt$
$= (t^3 + t)\mathbf{i} + (t^3 - 4t)\mathbf{j} + \mathbf{D}$
When $t = 1$, $\mathbf{r}_B = (2\mathbf{i} + 3\mathbf{j})$, so:
$2\mathbf{i} + 3\mathbf{j} = (1^3 + 1)\mathbf{i} + (1^3 - 4(1))\mathbf{j} + \mathbf{D}$
$2\mathbf{i} + 3\mathbf{j} = 2\mathbf{i} - 3\mathbf{j} + \mathbf{D}$
$\Rightarrow \mathbf{D} = 6\mathbf{j}$
So $\mathbf{r}_B = [(t^3 + t)\mathbf{i} + (t^3 - 4t + 6)\mathbf{j}]$ m

d) $r_B - r_A = [(t^3 + t)\mathbf{i} + (t^3 - 4t + 6)\mathbf{j}] -$
$[(t^3 - t^2 - 4t + 3)\mathbf{i} + (t^3 - 2t^2 + 3t - 7)\mathbf{j}]$
$= [(t^2 + 5t - 3)\mathbf{i} + (2t^2 - 7t + 13)\mathbf{j}]$ m

e) When $t = 4$, $r_B - r_A =$
$(4^2 + 5(4) - 3)\mathbf{i} + (2(4)^2 - 7(4) + 13)\mathbf{j}$
$= (33\mathbf{i} + 17\mathbf{j})$ m
Using Pythagoras' theorem:
distance $= \sqrt{33^2 + 17^2} = 37.1$ m (3 s.f.)

Exercise 3.2 — Forces

Q1 $\mathbf{a} = \dot{\mathbf{v}} = (3t^2\mathbf{i} - 8t\mathbf{j})$ ms^{-2}
When $t = 5$, $\mathbf{a} = 3(5)^2\mathbf{i} - 8(5)\mathbf{j} = (75\mathbf{i} - 40\mathbf{j})$ ms^{-2}
Using $\mathbf{F} = m\mathbf{a}$:
$15\mathbf{i} - 8\mathbf{j} = m(75\mathbf{i} - 40\mathbf{j})$
Equating $\mathbf{i}$-components:
$15 = 75m \Rightarrow m = 0.2$ kg

Q2 $\mathbf{a} = \ddot{\mathbf{r}} = \frac{d}{dt}[-2t\mathbf{i} + (6t + 1)\mathbf{j}] = (-2\mathbf{i} + 6\mathbf{j})$ ms^{-2}
So $\mathbf{a}$ doesn't depend on t, and as $\mathbf{F} = m\mathbf{a}$, and m
is constant, $\mathbf{F}$ doesn't depend on t either, so $\mathbf{F}$ is
constant.

Q3 **a)** $\mathbf{v} = \dot{\mathbf{r}} = [(2t - 4)\mathbf{i} + (2t - 4)\mathbf{j}]$ ms^{-1}
The object is at rest when $2t - 4 = 0$,
i.e. at time $t = 2$ seconds.

b) When $t = 2$:
$\mathbf{r} = ((2)^2 - 4(2) - 5)\mathbf{i} + ((2)^2 - 4(2) + 3)\mathbf{j}$
$= (-9\mathbf{i} - \mathbf{j})$ m
Using Pythagoras' theorem:
distance $= \sqrt{(-9)^2 + (-1)^2} = 9.06$ m (3 s.f.)

c) $\mathbf{a} = \dot{\mathbf{v}} = \frac{d}{dt}[(2t - 4)\mathbf{i} + (2t - 4)\mathbf{j}] = (2\mathbf{i} + 2\mathbf{j})$ ms^{-2}
$\mathbf{F} = m\mathbf{a} = 14(2\mathbf{i} + 2\mathbf{j}) = (28\mathbf{i} + 28\mathbf{j})$ N

Q4 **a)** When $t = 1$, $\mathbf{F} = 3\mathbf{i} + 6\mathbf{j}$
Using $\mathbf{F} = m\mathbf{a}$:
$3\mathbf{i} + 6\mathbf{j} = 3\mathbf{a}$
$\Rightarrow \mathbf{a} = (\mathbf{i} + 2\mathbf{j})$ ms^{-2}
Using Pythagoras' theorem:
magnitude $= \sqrt{1^2 + 2^2} = 2.24$ ms^{-2} (3 s.f.)

b) Using $\mathbf{F} = m\mathbf{a}$:
$3\mathbf{i} + 6t\mathbf{j} = 3\mathbf{a} \Rightarrow \mathbf{a} = (\mathbf{i} + 2t\mathbf{j})$ ms^{-2}
$\mathbf{v} = \int \mathbf{a}\ dt = \int (\mathbf{i} + 2t\mathbf{j})\ dt = (t\mathbf{i} + t^2\mathbf{j}) + \mathbf{C}$
When $t = 0$, $\mathbf{v} = -2\mathbf{i} + 5\mathbf{j}$, so:
$-2\mathbf{i} + 5\mathbf{j} = (0)\mathbf{i} + (0)^2\mathbf{j} + \mathbf{C}$
$\Rightarrow \mathbf{C} = -2\mathbf{i} + 5\mathbf{j}$
So $\mathbf{v} = [(t - 2)\mathbf{i} + (t^2 + 5)\mathbf{j}]$ ms^{-1}

c) The particle is moving parallel to $\mathbf{j}$ when the
$\mathbf{i}$-component of velocity is zero:
$t - 2 = 0 \Rightarrow t = 2$ s
When $t = 2$, the $\mathbf{j}$-component of velocity is:
$2^2 + 5 = 9 \neq 0$, so the particle is moving parallel
to $\mathbf{j}$ when $t = 2$.
Substitute this into the expression for $\mathbf{F}$:
$\mathbf{F} = 3\mathbf{i} + 6(2)\mathbf{j} = (3\mathbf{i} + 12\mathbf{j})$ N

d) $\mathbf{r} = \int \mathbf{v}\ dt = \int [(t - 2)\mathbf{i} + (t^2 + 5)\mathbf{j}]\ dt$
$= (\frac{1}{2}t^2 - 2t)\mathbf{i} + (\frac{1}{3}t^3 + 5t)\mathbf{j} + \mathbf{D}$
When $t = 0$, $\mathbf{r} = \mathbf{0}$, so:
$\mathbf{0} = (\frac{1}{2}(0)^2 - 2(0))\mathbf{i} + (\frac{1}{3}(0)^3 + 5(0))\mathbf{j} + \mathbf{D}$
$\Rightarrow \mathbf{D} = \mathbf{0}$
So $\mathbf{r} = [(\frac{1}{2}t^2 - 2t)\mathbf{i} + (\frac{1}{3}t^3 + 5t)\mathbf{j}]$ m

e) When $t = 3$, $\mathbf{r} = [\frac{1}{2}(3)^2 - 2(3)]\mathbf{i} + [\frac{1}{3}(3)^3 + 5(3)]\mathbf{j}$
$= (-1.5\mathbf{i} + 24\mathbf{j})$ m
Using Pythagoras' theorem:
distance $= \sqrt{(-1.5)^2 + 24^2} = 24.0$ m (3 s.f.)

Q5 **a)** $\mathbf{a} = \dot{\mathbf{v}} = (5\mathbf{i} + 6t\mathbf{j})$ ms^{-2}
$\mathbf{F} = m\mathbf{a} = 0.2(5\mathbf{i} + 6t\mathbf{j}) = (\mathbf{i} + 1.2t\mathbf{j})$ N

b) When $t = 2$, $\mathbf{F} = \mathbf{i} + 1.2(2)\mathbf{j} = (\mathbf{i} + 2.4\mathbf{j})$ N
Using Pythagoras' theorem:
magnitude $= \sqrt{1^2 + 2.4^2} = 2.6$ N

c) $\mathbf{r} = \int \mathbf{v}\ dt = \int [(5t - 2)\mathbf{i} + 3t^2\mathbf{j}]\ dt$
$= (\frac{5}{2}t^2 - 2t)\mathbf{i} + t^3\mathbf{j} + \mathbf{C}$
When $t = 1$, $\mathbf{r} = -16\mathbf{i} - 8\mathbf{j}$, so:
$-16\mathbf{i} - 8\mathbf{j} = (\frac{5}{2}(1)^2 - 2(1))\mathbf{i} + (1)^3\mathbf{j} + \mathbf{C}$
$-16\mathbf{i} - 8\mathbf{j} = 0.5\mathbf{i} + \mathbf{j} + \mathbf{C}$
$\Rightarrow \mathbf{C} = -16.5\mathbf{i} - 9\mathbf{j}$
So $\mathbf{r} = [(\frac{5}{2}t^2 - 2t - 16.5)\mathbf{i} + (t^3 - 9)\mathbf{j}]$ m

d) When the particle is directly above O, the
$\mathbf{i}$-component of its position vector is zero:
$\frac{5}{2}t^2 - 2t - 16.5 = 0$
$5t^2 - 4t - 33 = 0$
$(5t + 11)(t - 3) = 0$
$\Rightarrow t = -2.2$ and $t = 3$
When $t = 3$, the $\mathbf{j}$-component of $\mathbf{r}$ is:
$3^3 - 9 = 18 > 0$, so the particle is directly above O
at time $t = 3$ seconds.

Q6 **a)** Using $\mathbf{F} = m\mathbf{a}$:
$(3t - 4)\mathbf{i} + (t - 3t^2)\mathbf{j} = 0.5\mathbf{a}$
$\Rightarrow \mathbf{a} = [(6t - 8)\mathbf{i} + (2t - 6t^2)\mathbf{j}]$ ms^{-2}
$\mathbf{v} = \int \mathbf{a}\ dt = \int [(6t - 8)\mathbf{i} + (2t - 6t^2)\mathbf{j}]\ dt$
$= (3t^2 - 8t)\mathbf{i} + (t^2 - 2t^3)\mathbf{j} + \mathbf{C}$
When $t = 0$, $\mathbf{v} = -3\mathbf{i} + 45\mathbf{j}$, so:
$-3\mathbf{i} + 45\mathbf{j} = [3(0)^2 - 8(0)]\mathbf{i} + [0^2 - 2(0)^3]\mathbf{j} + \mathbf{C}$
$\Rightarrow -3\mathbf{i} + 45\mathbf{j} = \mathbf{C}$
So $\mathbf{v} = [(3t^2 - 8t - 3)\mathbf{i} + (t^2 - 2t^3 + 45)\mathbf{j}]$ ms^{-1}
When $t = 3$:
$\mathbf{v} = [3(3)^2 - 8(3) - 3]\mathbf{i} + [(3)^2 - 2(3)^3 + 45]\mathbf{j}$
$= (0\mathbf{i} + 0\mathbf{j})$ ms^{-1}
So the particle is stationary —
i.e. its speed is 0 ms^{-1}.

b) $\mathbf{r} = \int \mathbf{v}\ dt = \int [(3t^2 - 8t - 3)\mathbf{i} + (t^2 - 2t^3 + 45)\mathbf{j}]\ dt$
$= (t^3 - 4t^2 - 3t)\mathbf{i} + (\frac{1}{3}t^3 - \frac{1}{2}t^4 + 45t)\mathbf{j} + \mathbf{D}$
When $t = 0$, $\mathbf{r} = \mathbf{0}$, so:
$\mathbf{0} = [0^3 - 4(0)^2 - 3(0)]\mathbf{i} + [(\frac{1}{3}(0)^3 - \frac{1}{2}(0)^4 + 45(0)]\mathbf{j} + \mathbf{D}$
$\Rightarrow \mathbf{D} = \mathbf{0}$
So $\mathbf{r} = [(t^3 - 4t^2 - 3t)\mathbf{i} + (\frac{1}{3}t^3 - \frac{1}{2}t^4 + 45t)\mathbf{j}]$ m
Substituting in $t = 3$:
$\mathbf{r} = [(3)^3 - 4(3)^2 - 3(3)]\mathbf{i} + [\frac{1}{3}(3)^3 - \frac{1}{2}(3)^4 + 45(3)]\mathbf{j}$
$= (-18\mathbf{i} + 103.5\mathbf{j})$ m
Using Pythagoras' theorem:
distance $= \sqrt{(-18)^2 + 103.5^2} = 105$ m (3 s.f.)

Q7 **a)** When the projectile lands, the $\mathbf{j}$-component of its
position vector will be zero:
$19.6t - 4.9t^2 = 0$
$t(19.6 - 4.9t) = 0$
$\Rightarrow t = 0$ and $t = 19.6 \div 4.9 = 4$
So the projectile lands at time $t = 4$ s.
Substituting $t = 4$ into the $\mathbf{i}$-component of $\mathbf{r}$:
$8 \times 4 = 32$
So the horizontal range of the projectile is 32 m.

b) $\mathbf{v} = \dot{\mathbf{r}} = [8\mathbf{i} + (19.6 - 9.8t)\mathbf{j}]$ ms^{-1}

c) When the projectile reaches its maximum height, the **j**-component of its velocity will be zero:
$19.6 - 9.8t = 0 \Rightarrow t = 2$ s
Substituting $t = 2$ into the **j**-component of **r**:
$19.6(2) - 4.9(2)^2 = 19.6$
So the projectile's maximum height is 19.6 m.

d) $\mathbf{a} = \dot{\mathbf{v}} = \dfrac{\mathrm{d}}{\mathrm{d}t}[8\mathbf{i} + (19.6 - 9.8t)\mathbf{j}] = -9.8\mathbf{j}$ ms^{-2}
$\mathbf{F} = m\mathbf{a} = 2 \times -9.8\mathbf{j} = -19.6\mathbf{j}$ N
The force acting on the projectile is just the projectile's weight: F = W = mg.

Review Exercise — Chapter 1

Q1 Horizontal component = $u\cos\alpha$
Vertical component = $u\sin\alpha$

Q2 Resolving horizontally, taking right as positive:
$u = 120$, $s = 60$, $a = 0$, $t = t$
$s = ut + \frac{1}{2}at^2$
$60 = 120t$
$t = 0.5$ s
Resolving vertically, taking down as positive:
$u = 0$, $s = d$, $a = 9.8$, $t = 0.5$
$s = ut + \frac{1}{2}at^2$
$= (0 \times 0.5) + (\frac{1}{2} \times 9.8 \times 0.5^2)$
$= 1.23$ m (3 s.f.)

Q3 Resolving vertically, taking up as positive:
$u = 22\sin\alpha$, $a = -9.8$, $t = 4$, $s = 0$
s = 0 because the ball lands at the same vertical level it started at.
$s = ut + \frac{1}{2}at^2$
$0 = (22\sin\alpha \times 4) + (0.5 \times -9.8 \times 4^2)$
Rearranging: $\sin\alpha = \frac{78.4}{88}$
$\Rightarrow \alpha = 63.0°$ (3 s.f.)
There are other ways to answer this question — you could use v = u + at and use t = 2, which is the time taken to reach the highest point, when v = 0.

Q4 a) Resolving vertically, taking up as positive:
$u = 6.5\sin29°$, $a = -9.8$, $s = -0.3$, $t = t$
$s = ut + \frac{1}{2}at^2$
$-0.3 = 6.5\sin29°t - 4.9t^2$
$4.9t^2 - 6.5\sin29°t - 0.3 = 0$
Using the quadratic formula:
$t = \dfrac{6.5\sin29° \pm \sqrt{(-6.5\sin29°)^2 - (4 \times 4.9 \times -0.3)}}{9.8}$
$\Rightarrow t = 0.727...$ or $t = -0.084...$
Resolving horizontally, taking right as positive:
$u = 6.5\cos29°$, $a = 0$, $s = s$, $t = 0.727...$
$s = ut + \frac{1}{2}at^2$
$s = 6.5\cos29° \times 0.727... = 4.13$ m (3 s.f.)

b) Resolving vertically, taking up as positive:
$u = 6.5\sin29°$, $a = -9.8$, $s = -0.3$, $v = v_y$
$v^2 = u^2 + 2as$
$v_y^2 = (6.5\sin29°)^2 + (2 \times -9.8 \times -0.3)$
$v_y^2 = 15.810...$
Horizontally, $v_x = u_x = 6.5\cos29°$
speed $= \sqrt{(6.5\cos29°)^2 + 15.810...}$
$= 6.94$ ms^{-1} (3 s.f.)

Q5 a) $\mathbf{u} = (2\mathbf{i} + 11\mathbf{j})$, $\mathbf{v} = \mathbf{v}$, $\mathbf{a} = -9.8\mathbf{j}$, $t = 0.8$
$\mathbf{v} = \mathbf{u} + \mathbf{a}t$
$\mathbf{v} = (2\mathbf{i} + 11\mathbf{j}) + (-9.8\mathbf{j} \times 0.8) = (2\mathbf{i} + 3.16\mathbf{j})$ ms^{-1}

b) Resolving vertically, taking up as positive:
$u = 11$, $a = -9.8$, $s = 0$, $t = t$
$s = ut + \frac{1}{2}at^2$
$0 = 11t - 4.9t^2$
$0 = t(11 - 4.9t)$
$\Rightarrow t = 0$ and $t = 11 \div 4.9 = 2.244...$
So the time of flight of the body is 2.24 s (3 s.f.)

c) Resolving vertically, taking up as positive:
$u = 11$, $v = 0$, $a = -9.8$, $s = s$
$v^2 = u^2 + 2as$
$0 = 121 - 19.6s$
$\Rightarrow s = 6.17$ m (3 s.f.)

Q6 a) Resolving vertically, taking down as positive:
$u = 4$, $a = 9.8$, $s = 10$, $t = t$
$s = ut + \frac{1}{2}at^2$
$10 = 4t + 4.9t^2$
$4.9t^2 + 4t - 10 = 0$
Using the quadratic formula:
$t = \dfrac{-4 \pm \sqrt{4^2 - (4 \times 4.9 \times -10)}}{9.8}$
$\Rightarrow t = 1.077...$ or $t = -1.893...$
So the ball takes 1.08 s (3 s.f.) to land.

b) Resolving horizontally, taking right as positive:
$u = 20$, $a = 0$, $s = s$, $t = 1.077...$
$s = ut + \frac{1}{2}at^2$
$s = 20 \times 1.077... = 21.551...$ m
$21.551... - 21 = 0.551...$ m
So the ball overshoots the target by 0.551 m (3 s.f.)

c) Resolving horizontally, taking right as positive:
$u = 20$, $a = 0$, $s = 21$, $t = t$
$s = ut + \frac{1}{2}at^2$
$21 = 20t$
$\Rightarrow t = 1.05$ s
Resolving vertically, taking down as positive:
$u = 4$, $v = v_y$, $a = 9.8$, $t = 1.05$
$v = u + at$
$v_y = 4 + (9.8 \times 1.05) = 14.29$ ms^{-1}
Horizontally, $v_x = u_x = 20$
speed $= \sqrt{20^2 + 14.29^2} = 24.6$ ms^{-1} (3 s.f.)

Q7 a) $a = \dfrac{\mathrm{d}v}{\mathrm{d}t} = (16t - 2)$ ms^{-2}

b) $x = \int v\,\mathrm{d}t = \frac{8}{3}t^3 - t^2 + C$
When $t = 0$, $x = 0$, so:
$0 = \frac{8}{3}(0)^3 - (0)^2 + C$
$\Rightarrow C = 0$
So $x = (\frac{8}{3}t^3 - t^2)$ m

Q8 a) $a = \dfrac{\mathrm{d}v}{\mathrm{d}t} = (6t - 9)$ ms^{-2}

b) When $t = 3$, $a = 6(3) - 9 = 9$ ms^{-2}
$F = ma = 0.1 \times 9 = 0.9$ N

c) When $F = 0$, $a = 0$:
$6t - 9 = 0$
$\Rightarrow t = 1.5$ s

Q9 a) The particle's velocity in the region $0 \le t \le 2$ forms a u-shaped quadratic curve. The particle's maximum speed in this interval could either be at the curve's turning point, or at the upper or lower bounds of the interval.

When $t = 0$:
$v = (0)^2 - 3(0) = 0$ ms^{-1}

When $t = 2$:
$v = (2)^2 - 3(2) = -2$ ms^{-1}

Now considering the curve's turning point:
$a = \dfrac{dv}{dt} = (2t - 3)$ ms^{-2} $0 \le t \le 2$

$2t - 3 = 0 \Rightarrow t = 1.5$ s

When $t = 1.5$:
$v = (1.5)^2 - 3(1.5) = -2.25$ ms^{-1}

So the particle's maximum speed in the interval $0 \le t \le 2$ is 2.25 ms^{-1}.

b) For $0 \le t \le 2$, $x = \int (t^2 - 3t)\, dt = \frac{1}{3}t^3 - \frac{3}{2}t^2 + C$
When $t = 0$, $x = 0$, so:
$0 = \frac{1}{3}(0)^3 - \frac{3}{2}(0)^2 + C$
$\Rightarrow C = 0$
So $x = (\frac{1}{3}t^3 - \frac{3}{2}t^2)$ m for $0 \le t \le 2$
When $t = 2$, $x = \frac{1}{3}(2)^3 - \frac{3}{2}(2)^2 = -\frac{10}{3}$
$= -3.33$ m (3 s.f.)

c) For $t > 2$, $x = \int (2 - t^2)\, dt = 2t - \frac{1}{3}t^3 + D$
When $t = 2$, $x = -\frac{10}{3}$, so:
$-\frac{10}{3} = 2(2) - \frac{1}{3}(2)^3 + D$
$\Rightarrow D = -\frac{14}{3}$
So $x = (2t - \frac{1}{3}t^3 - \frac{14}{3})$ m for $t > 2$
When $t = 4$, $x = 2(4) - \frac{1}{3}(4)^3 - \frac{14}{3} = -18$ m

Q10 a) $a = \dfrac{dv}{dt} = (4\mathbf{i} + 2t\mathbf{j})$ ms^{-2}

b) $\mathbf{r} = \int \mathbf{v}\, dt = 2t^2\mathbf{i} + \frac{1}{3}t^3\mathbf{j} + \mathbf{C}$
When $t = 0$, $\mathbf{r} = \mathbf{0}$, so:
$0 = 2(0)^2\mathbf{i} + \frac{1}{3}(0)^3\mathbf{j} + \mathbf{C}$
$\Rightarrow \mathbf{C} = \mathbf{0}$
So $\mathbf{r} = (2t^2\mathbf{i} + \frac{1}{3}t^3\mathbf{j})$ m

Q11 a) When $t = 0$, $\mathbf{r} = (0^2 - 3(0) + 2)\mathbf{i} + (0^2 - 5)\mathbf{j}$
$= (2\mathbf{i} - 5\mathbf{j})$ m

b) When the particle is directly below O, the **i**-component of its position vector will be zero:
$t^2 - 3t + 2 = 0$
$(t - 1)(t - 2) = 0$
$\Rightarrow t = 1$ and $t = 2$
When $t = 1$, the **j**-component of $\mathbf{r}$ is:
$1^2 - 5 = -4 < 0$
When $t = 2$, the **j**-component of $\mathbf{r}$ is:
$2^2 - 5 = -1 < 0$
So the particle is directly below O when $t = 1$ s and $t = 2$ s.

c) $\mathbf{v} = \dot{\mathbf{r}} = [(2t - 3)\mathbf{i} + 2t\mathbf{j}]$ ms^{-1}
When $t = 4$, $\mathbf{v} = [2(4) - 3]\mathbf{i} + 2(4)\mathbf{j} = (5\mathbf{i} + 8\mathbf{j})$ ms^{-1}

Q12 a) $\mathbf{v} = \int \mathbf{a}\, dt = -10t\mathbf{j} + \mathbf{C}$
When $t = 0$, $\mathbf{v} = 15\mathbf{i} + 12\mathbf{j}$, so:
$15\mathbf{i} + 12\mathbf{j} = -10(0)\mathbf{j} + \mathbf{C}$
$\Rightarrow \mathbf{C} = 15\mathbf{i} + 12\mathbf{j}$
So $\mathbf{v} = [15\mathbf{i} + (12 - 10t)\mathbf{j}]$ ms^{-1}

b) $\mathbf{r} = \int \mathbf{v}\, dt = \int [15\mathbf{i} + (12 - 10t)\mathbf{j}]\, dt$
$= 15t\mathbf{i} + (12t - 5t^2)\mathbf{j} + \mathbf{D}$
When $t = 1$, $\mathbf{r} = (15\mathbf{i} + 16\mathbf{j})$, so:
$15\mathbf{i} + 16\mathbf{j} = 15(1)\mathbf{i} + [12(1) - 5(1)^2]\mathbf{j} + \mathbf{D}$
$15\mathbf{i} + 16\mathbf{j} = 15\mathbf{i} + 7\mathbf{j} + \mathbf{D}$
$\Rightarrow \mathbf{D} = 9\mathbf{j}$
So $\mathbf{r} = [15t\mathbf{i} + (12t - 5t^2 + 9)\mathbf{j}]$ m

c) When the body is due east of O, the **j**-component of its position vector will be zero:
$12t - 5t^2 + 9 = 0$
$5t^2 - 12t - 9 = 0$
$(5t + 3)(t - 3) = 0$
$\Rightarrow t = -0.6$ and $t = 3$
When $t = 3$, the **i**-component of $\mathbf{r}$ is:
$15 \times 3 = 45 > 0$, so the body is due east of O at time $t = 3$ seconds.
When $t = 3$, $\mathbf{v} = 15\mathbf{i} + [12 - 10(3)]\mathbf{j}$
$= (15\mathbf{i} - 18\mathbf{j})$ ms^{-1}

Q13 a) $\mathbf{a} = \dot{\mathbf{v}} = [(6t - 8)\mathbf{i} + 4\mathbf{j}]$ ms^{-1}
$\mathbf{F} = m\mathbf{a} = 7.5[(6t - 8)\mathbf{i} + 4\mathbf{j}]$
$= [(45t - 60)\mathbf{i} + 30\mathbf{j}]$ N

b) $\mathbf{r} = \int \mathbf{v}\, dt = \int [(3t^2 - 8t)\mathbf{i} + (6 + 4t)\mathbf{j}]\, dt$
$= (t^3 - 4t^2)\mathbf{i} + (6t + 2t^2)\mathbf{j} + \mathbf{C}$
When $t = 3$, $\mathbf{r} = -4\mathbf{i} + 32\mathbf{j}$, so:
$-4\mathbf{i} + 32\mathbf{j} = [3^3 - 4(3)^2]\mathbf{i} + [6(3) + 2(3)^2]\mathbf{j} + \mathbf{C}$
$-4\mathbf{i} + 32\mathbf{j} = -9\mathbf{i} + 36\mathbf{j} + \mathbf{C}$
$\Rightarrow \mathbf{C} = 5\mathbf{i} - 4\mathbf{j}$
So $\mathbf{r} = [(t^3 - 4t^2 + 5)\mathbf{i} + (6t + 2t^2 - 4)\mathbf{j}]$ m

Exam-Style Questions — Chapter 1

1 a) $\tan\alpha = \frac{3}{4} \Rightarrow \sin\alpha = \frac{3}{5}$ *[1 mark]*
Resolving vertically, taking down as positive:
$u = u_y = 15\sin\alpha = 9;$ *[1 mark]*
$s = 11;\ a = 9.8;\ t = t$
$s = ut + \frac{1}{2}at^2$ *[1 mark]*
$11 = 9t + 4.9t^2$ *[1 mark]*
Use the quadratic formula to find:
$t = 0.8389... = 0.839$ s (3 s.f.) *[1 mark]*
As usual, the negative value of t has been ignored.

b) Resolving horizontally, taking right as positive:
$u = u_x = 15\cos\alpha = 15 \times \frac{4}{5} = 12;$ *[1 mark]*
$s = s;\ t = 0.8389...$ s
$a = 0$, so $s = ut$
$\Rightarrow OB = 12 \times 0.8389...$ *[1 mark]*
$= 10.067...$ m
So distance HB is $10.067... - 9$
$= 1.07$ m (3 s.f.) *[1 mark]*

c) Resolving horizontally, taking right as positive:

$s = 9$; $u_x = u\cos\alpha$; $a = 0$; $t = t$

$s = u_x t + \frac{1}{2}at^2$ *[1 mark]*

$9 = (u\cos\alpha)t$

$\Rightarrow t = \dfrac{9}{u\cos\alpha}$ — call this **eqn 1**. *[1 mark]*

Now resolve vertically, taking down as positive:

$s = 11$; $u_y = u\sin\alpha$; $a = 9.8$; $t = t$

$s = u_y t + \frac{1}{2}at^2$

$11 = (u\sin\alpha)t + 4.9t^2$ — call this **eqn 2**. *[1 mark]*

t is the same both horizontally and vertically, so substitute **eqn 1** in **eqn 2** to eliminate t:

$11 = 9\left(\dfrac{u\sin\alpha}{u\cos\alpha}\right) + 4.9\left(\dfrac{9}{u\cos\alpha}\right)^2$ *[1 mark]*

$11 = 9\tan\alpha + \dfrac{4.9 \times 81}{u^2\cos^2\alpha}$

$\tan\alpha = \frac{3}{4}$ and $\cos\alpha = \frac{4}{5}$, so substituting and simplifying:

$u^2 = 145.919...$

so $u = 12.1$ ms^{-1} (3 s.f.) *[1 mark]*

2 a) $\mathbf{v} = \dot{\mathbf{r}} = [(6t^2 - 14t)\mathbf{i} + (6t - 12t^2)\mathbf{j}]$ ms^{-1}

[2 marks in total — 1 mark for attempting to differentiate the position vector, 1 mark for correctly differentiating both components]

b) $\mathbf{v} = \left(\frac{6}{4} - \frac{14}{2}\right)\mathbf{i} + \left(\frac{6}{2} - \frac{12}{4}\right)\mathbf{j}$ *[1 mark]*

$= (-5.5\mathbf{i} + 0\mathbf{j})$ ms^{-1}

Speed $= \sqrt{(-5.5)^2 + 0^2} = 5.5$ ms^{-1} *[1 mark]*

The component of velocity in the direction of north is zero, and the component in the direction of east is negative, so the particle is moving due west *[1 mark]*

c) $\mathbf{a} = \dot{\mathbf{v}}$ *[1 mark]*

$= [(12t - 14)\mathbf{i} + (6 - 24t)\mathbf{j}]$ ms^{-2} *[1 mark]*

At $t = 2$, $\mathbf{a} = (10\mathbf{i} - 42\mathbf{j})$ ms^{-2} *[1 mark]*

d) At $t = 2$, $|\mathbf{a}| = a = \sqrt{10^2 + (-42)^2}$

$= 43.174...$ ms^{-2} *[1 mark]*

Now use $F = ma$ to find the force at $t = 2$:

$F = (43.174...)m$ N *[1 mark]*

Magnitude of $\mathbf{F}$ at $t = 2$ is 170 N, so:

$(43.174...)m = 170$

$\Rightarrow m = 3.94$ kg (3 s.f.) *[1 mark]*

e) The vectors $\mathbf{F}$ and $\mathbf{a}$ always act in the same direction, so when $\mathbf{F}$ is acting parallel to $\mathbf{j}$, so is $\mathbf{a}$. *[1 mark]*

So, when $\mathbf{F}$ is acting parallel to $\mathbf{j}$, the component of $\mathbf{a}$ in direction of $\mathbf{i}$ will be zero *[1 mark]*

i.e. $12t - 14 = 0$

$\Rightarrow t = 1.166... = 1.17$ s (3 s.f.) *[1 mark]*

Checking that the $\mathbf{j}$-component of $\mathbf{a}$ is non-zero:

$6 - 24t = 6 - 24(1.166...) = -22 \neq 0$

So $\mathbf{F}$ is acting parallel to $\mathbf{j}$ at this time.

3 Resolving horizontally, taking right as positive:

$u = 20\cos30°$; $s = 30$; $a = 0$; $t = t$

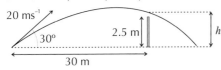

$s = ut + \frac{1}{2}at^2$ *[1 mark]*

$30 = (20\cos30° \times t)$

$t = 1.732...$ s *[1 mark]*

Resolving vertically, taking up as positive:

$s = h$; $u = 20\sin30°$; $t = 1.732...$; $a = -9.8$

$s = ut + \frac{1}{2}at^2$ *[1 mark]*

$h = (20\sin30° \times 1.732...) + (\frac{1}{2} \times -9.8 \times (1.732...)^2)$

$= 2.62$ m (to 3 s.f.) *[1 mark]*

Therefore the ball goes over the crossbar. *[1 mark]*

Assumptions: e.g. ball is a particle / no air or wind resistance / no spin on the ball / g is constant at 9.8 ms^{-2}. *[1 mark]*

4 a) v forms an n-shaped quadratic curve (because the coefficient of t^2 is negative), so v will be at a maximum either when $a = 0$ ms^{-2} (providing that the value of t for which this occurs is in the range $0 \leq t \leq 4$), or at one of the boundaries of the interval.

In the interval $0 \leq t \leq 4$:

$a = \dfrac{dv}{dt} = 9 - 6t$ *[1 mark]*

Set $a = 0$:

$0 = 9 - 6t \Rightarrow t = 1.5$ s *[1 mark]*

So, $v = (9 \times 1.5) - 3(1.5)^2 = 6.75$ ms^{-1} *[1 mark]*

Now check the boundaries:

When $t = 0$, $v = 9(0) - 3(0)^2 = 0$ ms^{-1}

When $t = 4$, $v = 9(4) - 3(4)^2 = -12$ ms^{-1} *[1 mark]*

So the particle's maximum speed in this interval is 12 ms^{-1}. *[1 mark]*

The question asks for the particle's maximum speed, so you're only interested in the magnitude of the particle's velocity — you can ignore the minus sign.

b) (i) $x = \int v \, dt = \frac{9}{2}t^2 - t^3 + c$ $\quad 0 \leq t \leq 4$ *[1 mark]*

When $t = 0$, $x = 0 \Rightarrow c = 0$ *[1 mark]*

$\Rightarrow x = \frac{9}{2}t^2 - t^3$

So, at $t = 4$:

$x = \frac{9}{2}(16) - 64 = 8$ m *[1 mark]*

(ii) $x = \int v \, dt = \left(\dfrac{192}{t}\right) + k$ $\quad t > 4$ *[1 mark]*

When $t = 4$, $s = 8$, so $8 = \left(\dfrac{192}{4}\right) + k$ *[1 mark]*

$\Rightarrow k = -40$ *[1 mark]*

$\Rightarrow x = \left(\dfrac{192}{t}\right) - 40$

When $t = 6$,

$s = \left(\dfrac{192}{6}\right) - 40 = -8$ m *[1 mark]*

5 a) Resolving horizontally, taking right as positive:

$u = 14$; $s = x$, $t = t$, $a = 0$

$s = ut + \frac{1}{2}at^2$ gives:

$x = 14t$, so $t = \frac{x}{14}$ — call this **eqn 1**. *[1 mark]*

Resolving vertically, taking up as positive:

$u = 35$; $s = y$; $t = t$; $a = -9.8$

$s = ut + \frac{1}{2}at^2$

$y = 35t - 4.9t^2$ — call this **eqn 2**. *[1 mark]*

Substitute **eqn 1** into **eqn 2** to eliminate t:

$y = 35\left(\dfrac{x}{14}\right) - 4.9\left(\dfrac{x}{14}\right)^2$ *[1 mark]*

Rearrange:

$y = \dfrac{5x}{2} - \dfrac{x^2}{40}$ *[1 mark]*

If you take down as positive in the working, then you have to use a = 9.8, s = −y (because y is defined as being positive), and u = −35.

b) Use formula from part a) with $y = -30$;
y = −30 because the ball lands 30 m below the point it's hit from and up was taken as positive when deriving the formula.
$-30 = \frac{5x}{2} - \frac{x^2}{40}$ *[1 mark]*
Rearrange: $x^2 - 100x - 1200 = 0$
Solve quadratic using quadratic formula *[1 mark]*
$x = 110.82...$ So $AB = 111$ m (3 s.f.) *[1 mark]*

c) Distance $AH = 110.82... - 7 = 103.82...$ m
Use formula from part a) with $x = 103.82...$ m:
$y = \frac{5 \times 103.82...}{2} - \frac{(103.82...)^2}{40} = -9.935...$ m
[1 mark]
So, when ball is vertically above H, it is 9.935... m below the level of O.
Now resolve vertically, taking up as positive:
$u = u_y = 35$; $s = -9.935...$; $a = -9.8$; $v = v_y$
$v^2 = u^2 + 2as \Rightarrow v_y^2 = 1419.7...$ *[1 mark]*
In this case, you don't need to take the square root to find the value of v_y as you'd have to square it again to find the speed.
No acceleration horizontally, so $v_x = u_x = 14$ ms^{-1}
Speed, $V = \sqrt{v_x^2 + v_y^2}$ *[1 mark]*
$= \sqrt{14^2 + 1419.7...} = 40.2$ ms^{-1} (3 s.f.) *[1 mark]*

Chapter 2: Centres of Mass

1. Particles

Exercise 1.1 — Particles in a line

Q1 $\Sigma mx = \overline{x}\Sigma m$
$(4 \times 3) + (6 \times 5) + (10 \times 7) = \overline{x}(4 + 6 + 10)$
$112 = 20\overline{x}$
$\Rightarrow \overline{x} = 5.6$
i.e. the centre of mass is at the point (5.6, 0)

Q2 $\Sigma mx = \overline{x}\Sigma m$
$(8 \times -3) + (4 \times 1) + (M \times 13) = 5(8 + 4 + M)$
$8M = 80$
$\Rightarrow M = 10$

Q3 $\Sigma mx = \overline{x}\Sigma m$
$(2 \times 1) + (1 \times 2.5) + (1.5 \times 3) = \overline{x}(2 + 1 + 1.5)$
$9 = 4.5\overline{x}$
$\Rightarrow \overline{x} = 2$ m

Q4 $\Sigma mx = \overline{x}\Sigma m$
$(1 \times 0.5) + (4 \times 1.4) + (3 \times 2) = \overline{x}(1 + 4 + 3)$
$12.1 = 8\overline{x}$
$\Rightarrow \overline{x} = 1.5125$ m

Q5 $\Sigma my = \overline{y}\Sigma m$
$(0.8 \times -2) + (1.2 \times -2.6) + (1.8 \times -3.5) + (2.1 \times -3.8)$
$= \overline{y}(0.8 + 1.2 + 1.8 + 2.1)$
$-19 = 5.9\overline{y}$
$\Rightarrow \overline{y} = -3.220...$
So the centre of mass is at (0, −3.22) (3 s.f.)

Q6 $\Sigma my = \overline{y}\Sigma m$
$(3 \times -7) + (2 \times -5) + (4 \times -1) + (1 \times 0) + (4 \times 6)$
$+ (6 \times 8) = \overline{y}(3 + 2 + 4 + 1 + 4 + 6)$
$37 = 20\overline{y}$
$\Rightarrow \overline{y} = 1.85$
So the centre of mass is at (0, 1.85)

Q7 The particles will be placed at the points:
(0, 0), (3, 0), (6, 0), (9, 0) and (12, 0).
$\Sigma mx = \overline{x}\Sigma m$
$(1 \times 0) + (2 \times 3) + (3 \times 6) + (4 \times 9) + (5 \times 12)$
$= \overline{x}(1 + 2 + 3 + 4 + 5)$
$120 = 15\overline{x}$
$\Rightarrow \overline{x} = 8$
So the centre of mass is at (8, 0)

Q8 $\Sigma my = \overline{y}\Sigma m$
$(M \times -3) + (2M \times 1) + (5 \times 2) = 0(M + 2M + 5)$
$-M + 10 = 0$
$\Rightarrow M = 10$

Q9 For string P:
$\Sigma my = \overline{y}\Sigma m$, where y is the distance of each point from the top of the string:
$(5 \times 1) + (4 \times 2) = \overline{y}_P(5 + 4)$
$13 = 9\overline{y}_P$
$\Rightarrow \overline{y}_P = 1.444...$
For string Q:
$\Sigma my = \overline{y}\Sigma m$
$(4 \times 1) + (5 \times 2) = \overline{y}_Q(4 + 5)$
$14 = 9\overline{y}_Q$
$\Rightarrow \overline{y}_Q = 1.555...$
$\overline{y}_Q - \overline{y}_P = 1.555... - 1.444... = 0.111...$
So the required distance is 0.111 m (3 s.f.)

Q10 $\Sigma mx = \overline{x}\Sigma m$, where x is the distance of each point from A:
$(1.5 \times 0) + (0.5 \times 1) + (2 \times 0.5) + (0.2 \times AC)$
$= AC(1.5 + 0.5 + 2 + 0.2)$
$1.5 + 0.2AC = 4.2AC$
$1.5 = 4AC$
$AC = 0.375$ m

Exercise 1.2 — Particles in two dimensions

Q1 $\Sigma m\overline{r} = \overline{r}\Sigma m$
$2\binom{3}{1} + 3\binom{2}{4} + 5\binom{5}{2} = \overline{r}(2 + 3 + 5)$
$\binom{37}{24} = 10\overline{r}$
$\Rightarrow \overline{r} = \binom{3.7}{2.4}$
So the coordinates are (3.7, 2.4)

Q2 $\Sigma m\overline{r} = \overline{r}\Sigma m$
$2\binom{1}{2} + 8\binom{2}{3} + 6\binom{6}{4} = \overline{r}(2 + 8 + 6)$
$\binom{54}{52} = 16\overline{r}$
$\Rightarrow \overline{r} = \binom{3.375}{3.25}$
So the coordinates are (3.375, 3.25)

Q3 $\Sigma m\mathbf{r} = \bar{\mathbf{r}}\Sigma m$

$3\binom{1}{2} + 4\binom{5}{1} + 5\binom{3}{6} + M\binom{0}{1} = (3 + 4 + 5 + M)\binom{1.9}{2.4}$

$\binom{38}{40 + M} = \binom{22.8 + 1.9M}{28.8 + 2.4M}$

Equating horizontal components:

$38 = 22.8 + 1.9M$

$\Rightarrow M = 15.2 \div 1.9 = 8$ kg

You can check your answer using the vertical components.

Q4 **a)** $\Sigma m\mathbf{r} = \bar{\mathbf{r}}\Sigma m$

$3\binom{2}{1} + 4\binom{4}{0} + M_1\binom{-4}{0} + M_2\binom{0}{-5}$

$= (3 + 4 + M_1 + M_2)\binom{0}{0}$

$\binom{22 - 4M_1}{3 - 5M_2} = \binom{0}{0}$

Equating horizontal components:

$22 - 4M_1 = 0$

$\Rightarrow M_1 = 5.5$ kg

b) Equating vertical components:

$3 - 5M_2 = 0$

$\Rightarrow M_2 = 0.6$ kg

Q5

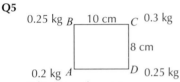

0.25 kg *B* — 10 cm — *C* 0.3 kg

8 cm

0.2 kg *A* — *D* 0.25 kg

Taking *A* as the origin:

$\Sigma m\mathbf{r} = \bar{\mathbf{r}}\Sigma m$

$0.2\binom{0}{0} + 0.25\binom{0}{8} + 0.3\binom{10}{8} + 0.25\binom{10}{0}$

$= (0.2 + 0.25 + 0.3 + 0.25)\bar{\mathbf{r}}$

$\binom{5.5}{4.4} = 1\bar{\mathbf{r}}$

$\Rightarrow \bar{\mathbf{r}} = \binom{5.5}{4.4}$

Using Pythagoras' theorem:

Distance from $A = |\bar{\mathbf{r}}| = \sqrt{5.5^2 + 4.4^2} = 7.04$ cm (3 s.f.)

Q6 $\Sigma m\mathbf{r} = \bar{\mathbf{r}}\Sigma m$

$2.5\binom{-3}{1} + 2\binom{-2}{-4} + 3\binom{4}{-3} + 1.5\binom{2}{3} + 1\mathbf{r}_5$

$= (2.5 + 2 + 3 + 1.5 + 1)\binom{0.65}{-0.8}$

$\binom{3.5}{-10} + \mathbf{r}_5 = \binom{6.5}{-8}$

$\Rightarrow \mathbf{r}_5 = \binom{6.5}{-8} - \binom{3.5}{-10} = \binom{3}{2}$

So the particle should be placed at (3, 2).

Q7 **a)**

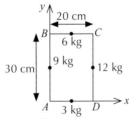

y

20 cm

B — *C*

6 kg

30 cm   9 kg   12 kg

A 3 kg *D* → *x*

$\Sigma m\mathbf{r} = \bar{\mathbf{r}}\Sigma m$

$9\binom{0}{15} + 6\binom{10}{30} + 12\binom{20}{15} + 3\binom{10}{0}$

$= (9 + 6 + 12 + 3)\bar{\mathbf{r}}$

$\binom{330}{495} = 30\bar{\mathbf{r}}$

$\Rightarrow \bar{\mathbf{r}} = \binom{11}{16.5}$

So the coordinates of the COM are (11, 16.5).

b) The *x*-coordinate of the centre of mass of the system is now $x = 10$.

$\Sigma mx = \bar{x}\Sigma m$

From part a), the *x*-coordinate of the centre of mass of the system without the *M* kg particle is 11, and its mass is 30 kg, so:

$(30 \times 11) + (M \times 0) = (30 + M) \times 10$

$330 = 300 + 10M$

$30 = 10M$

$\Rightarrow M = 3$ kg

You could also answer part b) using symmetry —
for the new centre of mass to lie on EF, the sum of the
masses of the particles on AB must equal the mass of
the particle on CD. i.e. $9 + M = 12 \Rightarrow M = 3$ kg.

Q8 **a)** *E* is the midpoint of *A*(0, 0) and *C*(0.8, 0.6).
So *E* has coordinates (0.4, 0.3).
F is the midpoint of *B*(0, 0.6) and *D*(1.2, 0).
So *F* has coordinates (0.6, 0.3).

b) $\Sigma m\mathbf{r} = \bar{\mathbf{r}}\Sigma m$

$0.5\binom{0.4}{0.3} + 0.75\binom{0.6}{0.3} + 0.25\binom{0.8}{0.6} + 1\binom{1.2}{0}$

$= (0.5 + 0.75 + 0.25 + 1)\bar{\mathbf{r}}$

$\binom{2.05}{0.525} = 2.5\bar{\mathbf{r}}$

$\Rightarrow \bar{\mathbf{r}} = \binom{0.82}{0.21}$

So the coordinates of the COM are (0.82, 0.21).

c) Call the new COM $\binom{p}{q}$.

$\Sigma m\mathbf{r} = \bar{\mathbf{r}}\Sigma m$

$2.5\binom{0.82}{0.21} + M\binom{0}{0.6} = (2.5 + M)\binom{p}{q}$

$\binom{2.05}{0.525 + 0.6M} = (2.5 + M)\binom{p}{q}$

Equating horizontal components:

$2.05 = p(2.5 + M)$ **eqn1**

Equating vertical components:

$0.525 + 0.6M = q(2.5 + M)$ **eqn2**

The gradient of *AC* is $\frac{0.6}{0.8} = \frac{3}{4}$, so the equation of the line *AC* is $y = \frac{3}{4}x$.

$\binom{p}{q}$ lies on this line, so $q = \frac{3}{4}p$, or $\frac{p}{q} = \frac{4}{3}$.

Dividing **eqn1** by **eqn2**:

$\frac{2.05}{0.525 + 0.6M} = \frac{p(2.5 + M)}{q(2.5 + M)}$

$\frac{2.05}{0.525 + 0.6M} = \frac{4}{3}$

$6.15 = 2.1 + 2.4M$

$\Rightarrow M = 1.6875$ kg

d) Using **eqn1**:

$2.05 = p(2.5 + M)$

$p = 2.05 \div (2.5 + 1.6875) = 0.4895...$

$q = \frac{3}{4}p = 0.3671...$

So the COM has coordinates (0.490, 0.367) (3 s.f.)

2. Laminas

Exercise 2.1 — Uniform laminas

Q1 The centre of mass is at the square's centre.
$\bar{x}$ is the *x*-coordinate of the midpoint of *AD* (or *BC*):
$\bar{x} = (1 + 4) \div 2 = 2.5$
$\bar{y}$ is the *y*-coordinate of the midpoint of *AB* (or *CD*):
$\bar{y} = (2 + 5) \div 2 = 3.5$
So the coordinates of the COM are (2.5, 3.5).

Q2 $(\overline{x}, \overline{y}) = \left(\frac{x_1 + x_2 + x_3}{3}, \frac{y_1 + y_2 + y_3}{3}\right)$

$= \left(\frac{(-3) + (-5) + (-7)}{3}, \frac{(-2) + (-6) + (-1)}{3}\right) = (-5, -3)$

Q3 **a)** $(\overline{x}, \overline{y}) = \left(\frac{2 + 4 + 6}{3}, \frac{5 + 1 + 3}{3}\right) = (4, 3)$

b) $(\overline{x}, \overline{y}) = \left(\frac{-3 + 2}{2}, \frac{-1 + 2}{2}\right) = (-0.5, 0.5)$

c) $(\overline{x}, \overline{y}) = \left(\frac{(-2) + 4 + 4}{3}, \frac{(-4) + (-4) + (-2)}{3}\right)$

$= (2, -3.33)$ (3 s.f.)

Q4 COM is at centre of circle — i.e. at midpoint of AB.

$(-5 + 1) \div 2 = -2$

$(-5 + 3) \div 2 = -1$

So coordinates of COM are $(-2, -1)$.

Q5 $r = 16$, $2\alpha = \pi$ $\Rightarrow$ $\alpha = \frac{\pi}{2}$

$\frac{2r\sin\alpha}{3\alpha} = \frac{32}{3\pi/2} = \frac{64}{3\pi} = 6.79$ cm (3 s.f.)

Q6

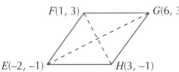

F(1, 3)   G(6, 3)

E(-2, -1)   H(3, -1)

The centre of mass of the parallelogram is the point that the diagonals intersect — i.e. the midpoint of EG or the midpoint of FH.

Midpoint of EG is at $\left(\frac{-2 + 6}{2}, \frac{-1 + 3}{2}\right) = (2, 1)$

So the COM is at $(2, 1)$.

Q7 $(\overline{x}, \overline{y}) = \left(\frac{x_1 + x_2 + x_3}{3}, \frac{y_1 + y_2 + y_3}{3}\right)$

$(2, 0) = \left(\frac{-2 + 7 + z_1}{3}, \frac{-3 + 0 + z_2}{3}\right)$

Equating x-coordinates:

$2 = \frac{-2 + 7 + z_1}{3}$

$6 = 5 + z_1$

$\Rightarrow z_1 = 1$

Equating y-coordinates:

$0 = \frac{-3 + 0 + z_2}{3}$

$0 = -3 + z_2$

$\Rightarrow z_2 = 3$

Q8 $r = 12$, $2\alpha = 90°$ $\Rightarrow$ $\alpha = 45° = \frac{\pi}{4}$ radians

$\frac{2r\sin\alpha}{3\alpha} = \frac{24/\sqrt{2}}{3\pi/4} = 7.20$ cm (3 s.f.)

Q9

2.5 cm   6.5 cm   5 cm

$\overline{x}$

Using Pythagoras' theorem:

$2.5^2 + x^2 = 6.5^2$

$x^2 = 36$

$x = 6$ cm

So the length of the longer side is 12 cm.

Q10 **a)** $r = 5$, $2\alpha = \frac{\pi}{3}$ $\Rightarrow$ $\alpha = \frac{\pi}{6}$

$\frac{2r\sin\alpha}{3\alpha} = \frac{5}{\pi/2} = 3.18$ cm (3 s.f.)

b) $r = 5$, $2\alpha = 2\pi - \frac{\pi}{3} = \frac{5\pi}{3}$ $\Rightarrow$ $\alpha = \frac{5\pi}{6}$

$\frac{2r\sin\alpha}{3\alpha} = \frac{10\sin(5\pi/6)}{5\pi/2} = 0.637$ cm (3 s.f.)

Q11 $2\alpha = \pi$ $\Rightarrow$ $\alpha = \frac{\pi}{2}$

$\frac{2r\sin\alpha}{3\alpha} = 5$

$\frac{2r}{3\pi/2} = 5$

$2r = \frac{15\pi}{2}$

$\Rightarrow r = \frac{15\pi}{4} = 11.8$ cm (3 s.f.)

Q12

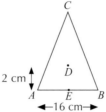

C

2 cm $\dot{D}$

A   E   B

←16 cm→

CE is a median of the triangle. D is $\frac{2}{3}$ of the way from C to E, so $CE = 3DE = 6$ cm.

Using Pythagoras' theorem on the triangle ACE:

$AC = \sqrt{8^2 + 6^2} = 10$ cm

Q13 $2\alpha = \frac{\pi}{5}$ $\Rightarrow$ $\alpha = \frac{\pi}{10}$

$\frac{2r\sin\alpha}{3\alpha} = 4.6$

$\frac{(0.6180...)r}{3\pi/10} = 4.6$

$(0.6180...)r = \frac{3\pi}{10} \times 4.6$

$\Rightarrow r = 7.014...$

So the required coordinates are $(7.01, 0)$ (3 s.f.)

Exercise 2.2 — Loaded laminas and composite shapes

Q1 By symmetry, the centre of mass of the lamina is at

$\left(\frac{1 + 7}{2}, \frac{1 + 7}{2}\right) = (4, 4)$

$\Sigma m\mathbf{r} = \overline{\mathbf{r}}\Sigma m$

$4.5\binom{4}{4} + 4\binom{5}{4} + 1.5\binom{2}{2} = \overline{\mathbf{r}}(4.5 + 4 + 1.5)$

$\binom{41}{37} = 10\overline{\mathbf{r}}$

$\Rightarrow \overline{\mathbf{r}} = \binom{4.1}{3.7}$

So the coordinates of the COM are $(4.1, 3.7)$.

Q2 Call the larger rectangle A and the smaller rectangle B. By symmetry, the COM of A is at $(2, 2.5)$ cm and the COM of B is at $(5, 3.5)$ cm.

The area of A is $5 \times 4 = 20$ cm^2 and the area of B is $3 \times 2 = 6$ cm^2. The rectangles are made from the same material, so their areas are proportional to their masses.

$\Sigma m\mathbf{r} = \overline{\mathbf{r}}\Sigma m$

$20\binom{2}{2.5} + 6\binom{5}{3.5} = \overline{\mathbf{r}}(20 + 6)$

$\binom{70}{71} = 26\overline{\mathbf{r}}$

$\Rightarrow \overline{\mathbf{r}} = \binom{2.692...}{2.730...}$ cm

So the coordinates of the COM are $(2.69, 2.73)$ cm (3 s.f.)

Q3 Call the original lamina A and the removed circle B.

By symmetry, the COM of A is at $\left(\frac{1+7}{2}, \frac{2+7}{2}\right)$
$= (4, 4.5)$ and its area is $(7 - 1) \times (7 - 2) = 30$.

By symmetry, the COM of B is at $(4, 5)$ and its area is $(\pi \times 1^2) = \pi$. A is uniform, so the masses of A and B are proportional to their areas.

Using the removal method:

$m_A r_A - m_B r_B = (m_A - m_B)\bar{r}$

$30\binom{4}{4.5} - \pi\binom{4}{5} = (30 - \pi)\bar{r}$

$\binom{120 - 4\pi}{135 - 5\pi} = (30 - \pi)\bar{r}$

$\Rightarrow \bar{r} = \binom{4}{4.441...}$

So the coordinates of the centre of mass of the resulting shape are $(4, 4.44)$ (3 s.f.)

The line $x = 4$ is a line of symmetry here — the COM of both shapes has an x-coordinate of 4, so you could've used symmetry to find the x-coordinate of the resultant shape, rather than performing any calculations.

Q4 Split the letter up as shown:

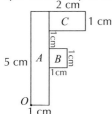

Taking O as the origin, by symmetry, A has COM $(0.5, 2.5)$ and area 5 cm². Similarly, B has COM $(1.5, 2.5)$ and area 1 cm², and C has COM $(2, 4.5)$ and area 2 cm². The whole shape is cut from one sheet of card, so the masses of A, B and C are proportional to their areas.

$\Sigma m r = \bar{r} \Sigma m$

$5\binom{0.5}{2.5} + 1\binom{1.5}{2.5} + 2\binom{2}{4.5} = \bar{r}(5 + 1 + 2)$

$\binom{8}{24} = 8\bar{r}$

$\Rightarrow \bar{r} = \frac{1}{8}\binom{8}{24} = \binom{1}{3}$

This is the position vector of the COM of the letter relative to O. You need to find the distance of the COM from O. Using Pythagoras' theorem:

$|\bar{r}| = \sqrt{1^2 + 3^2} = 3.16$ cm (3 s.f.)

You can split the shape up any way you like — it doesn't have to be in the way shown here.

Q5 a) Let h be the triangle's height.

The COM of the triangle is $\frac{2}{3}$ of the way down from Q to the triangle's base, i.e. $\frac{2}{3}h$ cm down from Q, or $\frac{1}{3}h$ cm up from the triangle's base.

The triangle's area is $\frac{1}{2} \times 12 \times h = 6h$ cm².

The COM of the semicircle is $\frac{2r\sin\alpha}{3\alpha}$ down from the triangle's base, where $r = 6$, $2\alpha = \pi \Rightarrow \alpha = \frac{\pi}{2}$.

$\frac{2r\sin\alpha}{3\alpha} = \frac{12}{3\pi/2} = \frac{8}{\pi}$, so the COM of the semicircle is $\frac{8}{\pi}$ cm down from the triangle's base.

The triangle and semicircle are made from the same material, so their masses are proportional to their areas.

The semicircle's area is $\frac{1}{2} \times \pi \times 6^2 = 18\pi$ cm².

The COM of the composite shape is at the midpoint of the base of the triangle. Model the triangle and semicircle as particles positioned at their individual centres of mass. Taking the midpoint of the base of the triangle as the origin:

$y_{\text{triangle}} = \frac{1}{3}h$ and $y_{\text{semicircle}} = -\frac{8}{\pi}$.

$\Sigma my = \bar{y}\Sigma m$

$(6h \times \frac{1}{3}h) + (18\pi \times -\frac{8}{\pi}) = 0 \times (6h + 18\pi)$

$2h^2 = 144$

$h^2 = 72$

$h = \sqrt{72} = 8.49$ cm (3 s.f.)

b) Taking Q as the origin:

$\Sigma my = \bar{y}\Sigma m$

$(2.6 \times \sqrt{72}) + (1.4 \times 0) = \bar{y}(2.6 + 1.4)$

$\Rightarrow \bar{y} = 22.061... \div 4 = 5.52$ cm (3 s.f.)

Q6 Let K be the larger disc and L be the smaller disc which is removed. Let A be the origin.

By symmetry, the COM of K is a horizontal distance of 12 cm from A.

The area of K is $\pi \times 12^2 = 144\pi$ cm².

By symmetry, the COM of L is a horizontal distance of 8 cm from A:

The area of L is $\pi \times 4^2 = 16\pi$ cm².

K is uniform, so the masses of K and L are proportional to their areas.

Using the removal method:

$m_K x_K - m_L x_L = \bar{x}(m_K - m_L)$

$(144\pi \times 12) - (16\pi \times 8) = AC(144\pi - 16\pi)$

$1600\pi = 128\pi AC$

$\Rightarrow AC = 12.5$ cm

Q7 The two rectangles form a square with its centre of mass 0.9 m from the base of the doors (by symmetry) and with area $1.8 \times 1.8 = 3.24$ m².

Considering the quarter-circles:

$r = 0.9$, $2\alpha = \frac{\pi}{2} \Rightarrow \alpha = \frac{\pi}{4}$

$\frac{2r\sin\alpha}{3\alpha} = \frac{1.8/\sqrt{2}}{3\pi/4} = \frac{1.2\sqrt{2}}{\pi}$

Using trigonometry:

$\sin\left(\frac{\pi}{4}\right) = \frac{y}{(1.2\sqrt{2}/\pi)}$

$\Rightarrow y = \frac{1}{\sqrt{2}} \times \frac{1.2\sqrt{2}}{\pi} = \frac{1.2}{\pi}$

So the COM of each quarter-circle is $\left(1.8 + \frac{1.2}{\pi}\right)$ m from the base of the doors.

Each quarter-circle has area $\frac{1}{4}\pi r^2 = \frac{1}{4} \times \pi \times 0.9^2$
$= 0.2025\pi$ m²
The door is modelled as a uniform lamina, so its mass is proportional to its area.
$\Sigma my = \bar{y}\Sigma m$
$(3.24 \times 0.9) + 2\left(0.2025\pi \times \left(1.8 + \frac{1.2}{\pi}\right)\right)$
$= \bar{y}(3.24 + 2(0.2025\pi))$
$\Rightarrow \bar{y} = 1.2614... = 1.26$ m (3 s.f.)
It's best to keep values in terms of π and $\sqrt{2}$ all the way through your working — but you can write them as decimals if you prefer, as long as you don't round them. It can be quite tricky to keep track of all the different decimals that way though.

Q8 a) Let P be the triangle and Q be the rectangle.
Let A be the origin.
Taking $A(0, 0)$, $B(0, 8)$ and $C(6, 0)$, the COM of P is at $\left(\frac{0+0+6}{3}, \frac{0+8+0}{3}\right) = \left(2, \frac{8}{3}\right)$.
The area of P is $\frac{1}{2} \times 6 \times 8 = 24$ cm².
By symmetry, the COM of Q is at $(2, 1.5)$.
The area of Q is 2 cm². P is uniform, so the masses of P and Q are proportional to their lengths. Using the removal method:
$m_P x_P - m_Q x_Q = \bar{x}(m_P - m_Q)$
$(24 \times 2) - (2 \times 2) = \bar{x}(24 - 2)$
$44 = 22\bar{x}$
$\Rightarrow \bar{x} = 2$ cm
You can also do this part using symmetry — the centres of mass of P and Q are 2 cm from AB, so the centre of mass of the template is also 2 cm from AB.

b) Using the removal method, with the y-coordinates found in part a):
$m_P y_P - m_Q y_Q = \bar{y}(m_P - m_Q)$
$(24 \times \frac{8}{3}) - (2 \times 1.5) = \bar{y}(24 - 2)$
$61 = 22\bar{y}$
$\Rightarrow \bar{y} = 2.772... = 2.77$ cm (3 s.f.)

c) Using $\Sigma mx = \bar{x}\Sigma m$, where x is measured as a horizontal distance from AB:
$m_{template}x_{template} + m_{particle}x_{particle} = \bar{x}(m_{template} + m_{particle})$
$(0.3 \times 2) + (m \times 6) = 3.5 \times (0.3 + m)$
$2.5m = 0.45$
$\Rightarrow m = 0.18$ kg

d) Using $\Sigma my = \bar{y}\Sigma m$, where y is measured as a vertical distance from AC:
$m_{template}y_{template} + m_{particle}y_{particle} = \bar{y}(m_{template} + m_{particle})$
$(0.3 \times 2.772...) + (0.18 \times 0) = \bar{y}(0.3 + 0.18)$
$0.831... = 0.48\bar{y}$
$\bar{y} = 1.73$ cm (3 s.f.)

3. Frameworks
Exercise 3.1 — Frameworks

Q1 a) Using the fact that all sides are made of the same uniform wire, the mass of each side is proportional to its length. By symmetry, the COM of each side is at its midpoint.
Let x be the distance of the COM of each side from AB.
$\Sigma mx = \bar{x}\Sigma m$
$m_{AB}x_{AB} + m_{BC}x_{BC} + m_{CD}x_{CD} + m_{DE}x_{DE} + m_{EF}x_{EF} + m_{AF}x_{AF} = \bar{x}(m_{AB} + m_{BC} + m_{CD} + m_{DE} + m_{EF} + m_{AF})$
$(5 \times 0) + (4 \times 2) + (1 \times 4) + (3 \times 2.5) + (4 \times 1) + (1 \times 0.5) = \bar{x}(5 + 4 + 1 + 3 + 4 + 1)$
$24 = 18\bar{x}$
$\Rightarrow \bar{x} = 1.33$ cm (3 s.f.)

b) Let y be the distance of the COM of each side from AF.
$\Sigma my = \bar{y}\Sigma m$
$m_{AB}y_{AB} + m_{BC}y_{BC} + m_{CD}y_{CD} + m_{DE}y_{DE} + m_{EF}y_{EF} + m_{AF}y_{AF} = \bar{y}(m_{AB} + m_{BC} + m_{CD} + m_{DE} + m_{EF} + m_{AF})$
$(5 \times 2.5) + (4 \times 5) + (1 \times 4.5) + (3 \times 4) + (4 \times 2) + (1 \times 0) = \bar{y}(5 + 4 + 1 + 3 + 4 + 1)$
$57 = 18\bar{y}$
$\Rightarrow \bar{y} = 3.17$ cm (3 s.f.)

Q2 a) All sides are made from the same uniform wire, so the mass of each side is proportional to its length. By symmetry, the COM of each side is at its midpoint. So:
$m_{AB} = 4, y_{AB} = 2$; $m_{BC} = 5, y_{BC} = 2$; $m_{AC} = 3, y_{AC} = 0$
$\Sigma my = \bar{y}\Sigma m$
$(4 \times 2) + (5 \times 2) + (3 \times 0) = \bar{y}(4 + 5 + 3)$
$18 = 12\bar{y}$
$\Rightarrow \bar{y} = 1.5$ m

b) The mass of the framework is $4 + 5 + 3 = 12$ kg.
$\Sigma my = \bar{y}\Sigma m$
$m_{frame}y_{frame} + m_{particle}y_{particle} = \bar{y}(m_{frame} + m_{particle})$
$(12 \times 1.5) + (M \times 4) = 2.4 \times (12 + M)$
$18 + 4M = 28.8 + 2.4M$
$1.6M = 10.8$
$\Rightarrow M = 6.75$ kg

c) First need to find distance of COM of unloaded framework ABC from AB.
$m_{AB} = 4, x_{AB} = 0$; $m_{BC} = 5, x_{BC} = 1.5$; $m_{AC} = 3, x_{AC} = 1.5$
$\Sigma mx = \bar{x}\Sigma m$
$(4 \times 0) + (5 \times 1.5) + (3 \times 1.5) = \bar{x}_{unloaded}(4 + 5 + 3)$
$12 = 12\bar{x}_{unloaded}$
$\Rightarrow \bar{x}_{unloaded} = 1$ m
Now considering the loaded framework:
$\Sigma mx = \bar{x}_{loaded}\Sigma m$
$m_{frame}x_{frame} + m_{particle}x_{particle} = \bar{x}_{loaded}(m_{frame} + m_{particle})$
$(12 \times 1) + (6.75 \times 0) = \bar{x}_{loaded}(12 + 6.75)$
$12 = 18.75\bar{x}_{loaded}$
$\Rightarrow \bar{x}_{loaded} = 0.64$ m
You could also have answered this question by modelling each side of the framework as a particle positioned at the side's COM, then combining them with the M kg particle and using the formula for the COM of a group of particles.

Q3

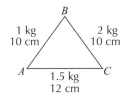

The rods are uniform, so you can use symmetry to say that the COM of each rod is at its midpoint.

Using Pythagoras' theorem, the height of the triangle is $\sqrt{10^2 - 6^2} = 8$ cm, so $y_{AB} = y_{BC} = 4$ cm, where y_{AB} and y_{BC} are the vertical distances of the midpoints of AB and BC from AC.

$\Sigma my = \overline{y}\,\Sigma m$

$m_{AB}y_{AB} + m_{BC}y_{BC} + m_{AC}y_{AC} = \overline{y}(m_{AB} + m_{BC} + m_{AC})$

$(1 \times 4) + (2 \times 4) + (1.5 \times 0) = \overline{y}(1 + 2 + 1.5)$

$12 = 4.5\,\overline{y}$

$\Rightarrow \overline{y} = 2.67$ cm (3 s.f.)

Q4 a) The rods are uniform, so you can use symmetry to say that the COM of each rod is at its midpoint.

$\Sigma mx = \overline{x}\,\Sigma m$

$m_{AB}x_{AB} + m_{BC}x_{BC} + m_{CD}x_{CD} + m_{AD}x_{AD} = \overline{x}(m_{AB} + m_{BC} + m_{CD} + m_{AD})$

$(M \times 0.12) + (2M \times 0.24) + (1.5M \times 0.12) + (m_{AD} \times 0) = 0.15 \times (M + 2M + 1.5M + m_{AD})$

$0.78M = 0.15 \times (4.5M + m_{AD})$

$0.105M = 0.15m_{AD}$

$\Rightarrow m_{AD} = 0.7M$ kg

b) $\Sigma my = \overline{y}\,\Sigma m$

$m_{AB}y_{AB} + m_{BC}y_{BC} + m_{CD}y_{CD} + m_{AD}y_{AD} = \overline{y}(m_{AB} + m_{BC} + m_{CD} + m_{AD})$

$(M \times 0) + (2M \times 0.09) + (1.5M \times 0.18) + (0.7M \times 0.09) = \overline{y}(M + 2M + 1.5M + 0.7M)$

$0.513 = 5.2\,\overline{y}$

$\Rightarrow \overline{y} = 0.0987$ m (3 s.f.)

Q5 a) The mass of each rod is proportional to its length. The rods are uniform, so you can use symmetry to say that the COM of each rod is at its midpoint.

Let x be the horizontal distance of the COM of each side of the framework from A.

$\Sigma mx = \overline{x}\,\Sigma m$

$m_{AB}x_{AB} + m_{BC}x_{BC} + m_{CD}x_{CD} + m_{DE}x_{DE} = \overline{x}(m_{AB} + m_{BC} + m_{CD} + m_{DE})$

$(9 \times 4.5) + (6 \times 9) + (9 \times 4.5) + (d \times 0) = 5.4 \times (9 + 6 + 9 + d)$

$135 = 129.6 + 5.4d$

$5.4 = 5.4d$

$\Rightarrow d = 1$ cm

b) Let y be the vertical distance of the COM of each side of the framework from A.

$y_{DE} = 6 - (1 \div 2) = 5.5$ cm

$\Sigma my = \overline{y}\,\Sigma m$

$m_{AB}y_{AB} + m_{BC}y_{BC} + m_{CD}y_{CD} + m_{DE}y_{DE} = \overline{y}(m_{AB} + m_{BC} + m_{CD} + m_{DE})$

$(9 \times 0) + (6 \times 3) + (9 \times 6) + (1 \times 5.5) = \overline{y}(9 + 6 + 9 + 1)$

$77.5 = 25\,\overline{y}$

$\Rightarrow \overline{y} = 3.1$ cm

Q6 a) The mass of each rod is proportional to its length. The rods are uniform, so, by symmetry, the COM of each rod is at its midpoint.

You need to find length of EF, so, using Pythagoras' theorem:

$EF = \sqrt{12^2 + 9^2} = 15$ cm

Let **r** be the position vector of the COM of each side of the framework relative to A.

$\mathbf{r}_{AC} = \begin{pmatrix} 0 \\ -7.5 \end{pmatrix};\ \mathbf{r}_{AB} = \begin{pmatrix} 10 \\ 0 \end{pmatrix};\ \mathbf{r}_{EF} = \mathbf{r}_{AF} = \begin{pmatrix} 6 \\ -4.5 \end{pmatrix};\ \mathbf{r}_{BD} = \begin{pmatrix} 20 \\ -2 \end{pmatrix}$

$\Sigma m\mathbf{r} = \overline{\mathbf{r}}\,\Sigma m$

$m_{AC}\mathbf{r}_{AC} + m_{AB}\mathbf{r}_{AB} + m_{EF}\mathbf{r}_{EF} + m_{BD}\mathbf{r}_{BD} = \overline{\mathbf{r}}(m_{AC} + m_{AB} + m_{EF} + m_{BD})$

$15\begin{pmatrix} 0 \\ -7.5 \end{pmatrix} + 20\begin{pmatrix} 10 \\ 0 \end{pmatrix} + 15\begin{pmatrix} 6 \\ -4.5 \end{pmatrix} + 4\begin{pmatrix} 20 \\ -2 \end{pmatrix} = \overline{\mathbf{r}}(15 + 20 + 15 + 4)$

$\begin{pmatrix} 370 \\ -188 \end{pmatrix} = 54\overline{\mathbf{r}}$

$\Rightarrow \overline{\mathbf{r}} = \frac{1}{54}\begin{pmatrix} 370 \\ -188 \end{pmatrix} = \begin{pmatrix} 6.851... \\ -3.481... \end{pmatrix}$ cm

This is the position vector of the COM of the bracket relative to A. The distance from A can be found using Pythagoras' theorem:

distance $= \sqrt{(6.851...)^2 + (-3.481...)^2}$
$= 7.69$ cm (3 s.f.)

b) Let the mass of the bracket be 1 and the mass of the basket be 2.

$\Sigma m\mathbf{r} = \overline{\mathbf{r}}\,\Sigma m$

$m_{\text{bracket}}\mathbf{r}_{\text{bracket}} + m_{\text{basket}}\mathbf{r}_{\text{basket}} = \overline{\mathbf{r}}(m_{\text{bracket}} + m_{\text{basket}})$

$1\begin{pmatrix} 6.851... \\ -3.481... \end{pmatrix} + 2\begin{pmatrix} 20 \\ -4 \end{pmatrix} = \overline{\mathbf{r}}(1 + 2)$

$\begin{pmatrix} 46.851... \\ -11.481... \end{pmatrix} = 3\overline{\mathbf{r}}$

$\Rightarrow \overline{\mathbf{r}} = \frac{1}{3}\begin{pmatrix} 46.851... \\ -11.481... \end{pmatrix} = \begin{pmatrix} 15.617... \\ -3.827... \end{pmatrix}$ cm

$\Rightarrow$ distance $= \sqrt{(15.617...)^2 + (-3.827...)^2}$
$= 16.1$ cm (3 s.f.)

Q7 a) The rods are uniform, so, by symmetry, the COM of each rod is at its midpoint.

Let x be the horizontal distance of the COM of each mass from A.

$\Sigma mx = \overline{x}\,\Sigma m$

$m_{AB}x_{AB} + m_{CD}x_{CD} + m_{P}x_{P} + m_{Q}x_{Q} = \overline{x}(m_{AB} + m_{CD} + m_{P} + m_{Q})$

$(M \times 6) + (M \times 6) + (4M \times 0) + (6M \times x_{Q}) = 6 \times (M + M + 4M + 6M)$

$12M + 6Mx_{Q} = 72M$

$6x_{Q} = 60$

$\Rightarrow x_{Q} = 10$ cm

So Q should be attached 10 cm from A.

You could also answer this by taking moments about C and ignoring the rods.

b) (i) Let y be the vertical distance of the COM of each mass from C.

$\Sigma my = \overline{y}\,\Sigma m$

$m_{AB}y_{AB} + m_{CD}y_{CD} + m_{P}y_{P} + m_{Q}y_{Q} = \overline{y}(m_{AB} + m_{CD} + m_{P} + m_{Q})$

$(M \times 0) + (M \times 6) + (4M \times 0) + (6M \times y_{Q}) = 4 \times (M + M + 4M + 6M)$

$6M + 6My_{Q} = 48M$

$6y_{Q} = 42$

$\Rightarrow y_{Q} = 7$ cm

So Q should be attached 7 cm from C.

(ii) Let x be the horizontal distance of the COM of each mass from CD.

$\Sigma mx = \bar{x}\Sigma m$

$m_{AB}x_{AB} + m_{CD}x_{CD} + m_P x_P + m_Q x_Q = \bar{x}(m_{AB} + m_{CD} + m_P + m_Q)$

$(M \times 0) + (M \times 0) + (4M \times -6) + (6M \times 0) = \bar{x} \times (M + M + 4M + 6M)$

$-24M = 12M\bar{x}$

$\Rightarrow \bar{x} = -2$ cm

So the COM is 2 cm from CD.

Exercise 3.2 — Arcs

Q1 Split the framework into two parts — let A be the arc and B be the straight side. Both made from the same wire, so the masses of A and B are proportional to their lengths. By symmetry, the COM of framework lies on the vertical line of symmetry passing through O.

Finding the COM of A:

$r = 5$, $2\alpha = \pi \Rightarrow \alpha = \dfrac{\pi}{2}$

$\dfrac{r\sin\alpha}{\alpha} = \dfrac{5}{\pi/2} = \dfrac{10}{\pi}$

So the COM of A is $\dfrac{10}{\pi}$ cm from O.

The length of A is $\pi r = 5\pi$ cm.

The COM of B is 0 cm from O, and B has length 10 cm.

$\Sigma my = \bar{y}\Sigma m$

$\left(5\pi \times \dfrac{10}{\pi}\right) + (10 \times 0) = \bar{y}(5\pi + 10)$

$\bar{y} = 50 \div (5\pi + 10) = 1.944... = 1.94$ cm (3 s.f.)

Q2 a) $r = 12$, $2\alpha = \dfrac{2\pi}{3} \Rightarrow \alpha = \dfrac{\pi}{3}$

$\dfrac{r\sin\alpha}{\alpha} = \dfrac{6\sqrt{3}}{\pi/3} = \dfrac{18\sqrt{3}}{\pi} = 9.923...$

So the COM is 9.92 cm (3 s.f.) from O.

b)

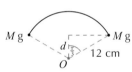

The vertical distance of each particle from O, labelled d in the diagram, is $d = 12\cos\left(\dfrac{\pi}{3}\right) = 6$ cm.

$\Sigma my = \bar{y}\Sigma m$

$(100 \times 9.923...) + 2(M \times 6) = 8(100 + 2M)$

$992.3... + 12M = 800 + 16M$

$192.3... = 4M$

$\Rightarrow M = 48.1$ g (3 s.f.)

Q3 By symmetry, the COM of each side is at its midpoint (the wires are uniform). The mass of each side is proportional to its length.

The COM of the semicircular arc is $\dfrac{r\sin\alpha}{\alpha}$ cm vertically below E, where $r = 3$ and $2\alpha = \pi \Rightarrow \alpha = \dfrac{\pi}{2}$

$\dfrac{r\sin\alpha}{\alpha} = \dfrac{3}{\pi/2} = \dfrac{6}{\pi}$

The length of the arc is $\pi r = 3\pi$ cm.

Let y be the vertical distance of the COM of each side from E. The COM of the framework, $\bar{y}$, is 3 cm below E (this is the radius of the semicircle).

$\Sigma my = \bar{y}\Sigma m$

$m_{arc}y_{arc} + m_{AB}y_{AB} + m_{BC}y_{BC} + m_{CD}y_{CD} = 3(m_{arc} + m_{AB} + m_{BC} + m_{CD})$

$\left(3\pi \times \dfrac{6}{\pi}\right) + \left(l \times \dfrac{l}{2}\right) + (6 \times l) + \left(l \times \dfrac{l}{2}\right) = 3(3\pi + l + 6 + l)$

$18 + l^2 + 6l = 6l + 18 + 9\pi$

$l^2 = 9\pi$

$\Rightarrow l = 5.317... = 5.32$ cm (3 s.f.)

Q4 a) The wires are uniform, so the COM of each wire is at its midpoint. The mass of each wire is proportional to its length.

Let A be the 20-unit radius arc, B be the 15-unit radius arc and C be the 5-unit radius arc.

A is centred at $(0, 0)$. Its COM is $\dfrac{r\sin\alpha}{\alpha}$ vertically above this, where $r = 20$ and $2\alpha = \pi \Rightarrow \alpha = \dfrac{\pi}{2}$.

$\dfrac{r\sin\alpha}{\alpha} = \dfrac{20}{\pi/2} = \dfrac{40}{\pi} = 12.7$ (3 s.f.).

So $\text{COM}_A = (0, 12.7)$ (3 s.f.).

B is centred at $(-5, 0)$. Its COM is $\dfrac{r\sin\alpha}{\alpha}$ vertically below this, where $r = 15$ and $\alpha = \dfrac{\pi}{2}$.

$\dfrac{r\sin\alpha}{\alpha} = \dfrac{15}{\pi/2} = \dfrac{30}{\pi} = 9.55$ (3 s.f.).

So $\text{COM}_B = (-5, -9.55)$ (3 s.f.).

C is centred at $(15, 0)$. Its COM is $\dfrac{r\sin\alpha}{\alpha}$ vertically below this, where $r = 5$ and $\alpha = \dfrac{\pi}{2}$.

$\dfrac{r\sin\alpha}{\alpha} = \dfrac{5}{\pi/2} = \dfrac{10}{\pi} = 3.18$ (3 s.f.).

So $\text{COM}_C = (15, -3.18)$ (3 s.f.).

b) A has length $\pi r = 20\pi$, B has length 15π and C has length 5π.

$\Sigma m\mathbf{r} = \bar{\mathbf{r}}\Sigma m$

$20\pi\begin{pmatrix}0 \\ 40/\pi\end{pmatrix} + 15\pi\begin{pmatrix}-5 \\ -30/\pi\end{pmatrix} + 5\pi\begin{pmatrix}15 \\ -10/\pi\end{pmatrix} = \bar{\mathbf{r}}(20\pi + 15\pi + 5\pi)$

$\begin{pmatrix}0 \\ 300\end{pmatrix} = 40\pi\bar{\mathbf{r}}$

$\Rightarrow \bar{\mathbf{r}} = \begin{pmatrix}0 \\ 2.387...\end{pmatrix}$

So the COM is at $(0, 2.39)$ (3 s.f.)

Q5 a) The wires are uniform, so the COM of each wire is at its midpoint.

The COM of arc AB is $\dfrac{r\sin\alpha}{\alpha}$ from O, on the line of symmetry of the shape, where $r = 24$ and

$2\alpha = \dfrac{\pi}{2} \Rightarrow \alpha = \dfrac{\pi}{4}$

$\dfrac{r\sin\alpha}{\alpha} = \dfrac{24/\sqrt{2}}{\pi/4} = \dfrac{12\sqrt{2}}{\pi/4} = \dfrac{48\sqrt{2}}{\pi}$

Use trigonometry to find the position vector of the COM of arc AB:

$\text{COM}_{AB} = \begin{pmatrix}(48\sqrt{2}/\pi)\cos(\pi/4) \\ (48\sqrt{2}/\pi)\sin(\pi/4)\end{pmatrix} = \begin{pmatrix}48/\pi \\ 48/\pi\end{pmatrix}$ m

$\Sigma m\mathbf{r} = \bar{\mathbf{r}}\Sigma m$

$m_{AB}\mathbf{r}_{AB} + m_{OA}\mathbf{r}_{OA} + m_{OB}\mathbf{r}_{OB} = \bar{\mathbf{r}}(m_{AB} + m_{OA} + m_{OB})$

$2\begin{pmatrix}48/\pi \\ 48/\pi\end{pmatrix} + \begin{pmatrix}0 \\ 12\end{pmatrix} + \begin{pmatrix}12 \\ 0\end{pmatrix} = \bar{\mathbf{r}}(2 + 1 + 1)$

$\begin{pmatrix}96/\pi + 12 \\ 96/\pi + 12\end{pmatrix} = 4\bar{\mathbf{r}}$

$\Rightarrow \bar{\mathbf{r}} = \begin{pmatrix}24/\pi + 3 \\ 24/\pi + 3\end{pmatrix}$ m, as required.

b) $\sum mr = \bar{r}\sum m$

$4\binom{24/\pi + 3}{24/\pi + 3} + p\binom{0}{24} + q\binom{24}{0} = \binom{12}{10}(4 + p + q)$

$\binom{96/\pi + 12 + 24q}{96/\pi + 12 + 24p} = \binom{48 + 12p + 12q}{40 + 10p + 10q}$

Equating horizontal components:

$\frac{96}{\pi} + 12 + 24q = 48 + 12p + 12q$

$\frac{96}{\pi} + 12q = 36 + 12p$

$\frac{8}{\pi} + q = 3 + p$

$q = 3 + p - \frac{8}{\pi}$ **eqn1**

Equating vertical components:

$\frac{96}{\pi} + 12 + 24p = 40 + 10p + 10q$

$\frac{96}{\pi} + 14p = 28 + 10q$

$\frac{48}{\pi} + 7p = 14 + 5q$ **eqn2**

Substituting **eqn1** into **eqn2**:

$\frac{48}{\pi} + 7p = 14 + 5(3 + p - \frac{8}{\pi})$

$\frac{48}{\pi} + 7p = 14 + 15 + 5p - \frac{40}{\pi}$

$2p = 29 - \frac{88}{\pi}$

$\Rightarrow p = 0.4943... = 0.494$ kg (3 s.f.)

Substituting this into **eqn1**:

$q = 3 + 0.4943... - \frac{8}{\pi} = 0.9478...$

$= 0.948$ kg (3 s.f.)

4. Laminas in Equilibrium
Exercise 4.1 — Laminas suspended from a point

Q1 a) Let A be the rectangular lamina and B be the removed square. By symmetry, the COM of A is at (3, 2.5) and the COM of B is at (4, 2). The area of A is $6 \times 5 = 30$ and the area of B is $2 \times 2 = 4$.
Using the removal method:

$m_A\mathbf{r}_A - m_B\mathbf{r}_B = \bar{\mathbf{r}}(m_A - m_B)$

$30\binom{3}{2.5} - 4\binom{4}{2} = \bar{\mathbf{r}}(30 - 4)$

$\binom{74}{67} = 26\bar{\mathbf{r}}$

$\Rightarrow \bar{\mathbf{r}} = \binom{2.846...}{2.576...}$

So the COM is at (2.85, 2.58) (3 s.f.)

b)

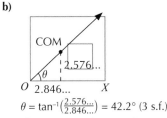

$\theta = \tan^{-1}\left(\frac{2.576...}{2.846...}\right) = 42.2°$ (3 s.f.)

Q2 a) The wire is uniform, so, by symmetry, the COM of each side is at its midpoint. The framework is made from a single wire, so the mass of each side is proportional to its length.

$\sum m\mathbf{r} = \bar{\mathbf{r}}\sum m$

$4\binom{0}{2} + 2\binom{1}{4} + 2\binom{2}{3} + 4\binom{4}{2} + 2\binom{6}{1} + 6\binom{3}{0}$

$= \bar{\mathbf{r}}(4 + 2 + 2 + 4 + 2 + 6)$

$\binom{52}{32} = 20\bar{\mathbf{r}}$

$\Rightarrow \bar{\mathbf{r}} = \binom{2.6}{1.6}$ So the COM is at (2.6, 1.6)

b)

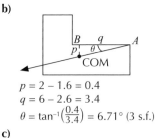

$p = 2 - 1.6 = 0.4$

$q = 6 - 2.6 = 3.4$

$\theta = \tan^{-1}\left(\frac{0.4}{3.4}\right) = 6.71°$ (3 s.f.)

c)

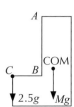

Taking moments about A,
moments clockwise = moments anticlockwise:

$(Mg \times 0.4) = (2.5g \times 2)$

$M = 5 \div 0.4 = 12.5$ kg

Q3

D(0, 8) ─────────── C(12, 8)

(9, 3) circle

(1, 1)

A(0, 0) ─────────── B(12, 0)

Let P be the rectangular lamina and Q be the circle removed. By symmetry, the COM of P is at (6, 4) and the COM of Q is at (9, 3). The area of P is $12 \times 8 = 96$ and the area of Q is $\pi \times 2^2 = 4\pi$.
Using the removal method:

$m_P\mathbf{r}_P - m_Q\mathbf{r}_Q = \bar{\mathbf{r}}(m_P - m_Q)$

$96\binom{6}{4} - 4\pi\binom{9}{3} = \bar{\mathbf{r}}(96 - 4\pi)$

$\binom{576 - 36\pi}{384 - 12\pi} = \bar{\mathbf{r}}(96 - 4\pi)$

$\Rightarrow \bar{\mathbf{r}} = \binom{5.548...}{4.150...}$

So the COM has coordinates (5.548..., 4.150...).
Draw an arrow from the pivot point (1, 1) to the COM, and form a right-angled triangle. You can find the horizontal and vertical side lengths of the triangle using the coordinates of the pivot point and COM:

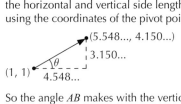

So the angle AB makes with the vertical is:

$\theta = \tan^{-1}\left(\frac{3.150...}{4.548...}\right) = 34.7°$ (3 s.f.)

Q4 a) Let P be the larger rectangle and Q be the smaller rectangle. By symmetry, the COM of each lamina is at its midpoint. P and Q are made from the same material, so their masses are proportional to their areas.

$x_P = 4$, $m_P = 8 \times 9 = 72$;

$x_Q = 8 + 2 = 10$, $m_Q = 4 \times 3 = 12$.

$\sum mx = \bar{x}\sum m$

$(72 \times 4) + (12 \times 10) = \bar{x}(72 + 12)$

$\Rightarrow \bar{x} = 4.857... = 4.86$ cm (3 s.f.)

b) $y_P = 4.5$; $y_Q = 1.5$.
$\Sigma my = \bar{y}\Sigma m$
$(72 \times 4.5) + (12 \times 1.5) = \bar{x}(72 + 12)$
$\Rightarrow \bar{y} = 4.071... = 4.07$ cm (3 s.f.)

c)

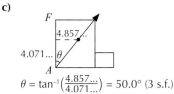

$\theta = \tan^{-1}\left(\frac{4.857...}{4.071...}\right) = 50.0°$ (3 s.f.)

d)

$d = 9 - 4.071... = 4.928...$
$\alpha = \tan^{-1}\left(\frac{4.857...}{4.928...}\right) = 44.6°$ (3 s.f.)

Q5 The composite shape has a vertical line of symmetry on which its COM lies. Call the square P and the triangle Q. P and Q are made from same material, so their masses are proportional to their areas.
By symmetry, the COM of each shape is at its midpoint. Let y be the vertical distance of each individual COM from AB.

$\tan\theta = \frac{\bar{y}}{8}$
$1.25 = \frac{\bar{y}}{8}$
$\Rightarrow \bar{y} = 10$ cm
$y_P = 8$, $m_P = 16 \times 16 = 256$.
The COM of Q is $\frac{1}{3}$ of the way up from its base, so
$y_Q = 16 + \frac{1}{3}h$, and $m_Q = \frac{1}{2} \times 16 \times h = 8h$.
$\Sigma my = \bar{y}\Sigma m$
$(256 \times 8) + (8h \times (16 + \frac{1}{3}h)) = 10 \times (256 + 8h)$
$2048 + 128h + \frac{8}{3}h^2 = 2560 + 80h$
$\frac{8}{3}h^2 + 48h - 512 = 0$
$h^2 + 18h - 192 = 0$
Solve using the quadratic formula or by completing the square:
$(h + 9)^2 - 273 = 0$
$h = -9 \pm \sqrt{273}$
h must be positive, so take $h = -9 + \sqrt{273} = 7.522...$
So the height of the triangle is 7.52 cm (3 s.f.)

Q6 a) Let P be the 10-unit radius circle, and Q be the 2-unit radius circle.
By symmetry, the COM of each circle is at its centre.
P has area $\pi \times 10^2 = 100\pi$ and Q has area $\pi \times 2^2 = 4\pi$.
Using the removal method:
$m_P\mathbf{r}_P - m_Q\mathbf{r}_Q = \bar{\mathbf{r}}(m_P - m_Q)$
$100\pi\begin{pmatrix}0\\0\end{pmatrix} - 4\pi\begin{pmatrix}2\\-4\end{pmatrix} = \bar{\mathbf{r}}(100\pi - 4\pi)$
$\begin{pmatrix}-8\pi\\16\pi\end{pmatrix} = 96\pi\bar{\mathbf{r}}$
$\Rightarrow \bar{\mathbf{r}} = \begin{pmatrix}-0.083...\\0.166...\end{pmatrix}$

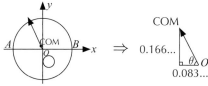

$\theta = \tan^{-1}\left(\frac{0.166...}{0.083...}\right) = 63.4°$ (3 s.f.)

b) $\Sigma m\mathbf{r} = \bar{\mathbf{r}}\Sigma m$
$m_{lamina}\mathbf{r}_{lamina} + m_{particle}\mathbf{r}_{particle} = \bar{\mathbf{r}}(m_{lamina} + m_{particle})$
$0.7\begin{pmatrix}-0.083...\\0.166...\end{pmatrix} + 0.9\begin{pmatrix}10\\0\end{pmatrix} = \bar{\mathbf{r}}(0.7 + 0.9)$
$\begin{pmatrix}8.941...\\0.116...\end{pmatrix} = 1.6\bar{\mathbf{r}}$
$\Rightarrow \bar{\mathbf{r}} = \begin{pmatrix}5.588...\\0.0729...\end{pmatrix}$

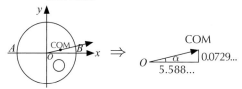

$\alpha = \tan^{-1}\left(\frac{0.0729...}{5.588...}\right) = 0.748°$ (3 s.f.)

Q7 First find the length of side BC:
$\tan25° = \frac{BC}{50}$
$\Rightarrow BC = 50\tan25° = 23.315...$ cm

Take D as the origin. The COM of the unloaded lamina is at its centre, i.e. at $\left(\frac{50}{2}, \frac{23.315...}{2}\right)$
$= (25, 11.657...)$
So, finding $\bar{\mathbf{r}}$, the COM of the loaded lamina:
$\Sigma m\mathbf{r} = \bar{\mathbf{r}}\Sigma m$
$0.5\begin{pmatrix}25\\11.657...\end{pmatrix} + 0.2\begin{pmatrix}0\\0\end{pmatrix} = \bar{\mathbf{r}}(0.5 + 0.2)$
$\begin{pmatrix}12.5\\5.828...\end{pmatrix} = 0.7\bar{\mathbf{r}}$
$\Rightarrow \bar{\mathbf{r}} = \begin{pmatrix}17.857...\\8.326...\end{pmatrix}$

$d = 23.315... - 8.326... = 14.988...$
$\theta = \tan^{-1}\left(\frac{14.988...}{17.857...}\right) = 40.0°$ (3 s.f.)

Exercise 4.2 — Laminas on an inclined plane

Q1 a) The COM of the rectangle is at its midpoint, i.e. $15 \div 2 = 7.5$ m along the slope from its bottom corner, and $10 \div 2 = 5$ m measured perpendicular to the slope from its bottom corner.

$\alpha = \tan^{-1}\left(\frac{7.5}{5}\right) = 56.3°$ (3 s.f.)

b) The height of the triangle is $\sqrt{13^2 - 5^2} = 12$ cm. The COM of the triangle is $\frac{1}{3}$ of the way up from its base, on the line of symmetry, i.e. $10 \div 2 = 5$ cm along the slope from the bottom corner, and $12 \div 3 = 4$ cm measured perpendicular to the slope from the bottom corner.

$\alpha = \tan^{-1}\left(\frac{5}{4}\right) = 51.3°$ (3 s.f.)

Q2 a) Split the shape into two rectangles. For example:

COM of A is at $\binom{0.5}{2}$, area of A is $4 \times 1 = 4$.
COM of B is at $\binom{2}{0.5}$, area of B is $1 \times 2 = 2$.
$\sum m\mathbf{r} = \bar{\mathbf{r}}\sum m$
$4\binom{0.5}{2} + 2\binom{2}{0.5} = \bar{\mathbf{r}}(4 + 2)$
$\binom{6}{9} = 6\bar{\mathbf{r}}$
$\Rightarrow \bar{\mathbf{r}} = \binom{1}{1.5}$ m

b)

$\alpha = \tan^{-1}\left(\frac{1}{1.5}\right) = 33.7°$ (3 s.f.)

Q3 a) (i) Let P be the rectangle and Q be the quarter-circle. By symmetry, the COM of P is 4 cm from AB. The area of P is $6 \times 8 = 48$ cm². Finding $x_{Q'}$ the distance of the COM of Q from AB:

$r = 3$, $2\alpha = \frac{\pi}{2} \Rightarrow \alpha = \frac{\pi}{4}$

$\frac{2r\sin\alpha}{3\alpha} = \frac{6/\sqrt{2}}{3\pi/4} = \frac{3\sqrt{2}}{3\pi/4} = \frac{4\sqrt{2}}{\pi}$

So the COM of Q is $\frac{4\sqrt{2}}{\pi}$ cm from the centre of the quarter circle, on Q's line of symmetry. Using trigonometry:

$\frac{4\sqrt{2}}{\pi}\cos\left(\frac{\pi}{4}\right) = \frac{4}{\pi}$

So the COM of Q is $\frac{4}{\pi}$ cm horizontally from DE, or $(8 - \frac{4}{\pi})$ cm horizontally from AB. The area of Q is $\frac{1}{4} \times \pi \times r^2 = \frac{9}{4}\pi$. Using the removal method:

$m_P x_P - m_Q x_Q = \bar{x}(m_P - m_Q)$
$(48 \times 4) - (\frac{9}{4}\pi \times (8 - \frac{4}{\pi})) = \bar{x}(48 - \frac{9}{4}\pi)$
$\Rightarrow \bar{x} = 144.451... \div 40.931... = 3.529...$
$= 3.53$ cm (3 s.f.)

(ii) The COM of P is 3 cm from AE. Now finding $y_{Q'}$ the distance of the COM of Q from AE: Using trigonometry:

$\frac{4\sqrt{2}}{\pi}\sin\left(\frac{\pi}{4}\right) = \frac{4}{\pi}$

So the COM of Q is $\frac{4}{\pi}$ cm vertically from BC, or $(6 - \frac{4}{\pi})$ cm vertically from AE. Using the removal method:

$m_P y_P - m_Q y_Q = \bar{y}(m_P - m_Q)$
$(48 \times 3) - (\frac{9}{4}\pi \times (6 - \frac{4}{\pi})) = \bar{y}(48 - \frac{9}{4}\pi)$
$\Rightarrow \bar{y} = 110.588... \div 40.931... = 2.701...$
$= 2.70$ cm (3 s.f.)

b) $\alpha = \tan^{-1}\left(\frac{3.529...}{2.701...}\right) = 52.563...°$
The shape will topple when it is tilted at more than 52.6° (3 s.f.). So it will not topple at 50°.

Q4 a) Let P be the square and Q be the circle. By symmetry, the COM, relative to A, of P is at $(3, 3)$ and the COM of Q is at $(4, 2)$. The area of P is $6 \times 6 = 36$ and the area of Q is $\pi r^2 = \pi \times 1^2 = \pi$. Using the removal method:

$m_P \mathbf{r}_P - m_Q \mathbf{r}_Q = \bar{\mathbf{r}}(m_P - m_Q)$
$36\binom{3}{3} - \pi\binom{4}{2} = \bar{\mathbf{r}}(36 - \pi)$
$\binom{108 - 4\pi}{108 - 2\pi} = \bar{\mathbf{r}}(36 - \pi)$
$\Rightarrow \bar{\mathbf{r}} = \binom{2.904...}{3.095...}$
So the COM is at $(2.90, 3.10)$ (3 s.f.)

b) $\alpha = \tan^{-1}\left(\frac{2.904...}{3.095...}\right) = 43.174...°$
The shape will topple when it is tilted at more than 43.2° (3 s.f.). Therefore, it will topple at 44°.

c) You know the distance of the COM from AB is 2.90 m (3 s.f.), but you need to find the distance of the COM from CD. The square has side length 6 units, so:
$6 - 2.904... = 3.095...$
$\beta = \tan^{-1}\left(\frac{3.095...}{3.095...}\right) = 45°$
So the shape will topple when it is tilted at more than 45°. Therefore, it will not topple at 44°.

Q5 a) Let P be the square and Q be the triangle.
Let O be the origin.
By symmetry, the COM of P is at $(0.5, 0.5)$.
The area of P is 1 m². Q has vertices at $(0.5, 0)$,
$(1, 0.5)$ and $(1, 0)$. The COM of Q is therefore at
$\left(\dfrac{0.5 + 1 + 1}{3}, \dfrac{0 + 0.5 + 0}{3}\right) = (0.833..., 0.166...)$
The area of Q is $\frac{1}{2} \times 0.5 \times 0.5 = 0.125$ m³.
Using the removal method:
$m_P \mathbf{r}_P - m_Q \mathbf{r}_Q = \bar{\mathbf{r}}(m_P - m_Q)$
$1\binom{0.5}{0.5} - 0.125\binom{0.833...}{0.166...} = \bar{\mathbf{r}}(1 - 0.125)$
$\binom{0.395...}{0.479...} = 0.875\bar{\mathbf{r}}$
$\Rightarrow \bar{\mathbf{r}} = \binom{0.452...}{0.547...}$ m
So the COM is 0.452 m (3 s.f.) to the right of O
and 0.548 m (3 s.f.) above O.

b) Let x be the horizontal distance of each COM
from O. When the loaded shape is on the point
of toppling about A, its COM is directly above A,
i.e. $\bar{x} = 0.5$.
$\Sigma mx = \bar{x}\Sigma m$
$(2 \times 0.452...) + (M \times 1) = 0.5(2 + M)$
$0.904... + M = 1 + 0.5M$
$0.5M = 0.0952...$
$\Rightarrow M = 0.190$ kg (3 s.f.)
*Be careful here — in part a), you were using areas
in your calculations (because the shape's area is
proportional to its mass), but in part b) you need to use
the actual masses given in the question.*

Q6

$\alpha = 35° \Rightarrow \tan 35° = \dfrac{x}{y}$
$\Rightarrow \dfrac{y}{x} = \dfrac{1}{\tan 35°} = 1.428...$
Now with CD in contact with the plane:

$\alpha = \tan^{-1}\left(\dfrac{y}{x}\right) = \tan^{-1}(1.428...) = 55°$

Review Exercise — Chapter 2

Q1 a) $\Sigma mx = \bar{x}\Sigma m$
$m_1 x_1 + m_2 x_2 + m_3 x_3 = \bar{x}(m_1 + m_2 + m_3)$
$(1 \times 1) + (2 \times 2) + (3 \times 3) = \bar{x}(1 + 2 + 3)$
$\Rightarrow 14 = 6\bar{x} \Rightarrow \bar{x} = 14 \div 6 = 2.333...$
So the coordinates are $(2.33, 0)$ (3 s.f.)

b) $\Sigma my = \bar{y}\Sigma m$
$m_1 y_1 + m_2 y_2 + m_3 y_3 = \bar{y}(m_1 + m_2 + m_3)$
$(1 \times 3) + (2 \times 2) + (3 \times 1) = \bar{y}(1 + 2 + 3)$
$\Rightarrow 10 = 6\bar{y} \Rightarrow \bar{y} = 10 \div 6 = 1.666...$
So the coordinates are $(0, 1.67)$ (3 s.f.)

c) $\Sigma m\mathbf{r} = \bar{\mathbf{r}}\Sigma m$
$m_1\mathbf{r}_1 + m_2\mathbf{r}_2 + m_3\mathbf{r}_3 = \bar{\mathbf{r}}(m_1 + m_2 + m_3)$
$1\binom{3}{4} + 2\binom{3}{1} + 3\binom{1}{0} = \bar{\mathbf{r}}(1 + 2 + 3)$
$\binom{12}{6} = 6\bar{\mathbf{r}}$
$\Rightarrow \bar{\mathbf{r}} = \binom{12}{6} \div 6 = \binom{2}{1}$
So the coordinates are $(2, 1)$.

Q2 $\Sigma m\mathbf{r} = \bar{\mathbf{r}}\Sigma m$
$m\binom{0}{0} + 2m\binom{0}{4} + 3m\binom{5}{4} + 12\binom{5}{0}$
$= (m + 2m + 3m + 12)\binom{3.5}{2}$
$\binom{15m + 60}{20m} = \binom{21m + 42}{12m + 24}$
Equating vertical components:
$20m = 12m + 24$
$8m = 24$
$\Rightarrow m = 24 \div 8 = 3$ kg

Q3 a) Triangle (1) has area $\frac{1}{2} \times 4 \times 3 = 6$, so $m_1 = 6$.
$x_1 = 2$ (by symmetry) and $y_1 = 5 - (\frac{2}{3} \times 3) = 3$
($\frac{2}{3}$ down the median from the top vertex).
Rectangle (2) has area $1 \times 2 = 2$, so $m_2 = 2$.
$x_2 = 2$ and $y_2 = 1.5$ (by symmetry).
Combined shape has $\bar{x} = 2$ (by symmetry) and:
$\Sigma my = \bar{y}\Sigma m$
$m_1 y_1 + m_2 y_2 = \bar{y}(m_1 + m_2)$
$(6 \times 3) + (2 \times 1.5) = (6 + 2)\bar{y}$
$21 = 8\bar{y}$
$\Rightarrow \bar{y} = 21 \div 8 = 2.625$.
So the coordinates are $(2, 2.625)$.

b) Semicircle (1) has area $\frac{1}{2} \times \pi \times 3^2 = 4.5\pi$,
so $m_1 = 4.5\pi$.
$x_1 = 8$ (by symmetry) and $y_1 = 1 + \dfrac{2 \times 3 \times \sin \frac{\pi}{2}}{3 \frac{\pi}{2}}$
$= \dfrac{4 + \pi}{\pi}$
(COM is $\dfrac{2r\sin\alpha}{3\alpha}$ up from the centre of the circle,
where $2\alpha = \pi$).
Triangle (2) has area $\frac{1}{2} \times 2 \times 1 = 1$, so $m_2 = 1$.
$x_2 = 8$ (by symmetry) and $y_2 = \frac{2}{3} \times 1 = \frac{2}{3}$ ($\frac{2}{3}$ up
the median from the bottom vertex).
Combined shape has $\bar{x} = 8$ (by symmetry) and:
$m_1 y_1 + m_2 y_2 = \bar{y}(m_1 + m_2)$
$(4.5\pi \times \frac{4 + \pi}{\pi}) + (1 \times \frac{2}{3}) = (4.5\pi + 1)\bar{y}$
$18\frac{2}{3} + 4.5\pi = (4.5\pi + 1)\bar{y}$
$\Rightarrow \bar{y} = (18\frac{2}{3} + 4.5\pi) \div (4.5\pi + 1) = 2.17$ (3 s.f.)
So the coordinates are $(8, 2.17)$ (3 s.f.)

c) Circle (1) has area $\pi \times 2^2 = 4\pi$, so $m_1 = 4\pi$.
$x_1 = 14$ and $y_1 = 2$ (by symmetry).
Square (2) has area $1 \times 1 = 1$, so $m_2 = 1$.
$x_2 = 14.5$ and $y_2 = 2.5$ (by symmetry).
Using the removal method:
$m_1\mathbf{r}_1 - m_2\mathbf{r}_2 = \bar{\mathbf{r}}(m_1 - m_2)$
$4\pi\binom{14}{2} - \binom{14.5}{2.5} = (4\pi - 1)\bar{\mathbf{r}}$
$\binom{56\pi - 14.5}{8\pi - 2.5} = (4\pi - 1)\bar{\mathbf{r}}$
$\Rightarrow \bar{\mathbf{r}} = \binom{56\pi - 14.5}{8\pi - 2.5} \div (4\pi - 1) = \binom{14.0}{1.96}$ (3 s.f.)
So the coordinates are $(14.0, 1.96)$ (3 s.f.)

Q4

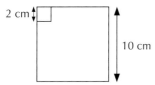

Large square (1) has area $10 \times 10 = 100$, so $m_1 = 100$.
$y_1 = 5$ cm from top edge (by symmetry).
Small square (2) has area $2 \times 2 = 4$, so $m_2 = 4$.
$y_2 = 1$ cm from top edge (by symmetry).
Using the removal method:
$m_1 y_1 - m_2 y_2 = \overline{y}(m_1 - m_2)$
$(100 \times 5) - (4 \times 1) = (100 - 4)\overline{y}$
$496 = 96\overline{y}$
$\Rightarrow \overline{y} = 496 \div 96 = 5.17$ cm from the top edge (3 s.f.)

Q5 a) The COM lies on the vertical line of symmetry of the shape.
The COM of the arc is $\frac{r\sin\alpha}{\alpha}$ from A, where
$r = 10$ and $2\alpha = \frac{\pi}{2} \Rightarrow \alpha = \frac{\pi}{4}$.
$\frac{r\sin\alpha}{\alpha} = \frac{10/\sqrt{2}}{\pi/4} = \frac{5\sqrt{2}}{\pi/4} = \frac{20\sqrt{2}}{\pi}$ cm
The length of the arc is $r\theta = 10 \times \frac{\pi}{2} = 5\pi$ cm.
Using trigonometry, the COM of AB is a vertical distance of $5\cos\left(\frac{\pi}{4}\right) = \frac{5}{\sqrt{2}} = 2.5\sqrt{2}$ cm from A, as is the COM of AC.
The framework is made from a single wire, so the mass of each side is proportional to its length.
$\Sigma my = \overline{y}\Sigma m$
$\left(5\pi \times \frac{20\sqrt{2}}{\pi}\right) + 2\left(10 \times \frac{5}{\sqrt{2}}\right) = \overline{y}(5\pi + 10 + 10)$
$\Rightarrow \overline{y} = 212.13... \div 35.70... = 5.94...$
$= 5.94$ cm (3 s.f.)

b) Vertical distance of B and C from A is
$10\cos\left(\frac{\pi}{4}\right) = \frac{10}{\sqrt{2}} = 5\sqrt{2}$ cm.
$\Sigma my = \overline{y}\Sigma m$
$(0.1 \times 5.94...) + (0.3 \times 5\sqrt{2}) + (0.4 \times 5\sqrt{2})$
$= \overline{y}(0.1 + 0.3 + 0.4)$
$\Rightarrow \overline{y} = 5.54... \div 0.8 = 6.929...$ cm
Horizontal distance of B and C from A is
$10\sin\left(\frac{\pi}{4}\right) = \frac{10}{\sqrt{2}} = 5\sqrt{2}$ cm.
The COM of unloaded ABC lies on the vertical line of symmetry passing through A.
$\Sigma mx = \overline{x}\Sigma m$
$(0.1 \times 0) + (0.3 \times -5\sqrt{2}) + (0.4 \times 5\sqrt{2})$
$= \overline{x}(0.1 + 0.3 + 0.4)$
$\Rightarrow \overline{x} = 0.707... \div 0.8 = 0.883...$ cm
Using Pythagoras' theorem:
distance $= \sqrt{(0.883...)^2 + (6.929...)^2}$
$= 6.99$ cm (3 s.f.)

Q6 a) (i) $m_1 y_1 + m_2 y_2 + m_3 y_3 + m_4 y_4$
$= \overline{y}(m_1 + m_2 + m_3 + m_4)$
$(7 \times 0) + (12 \times 5) + (10 \times 5) + (6 \times 0)$
$= \overline{y}(7 + 12 + 10 + 6)$
$110 = 35\overline{y}$
$\Rightarrow \overline{y} = 3.142... = 3.14$ cm (3 s.f.).
The framework is 'light' so it has no mass.

(ii) $m_1 x_1 + m_2 x_2 + m_3 x_3 + m_4 x_4$
$= \overline{x}(m_1 + m_2 + m_3 + m_4)$
$(7 \times 0) + (12 \times 0) + (10 \times 5) + (6 \times 5)$
$= \overline{x}(7 + 12 + 10 + 6)$
$80 = 35\overline{x}$
$\Rightarrow \overline{x} = 2.285... = 2.29$ cm (3 s.f.)

b) $\alpha = \tan^{-1}\left(\frac{2.285...}{3.142...}\right) = 36.0°$ (3 s.f.)

Q7 a)

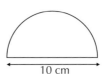

Straight wire (1) has length 10 cm so $m_1 = 10$.
$y_1 = 0$ (as it lies on the straight edge).
Arc (2) has length $\frac{10}{2} \times \pi$, so $m_2 = 5\pi$.
$y_2 = \frac{5 \times \sin^{\pi/2}}{\pi/2} = \frac{10}{\pi}$ (COM is $\frac{r\sin\alpha}{\alpha}$ up from the
centre of the circle, where $2\alpha = \pi$).
Combined frame:
$m_1 y_1 + m_2 y_2 = \overline{y}(m_1 + m_2)$
$(10 \times 0) + (5\pi \times \frac{10}{\pi}) = (10 + 5\pi)\overline{y}$
$50 = (10 + 5\pi)\overline{y}$
$\Rightarrow \overline{y} = 50 \div (10 + 5\pi) = 1.944...$
$= 1.94$ cm (to 3 s.f.)

b)

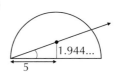

Drawing a line to represent the vertical through the COM (shown) gives a right-angled triangle.
If α is the angle between the straight edge and the vertical then:
$\alpha = \tan^{-1}\left(\frac{1.944...}{5}\right) = 21.3°$ (3 s.f.)

Q8 a) (i)

The COM is the point at which the two arrows intersect, marked E on the diagram.
Angle $AED = 180° - 45° - 60° = 75°$.
By the sine rule:
$\frac{AE}{\sin 60°} = \frac{70}{\sin 75°}$
$\Rightarrow AE = 62.76...$ cm
So, using trigonometry, the distance of the COM from AD is $(62.76...)\sin 45° = 44.37...$
$= 44.4$ cm (3 s.f.)

(ii) Resolving horizontally, the distance of the COM from AB is $(62.76...)\cos 45° = 44.37...$
$= 44.4$ cm (3 s.f.)

b)

$d = 60 - 44.37... = 15.62...$ cm

$\alpha = \tan^{-1}\left(\frac{15.62...}{44.37...}\right) = 19.4°$ (3 s.f.)

Q9 a) Splitting up the shape into a circle (1), large square (2) and small square (3) and taking the point A as the origin, the position vectors of the centres of mass of each shape are as follows:
Circle:
$x_1 = 25$ and $y_1 = 50 + (40 - 35) = 55$
(by symmetry) so $\mathbf{r}_1 = \binom{25}{55}$.
Large Square:
$x_2 = 25$ and $y_2 = 25$ (by symmetry) so $\mathbf{r}_2 = \binom{25}{25}$.
Small Square:
$x_3 = 50 + 5 = 55$ and $y_3 = 5$ (by symmetry)
so $\mathbf{r}_3 = \binom{55}{5}$.
$\Sigma mr = \bar{\mathbf{r}}\Sigma m$
$m_1\mathbf{r}_1 + m_2\mathbf{r}_2 + m_3\mathbf{r}_3 = \bar{\mathbf{r}}(m_1 + m_2 + m_3)$
$5\binom{25}{55} + 4\binom{25}{25} + 1\binom{55}{5} = \bar{\mathbf{r}}(5 + 4 + 1)$
$\binom{125 + 100 + 55}{275 + 100 + 5} = 10\bar{\mathbf{r}}$
$\Rightarrow \bar{\mathbf{r}} = \binom{280}{380} \div 10 = \binom{28}{38}$.
The centre of mass of the sign is 28 cm from AB and 38 cm from AF.

b)

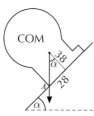

$\alpha = \tan^{-1}\left(\frac{28}{38}\right) = 36.4°$ (3 s.f.)

Q10

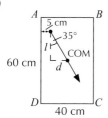

The COM is at the centre of the rectangle, i.e. 20 cm from AD and 30 cm from AB.
$d = 20 - 5 = 15$ cm
$\tan 35° = \frac{d}{l}$
$\Rightarrow l = \frac{15}{\tan 35°} = 21.42...$ cm
So the distance of the pivot from AB is:
$30 - 21.42... = 8.58$ cm (3 s.f.)

Exam-Style Questions — Chapter 2

Q1 a) Using the formula $\Sigma my = \bar{y}\Sigma m$
$m_1y_1 + m_2y_2 + m_3y_3 = \bar{y}(m_1 + m_2 + m_3)$
$(4 \times 3) + (3 \times 1) + (2 \times y) = 2 \times (4 + 3 + 2)$
[1 mark]
$15 + 2y = 18$ *[1 mark]*
$\Rightarrow y = (18 - 15) \div 2 = 1.5$ *[1 mark]*.

b) Using the formula $\Sigma mx = \bar{x}\Sigma m$
$m_1x_1 + m_2x_2 + m_3x_3 = \bar{x}(m_1 + m_2 + m_3)$
$(4 \times 1) + (3 \times 5) + (2 \times 4) = \bar{x}(4 + 3 + 2)$ *[1 mark]*
$27 = 9\bar{x}$ *[1 mark]*
$\Rightarrow \bar{x} = 27 \div 9 = 3$ *[1 mark]*.

c) The centre of mass of the lamina is at (3.5, 2.5), due to the symmetry of the shape, and
$m_{lamina} = 6$ kg.
The centre of mass of the group of particles is (3, 2) (from part b)) and $m_{particles} = 4 + 3 + 2 = 9$ kg. Using $\Sigma m\mathbf{r} = \bar{\mathbf{r}}\Sigma m$:
$m_{lamina}\mathbf{r}_{lamina} + m_{particles}\mathbf{r}_{particles} = \bar{\mathbf{r}}(m_{lamina} + m_{particles})$
$6\binom{3.5}{2.5} + 9\binom{3}{2} = \bar{\mathbf{r}}(6 + 9)$
$\binom{21 + 27}{15 + 18} = 15\bar{\mathbf{r}}$
$\Rightarrow \bar{\mathbf{r}} = \binom{48}{33} \div 15 = \binom{3.2}{2.2}$
So the coordinates are (3.2, 2.2).
[6 marks available — 1 mark for correct x_{lamina}, 1 mark for correct y_{lamina}, 1 mark for correct entry of horizontal positions in the formula, 1 mark for correct entry of vertical positions in the formula, 1 mark for x-coordinate of 3.2, 1 mark for y-coordinate of 2.2.]

2 a) (i) Setting M as the origin, the distance of the centre of mass from MP is the horizontal distance $\bar{x}$.
For each element the masses and centres are:
Particle at A: $m_A = 3m$ and $x_A = -10$ (since A is 10 cm to the left of M).
Particle at B: $m_B = 4m$ and $x_B = 10$.
Straight rod: $m_{rod} = 2m$ and $x_{rod} = 0$ (M is the midpoint of the rod, which is the centre of its mass).
Arc: $m_{arc} = \pi m$ and $x_{arc} = 0$ (due to the symmetry of the semicircular arc).
Don't forget to include the masses of all the rods and arcs — unless you're told that they're 'light'.
Combining these elements in the formula $\Sigma mx = \bar{x}\Sigma m$
$m_Ax_A + m_Bx_B + m_{rod}x_{rod} + m_{arc}x_{arc} = \bar{x}(m_A + m_B + m_{rod} + m_{arc})$
$(3m \times -10) + (4m \times 10) + (2m \times 0) + (\pi m \times 0) = \bar{x}(3m + 4m + 2m + \pi m)$
$-30m + 40m = (9 + \pi)m\bar{x}$
$\Rightarrow \bar{x} = 10 \div (9 + \pi) = 0.82361...$
$= 0.8236$ cm (4 d.p.)

[3 marks available — 1 mark for correct total mass of system, 1 mark for correct entry into formula, 1 mark for correct final answer.]

(ii) With M as the origin, the distance of the centre of mass of AB is the vertical distance $\overline{y}$. So: $y_A = y_B = y_{rod} = 0$, since all three lie on the line AB.

For the arc, use the formula $y_{arc} = \frac{r\sin\alpha}{\alpha}$, where $r = 10$, and $\alpha = \frac{\pi}{2}$ (since the angle at the centre $(2\alpha) = \pi$), so $y_{arc} = \frac{10\sin\frac{\pi}{2}}{\frac{\pi}{2}} = \frac{20}{\pi}$.

Combining these in the formula $\Sigma my = \overline{y}\Sigma m$:
$$m_A y_A + m_B y_B + m_{rod}y_{rod} + m_{arc}y_{arc} = \overline{y}(m_A + m_B + m_{rod} + m_{arc})$$
$$(\pi m \times \frac{20}{\pi}) = (9 + \pi)m\,\overline{y}$$
$$\Rightarrow \overline{y} = 20 \div (9 + \pi) = 1.64723...$$
$$= 1.6472 \text{ cm (4 d.p.)}$$

[3 marks available — 1 mark for correct value of y_{arc}, 1 mark for correct entry into formula, 1 mark for correct final answer.]

b) On a sketch, draw a line from P to the centre of mass to represent the vertical, and label relevant lengths and angles:

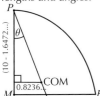

The vertical distance between P and COM $=$ $10 - 1.6472...$ (from a)(ii)) $= 8.3527...$ cm
[1 mark]
Using trig:
$$\theta = \tan^{-1}\left(\frac{0.8236...}{8.3527...}\right) \text{ [1 mark]}$$
$$= 5.63° \text{ (3 s.f.) [1 mark]}.$$

3 a) Splitting up the shape into a triangle (1), large square (2) and small square (3), where the mass of each shape is proportional to the area, gives the following masses:
$$m_1 = \frac{1}{2} \times 70 \times 30 = 1050$$
$$m_2 = 50 \times 50 = 2500$$
$$m_3 = 10 \times 10 = 100$$
Taking the point A as the origin, the position vectors of the centres of mass of each shape are as follows:
Triangle:
$x_1 = 25$ (due to the symmetry of the shape) and $y_1 = 50 + (\frac{1}{3} \times 30) = 60$ (since the COM of a triangle is $\frac{2}{3}$ down the median from the vertex, and so $\frac{1}{3}$ up from the edge). So $\mathbf{r}_1 = \binom{25}{60}$.
Large Square:
$x_2 = 25$ and $y_2 = 25$ (due to the symmetry of the shape). So $\mathbf{r}_2 = \binom{25}{25}$.
Small Square:
$x_3 = 50 + 5 = 55$ and $y_3 = 5$ (due to the symmetry of the shape). So $\mathbf{r}_3 = \binom{55}{5}$.

Using the formula $\Sigma m\mathbf{r} = \overline{\mathbf{r}}\Sigma m$
$$m_1\mathbf{r}_1 + m_2\mathbf{r}_2 + m_3\mathbf{r}_3 = \overline{\mathbf{r}}(m_1 + m_2 + m_3)$$
$$1050\binom{25}{60} + 2500\binom{25}{25} + 100\binom{55}{5}$$
$$= \overline{\mathbf{r}}(1050 + 2500 + 100)$$
$$\binom{26250 + 62500 + 5500}{63000 + 62500 + 500} = 3650\overline{\mathbf{r}}$$
$$\Rightarrow \overline{\mathbf{r}} = \binom{94250}{126000} \div 3650 = \binom{25.8219...}{34.5205...}.$$
So, to 3 s.f., the centre of mass of the sign is 25.8 cm from AB and 34.5 cm from AI.
[6 marks available — 1 mark for masses in the correct proportion, 1 mark for each individual centre of mass entered correctly into the formula, 1 mark for correct working to find distance from AB, 1 mark for correct working to find distance from AI.]

b) For the sign to hang with AI horizontal, the centre of mass of the whole system (sign + particle) must be vertically below D, i.e. $\overline{x}$ must be 25 (taking A as the origin again).
Given that $m_{sign} = 1$ kg and $x_{sign} = 25.8219...$ (from a)), and $x_{particle} = 0$ (since it's attached at the origin):
$$m_{sign}x_{sign} + m_{particle}x_{particle} = \overline{x}(m_{sign} + m_{particle})$$
$$(1 \times 25.8219...) + 0 = 25(1 + m_{particle})$$
$$25.8219... \div 25 = 1 + m_{particle}$$
$$1.0328... - 1 = m_{particle}$$
$$\Rightarrow m_{particle} = 0.03287... = 0.0329 \text{ kg (3 s.f.)}$$
[3 marks available — 1 mark for stating the correct required value of $\overline{x}$, 1 mark for correct entry of values into the formula, 1 mark for correct final answer.]

4 a) The stencil is a rectangle (1) with a quarter circle (2) of radius $(10 - 2) = 8$ cm removed. The lamina is uniform so mass is proportional to area, so $m_1 = 12 \times 10 = 120$, and $m_2 = \frac{1}{4} \times \pi \times 8^2 = 16\pi$.
Taking O as the origin, the position of the centre of mass of the rectangle, $\mathbf{r}_1 = \binom{6}{5}$ (from the symmetry of the shape).
The sector angle $2\alpha = \frac{\pi}{2}$, so $\alpha = \frac{\pi}{4}$, and the centre of mass of the sector is $\frac{2r\sin\alpha}{3\alpha}$ from O along the axis of symmetry $= \frac{2 \times 8 \times \sin\frac{\pi}{4}}{3\pi/4}$
$$= \frac{64}{3\pi\sqrt{2}} = \frac{32\sqrt{2}}{3\pi} \text{ cm}.$$

Using trigonometry, the position vector of the COM of the sector, $\mathbf{r}_2 = \begin{pmatrix} \frac{32\sqrt{2}}{3\pi} \times \cos\frac{\pi}{4} \\ \frac{32\sqrt{2}}{3\pi} \times \sin\frac{\pi}{4} \end{pmatrix} = \begin{pmatrix} \frac{32}{3\pi} \\ \frac{32}{3\pi} \end{pmatrix}.$

Using the removal method:
$$m_1\mathbf{r}_1 - m_2\mathbf{r}_2 = \bar{\mathbf{r}}(m_1 - m_2)$$

$$120\binom{6}{5} - 16\pi\binom{\frac{32}{3\pi}}{\frac{32}{3\pi}} = \bar{\mathbf{r}}(120 - 16\pi)$$

$$\binom{720 - \frac{512}{3}}{600 - \frac{512}{3}} = \bar{\mathbf{r}}(120 - 16\pi)$$

$$\binom{\frac{1648}{3}}{\frac{1288}{3}} \div (120 - 16\pi) = \bar{\mathbf{r}}$$

$$\Rightarrow \bar{\mathbf{r}} = \binom{7.8774...}{6.1566...} \text{ cm}$$

So, to 3 s.f., the coordinates of the centre of mass of the stencil are (7.88, 6.16) cm.
[7 marks available — 1 mark for the correct total mass, 1 mark for correct r_y, 1 mark for correct r_x, 1 mark for correct entry of horizontal positions in the formula, 1 mark for correct entry of vertical positions in the formula, 1 mark for x-coordinate of 7.88, 1 mark for y-coordinate of 6.16.]

b) At the point of toppling, the centre of mass will be vertically above the point *D*, as shown:

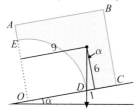

Horizontal distance from *D* to the centre of mass = 9 − 8 = 1 cm *[1 mark]*.

$\alpha = \tan^{-1}\left(\frac{1}{6}\right)$ *[1 mark]* = 9.46° (3 s.f.) *[1 mark]*.

Chapter 3: Work, Energy and Power

1. Work Done

Exercise 1.1 — Work done

Q1 Work done = *Fs*
Work done = 500 × 300 = 150 000 J
Remember to convert the distance into metres.

Q2 Work done = *F* × *s*
8 = *P* × 1.6
⇒ *P* = 8 ÷ 1.6 = 5 N

Q3 Work done = *Fs*
0.428 = 84 × *d*
⇒ *d* = 0.428 ÷ 84 = 5.10 × 10⁻³ m (3 s.f.)

Q4 a) Work done against friction = 50 × 0.7 = 35 J

b) The resultant force is 350 N − 50 N = 300 N in the direction of motion.
So work done = 300 × 0.7 = 210 J

Q5 Resolving horizontally:
F = 2000cos18°
Work done = *Fs* = 2000cos18° × 1150
= 2 190 000 J (3 s.f.)

Q6 Resolving horizontally, taking direction of motion as positive, and using $F_{net} = ma$:
*P*cos30° − *F* = *m* × 0
⇒ *F* = *P*cos30°, where *F* is the frictional force acting between the particle and the plane.
So, using 'Work done = Force × distance':
Work done against friction = *F* × 25
Substituting in *F* = *P*cos30°:
55 = *P*cos30° × 25
⇒ *P* = 55 ÷ 25cos30° = 2.54 N (3 s.f.)

Q7 a)

Resolving vertically:
R + 2.2sin24° = 0.15*g*
⇒ *R* = 0.575... N
Using *F* = μ*R*:
F = 0.14 × 0.575... = 0.0805... N
Work done against friction = *Fs*
= 0.0805... × 6 = 0.483 J (3 s.f.)

b) Resolving horizontally, taking direction of motion as positive, and using formula for work done:
Work done = (2.2cos24° − 0.0805...) × 6
= 11.6 J (3 s.f.)

Q8 a)

Resolving vertically:
R + 32sin15° = 12*g*
⇒ *R* = 109.317... N
Using *F* = μ*R*:
F = 0.18 × 109.317... = 19.677... N
Work done against friction = *Fs*
45 = 19.677... × *s*
⇒ *s* = 2.286... = 2.29 m (3 s.f.)

b) Resolving horizontally, taking direction of motion as positive, and using formula for work done:
Work done = (32cos15° − 19.677...) × 2.286...
= 25.7 J (3 s.f.)

Q9 Using 'Work done = Force × distance':
28 = (60cos40° − *F*) × 3.5
8 = 60cos40° − *F*
⇒ *F* = 37.962... N
Resolving vertically:
R = 60sin40° + 28*g* = 312.967... N
Using *F* = μ*R*:
37.962... = μ × 312.967...
⇒ μ = 0.121 (3 s.f.)

Exercise 1.2 — Gravity

Q1 Work done by gravity $= mgh$
$= 0.0013 \times 9.8 \times 37 = 0.472$ J (3 s.f.)
You need to change the mass from grams to kilograms to get an answer in joules.

Q2 Work done against gravity $= mgh$
$16\,367 = 57 \times 9.8 \times h$
$\Rightarrow h = 16\,367 \div (57 \times 9.8) = 29.3$ m (3 s.f.)

Q3 Work done against gravity $= mgh$
$22\,491 = m \times 9.8 \times 2.7$
$\Rightarrow m = 22\,491 \div (9.8 \times 2.7) = 850$ kg

Q4 Gravity only does work vertically, so you only need to take the vertical motion into account.
Work done $= mgh = 48 \times 9.8 \times 3 = 1410$ J (3 s.f.)

Q5 **a)** **(i)** Resolving vertically and using $F = ma$:
$T - mg = m \times 0$
$\Rightarrow T = mg = 3 \times 9.8 = 29.4$ N

(ii) Work done $= F \times s = T \times h$
$= 29.4 \times 9.5 = 279.3$ J
You could also do this using the fact that the work done by the rope is equal to the work done against gravity, so Work done = mgh.

b) **(i)** Resolving vertically and using $F_{net} = ma$:
$T - mg = ma$
$\Rightarrow T = ma + mg = m(a + g)$
$= 3(1.5 + 9.8) = 33.9$ N

(ii) Work done $= F_{net} \times h$
$= (T - mg) \times h = (33.9 - 3g) \times 9.5$
$= 42.75$ J

Q6 **a)** Using $s = ut + \frac{1}{2}at^2$, taking down as positive:
$s = (0 \times 3) + \frac{1}{2} \times 9.8 \times 3^2 = 44.1$ m

b) Work done by gravity $= mgh = 2 \times 9.8 \times 44.1$
$= 864.36$ J

c) E.g. there is no air resistance or any other external forces, the stone is a particle, g is constant at 9.8 ms^{-2}.

Q7 **a)** Resolving vertically, taking up as positive, and using $F = ma$:
$44 - mg = m \times 0.16$
$44 = m(0.16 + 9.8)$
$\Rightarrow m = 4.417... = 4.42$ kg (3 s.f.)

b) Resolving vertically, taking up as positive, and using the formula for work done:
Work done $= (44 - (4.417...)g) \times 9$
$= 6.3614... = 6.36$ J (3 s.f.)

Q8 **a)** $u = 0$, $v = 4.2$, $s = s$, $t = 10$
Using $s = \left(\frac{u + v}{2}\right)t$:
$s = 2.1 \times 10 = 21$ m
Work done against gravity $= mgh$
$= 25 \times 9.8 \times 21 = 5145$ J

b) $u = 0$, $v = 4.2$, $a = a$, $t = 10$
Using $v = u + at$:
$4.2 = 10a$
$\Rightarrow a = 0.42$ ms^{-2}
Resolving vertically, taking up as positive, and using $F = ma$:
$T - 25g = 25 \times 0.42$
$\Rightarrow T = 255.5$ N

c) Work done $=$ Force $\times$ distance
$= 255.5 \times 21 = 5365.5$ J

Exercise 1.3 — Friction and gravity

Q1 Resolving vertically, the body travels a vertical distance of $1.4\sin70°$ m.
Work done $= mgh = 90 \times 9.8 \times 1.4\sin70°$
$= 1160$ J (3 s.f.)

Q2 **a)** Work done by gravity $= mgh$
$= 0.45 \times 9.8 \times 2\sin25° = 3.73$ J (3 s.f.)

b) Resolving perpendicular to the plane:
$R = 0.45g\cos25° = 3.996...$ N
$F = \mu R = 0.37 \times 3.996... = 1.478...$ N
Work done against friction $= Fs$
$= 1.478... \times 2 = 2.96$ J (3 s.f.)

Q3 **a)**

Work done against gravity $= mgh$
$= 8 \times 9.8 \times 1.5\sin22° = 44.1$ J (3 s.f.)

b) Resolving perpendicular to the plane:
$R = 8g\cos22° = 72.691...$ N
$F = \mu R = 0.55 \times 72.691... = 39.980...$ N
Work done against friction $= Fs$
$= 39.980... \times 1.5 = 60.0$ J (3 s.f.)

Q4 Resolving perpendicular to the plane:
$R = 11g\cos5° = 107.389...$ N
$F = \mu R = 0.08 \times 107.389... = 8.591...$ N
Resolving parallel to the plane, taking up the plane as positive, and using $F_{net} = ma$:
$P - 8.591... - 11g\sin5° = 11 \times 0$
$\Rightarrow P = 8.591... + 11g\sin5° = 17.986...$ N
So, using 'Work done = Force × distance':
Work done by $P = 17.986... \times 16 = 287.785...$
$= 288$ J (3 s.f.)

Q5 $u = 0$, $v = 5$, $a = a$, $s = 4.5$
$v^2 = u^2 + 2as$
$25 = 9a$
$\Rightarrow a = 2.777...$ ms^{-2}
Resolving parallel to the plane, taking up the plane as positive, and using $F_{net} = ma$:
$F_{net} = 1.2 \times 2.777... = 3.333...$ N
Work done $=$ Force $\times$ distance
$= 3.333... \times 4.5 = 15$ J

Q6 **a)** Resolving perpendicular to the plane:
$R = 23g\cos18° = 214.368...$ N
$F = \mu R = 0.36 \times 214.368... = 77.172...$ N
Resolving parallel to the plane, taking up the plane as positive, and using $F_{net} = ma$:
$T - 23g\sin18° - 77.172... = 23 \times 0.95$
$\Rightarrow T = 21.85 + 146.824... = 168.674...$ N
$= 169$ N (3 s.f.)

b) Work done = Force × distance = mas
$= 23 \times 0.95 \times 0.75 = 16.3875$ J

2. Kinetic and Potential Energy

Exercise 2.1 — Kinetic energy

Q1 K.E. $= \frac{1}{2}mv^2 = \frac{1}{2} \times 0.045 \times 20^2 = 9$ J

Don't forget to convert grams to kilograms.

Q2 K.E. $= \frac{1}{2}mv^2$
$94\,080 = \frac{1}{2} \times 60 \times v^2$
$v^2 = 3136$
$\Rightarrow v = 56$ ms^{-1}

Q3 $1462 \times 1000 \div 3600 = 406.11...$ ms^{-1}
K.E. $= \frac{1}{2}mv^2 = \frac{1}{2} \times 11\,249 \times (406.11...)^2$
$= 9.28 \times 10^8$ J (to 3 s.f.)

Q4 K.E. $= \frac{1}{2}mv^2 = \frac{1}{2} \times (6.64 \times 10^{-27}) \times (1.5 \times 10^6)^2$
$= 7.47 \times 10^{-15}$ J

Q5 $v = \frac{s}{t} = 14 \div 3.5 = 4$ ms^{-1}
K.E. $= \frac{1}{2}m(4)^2 = 22$
$\Rightarrow m = 22 \div 8 = 2.75$ kg

Q6 Let v be the velocity of B. The velocity of A is then $2v$. The ratio of K.E. is:
$\frac{1}{2}m(2v)^2 : \frac{1}{2}mv^2$
$(2v)^2 : v^2$
$4v^2 : v^2$
$4 : 1$

Exercise 2.2 — Kinetic energy and work done

Q1 **a)**

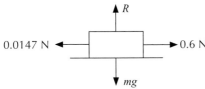

Change in K.E. = Work done on the particle
3.62×10^{-3} = Force × Distance
$3.62 \times 10^{-3} = F_{net} \times s$
Resolving horizontally, taking direction of motion as positive:
$F_{net} = 0.6 - 0.0147 = 0.5853$ N
So:
$3.62 \times 10^{-3} = 0.5853s$
$\Rightarrow s = 6.18 \times 10^{-3}$ m (3 s.f.) = 6.18 mm (3 s.f.)

b) Work done $= \frac{1}{2}m(v^2 - u^2)$
$3.62 \times 10^{-3} = \frac{1}{2}m(1.222^2 - 0.210^2)$
$\Rightarrow m = 4.995... \times 10^{-3}$ kg
$= 5.00 \times 10^{-3}$ kg (3 s.f.) = 5.00 g (3 s.f.)

Q2 Work done = change in K.E.
So, Work done $= \frac{1}{2}m(v^2 - u^2)$
$= \frac{1}{2} \times 1800(0^2 - 11^2) = -108\,900$ J
So there is a loss in K.E. of 108 900 J.
Therefore, the work done is 108 900 J.
Work done = Force × Distance
$108\,900 = R \times 96$
$\Rightarrow R = 1134.375$ N = 1130 N (3 s.f.)

Q3 **a)** Change in K.E. $= \frac{1}{2}m(v^2 - u^2)$
$= \frac{1}{2} \times 3(7^2 - 3^2) = 60$ J

b) $R = mg = 3 \times 9.8 = 29.4$ N
$F = \mu R = 0.2 \times 29.4 = 5.88$ N

c) Work done = change in K.E.
$(T - F) \times s = 60$
$(15.88 - 5.88) \times s = 60$
$\Rightarrow s = 6$ m

Q4 **a)** K.E. $= \frac{1}{2}mv^2 = \frac{1}{2} \times 0.022 \times 8^2 = 0.704$ J

b) Work done = change in K.E.
Final velocity is zero, so change in K.E. is the same as the initial K.E.
So the work done = 0.704 J.

c) Work done = Fs
$0.704 = F \times 0.005$
$\Rightarrow F = 140.8$ N

Q5

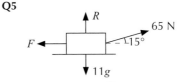

Resolving vertically:
$R + 65\sin15° = 11 \times 9.8$
$\Rightarrow R = 90.976...$ N
So $F = \mu R = 0.19 \times 90.976... = 17.285...$ N
Change in K.E. $= \frac{1}{2}m(v^2 - u^2)$
$= \frac{1}{2} \times 11 \times (14^2 - 2^2) = 1056$ J
Change in K.E. = Work done
1056 = Force × distance
$1056 = (65\cos15° - 17.285...) \times s$
$1056 = 45.499... \times s$
$\Rightarrow s = 23.2$ m (3 s.f.)

Exercise 2.3 — Potential energy

Q1 Gain in P.E. = mgh
$= 3.7 \times 9.8 \times (0.73 - 0.41)$
$= 11.6032$ J = 11.6 J (3 s.f.)

Q2 Loss of P.E. = mgh
$7.2 \times 10^{-5} = m \times 9.8 \times (1.63 - 1.02)$
$\Rightarrow m = 1.204... \times 10^{-5} = 1.20 \times 10^{-5}$ kg (3 s.f.)

Q3 Gain in P.E. = mgh
$5 \times 10^{12} = 3\,039\,000 \times 9.8 \times h$
$\Rightarrow h = 1.678... \times 10^5 = 168$ km (to nearest km)

Q4 The vertical component of the distance travelled, h, is
$3.7 \sin \theta = 3.7 \sin\left(\arcsin\frac{1}{8}\right) = 3.7 \times \frac{1}{8} = 0.4625$ m.
So P.E. = $mgh = 20 \times 9.8 \times 0.4625 = 90.65$ J

Q5 The vertical component of the distance travelled, h, is
$240\sin13°$.
P.E. = mgh
$1\,000\,000 = m \times 9.8 \times 240 \times \sin13°$
$\Rightarrow m = 1890.055... = 1890$ kg (3 s.f.)

Q6

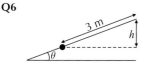

The vertical component of the distance travelled,
h, is $3\sin\theta$.
Loss of P.E. = mgh
$6.032 = 0.6 \times 9.8 \times 3 \times \sin\theta$
$\sin\theta = 0.341...$
$\Rightarrow \theta = 19.995... = 20.0°$ (3 s.f.)

Q7

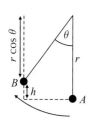

Using trigonometry, the height gained by the
pendulum, h, is $(r - r\cos\theta)$. So:
Gain in P.E. = $mgh = mg(r - r\cos\theta)$
$= mgr(1 - \cos\theta)$

3. The Work-Energy Principle
Exercise 3.1 — The principle of conservation of mechanical energy

Q1 Total mechanical energy is conserved, so
total M.E. at the top = total M.E. at the bottom
$= $ K.E. + P.E.
So P.E. at bottom = total M.E. at top – K.E. at bottom
$= 70\,560 - 52\,920 = 17\,640$ J

Q2 **a)** Total M.E. = K.E. + P.E. = $0 + mgh$
$= 0.057 \times 9.8 \times 1.13 = 0.631218$
$= 0.631$ J (3 s.f.)

b) When it hits the ground, P.E. is zero, so, using the
fact that total mechanical energy is conserved:
Total M.E. before = Total M.E. after
$0.631218 = \frac{1}{2}mv^2 + mgh$
$0.631218 = (\frac{1}{2} \times 0.057 \times v^2) + 0$
$v^2 = 22.148$
$\Rightarrow v = 4.71$ ms⁻¹ (3 s.f.)

Q3 At the instant it is dropped, the object has P.E. but no
K.E., and at the instant it hits the ground, it has K.E.
but no P.E.
Total mechanical energy is conserved, so:
P.E. lost = K.E. gained
$mgh = \frac{1}{2}mv^2$
$gh = \frac{1}{2}v^2$
$h = (\frac{1}{2} \times 11^2) \div 9.8 = 6.17$ m (3 s.f.)

Q4 Loss in K.E. = gain in P.E.
$1.47 \times 10^{-3} = mgh$
Using trigonometry, the bead moves a distance of
$(0.06\sin30°)$ m vertically upwards.
$1.47 \times 10^{-3} = m \times 9.8 \times 0.06\sin30°$
$\Rightarrow m = 0.005$ kg $= 5$ g

Q5 **a)** Total mechanical energy = K.E. + P.E.
$= \frac{1}{2}mv^2 + mgh$
$= (\frac{1}{2} \times 0.05 \times 10.1^2) + (0.05 \times 9.8 \times 52)$
$= 28.03025$ J $= 28.0$ J (3 s.f.)

b) When it reaches its maximum height, it will
momentarily be at rest, so it will have no K.E.
As total mechanical energy is conserved:
P.E. at highest point = 28.03025
$mgh = 28.03025$
$\Rightarrow h = 28.03025 \div (0.05 \times 9.8)$
$= 57.2$ m (3 s.f.)

c) It is projected from ground level, so it will have
no P.E. at the instant it is projected.
As total mechanical energy is conserved:
K.E. at projection = 28.03025
$\frac{1}{2}mv^2 = 28.03025$
$\frac{1}{2} \times 0.05 \times v^2 = 28.03025$
$v^2 = 1121.21$
$\Rightarrow v = 33.5$ ms⁻¹ (3 s.f.)

Q6 **a)** Change in P.E. = $4 \times 9.8 \times 7 \times \sin40°$
$= 176.380... = 176$ J (3 s.f.)

b) Mechanical energy is conserved, so:
gain in K.E. = loss in P.E.
$\frac{1}{2}m(v^2 - u^2) = 176.380...$ J
$\frac{1}{2} \times 4 \times (v^2 - 3^2) = 176.380...$
$v^2 = 97.190...$
$\Rightarrow v = 9.86$ ms⁻¹ (3 s.f.)

Q7 Mechanical energy is conserved, so:
gain in K.E. = loss in P.E.
$\frac{1}{2}m(v^2 - u^2) = mgh$
$\frac{1}{2}(v^2 - u^2) = gh$
$\frac{1}{2}(4.5^2 - 0^2) = 9.8h$
$\Rightarrow h = 1.033...$ m
This is the vertical distance travelled by the body.
Using trigonometry:
$x\sin19° = 1.033...$ (where x is the length of the sloped
surface of the ramp)
So $x = 1.033... \div \sin19° = 3.17$ m (3 s.f.)

Q8 a) Take the bottom of the plane as the base level (i.e. the point where the particle's height is measured from).
At the bottom of the plane, when it is fired, it has K.E. but no P.E.
At the point it comes to rest, it has P.E. but no K.E.
Change in K.E. $= \frac{1}{2}m(v^2 - u^2)$
$= \frac{1}{2} \times 13 \times (0^2 - 16^2) = -1664$ J
So 1664 J of K.E. has been lost.
Change in P.E. $= mgh$
$= 13 \times 9.8 \times h = 127.4h$ J
K.E. lost = P.E. gained
$1664 = 127.4h$
$\Rightarrow h = 13.061...$ m
This is the vertical distance travelled.
Using trigonometry, the distance travelled up the plane, x, satisfies:
$x\sin 25° = 13.061...$
$\Rightarrow x = 30.9$ m (3 s.f.)

b) Change in K.E. $= \frac{1}{2}m(v^2 - u^2)$
$= \frac{1}{2} \times 13 \times (10^2 - 16^2) = -1014$ J
As in part a), change in P.E. is $127.4h$ J
K.E. lost = P.E. gained
$1014 = 127.4h$
$\Rightarrow h = 7.959...$ m
This is the vertical distance travelled.
Using trigonometry, the distance travelled up the plane, x, satisfies:
$x\sin 25° = 7.959...$
$\Rightarrow x = 18.8$ m (3 s.f.)

Exercise 3.2 — The work-energy principle

Q1 Take the block's position when it has moved 12 m down the ramp as the 'base level' — the point where the block's height is measured from, and where it has no potential energy.
First, you need to find the block's initial mechanical energy — i.e. its mechanical energy at the top of the ramp:
Initial Mechanical Energy = Initial K.E. + Initial P.E.
$= \frac{1}{2}mu^2 + mgh_{initial}$
$= (\frac{1}{2} \times 5 \times 0^2) + (5 \times 9.8 \times 12\sin 10°) = 102.105...$ J
Next, find the block's final mechanical energy — i.e. its mechanical energy when it has moved 12 m down the ramp:
Final Mechanical Energy = Final K.E. + Final P.E.
$= \frac{1}{2}mv^2 + mgh_{final}$
$= (\frac{1}{2} \times 5 \times 3.5^2) + (5 \times 9.8 \times 0) = 30.625$ J
Now, using the work-energy principle:
Initial Mechanical Energy – Final Mechanical Energy = Work done against friction
$102.105... - 30.625 = 71.480... = 71.5$ J (3 s.f.)

Q2 a) Take the body's initial position as the 'base level'.
Initial M.E. = Initial K.E. + Initial P.E.
$= \frac{1}{2}mu^2 + mgh_{initial}$
$= (\frac{1}{2} \times 50 \times 8^2) + (50 \times 9.8 \times 0) = 1600$ J
Final M.E. = Final K.E. + Final P.E.
$= \frac{1}{2}mv^2 + mgh_{final}$
$= (\frac{1}{2} \times 50 \times 1.5^2) + (50 \times 9.8 \times 3.4\sin 30°)$
$= 889.25$ J
Now, using the work-energy principle:
Initial Mechanical Energy – Final Mechanical Energy = Work done against friction
$1600 - 889.25 = 710.75$ J

b) Work done $= Fs$
$710.75 = F \times 3.4$
$\Rightarrow F = 209.044... = 209$ N (3 s.f.)

Q3 a) Take the body's final position (i.e. 5 m down the slide) as the 'base level'.
Initial M.E. = Initial K.E. + Initial P.E.
$= \frac{1}{2}mu^2 + mgh_{initial}$
$= (\frac{1}{2} \times 7.9 \times 0^2) + (7.9 \times 9.8 \times 5\sin 45°) = 273.721...$ J
Final M.E. = Final K.E. + Final P.E.
$= \frac{1}{2}mv^2 + mgh_{final}$
$= (\frac{1}{2} \times 7.9 \times 6^2) + (7.9 \times 9.8 \times 0) = 142.2$ J
Now, using the work-energy principle:
Initial Mechanical Energy – Final Mechanical Energy = Work done against friction
$273.721... - 142.2 = 131.521... = 132$ J (3 s.f.)

b) Work done $= Fs$
$131.521... = F \times 5$
$\Rightarrow F = 26.304...$ N
Resolving perpendicular to the slope:
$R = 7.9g\cos 45° = 54.744...$ N
$F = \mu R$
$\Rightarrow \mu = F \div R = 26.304... \div 54.744...$
$= 0.48$ (2 d.p.)

Q4 Initial M.E. = Initial K.E. + Initial P.E.
$= \frac{1}{2}mu^2 + mgh_{initial}$
$= (\frac{1}{2} \times 0.025 \times 0^2) + (0.025 \times 9.8 \times 0.3) = 0.0735$ J
Final M.E. = Final K.E. + Final P.E.
$= \frac{1}{2}mv^2 + mgh_{final}$
$= (\frac{1}{2} \times 0.025 \times 0.7^2) + (0.025 \times 9.8 \times 0.1)$
$= 0.030625$ J
Now, using the work-energy principle:
Initial Mechanical Energy – Final Mechanical Energy = Work done against friction
$0.0735 - 0.030625 = 0.042875$ J
You could answer this question by redefining the base level as being 0.1 m above the ground — it would make the calculation a bit simpler.

Q5 a) Initial M.E. = Initial K.E. + Initial P.E.

$= \frac{1}{2}mu^2 + mgh_{\text{initial}}$

$= (\frac{1}{2} \times 9 \times 14^2) + (9 \times 9.8 \times 0) = 882$ J

Final M.E. = Final K.E. + Final P.E.

$= \frac{1}{2}mv^2 + mgh_{\text{final}}$

$= (\frac{1}{2} \times 9 \times 0^2) + (9 \times 9.8 \times 9) = 793.8$ J

Now, using the work-energy principle:
Initial Mechanical Energy – Final Mechanical Energy = Work done against resistive force
882 – 793.8 = 88.2 J

b) The work done by the resistive force as the particle travels upwards and back down again will be 2 × 88.2 = 176.4 J.
Using the work-energy principle:
Initial Mechanical Energy – Final Mechanical Energy = Work done against resistive force
882 – Final M.E. = 176.4
$\Rightarrow$ Final M.E. = 705.6 J
When the particle lands, it will have K.E., but no P.E., so:

$705.6 = \frac{1}{2}mv^2$

$705.6 = \frac{1}{2} \times 9 \times v^2$

$v^2 = 156.8$

$\Rightarrow v = 12.5$ ms⁻¹ (3 s.f.)

Q6 a)

Let x be the distance travelled before the object comes to rest.
Initial M.E. = Initial K.E. + Initial P.E.

$= \frac{1}{2}mu^2 + mgh_{\text{initial}}$

$= (\frac{1}{2} \times 5.5 \times 6.25^2) + (5.5 \times 9.8 \times 0)$

$= 107.421...$ J

Final M.E. = Final K.E. + Final P.E.

$= \frac{1}{2}mv^2 + mgh_{\text{final}}$

$= (\frac{1}{2} \times 5.5 \times 0^2) + (5.5 \times 9.8 \times x\sin17°)$

$= (15.758...)x$ J

Work done by friction = $Fx = \mu Rx$

$= 0.22 \times 5.5g\cos17° \times x = (11.339...)x$ J

Now, using the work-energy principle:
Initial Mechanical Energy – Final Mechanical Energy = Work done against friction
$107.421... - (15.758...)x = (11.339...)x$
$107.421... = (27.098...)x$
$\Rightarrow x = 3.964... = 3.96$ m (3 s.f.)

b) The object's initial M.E. (i.e. when it is first projected) = 107.421... J
The object's final M.E. (i.e. when it returns to its point of projection) is given by:

Final M.E. $= \frac{1}{2}mv^2 + mgh_{\text{final}}$

$= (\frac{1}{2} \times 5.5 \times v^2) + (5.5 \times 9.8 \times 0)$

$= 2.75v^2$ J

The work done by friction as the particle moves up the slope and back down again is given by:
Work done = Force × distance
$= F \times 2x = \mu R \times 2x$
$= 0.22 \times 5.5g\cos17° \times 2(3.964...) = 89.904...$ J

Now, using the work-energy principle:
Initial Mechanical Energy – Final Mechanical Energy = Work done against friction
$107.421... - 2.75v^2 = 89.904...$
$v^2 = 6.369...$
$\Rightarrow v = 2.52$ ms⁻¹

Q7 Let B be the 'base level'.
Initial M.E. = Initial K.E. + Initial P.E.

$= \frac{1}{2}mu^2 + mgh_{\text{initial}}$

$= (\frac{1}{2} \times 980 \times U^2) + (980 \times 9.8 \times 65\sin10°)$

$= (490U^2 + 108\,401.6...)$ J

Final M.E. = Final K.E. + Final P.E.

$= \frac{1}{2}mv^2 + mgh_{\text{final}}$

$= (\frac{1}{2} \times 980 \times 10^2) + (980 \times 9.8 \times 0) = 49\,000$ J

Work done = Force × distance
$= F \times 65 = \mu R \times 65$
$= 0.32 \times 980g\cos10° \times 65 = 196\,728.3...$ J

Now, using the work-energy principle:
Initial Mechanical Energy – Final Mechanical Energy = Work done against friction
$490U^2 + 108\,401.6... - 49\,000 = 196\,728.3...$
$U^2 = 280.258...$
$U = 16.7$ ms⁻¹ (3 s.f.)

Q8 a) Take the particles' initial position as 'base level'.
Then both particles have no P.E. initially.
They also have no K.E. initially, as the system is at rest. So: Initial M.E. = 0
Now consider P once it has moved 2.5 m:
(Final M.E.)$_P$ = (Final K.E.)$_P$ + (Final P.E.)$_P$

$= \frac{1}{2}mv^2 + mgh_{\text{final}}$

$= (\frac{1}{2} \times 5 \times 4^2) + (5 \times 9.8 \times 2.5\sin30°) = 101.25$ J

Now consider Q once it has moved 2.5 m:
(Final M.E.)$_Q$ = (Final K.E.)$_Q$ + (Final P.E.)$_Q$

$= \frac{1}{2}mv^2 + mgh_{\text{final}}$

$= (\frac{1}{2} \times 8 \times 4^2) + (8 \times 9.8 \times -2.5) = -132$ J

Q moves downwards, so the change in height is negative.

So the overall mechanical energy of the whole system after the particles have moved 2.5 m is:
$101.25 - 132 = -30.75$ J
Therefore, the mechanical energy lost from the system is 30.75 J.

b) Using the work-energy principle:
Initial Mechanical Energy – Final Mechanical
Energy = Work done against friction
$0 - (-30.75)$ = Force × distance
$30.75 = F \times 2.5$
$\Rightarrow F = 12.3$ N
Resolving perpendicular to the plane:
$R = 5g\cos30° = 42.435...$ N
$F = \mu R$
$\Rightarrow \mu = F \div R = 12.3 \div 42.435...$
$= 0.29$ (2 d.p.)

4. Power

Exercise 4.1 — Power

Q1 $v = 144$ kmh^{-1} = $(144 \div 3600 \times 1000)$ ms^{-1} = 40 ms^{-1}
$P = Fv = 65\,000 \times 40 = 2\,600\,000$ W = 2600 kW

Q2 At maximum speed, the acceleration is zero, and so
the resultant force is zero. Therefore:
Driving force = resistance to motion = 85 N.
$P = Fv = 85 \times 1.8 = 153$ W

Q3 $P = Fv$
$130\,000 = F \times 19$
$\Rightarrow F = 6840$ N (3 s.f.)

Q4 $P = Fv$
$23\,100 = F \times 11$
$\Rightarrow F = 2100$ N
Resolving horizontally in the direction of motion:
$F - 1140 = ma$
$2100 - 1140 = 900 \times a$
$a = 1.066666.... = 1.07$ ms^{-2} (3 s.f.)

Q5 **a)** Find the driving force F using $P = Fv$:
$96\,000 = F \times 32$
$\Rightarrow F = 3000$ N
Resolving horizontally in the direction of motion,
where there is no acceleration:
$F - R = ma = 0$
$\Rightarrow R = F = 3000$ N

b) Going up the hill you need to include a
component of the weight opposing the motion,
so resolving parallel to the slope, with no
acceleration, gives:
$F - R - mg\sin\theta = ma$
$F - 3000 - (250 \times 9.8\sin\theta) = 0$
$F = 3000 + 2450\sin\theta$
$P = Fv$
$96\,000 = F \times 28$
$\Rightarrow F = 3428.5...$ N
So $3000 + 2450\sin\theta = 3428.5...$
$\sin\theta = 0.174...$
$\Rightarrow \theta = 10.1°$ (3 s.f.)

Q6 Resolving vertically, taking up as positive, and using
$F_{net} = ma$:
$T - 52 - 4.2 = m \times 0$
$\Rightarrow T = 56.2$ N
(where T is the tension in the rope).
So, work done in lifting the object = Force × distance
$= 56.2 \times 2.4 = 134.88$ J
Power $= \dfrac{\text{Work Done}}{\text{Time}} = \dfrac{134.88}{11}$
$= 12.261... = 12.3$ W (3 s.f.)
*You could answer this question by finding the object's velocity,
and then using Power = Force × Velocity.*

Q7 Power $= Fv_{max}$
$29\,000 = F \times 8 \Rightarrow F = 3625$ N
At the maximum speed the acceleration is zero, so
resolving parallel to the slope, taking up the slope as
positive:
$F - R - 1300g\sin\theta = 0$
$R = F - 1300g\sin\theta$
$\tan\theta = \dfrac{1}{2\sqrt{6}}$, so, using trigonometry and Pythagoras'
theorem:

$\sin\theta = \dfrac{1}{5}$
So $R = 3625 - (1300 \times 9.8 \times \dfrac{1}{5}) = 1077$ N

Q8 **a)**

When travelling at max speed, acceleration is
zero, so resolving parallel to the ramp, taking up
the ramp as positive, and using $F_{net} = ma$:
$F - 140 - 660g\sin17° = 660 \times 0$
$\Rightarrow F = 2031.0...$ N
$P = Fv$
$16\,000 = 2031.0... \times v$
$\Rightarrow v = 7.877... = 7.88$ ms^{-1} (3 s.f.)

b)

140 N   17°   660g

Resolving parallel to the ramp, taking up the
ramp as positive, and using $F_{net} = ma$:
$-140 - 660g\sin17° = 660a$
$\Rightarrow a = -3.077...$ ms^{-2}
$u = 7.877..., v = 0, a = -3.077..., s = s$
$v^2 = u^2 + 2as$
$0 = (7.877...)^2 + 2(-3.077...)s$
$\Rightarrow s = 62.057... \div 6.154... = 10.1$ m (3 s.f.)

Q9

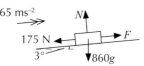

Resolving parallel to the ramp, taking up the ramp as positive, and using $F_{net} = ma$:
$F - 305 - 1230g\sin25° = 1230 \times -0.28$
$\Rightarrow F = 5054.8... \text{ N}$
$P = Fv$
$P = 5054.8... \times 8 = 40\,438.7... = 40.4 \text{ kW (3 s.f.)}$

Q10 Resolving parallel to the slope, taking down the slope as positive, and using $F_{net} = ma$:
$F + 720\sin5° - 25 = (720 \div 9.8) \times 0.733$
$\Rightarrow F = 16.100... \text{ N}$
$P = Fv = 16.100... \times 6.5$
$= 104.656... = 105 \text{ W (3 s.f.)}$

Q11 a)

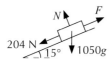

Resolving parallel to the slope, taking up the slope as positive, and using $F_{net} = ma$:
$F - 175 - 860g\sin3° = 860 \times 0.65$
$\Rightarrow F = 1175.0... \text{ N}$
$P = Fv$
$P = 1175.0... \times 16 = 18\,801.3... \text{ W}$
$= 18.8 \text{ kW (3 s.f.)}$

b)

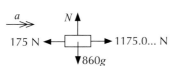

Resolving horizontally, taking direction of motion as positive:
$F_{net} = ma$
$1175.0... - 175 = 860a$
$\Rightarrow a = 1.16 \text{ ms}^{-2} \text{ (3 s.f.)}$

Q12 a)

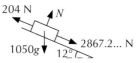

Resolving parallel to the slope, taking up the slope as positive, and using $F_{net} = ma$:
$F - 204 - 1050g\sin15° = 1050 \times 0$
$\Rightarrow F = 2867.2... \text{ N}$
$P = Fv$
$P = 2867.2... \times 8 = 22\,937.9... \text{ W}$
$= 22.9 \text{ kW (3 s.f.)}$

b)

204 N ↖ / N

$1050g$ ↓ / 2867.2... N / 12°

Resolving parallel to the slope, taking down the slope as positive, and using $F_{net} = ma$:
$2867.2... + 1050g\sin12° - 204 = 1050a$
$\Rightarrow a = 4.57 \text{ ms}^{-2}$

Q13

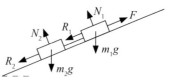

$P = Fv$, so driving force $= \dfrac{P}{v}$.

Resolving parallel to the slope, taking up the slope as positive, and using $F_{net} = ma$:
$\dfrac{P}{v} - (R_1 + R_2) - (m_1 + m_2)g\sin\theta = 0$

Where $\sin\theta = \dfrac{1}{25}$, so:
$\dfrac{P}{v} - (R_1 + R_2) - (m_1 + m_2)g\left(\dfrac{1}{25}\right) = 0$

Multiplying through by v gives:
$P - v(R_1 + R_2) - v(m_1 + m_2)g\left(\dfrac{1}{25}\right) = 0$
$\Rightarrow P = v(R_1 + R_2) + v(m_1 + m_2)g\left(\dfrac{1}{25}\right)$
$\Rightarrow P = v\left(R_1 + R_2 + \dfrac{(m_1 + m_2)g}{25}\right)$

The vehicle and the trailer are connected by a light, inextensible rope, so they can be considered as one particle (you covered this in M1). This means that the tension in the rope can be ignored, as it is just an internal force within the system.

Review Exercise — Chapter 3

Q1 Work done $= Fs = 250 \times 3 = 750 \text{ J}$

Q2 Work done $= Fs$
$1.3 = T\cos60° \times 0.4$
$\Rightarrow T = 6.5 \text{ N}$

Q3 $s = vt = 363 \times 40 = 14\,520 \text{ m}$
Work done $= Fs = 105\,000 \times 14\,520$
$= 1\,524\,600\,000 \text{ J } (= 1524.6 \text{ MJ})$

Q4 Work done against gravity $= mgh$
$34\,000 = m \times 9.8 \times 12$
$\Rightarrow m = 289 \text{ kg (3 s.f.)}$

Q5 Work done against gravity $= mgh$
$2.92 = 3 \times g_{moon} \times 0.6$
$\Rightarrow g_{moon} = 1.62 \text{ ms}^{-2} \text{ (3 s.f.)}$

Q6

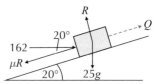

Resolving forces parallel to the plane to find the resultant force Q gives:
$Q = 162\cos20° - \mu R - 25g\sin20°$

Resolving perpendicular to the plane to find R gives:
$R = 25g\cos20° + 162\sin20° = 285.6319... \text{ N}$

So:
$Q = 162\cos20° - (0.19 \times 285.6319...) - 25g\sin20°$
$= 14.16519... \text{ N}$

Work done by $Q = Qs$
$= 14.16519... \times 10 = 142 \text{ J (3 s.f.)}$

Q7 Kinetic Energy $= \frac{1}{2}mv^2 = \frac{1}{2} \times 450 \times 13^2$
  $= 38\ 025$ J $= 38.0$ kJ (3 s.f.)

Q8 Work done = Change in Kinetic Energy
  $800 = \frac{1}{2}m(v^2 - u^2)$
  $u = 0$ and $m = 65$, so:
  $v^2 = \frac{1600}{65}$
  $\Rightarrow v = 4.96$ ms^{-1} (3 s.f.)

Q9 a) To find the work done you need to know the stopping distance. You can find this using constant acceleration equations, as long as you know the acceleration. Acceleration can be found by resolving forces horizontally, in the opposite direction to motion:
  $F_{net} = ma$
  $590 + 8500 = 1000a$
  $\Rightarrow a = 9.09$ ms^{-2} $(= -9.09$ in direction of motion)
  Now using $v^2 = u^2 + 2as$:
  $0^2 = 100^2 + (2 \times -9.09 \times s)$
  $\Rightarrow s = 550.055...$ m
  So work done by braking force $= Fs$
  $= 8500 \times 550.055... = 4\ 675\ 467.5...$
  $= 4.68$ MJ (3 s.f.)

b) Work done by resistance $= Fs$
  $= 590 \times 550.055... = 324\ 532.4...$
  $= 325$ kJ (3 s.f.)

c) Work done by resultant force $= Fs$
  $= (8500 + 590) \times 550.055... = 5\ 000\ 000$ J $= 5$ MJ
  Change in K.E. $= \frac{1}{2}m(u^2 - v^2)$
  $= \frac{1}{2} \times 1000 \times (100^2 - 0) = 5\ 000\ 000$ J $= 5$ MJ
  So the work done by the resultant force = change in K.E.

Q10 Increase in P.E. $= mg \times$ increase in height
  $= 0.5 \times 9.8 \times 150 = 735$ J

Q11 P.E. at $A = mgh = 680 \times 9.8 \times 7.5 = 49\ 980$ J
  P.E. at $B = 680 \times 9.8 \times 15.6 = 103\ 958.4$ J
  P.E. at $C = 680 \times 9.8 \times 1.8 = 11\ 995.2$ J

  So between A and B the car gains 53 978.4 J and between B and C loses 91 963.2, and overall between A and C it loses 37 984.8 J of P.E.

Q12 When the hat reaches its maximum height, its velocity will be zero. Using conservation of energy:
  Change in P.E. = Change in K.E.
  $mgh = \frac{1}{2}m(u^2 - v^2)$
  Cancel m from both sides, and substitute $u = 5$, $v = 0$ and $g = 9.8$:
  $9.8h = \frac{1}{2} \times 25$
  $\Rightarrow h = 1.28$ m (3 s.f.)

Q13 Using the principle of conservation of mechanical energy, Initial M.E. = Final M.E., so:

  Initial K.E. + Initial P.E. = Final K.E. + Final P.E.
  Final K.E. = Initial K.E. + Initial P.E. − Final P.E.
  $= 39.2 + 0 - mgh$
  (assuming the ball is kicked from the ground so initial P.E. = 0).
  Final K.E. $= 39.2 - (0.4 \times 9.8 \times 1.94) = 31.6$ J (3 s.f.)

Q14

Take the bottom of the ramp as the 'base level'.
Initial M.E. = Initial K.E. + Initial P.E.
  $= \frac{1}{2}mu^2 + mgh_{initial}$
  $= (\frac{1}{2} \times 15 \times 0^2) + (15 \times 9.8 \times 9\sin 11°) = 252.440...$ J
Final M.E. = Final K.E. + Final P.E.
  $= \frac{1}{2}mv^2 + mgh_{final}$
  $= (\frac{1}{2} \times 15 \times 4.2^2) + (15 \times 9.8 \times 0) = 132.3$ J
Now, using the work-energy principle:
Initial Mechanical Energy − Final Mechanical Energy
= Work done against friction
$252.440... - 132.3 = 120.140... = 120$ J (3 s.f.)

Q15 a) Take the body's initial position as the 'base level'.
  Initial M.E. = Initial K.E. + Initial P.E.
  $= \frac{1}{2}mu^2 + mgh_{initial}$
  $= (\frac{1}{2} \times 14 \times 5.5^2) + (14 \times 9.8 \times 0) = 211.75$ J
  Final M.E. = Final K.E. + Final P.E.
  $= \frac{1}{2}mv^2 + mgh_{final}$
  $= (\frac{1}{2} \times 14 \times 0.4^2) + (14 \times 9.8 \times 2.5\sin 30°)$
  $= 172.62$ J
  Now, using the work-energy principle:
  Initial Mechanical Energy − Final Mechanical Energy = Work done against friction
  $211.75 - 172.62 = 39.13$ J

b) Work done $= Fs$
  $39.13 = F \times 2.5$
  $\Rightarrow F = 15.652$ N
  Resolving perpendicular to the slope:
  $R = 14g\cos 30° = 118.818...$ N
  $F = \mu R$
  $\Rightarrow \mu = F \div R = 15.652 \div 118.818...$
  $= 0.131... = 0.132$ (3 s.f.)

Q16 Power of engine = driving force $\times$ velocity
  $350\ 000 = F \times 22$
  $\Rightarrow F = 15\ 900$ N (3 s.f.)

Q17

0.75 ms^{-2} N F 188 N   5°   820g

Resolving parallel to the slope, taking down the slope as positive, and using $F_{net} = ma$:
  $F + 820g\sin 5° - 188 = 820 \times 0.75$
  $\Rightarrow F = 102.616...$ N
  $P = Fv$
  $P = 102.616... \times 10 = 1026.1...$
  $= 1.03$ kW (3 s.f.)

Q18

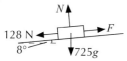

When moving with max speed, acceleration is zero. Resolving parallel to the slope, taking up the slope as positive, and using $F_{net} = ma$:

$F - 128 - 725g\sin8° = 725 \times 0$

$\Rightarrow F = 1116.8...$ N

$P = Fv$

$25\,000 = 1116.8... \times v$

$\Rightarrow v = 22.4$ ms^{-1} (3 s.f.)

Exam-Style Questions — Chapter 3

Q1 a) Take B as the 'base level'.

Initial M.E. = Initial K.E. + Initial P.E.

$= \frac{1}{2}mu^2 + mgh_{initial}$

$= (\frac{1}{2} \times 90 \times 8^2) + (90 \times 9.8 \times 100\sin20°)$

[1 mark]

$= 33\,046.1...$ J

Final M.E. = Final K.E. + Final P.E.

$= \frac{1}{2}mv^2 + mgh_{final}$

$= (\frac{1}{2} \times 90 \times 7^2) + (90 \times 9.8 \times 0)$ *[1 mark]*

$= 2205$ J

Initial M.E. – Final M.E. = 33 046.1... – 2205

$= 30\,841.1...$ J

$= 30\,800$ J (3 s.f.) *[1 mark]*

b) Using the work-energy principle:
change in mechanical energy = work done against friction

So, using 'Work done = Force × distance':

$30\,841.1... = F \times 100$ *[1 mark]*

$\Rightarrow F = 308.411...$ N *[1 mark]*

Resolving perpendicular to the plane:

$R = 90g\cos20° = 828.808...$ N *[1 mark]*

(where R is the normal reaction force of the plane on the man)

So, using $F = \mu R$:

$308.411... = \mu \times 828.808...$ *[1 mark]*

$\Rightarrow \mu = 0.372$ (3 s.f.) *[1 mark]*

Q2 a) K.E. $= \frac{1}{2}mv^2 = \frac{1}{2} \times 0.3 \times 20^2$ *[1 mark]*

$= 60$ J *[1 mark]*

b) The only force acting on the stone is its weight, so use conservation of mechanical energy.

Take the surface of the water as the 'base level'. Immediately before it is dropped, the stone has P.E. but no K.E. When it hits the surface of the water, it has K.E. but no P.E. Therefore:

Gain in K.E. = Loss in P.E. *[1 mark]*

$60 = 0.3 \times 9.8 \times h$ *[1 mark]*

$\Rightarrow h = 20.4$ m (3 s.f.) *[1 mark]*

c) Let the depth the stone sinks be y.

Work done by resistive forces = Force × Distance

$= 23y$ J *[1 mark]*

Now find the change in mechanical energy. Take the depth of the stone when its speed has been reduced to 1 ms^{-1} as the 'base level'. First find the initial mechanical energy (i.e. the mechanical energy when it hits the surface of the water):

Initial M.E. = Initial K.E. + Initial P.E.

$= \frac{1}{2}mu^2 + mgh_{initial}$

$= (\frac{1}{2} \times 0.3 \times 20^2) + (0.3 \times 9.8 \times y)$ *[1 mark]*

$= (60 + 2.94y)$ J

Now find final mechanical energy (i.e. mechanical energy when speed has been reduced to 1 ms^{-1}).

Final M.E. = Final K.E. + Final P.E.

$= \frac{1}{2}mv^2 + mgh_{final}$

$= (\frac{1}{2} \times 0.3 \times 1^2) + (0.3 \times 9.8 \times 0)$ *[1 mark]*

$= 0.15$ J

Now using the work-energy principle:

Initial Mechanical Energy – Final Mechanical Energy = Work done against resistive force

$60 + 2.94y - 0.15 = 23y$ *[1 mark]*

$59.85 = 20.06y$

$\Rightarrow y = 2.98$ m (3 s.f.) *[1 mark]*

Q3 a)

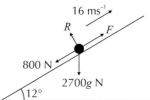

Let F be the driving force of the van's engine. Resolving parallel to the slope, taking up the slope as positive, and using $F_{net} = ma$ with $a = 0$:

$F - 800 - 2700g\sin12° = 0$ *[1 mark]*

$\Rightarrow F = 6301.343...$ *[1 mark]*

Power of engine = Fv *[1 mark]*

$= 6301.343... \times 16 = 101$ kW (3 s.f.) *[1 mark]*

b) Work done against resistive force = $800x$ *[1 mark]*

Take A as the 'base level'.

First find initial mechanical energy (i.e. mechanical energy at A):

Initial M.E. = Initial K.E. + Initial P.E.

$= \frac{1}{2}mu^2 + mgh_{initial}$

$= (\frac{1}{2} \times 2700 \times 16^2) + (2700 \times 9.8 \times 0)$ *[1 mark]*

$= 345\,600$ J

Now find final mechanical energy:

Final M.E. = Final K.E. + Final P.E.

$= \frac{1}{2}mv^2 + mgh_{final}$

$= (\frac{1}{2} \times 2700 \times 0^2) + (2700 \times 9.8 \times x\sin12°)$

[1 mark]

$= (5501.343...)x$ J

Now using the work-energy principle:
Initial mechanical energy – Final mechanical energy = Work done against resistive force
$345\ 600 - (5501.343...)x = 800x$ *[1 mark]*
$345\ 600 = (6301.343...)x$
$\Rightarrow x = 54.8$ m (3 s.f.) *[1 mark]*

c) Resolve parallel to the slope using $F = ma$ to find a:
$-800 - 2700g\sin12° = 2700a$ *[1 mark]*
$a = -2.333...$ ms^{-2} *[1 mark]*
Use $v = u + at$ to find the time taken to come to rest:
$0 = 16 - (2.333...)t$ *[1 mark]*
$t = 16 \div 2.333... = 6.86$ s (3 s.f.) *[1 mark]*

Q4 a) Work done = Force × distance moved
$= 800\cos40° \times 320 = 196$ kJ (3 s.f.)
[3 marks available in total]:
- *1 mark for using the horizontal component of the force*
- *1 mark for correct use of formula for work done*
- *1 mark for correct final answer.*

b)

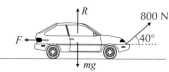

Resolving vertically:
$R + 800\sin40° = mg$
$R = 1500g - 800\sin40° = 14\ 185.7...$ N
[1 mark]
$F = \mu R = (14\ 185.7...)\mu$
The car is moving only horizontally, so:
Work done on car = change in kinetic energy
[1 mark]
Force × distance $= \frac{1}{2}m(v^2 - u^2)$
Resolving horizontally:
$(800\cos40° - (14\ 185.7...)\mu) \times 320$
$= \frac{1}{2} \times 1500 \times (16^2 - 11^2)$ *[1 mark]*
$\Rightarrow 94857.3... = (4\ 539\ 446.3...)\mu$
$\Rightarrow \mu = 0.0209$ (3 s.f.) *[1 mark]*

Q5 a) Use $P = Fv$ to find the 'driving' force, F, of the cyclist:
$250 = F \times 4$ *[1 mark]*
$\Rightarrow F = 62.5$ N *[1 mark]*
Resolving parallel to the slope, taking up the slope as positive, and using $F_{net} = ma$:
$62.5 - 35 - 88g\sin\alpha = m \times 0$ *[1 mark]*
$\alpha = \sin^{-1}\frac{27.5}{88g} = 1.83°$ (3 s.f.) *[1 mark]*

b) Use $P = Fv$ to find the new 'driving' force, F':
$370 = F' \times 4$ *[1 mark]*
$F' = 92.5$ N *[1 mark]*
Resolving parallel to the slope, taking up the slope as positive, and using $F_{net} = ma$:
$92.5 - 35 - 88g\sin\alpha = 88a$ *[1 mark]*
$a = 0.341$ ms^{-2} (3 s.f.) *[1 mark]*

Chapter 4: Collisions

1. Momentum and Impulse

Exercise 1.1 — Impulse

Q1 $\mathbf{I} = m\mathbf{v} - m\mathbf{u} = m(\mathbf{v} - \mathbf{u})$
$\mathbf{I} = 0.05(5\mathbf{i} + 3\mathbf{j} - 2\mathbf{i} + 3\mathbf{j}) = (0.15\mathbf{i} + 0.3\mathbf{j})$ Ns

Q2 $\mathbf{I} = m(\mathbf{v} - \mathbf{u})$
$60\mathbf{j} = 12(\mathbf{v} + 4\mathbf{i} - 7\mathbf{j})$
$60\mathbf{j} = 12\mathbf{v} + 48\mathbf{i} - 84\mathbf{j}$
$\mathbf{v} = (-4\mathbf{i} + 12\mathbf{j})$ ms^{-1}

Q3 $\mathbf{Q} = 9(-7\mathbf{i} - \mathbf{j} - 3\mathbf{i} - 4\mathbf{j}) = (-90\mathbf{i} - 45\mathbf{j})$ Ns

Q4 $\mathbf{I} = 0.3(-5\mathbf{i} - 2\mathbf{j} - 3\mathbf{i} - 4\mathbf{j}) = (-2.4\mathbf{i} - 1.8\mathbf{j})$ Ns

Q5 $4\mathbf{i} - 6\mathbf{j} = 0.2(-10\mathbf{i} + 20\mathbf{j} - \mathbf{u})$
$4\mathbf{i} - 6\mathbf{j} = -2\mathbf{i} + 4\mathbf{j} - 0.2\mathbf{u}$
$\mathbf{u} = (-30\mathbf{i} + 50\mathbf{j})$ ms^{-1}

Q6 $9\mathbf{i} + 6\mathbf{j} = m(6\mathbf{i} - 2\mathbf{j} - 3\mathbf{i} + 4\mathbf{j})$
$9\mathbf{i} + 6\mathbf{j} = m(3\mathbf{i} + 2\mathbf{j})$
$m = 3$ kg

Q7 $\mathbf{I} = 0.015(2\mathbf{j} + 0.2\mathbf{j}) = 0.033\mathbf{j}$ Ns
As there is no $\mathbf{i}$ component, the magnitude is just 0.033 Ns.

Q8 $\mathbf{Q} = 0.2(3\mathbf{i} - 4\mathbf{j} + 9\mathbf{i} - 4\mathbf{j}) = (2.4\mathbf{i} - 1.6\mathbf{j})$ Ns

$|\mathbf{Q}| = \sqrt{2.4^2 + 1.6^2} = 2.88$ Ns (3 s.f.)
$\theta = \tan^{-1}\left(\frac{1.6}{2.4}\right) = 33.7°$ (3 s.f.)

Q9 $45\mathbf{i} - 30\mathbf{j} = 7.5(4\mathbf{i} - 6\mathbf{j} - \mathbf{u})$
$45\mathbf{i} - 30\mathbf{j} = 30\mathbf{i} - 45\mathbf{j} - 7.5\mathbf{u}$
$\mathbf{u} = (-2\mathbf{i} - 2\mathbf{j})$ ms^{-1}

$|\mathbf{u}| = \sqrt{2^2 + 2^2} = 2\sqrt{2} = 2.83$ ms^{-1} (3 s.f.)
$\theta = \tan^{-1}\left(\frac{2}{2}\right) = 45°$, so its initial direction of motion is 45° below $-\mathbf{i}$.

Q10 a) $\mathbf{I} = 0.16(-30\mathbf{i} - 40\mathbf{j} - 50\mathbf{i}) = (-12.8\mathbf{i} - 6.4\mathbf{j})$ Ns
$|\mathbf{I}| = \sqrt{(-12.8)^2 + (-6.4)^2} = 14.3$ Ns (3 s.f.)

b) Initially the ball is travelling at 50$\mathbf{i}$ ms^{-1} — there is no $\mathbf{j}$ component so the ball is travelling in the positive $\mathbf{i}$ direction.

After being hit the ball travels at an angle θ below $-\mathbf{i}$:

$\theta = \tan^{-1}\left(\frac{40}{30}\right) = 53.130...°$

So the angle between the ball's path before and after being hit is $180° - 53.130...° = 127°$ (3 s.f.)

Q11 a) First find **u** and **v** by working out the change in position vector in the given times:

$$\mathbf{u} = \frac{12\mathbf{i} + 5\mathbf{j} - 4\mathbf{i} + 7\mathbf{j}}{4} = (2\mathbf{i} + 3\mathbf{j}) \text{ ms}^{-1}$$

$$\mathbf{v} = \frac{2\mathbf{i} - 10\mathbf{j} - 12\mathbf{i} - 5\mathbf{j}}{5} = (-2\mathbf{i} - 3\mathbf{j}) \text{ ms}^{-1}$$

Now use these to work out **I**:

$$\mathbf{I} = 0.5(-2\mathbf{i} - 3\mathbf{j} - 2\mathbf{i} - 3\mathbf{j}) = (-2\mathbf{i} - 3\mathbf{j}) \text{ Ns}$$

$$|\mathbf{I}| = \sqrt{(-2)^2 + (-3)^2} = 3.61 \text{ Ns (3 s.f.)}$$

b) You can see from the diagram below that the particle has been turned though 180° by the impulse:

Q12 $-3\mathbf{i} + 4\mathbf{j} = 0.17(\mathbf{v} - 7\mathbf{i} + 8\mathbf{j})$

$-3\mathbf{i} + 4\mathbf{j} = 0.17\mathbf{v} - 1.19\mathbf{i} + 1.36\mathbf{j}$

$\mathbf{v} = (-10.6...\mathbf{i} + 15.5...\mathbf{j}) \text{ ms}^{-1}$

Change in direction (clockwise) = $(180° - \theta) + \alpha$

$= (180° - \tan^{-1}\left(\frac{8}{7}\right)) + \tan^{-1}\left(\frac{15.5...}{10.6...}\right) = 187° \text{ (3 s.f.)}$

Q13 First use one of the constant acceleration equations to find the initial velocity u_i, which is the final velocity of a vertical fall of 1 m under gravity, taking down as positive:

$v^2 = u^2 + 2as \Rightarrow u_i^2 = 0^2 + (2 \times 9.8 \times 1)$

$\Rightarrow u_i = \sqrt{0^2 + (2 \times 9.8 \times 1)} = 4.427... \text{ ms}^{-1}$

The ball is falling vertically downwards at this velocity, so $\mathbf{u} = -4.427...\mathbf{j} \text{ ms}^{-1}$

$\mathbf{Q} = 0.06(40\mathbf{i} + 16\mathbf{j} + 4.427...\mathbf{j}) = (2.4\mathbf{i} + 1.225...\mathbf{j}) \text{ Ns}$

$|\mathbf{Q}| = \sqrt{2.4^2 + 1.225...^2} = 2.69 \text{ Ns (3 s.f.)}$

$\theta = \tan^{-1}\left(\frac{1.225...}{2.4}\right) = 27.1° \text{ (3 s.f.)}$

Exercise 1.2 — Conservation of momentum

Q1 a) $m_A\mathbf{u}_A + m_B\mathbf{u}_B = m_A\mathbf{v}_A + m_B\mathbf{v}_B$

$2(2\mathbf{i} + 3\mathbf{j}) + 3(-5\mathbf{i} + 2\mathbf{j}) = 2\mathbf{v}_A + 3(-2\mathbf{i})$

$4\mathbf{i} + 6\mathbf{j} - 15\mathbf{i} + 6\mathbf{j} = 2\mathbf{v}_A - 6\mathbf{i}$

$2\mathbf{v}_A = -5\mathbf{i} + 12\mathbf{j}$

$\mathbf{v}_A = (-2.5\mathbf{i} + 6\mathbf{j}) \text{ ms}^{-1}$

b) $m_A\mathbf{u}_A + m_B\mathbf{u}_B = m_A\mathbf{v}_A + m_B\mathbf{v}_B$

$4(3\mathbf{i} - 4\mathbf{j}) + m(-8\mathbf{i} + 11\mathbf{j}) = 4(-2\mathbf{i} + 6\mathbf{j}) + m(-3\mathbf{i} + \mathbf{j})$

$m(-8\mathbf{i} + 11\mathbf{j}) - m(-3\mathbf{i} + \mathbf{j}) = 4(-2\mathbf{i} + 6\mathbf{j} - 3\mathbf{i} + 4\mathbf{j})$

$m(-8\mathbf{i} + 11\mathbf{j} + 3\mathbf{i} - \mathbf{j}) = -20\mathbf{i} + 40\mathbf{j}$

$m(-5\mathbf{i} + 10\mathbf{j}) = -20\mathbf{i} + 40\mathbf{j}$

$m = 4 \text{ kg}$

c) $m_A\mathbf{u}_A + m_B\mathbf{u}_B = (m_A + m_B)\mathbf{v}$

$1(-4\mathbf{i} + 6\mathbf{j}) + 2(3\mathbf{i} - 3\mathbf{j}) = (1 + 2)\mathbf{v}$

$2\mathbf{i} = 3\mathbf{v}$

$\mathbf{v} = \frac{2}{3}\mathbf{i} \text{ ms}^{-1}$

Q2 $m_A\mathbf{u}_A + m_B\mathbf{u}_B = (m_A + m_B)\mathbf{v}$

$3m(3\mathbf{i} - \mathbf{j}) + 2m\mathbf{u}_B = (3m + 2m)(-\mathbf{i} + \mathbf{j})$

$9\mathbf{i} - 3\mathbf{j} + 2\mathbf{u}_B = -5\mathbf{i} + 5\mathbf{j}$

$\mathbf{u}_B = (-7\mathbf{i} + 4\mathbf{j}) \text{ ms}^{-1}$

Note that you can just divide through by m to get rid of it from each term.

Q3 $m_A\mathbf{u}_A + m_B\mathbf{u}_B = (m_A + m_B)\mathbf{v}$

$m(5\mathbf{i} - 3\mathbf{j}) + 0 = 2m\mathbf{v}$

$\mathbf{v} = (2.5\mathbf{i} - 1.5\mathbf{j}) \text{ ms}^{-1}$

Both particles have the same mass, so just call this mass 'm', and since B is initially stationary, $m_B\mathbf{u}_B = \mathbf{O}$.

Q4 $m_A\mathbf{u}_A + m_B\mathbf{u}_B = m_A\mathbf{v}_A + m_B\mathbf{v}_B$

$10(7\mathbf{i} - 10\mathbf{j}) + m(-5\mathbf{i} + 8\mathbf{j}) = 10(2\mathbf{i} - 5\mathbf{j}) + m(5\mathbf{i} - 2\mathbf{j})$

$m(-5\mathbf{i} + 8\mathbf{j}) - m(5\mathbf{i} - 2\mathbf{j}) = 10(2\mathbf{i} - 5\mathbf{j} - 7\mathbf{i} + 10\mathbf{j})$

$m(-10\mathbf{i} + 10\mathbf{j}) = -50\mathbf{i} + 50\mathbf{j}$

$m = 5 \text{ kg}$

Q5 $m_A\mathbf{u}_A + m_B\mathbf{u}_B = m_A\mathbf{v}_A + m_B\mathbf{v}_B$

$0.6(6\mathbf{i} - 2\mathbf{j}) + 0.4\mathbf{u}_B = \mathbf{0}$

$0.4\mathbf{u}_B = -3.6\mathbf{i} + 1.2\mathbf{j}$

$\mathbf{u}_B = (-9\mathbf{i} + 3\mathbf{j}) \text{ ms}^{-1}$

Q6 $m_A\mathbf{u}_A + m_B\mathbf{u}_B = m_A\mathbf{v}_A + m_B\mathbf{v}_B$

$m(4\mathbf{i} - 6\mathbf{j}) + m\mathbf{u}_B = m(3\mathbf{i} - 8\mathbf{j}) + m(-5\mathbf{i} + 7\mathbf{j})$

$4\mathbf{i} - 6\mathbf{j} + \mathbf{u}_B = -2\mathbf{i} - \mathbf{j}$

$\mathbf{u}_B = (-6\mathbf{i} + 5\mathbf{j}) \text{ ms}^{-1}$

The speed of B is the magnitude of the velocity, i.e.
Speed $= \sqrt{(-6)^2 + 5^2} = 7.81 \text{ ms}^{-1} \text{ (3 s.f.)}$

Q7 $m_A\mathbf{u}_A + m_B\mathbf{u}_B = m_A\mathbf{v}_A + m_B\mathbf{v}_B$

$20(5\mathbf{j}) + 0 = 20(0.2\mathbf{i} + 2\mathbf{j}) + 24\mathbf{v}_B$

$100\mathbf{j} = 4\mathbf{i} + 40\mathbf{j} + 24\mathbf{v}_B$

$\mathbf{v}_B = (-\frac{1}{6}\mathbf{i} + 2.5\mathbf{j}) \text{ ms}^{-1}$

Speed $= \sqrt{(-\frac{1}{6})^2 + 2.5^2} = 2.51 \text{ ms}^{-1} \text{ (3 s.f.)}$

Angle above $-\mathbf{i}$, $\theta = \tan^{-1}\left(\frac{2.5}{\frac{1}{6}}\right) = 86.2° \text{ (3 s.f.)}$

Q8 $m_A\mathbf{u}_A + m_B\mathbf{u}_B = m_A\mathbf{v}_A + m_B\mathbf{v}_B$

$m((t - 8)\mathbf{i} + 2t\mathbf{j}) + m((3t + 2)\mathbf{i} - t^2\mathbf{j})$
$= m(12\mathbf{i} + 2\mathbf{j}) + m(-6\mathbf{i} - 5\mathbf{j})$

$(4t - 6)\mathbf{i} + (2t - t^2)\mathbf{j} = 6\mathbf{i} - 3\mathbf{j}$

So $4t - 6 = 6 \Rightarrow t = 3 \text{ s}$

(Check this works in the **j** component too:
$2(3) - 3^2 = -3$, so yes it works.)

Q9 Before using the formula for the conservation of momentum you need to work out $\mathbf{u}_A$ and $\mathbf{v}_B$ in $\mathbf{i}$ and $\mathbf{j}$ form:

Before	After
$\mathbf{u}_B = 0$	$|\mathbf{v}_B| = 0.5$ ms^{-1}
$\mathbf{u}_A = (2 \text{ ms}^{-2} \times 0.4 \text{ s})\mathbf{j}$	So $\mathbf{v}_B = (0.5 \sin 60°)\mathbf{i} +$
$= 0.8\mathbf{j}$ ms^{-1}	$(0.5 \cos 60°)\mathbf{j}$ ms^{-1}

$m_A\mathbf{u}_A + m_B\mathbf{u}_B = m_A\mathbf{v}_A + m_B\mathbf{v}_B$

$m(0.8\mathbf{j}) + \mathbf{0} = m\mathbf{v}_A + m((0.5 \sin 60°)\mathbf{i} + (0.5 \cos 60°)\mathbf{j})$

$0.8\mathbf{j} = \mathbf{v}_A + \dfrac{\sqrt{3}}{4}\mathbf{i} + 0.25\mathbf{j}$

$\mathbf{v}_A = (-0.433\mathbf{i} + 0.55\mathbf{j})$ ms^{-1} (3 s.f.)

Q10 a) First find $\mathbf{u}_A$ following the impulse given to it by the snooker cue using $\mathbf{I} = m(\mathbf{v} - \mathbf{u})$:

$0.25\mathbf{i} - 0.125\mathbf{j} = 0.16(\mathbf{u}_A - \mathbf{0})$

$\Rightarrow \mathbf{u}_A = (1.5625\mathbf{i} - 0.78125\mathbf{j})$ ms^{-1}

Now use the conservation of momentum formula to find the velocity of the red ball, $\mathbf{v}_B$:

$m_A\mathbf{u}_A + m_B\mathbf{u}_B = m_A\mathbf{v}_A + m_B\mathbf{v}_B$

$m(1.5625\mathbf{i} - 0.78125\mathbf{j}) + \mathbf{0} = m(0.3\mathbf{i} - 0.4\mathbf{j}) + m\mathbf{v}_B$

$\mathbf{v}_B = (1.2625\mathbf{i} - 0.38125\mathbf{j})$ ms^{-1}

b) Original path of white ball is an angle θ below $\mathbf{i}$, where:

$\theta = \tan^{-1}\left(\dfrac{0.78125}{1.5625}\right) = 26.6°$ (3 s.f.)

Path of the red ball is an angle α below $\mathbf{i}$, where:

$\alpha = \tan^{-1}\left(\dfrac{0.38125}{1.2625}\right) = 16.8°$ (3 s.f.)

These angles are not within 5° of each other, so the ball does not go in the pocket.

2. Collisions

Exercise 2.1 — Newton's law of restitution

Q1 **a)** $e = \dfrac{v_B - v_A}{u_A - u_B} = \dfrac{2 - (-2)}{5 - 0} = 0.8$

b) $e = \dfrac{-1 - (-4)}{-2 - (-7)} = 0.6$

c) $e = \dfrac{8 - 1.5}{10 - (-3)} = 0.5$

d) $e = \dfrac{11 - 5}{12 - 3} = \dfrac{2}{3} = 0.667$ (3 s.f.)

Q2 **a)** $e = \dfrac{v_B - v_A}{u_A - u_B}$

$\Rightarrow 0.25 = \dfrac{2 - v_A}{5 - (-1)} \Rightarrow v_A = 0.5$ ms^{-1}

b) $e = \dfrac{v_B - v_A}{u_A - u_B}$

$\Rightarrow 0.1 = \dfrac{-2 - (-3)}{-5 - u_B} \Rightarrow u_B = -15$ ms^{-1}

c) $e = \dfrac{v_B - v_A}{u_A - u_B}$

$\Rightarrow 0.5 = \dfrac{0 - v_A}{1 - (-7)} \Rightarrow v_A = -4$ ms^{-1}

d) $e = \dfrac{v_B - v_A}{u_A - u_B}$

$\Rightarrow 0.8 = \dfrac{v_B - (-4)}{15 - 3} \Rightarrow v_B = 5.6$ ms^{-1}

Exercise 2.2 — Finding velocities

Q1 **a)** $e = \dfrac{v_B - v_A}{u_A - u_B}$

$\Rightarrow 0.5 = \dfrac{2 - v_A}{u_A - (-3)}$

$\Rightarrow u_A = 1 - 2v_A$ ...[1]

$m_A u_A + m_B u_B = m_A v_A + m_B v_B$

$\Rightarrow 4u_A + (2 \times -3) = 4v_A + (2 \times 2)$

$\Rightarrow 4u_A - 6 = 4v_A + 4$

$\Rightarrow u_A = v_A + 2.5$ ...[2]

Equating [1] and [2] gives:

$1 - 2v_A = v_A + 2.5 \Rightarrow v_A = -0.5$ ms^{-1}

Substituting in [1] gives:

$u_A = 1 - 2(-0.5) = 2$ ms^{-1}

b) $e = \dfrac{v_B - v_A}{u_A - u_B}$

$\Rightarrow 0.1 = \dfrac{v_B - v_A}{2.5 - (-4)}$

$\Rightarrow v_A = v_B - 0.65$ ...[1]

$m_A u_A + m_B u_B = m_A v_A + m_B v_B$

$\Rightarrow (2 \times 2.5) + (3 \times -4) = 2v_A + 3v_B$

$\Rightarrow -7 = 2v_A + 3v_B$ ...[2]

Substituting [1] into [2] gives:

$-7 = 2(v_B - 0.65) + 3v_B \Rightarrow v_B = -1.14$ ms^{-1}

Substituting in [1] gives:

$v_A = -1.14 - 0.65 = -1.79$ ms^{-1}

Q2 Call the white ball A and the blue ball B. Then $u_A = 1.5$, $u_B = 0$, and v_A and v_B are defined to be in the positive direction.

$e = \dfrac{v_B - v_A}{u_A - u_B}$

$\Rightarrow 0.8 = \dfrac{v_B - v_A}{1.5 - 0}$

$\Rightarrow v_A = v_B - 1.2$ ...[1]

$m_A u_A + m_B u_B = m_A v_A + m_B v_B$

$\Rightarrow 1.5m + 0 = m(v_A + v_B)$

$\Rightarrow v_A = 1.5 - v_B$ ...[2]

Equating [1] and [2] gives:

$v_B - 1.2 = 1.5 - v_B \Rightarrow v_B = 1.35$ ms^{-1}

Substituting in [1] gives:

$v_A = 1.35 - 1.2 = 0.15$ ms^{-1}

Q3 Call the 3000 kg truck A and the other truck B. Then $m_A = 3000$, $m_B = 4000$, $u_B = 0$, $v_B = 6$, and u_A and v_A are defined to be in the positive direction.

$e = \dfrac{v_B - v_A}{u_A - u_B}$

$\Rightarrow 0.6 = \dfrac{6 - v_A}{u_A - 0}$

$\Rightarrow v_A = 6 - 0.6u_A$ ...[1]

$m_A u_A + m_B u_B = m_A v_A + m_B v_B$

$\Rightarrow 3000u_A + 0 = 3000v_A + (4000 \times 6)$

$\Rightarrow v_A = u_A - 8$ ...[2]

Equating [1] and [2] gives:

$6 - 0.6u_A = u_A - 8 \Rightarrow u_A = 8.75$ ms^{-1}

Substituting in [1] gives:

$v_A = 6 - (0.6 \times 8.75) = 0.75$ ms^{-1}

Q4 a) $e = \dfrac{v_B - v_A}{u_A - u_B}$

$\Rightarrow 0.05 = \dfrac{v_B - v_A}{50 - (-30)}$

$\Rightarrow v_A = v_B - 4 \;...[1]$

$m_A u_A + m_B u_B = m_A v_A + m_B v_B$

$\Rightarrow (45 \times 50) + (60 \times -30) = 45v_A + 60v_B$

$\Rightarrow 450 = 45v_A + 60v_B \;...[2]$

Substituting [1] into [2] gives:
$450 = 45(v_B - 4) + 60v_B \Rightarrow v_B = 6 \text{ ms}^{-1}$

Substituting in [1] gives:
$v_A = 6 - 4 = 2 \text{ ms}^{-1}$

b) Changing the value of e only affects equation [1] from part a), which becomes:

$0.95 = \dfrac{v_B - v_A}{50 - (-30)} \Rightarrow v_A = v_B - 76 \;...[1]$

Substituting new eqn [1] into [2] from a) gives:
$450 = 45(v_B - 76) + 60v_B \Rightarrow v_B = 36.9 \text{ ms}^{-1}\text{ (3 s.f.)}$

Substituting in [1] gives:
$v_A = 36.85... - 76 = -39.1 \text{ ms}^{-1}\text{ (3 s.f.)}$

(i.e. 39.1 ms^{-1} (3 s.f.) in the opposite direction to before the collision.)

Q5 Call the first marble A and the second B.
Then $m_A = 0.04$, $m_B = 0.02$, $u_A = 1.5$, $u_B = 0$, and assume v_A and v_B are both in the positive direction.

$e = \dfrac{v_B - v_A}{u_A - u_B}$

$\Rightarrow 0.9 = \dfrac{v_B - v_A}{1.5 - 0}$

$\Rightarrow v_A = v_B - 1.35 \;...[1]$

$m_A u_A + m_B u_B = m_A v_A + m_B v_B$

$\Rightarrow (0.04 \times 1.5) + 0 = 0.04v_A + 0.02v_B$

$\Rightarrow 0.06 = 0.04v_A + 0.02v_B \;...[2]$

Substituting [1] into [2] gives:
$0.06 = 0.04(v_B - 1.35) + 0.02v_B \Rightarrow v_B = 1.9 \text{ ms}^{-1}$

Substituting in [1] gives:
$v_A = 1.9 - 1.35 = 0.55 \text{ ms}^{-1}$

Q6 a) Taking the initial direction of A to be positive, and assuming both particles move off in the positive direction:

$e = \dfrac{v_B - v_A}{u_A - u_B}$

$\Rightarrow 0.8 = \dfrac{v_B - v_A}{16 - 10}$

$\Rightarrow v_A = v_B - 4.8 \;...[1]$

$m_A u_A + m_B u_B = m_A v_A + m_B v_B$

$\Rightarrow (5 \times 16) + (3 \times 10) = 5v_A + 3v_B$

$\Rightarrow 110 = 5v_A + 3v_B \;...[2]$

Substituting [1] into [2] gives:
$110 = 5(v_B - 4.8) + 3v_B \Rightarrow v_B = 16.75 \text{ ms}^{-1}$

Substituting in [1] gives:
$v_A = 16.75 - 4.8 = 11.95 \text{ ms}^{-1}$

b) $e = \dfrac{v_B - v_A}{u_A - u_B}$

$\Rightarrow 0.8 = \dfrac{v_B - v_A}{16 - (-10)}$

$\Rightarrow v_A = v_B - 20.8 \;...[1]$

$m_A u_A + m_B u_B = m_A v_A + m_B v_B$

$\Rightarrow (5 \times 16) + (3 \times -10) = 5v_A + 3v_B$

$\Rightarrow 50 = 5v_A + 3v_B \;...[2]$

Substituting [1] into [2] gives:
$50 = 5(v_B - 20.8) + 3v_B \Rightarrow v_B = 19.25 \text{ ms}^{-1}$

Substituting in [1] gives:
$v_A = 19.25 - 20.8 = -1.55 \text{ ms}^{-1}$

So this time the direction of A is reversed in the collision.

Q7 a) $e = \dfrac{v_B - v_A}{u_A - u_B}$

$\Rightarrow 0.4 = \dfrac{v_B - v_A}{u - (-u)}$

$\Rightarrow v_A = v_B - 0.8u \;...[1]$

$m_A u_A + m_B u_B = m_A v_A + m_B v_B$

$\Rightarrow 4mu - mu = 4mv_A + mv_B$

$\Rightarrow 3u = 4v_A + v_B \;...[2]$

Substituting [1] into [2] gives:
$3u = 4(v_B - 0.8u) + v_B \Rightarrow v_B = 1.24u$

Substituting in [1] gives:
$v_A = 1.24u - 0.8u = 0.44u$

So they both move off in the same direction as A was travelling initially.

b) Changing the masses only affects equation [2] from part a), which becomes:

$mu - 9mu = mv_A + 9mv_B$

$\Rightarrow -8u = v_A + 9v_B \;...[2]$

Substituting [1] into [2] gives:
$-8u = v_B - 0.8u + 9v_B \Rightarrow v_B = -0.72u$

Substituting in [1] gives:
$v_A = -0.72u - 0.8u = -1.52u$

So they both move off in the same direction as B was travelling initially.

Q8 Let V and W be the speeds of A and B respectively following the collision.

$e = \dfrac{v_B - v_A}{u_A - u_B}$

$\Rightarrow e = \dfrac{W - (-V)}{4u - (-u)}$

$\Rightarrow V = 5eu - W \;...[1]$

$m_A u_A + m_B u_B = m_A v_A + m_B v_B$

$\Rightarrow 4mu - 3mu = -mV + 3mW$

$\Rightarrow u = 3W - V \;...[2]$

Substituting [1] into [2] gives:
$u = 3W - 5eu + W \Rightarrow W = \dfrac{(1 + 5e)u}{4}$

Substituting in [1] gives:
$V = 5eu - \dfrac{(1 + 5e)u}{4} = \dfrac{(15e - 1)u}{4}$

Q9 a) $e = \dfrac{v_Q - v_P}{u_P - u_Q}$

$\Rightarrow e = \dfrac{v_Q - v}{u_P - 0}$

$\Rightarrow v_Q = eu_P + v$ ...[1]

$m_P u_P + m_Q u_Q = m_P v_P + m_Q v_Q$

$\Rightarrow 5mu_P + 0 = 5mv + mv_Q$

$\Rightarrow v_Q = 5u_P - 5v$ ...[2]

Equating [1] and [2] gives:

$eu_P + v = 5u_P - 5v \Rightarrow 5u_P - eu_P = 6v$

$\Rightarrow u_P = \dfrac{6v}{5 - e}$

b) Substituting the expression for u_P in [1] gives:

$v_Q = \dfrac{6ev}{5 - e} + v = \dfrac{5v(e + 1)}{5 - e}$

Exercise 2.3 — Collisions with smooth planes

Q1 a) $e = \dfrac{v}{u}$, so $v = eu = 0.8 \times 3 = 2.4$ ms^{-1}

b) $e = \dfrac{v}{u}$, so $u = \dfrac{v}{e} = \dfrac{5}{0.3} = 16.7$ ms^{-1} (3 s.f.)

c) $e = \dfrac{v}{u} = \dfrac{5}{6} = 0.833$ (3 s.f.)

Q2 $e = \dfrac{5}{50} = 0.1$

Q3 $e = \dfrac{8}{10} = 0.8$

So when $u = 12$, $v = eu = 0.8 \times 12 = 9.6$ ms^{-1}.

Q4 $u = \dfrac{v}{e} = \dfrac{1.5}{0.6} = 2.5$ ms^{-1}

Impulse $= m(v - u) = 3(-1.5 - 2.5) = -12$ Ns, so the magnitude of the impulse is 12 Ns.

Q5 Use constant acceleration equations to find v and u:

$v^2 = u^2 + 2as$

$\Rightarrow u^2 = 0 + (2 \times 0.4 \times 8) \Rightarrow u = \sqrt{6.4}$ ms^{-1}

The ball rebounds at constant speed so

$v = \dfrac{s}{t} = \dfrac{8}{4.5} = \dfrac{16}{9}$.

So $e = \dfrac{16}{9\sqrt{6.4}} = 0.703$ (3 s.f.)

Q6 a) Use a constant acceleration equation to find v_1:

$v^2 = u^2 + 2as$

$\Rightarrow v_1^2 = 0 + (2 \times 9.8 \times 2)$

$\Rightarrow v_1 = 6.260... = 6.26$ ms^{-1} (3 s.f.)

$u_2 = ev_1 = 0.2 \times 6.260...$

$= 1.252... = 1.25$ ms^{-1} (3 s.f.)

b) $v^2 = u^2 + 2as$

$\Rightarrow 0 = 1.252...^2 + (2 \times -9.8)s_2 \Rightarrow s_2 = 0.08$ m

Q7 a) $v^2 = u^2 + 2as$

$\Rightarrow 0 = u_2^2 + (2 \times -9.8 \times 0.5)$

$\Rightarrow u_2 = 3.130... = 3.13$ ms^{-1} (3 s.f.)

$v_1 = \dfrac{u_2}{e} = \dfrac{3.130...}{0.75} = 4.173... = 4.17$ ms^{-1} (3 s.f.)

b) $v^2 = u^2 + 2as$

$\Rightarrow 4.173...^2 = 0 + (2 \times 9.8)s_1$

$\Rightarrow s_1 = 0.889$ m (3 s.f.)

Q8 First find the speed of approach (v_1) and speed of rebound (u_2) using a constant acceleration equation:

$v^2 = u^2 + 2as$

$\Rightarrow v_1^2 = 0 + (2 \times 9.8 \times 3)$

$\Rightarrow v_1 = 7.668...$ ms^{-1}

$v^2 = u^2 + 2as$

$\Rightarrow 0 = u_2^2 + (2 \times -9.8 \times 1)$

$\Rightarrow u_2 = 4.427...$ ms^{-1}

So $e = \dfrac{4.427...}{7.668...} = 0.577$ (3 s.f.)

Q9 a) First find the speed of approach (v_1) using a constant acceleration equation:

$v = u + at$

$\Rightarrow v_1 = 0 + (9.8 \times 1.5) = 14.7$ ms^{-1}

Then use $u_2 = ev_1$ to find the rebound speed:

$u_2 = 0.05 \times 14.7 = 0.735$ ms^{-1}

Then to find the height of rebound, s, use:

$v^2 = u^2 + 2as$

$\Rightarrow 0 = 0.735^2 + (2 \times -9.8)s$

$\Rightarrow s = 0.0276$ m (3 s.f.) = 2.76 cm

b) Any three from, e.g., the car can be modelled as a particle / $g = 9.8$ ms^{-2} / the floor is smooth / the floor is horizontal / the car strikes the floor vertically / the car rebounds vertically / there is no air resistance / the car doesn't rotate as it falls / the car doesn't break on impact.

3. Complex Collisions

Exercise 3.1 — Successive collisions

Q1 For collision 1, between A and B:

$e = \dfrac{v_B - v_A}{u_A - u_B}$

$\Rightarrow 0.4 = \dfrac{v_{B1} - v_{A1}}{10 - 0} \Rightarrow v_{A1} = v_{B1} - 4$ ...[1]

$m_A u_A + m_B u_B = m_A v_A + m_B v_B$

$\Rightarrow (2 \times 10) + 0 = 2v_{A1} + 3v_{B1}$

$\Rightarrow 20 = 2v_{A1} + 3v_{B1}$ ...[2]

Substituting [1] into [2] gives:

$20 = 2(v_{B1} - 4) + 3v_{B1} \Rightarrow v_{B1} = 5.6$ ms^{-1}

For collision 2, between B and C, $u_{B2} = v_{B1} = 5.6$ ms^{-1}, so:

$e = \dfrac{v_C - v_B}{u_B - u_C}$

$\Rightarrow 0.5 = \dfrac{v_{C2} - v_{B2}}{5.6 - 0} \Rightarrow v_{B2} = v_{C2} - 2.8$ ...[1]

$m_B u_B + m_C u_C = m_B v_B + m_C v_C$

$\Rightarrow (3 \times 5.6) + 0 = 3v_{B2} + v_{C2}$

$\Rightarrow 16.8 = 3v_{B2} + v_{C2}$ ...[2]

Substituting [1] into [2] gives:

$16.8 = 3(v_{C2} - 2.8) + v_{C2} \Rightarrow v_{C2} = 6.3$ ms^{-1}

So the speed of C after the second collision is 6.3 ms^{-1}.

You don't need to find v_{A1} or v_{B2} for this question, but if you did need to know them you could work them out from the simultaneous equations you set up.

Q2 For collision 1, between A and B:

$e = \dfrac{v_B - v_A}{u_A - u_B}$

$\Rightarrow 0.3 = \dfrac{v_{B1} - v_{A1}}{4 - 0} \Rightarrow v_{A1} = v_{B1} - 1.2$ ...[1]

$m_A u_A + m_B u_B = m_A v_A + m_B v_B$

$\Rightarrow (60 \times 4) + 0 = 60v_{A1} + 20v_{B1}$

$\Rightarrow 240 = 60v_{A1} + 20v_{B1}$ ...[2]

Substituting [1] into [2] gives:
$240 = 60(v_{B1} - 1.2) + 20v_{B1} \Rightarrow v_{B1} = 3.9$ ms^{-1}

For collision 2, between B and the wall,
$u_{B2} = v_{B1} = 3.9$ ms^{-1}, so:

$e = \dfrac{v}{u} \Rightarrow 0.7 = \dfrac{v_{B2}}{3.9} \Rightarrow v_{B2} = 2.73$ ms^{-1}

So the rebound speed of B after the second collision is 2.73 ms^{-1}.

Q3 Call the white ball A and the red ball B.

For collision 2, between B and the cushion:

$e = \dfrac{v}{u} \Rightarrow 0.5 = \dfrac{1.2}{u_{B2}} \Rightarrow u_{B2} = 2.4$ ms^{-1}

For collision 1, between A and B, $v_{B1} = u_{B2} = 2.4$ ms^{-1},
so:

$e = \dfrac{v_B - v_A}{u_A - u_B}$

$\Rightarrow 0.8 = \dfrac{2.4 - v_{A1}}{u_{A1} - 0} \Rightarrow v_{A1} = 2.4 - 0.8u_{A1}$ ...[1]

$m_A u_A + m_B u_B = m_A v_A + m_B v_B$

$\Rightarrow mu_{A1} + 0 = mv_{A1} + 2.4m$

$\Rightarrow v_{A1} = u_{A1} - 2.4$ ...[2]

Equating [1] and [2] gives:
$2.4 - 0.8u_{A1} = u_{A1} - 2.4 \Rightarrow u_{A1} = 2.67$ ms^{-1} (3 s.f.)

So the initial speed of the white ball is 2.67 ms^{-1} (to 3 s.f.).
You can save yourself a bit of work by doing the calculations in a different order than usual — so try and think it through before you start.

Q4 For collision 1, between A and the wall:

$e = \dfrac{v}{u} \Rightarrow 0.5 = \dfrac{v_{A1}}{16} \Rightarrow v_{A1} = 8$ ms^{-1}

For collision 2, between A and B, $u_{A2} = v_{A1} = 8$ ms^{-1},
but this is in the opposite direction to B, so:

$m_A u_A + m_B u_B = m_A v_A + m_B v_B$

$\Rightarrow (2 \times -8) + (5 \times 3) = 0 + 5v_{B2}$

$\Rightarrow v_{B2} = -0.2$ ms^{-1}

$e = \dfrac{v_B - v_A}{u_A - u_B} \Rightarrow e = \dfrac{-0.2 - 0}{-8 - 3} = 0.0182$ (3 s.f.)

Q5 For collision 2, between B and C:

$e = \dfrac{v_C - v_B}{u_B - u_C}$

$\Rightarrow 0.75 = \dfrac{3 - v_{B2}}{u_{B2} - 0} \Rightarrow 0.75u_{B2} = 3 - v_{B2}$ ...[1]

$m_B u_B + m_C u_C = m_B v_B + m_C v_C$

$\Rightarrow 5u_{B2} + 0 = 5v_{B2} + (2 \times 3)$

$\Rightarrow u_{B2} = v_{B2} + 1.2$ ...[2]

Substituting [2] into [1] gives:
$0.75(v_{B2} + 1.2) = 3 - v_{B2} \Rightarrow v_{B2} = 1.2$ ms^{-1}

So the speed of B after collision 2 is 1.2 ms^{-1}.
You still need to find u_{B2} though as you need it to work out values from the first collision...

Putting v_{B2} into [2] gives:
$u_{B2} = 1.2 + 1.2 = 2.4$ ms^{-1}

For collision 1, between A and B, $v_{B1} = u_{B2} = 2.4$ ms^{-1},
so:

$m_A u_A + m_B u_B = m_A v_A + m_B v_B$

$\Rightarrow (6 \times 3) + 0 = 6v_{A1} + (5 \times 2.4)$

$\Rightarrow v_{A1} = 1$ ms^{-1}

So the speed of A after collision 1 is 1 ms^{-1}.
Assuming that it continues at this speed (it shouldn't collide again with B as it is moving slower) this is also the speed of A after collision 2. Finally:

$e = \dfrac{v_B - v_A}{u_A - u_B} = \dfrac{2.4 - 1}{3 - 0} = 0.467$ (3 s.f.)

Q6 a) There will be a collision between B and C if the direction of B is changed, i.e. if v_{B1} is positive (taking the initial direction of A to be positive).

For collision 1 between A and B:

$e = \dfrac{v_B - v_A}{u_A - u_B}$

$\Rightarrow 0.25 = \dfrac{v_{B1} - v_{A1}}{2 - (-1)} \Rightarrow v_{A1} = v_{B1} - 0.75$ ...[1]

$m_A u_A + m_B u_B = m_A v_A + m_B v_B$

$\Rightarrow (3 \times 2) + (2 \times -1) = 3v_{A1} + 2v_{B1}$

$\Rightarrow 4 = 3v_{A1} + 2v_{B1}$ ...[2]

Substituting [1] into [2] gives:
$4 = 3(v_{B1} - 0.75) + 2v_{B1} \Rightarrow v_{B1} = 1.25$ ms^{-1}

This is positive so B moves off in the initial direction of A and hence will collide with C.

b) If B changes direction after the second collision then v_{B2} will be negative, i.e. $v_{B2} < 0$.

For the collision between B and C:

$m_B u_B + m_C u_C = m_B v_B + m_C v_C$

$\Rightarrow (2 \times 1.25) + 0 = 2v_{B2} + 4v_{C2}$

$\Rightarrow 2.5 = 2v_{B2} + 4v_{C2}$ ...[1]

$e = \dfrac{v_C - v_B}{u_B - u_C}$

$\Rightarrow e = \dfrac{v_{C2} - v_{B2}}{1.25 - 0} \Rightarrow v_{C2} = v_{B2} + 1.25e$ ...[2]

Substituting [2] into [1] gives:
$2.5 = 2v_{B2} + 4(v_{B2} + 1.25e)$

$\Rightarrow 6v_{B2} = 2.5 - 5e \Rightarrow v_{B2} = \dfrac{2.5 - 5e}{6}$

So if B changes direction, $\dfrac{2.5 - 5e}{6} < 0$, and so:
$2.5 - 5e < 0 \Rightarrow 5e > 2.5 \Rightarrow e > 0.5$.

Q7 a) There will be a further collision between A and B if either A carries on in the same direction after the first collision (v_{A1} is positive) or the rebound speed of B from the wall is faster than the rebound speed of A, if the direction of A is reversed ($|v_{B2}| > |v_{A1}|$).

For collision 1, between A and B:

$e = \dfrac{v_B - v_A}{u_A - u_B}$

$\Rightarrow 0.9 = \dfrac{v_{B1} - v_{A1}}{2 - (-4)} \Rightarrow v_{B1} = 5.4 + v_{A1}$ ...[1]

$m_A u_A + m_B u_B = m_A v_A + m_B v_B$

$\Rightarrow (6 \times 2) + (4 \times -4) = 6v_{A1} + 4v_{B1}$

$\Rightarrow -4 = 6v_{A1} + 4v_{B1}$ ...[2]

Substituting [1] into [2] gives:
$-4 = 6v_{A1} + 4(5.4 + v_{A1}) \Rightarrow v_{A1} = -2.56$ ms^{-1}

Putting this into [1] gives:

$v_{B1} = 5.4 - 2.56 = 2.84$ ms^{-1}

Since v_{A1} is not positive (i.e. it moves off in the opposite direction) we need to look at the second collision to check whether $|v_{B2}| > |v_{A1}|$.

For collision 2, between B and the wall:

$e = \dfrac{v}{u} \Rightarrow 0.95 = \dfrac{v_{B2}}{2.84} \Rightarrow v_{B2} = 2.698$ ms^{-1}

This is faster than the speed of A, so B should catch up with A to collide again.

b) Following collision 1, B is travelling at a constant speed of 2.84 ms^{-1} towards the wall, 5.68 m away.

This takes a time, t, where $t = \dfrac{5.68}{2.84} = 2$ s.

In this time, A has been travelling away from the wall at a constant speed of 2.56 ms^{-1}, so it has moved a distance of $2.56 \times 2 = 5.12$ m from the point of collision 1. But it was already 5.68 m from the wall at this point, so it will then be a total of $5.12 + 5.68 = 10.8$ m away from the wall.

Q8 For collision 1, between P and Q:

$e = \dfrac{v_Q - v_P}{u_P - u_Q}$

$\Rightarrow 0.15 = \dfrac{v_{Q1} - v_{P1}}{3 - 2} \Rightarrow v_{Q1} = 0.15 + v_{P1}$ ...[1]

$m_P u_P + m_Q u_Q = m_P v_P + m_Q v_Q$

$\Rightarrow (1.5 \times 3) + (3 \times 2) = 1.5v_{P1} + 3v_{Q1}$

$\Rightarrow 10.5 = 1.5v_{P1} + 3v_{Q1}$ ...[2]

Substituting [1] into [2] gives:
$10.5 = 1.5v_{P1} + 3(0.15 + v_{P1}) \Rightarrow v_{P1} = 2.23333...$ ms^{-1}

Putting this into [1] gives:

$v_{Q1} = 0.15 + 2.23333... = 2.38333...$ ms^{-1}

For collision 2, between Q and R, where $u_{Q2} = v_{Q1} = 2.38333...$ ms^{-1}:

$e = \dfrac{v_R - v_Q}{u_Q - u_R}$

$\Rightarrow 0.25 = \dfrac{v_{R2} - v_{Q2}}{2.38333... - 1}$

$\Rightarrow v_{R2} = 0.34583... + v_{Q2}$ ...[1]

$m_Q u_Q + m_R u_R = m_Q v_Q + m_R v_R$

$\Rightarrow (3 \times 2.38333...) + (4 \times 1) = 3v_{Q2} + 4v_{R2}$

$\Rightarrow 11.15 = 3v_{Q2} + 4v_{R2}$ ...[2]

Substituting [1] into [2] gives:
$11.15 = 3v_{Q2} + 4(0.34583... + v_{Q2})$
$\Rightarrow v_{Q2} = 1.39523...$ ms^{-1}

Putting this into [1] gives:

$v_{R2} = 0.34583... + 1.39523... = 1.74107...$ ms^{-1}

So to 3 s.f. the speeds of P, Q and R after collision 2 are, respectively, 2.23 ms^{-1}, 1.40 ms^{-1} and 1.74 ms^{-1}.

Q9 There will be a further collision between A and B if either A carries on in the same direction after the first collision (v_{A1} is positive) or the rebound speed of B from the wall is faster than the rebound speed of A, if the direction of A is reversed ($|v_{B2}| > |v_{A1}|$).

For collision 1, between A and B:

$e = \dfrac{v_B - v_A}{u_A - u_B}$

$\Rightarrow e = \dfrac{v_{B1} - v_{A1}}{5 - 0} \Rightarrow v_{B1} = 5e + v_{A1}$ ...[1]

$m_A u_A + m_B u_B = m_A v_A + m_B v_B$

$\Rightarrow 5m + 0 = mv_{A1} + 3mv_{B1}$

$\Rightarrow 5 = v_{A1} + 3v_{B1}$ ...[2]

Substituting [1] into [2] gives:
$5 = v_{A1} + 3(5e + v_{A1}) \Rightarrow v_{A1} = \dfrac{5 - 15e}{4}$

So A and B will collide again if A is moving towards the wall, i.e. if $\dfrac{5 - 15e}{4} > 0 \Rightarrow e < \dfrac{1}{3}$.

Putting the expression for v_{A1} into [1] gives:

$v_{B1} = 5e + \dfrac{5 - 15e}{4} = 1.25(e + 1)$

For collision 2, between B and the wall:

$e = \dfrac{v}{u} \Rightarrow 0.85 = \dfrac{8v_{B2}}{1.25(e + 1)} \Rightarrow v_{B2} = 1.0625(e + 1)$

If A is moving away from the wall following its first collision with B, then $v_{A1} < 0$, i.e. the speed of A is $\dfrac{15e - 5}{4}$ and $e > \dfrac{1}{3}$.

So A and B will also collide again if:

$1.0625(e + 1) > \dfrac{15e - 5}{4}$

$4.25e + 4.25 > 15e - 5$

$9.25 > 10.75e$

$\Rightarrow e < 0.8604...$

So, combining with previous result, $e < 0.860$ (3 s.f.)

Exercise 3.2 — Successive rebounds

Q1 a) <u>Bounce 1</u>:

Using $v^2 = u^2 + 2as$, where $v = u_1$, $u = 0$, $a = 9.8$ and $s = 20$ (taking down as positive):
$u_1^2 = 2 \times 9.8 \times 20 = 392$

$\Rightarrow u_1 = \sqrt{392} = 19.7989...$

Using $e = \dfrac{v}{u}$, $v = eu$, where $v = v_1$, $e = 0.75$ and $u = u_1$:
$v_1 = 0.75 \times 19.7989... = 14.8492...$

Then $v^2 = u^2 + 2as$, where $v = 0$, $u = v_1$ and $a = -9.8$ (taking up as positive):
$0 = 14.8492...^2 + (2 \times -9.8)s_1$

$\Rightarrow s_1 = 11.25$ m.

b) Bounce 2:

From the symmetry of the vertical motion,
$u_2 = v_1 = 14.8492...$

$v = eu$, where $v = v_2$, $e = 0.75$ and $u = u_2$:
$v_2 = 0.75 \times 14.8492... = 11.1369...$

So $v_2 = 11.1$ ms^{-1} to 3 s.f

c) $v^2 = u^2 + 2as$, where $v = 0$, $u = v_2$ and $a = -9.8$
(taking up as positive):
$0 = 11.1369...^2 + (2 \times -9.8)s_2$
$\Rightarrow s_2 = 6.328125 = 6.33$ m (3 s.f.)

Q2 a) Bounce 1:

Using $v^2 = u^2 + 2as$, where $v = u_1$, $u = 0$, $a = 9.8$
and $s = 3$ (taking down as positive):
$u_1^2 = 2 \times 9.8 \times 3 = 58.8$
$\Rightarrow u_1 = \sqrt{58.8} = 7.6681...$

Then for the rebound, $v^2 = u^2 + 2as$, where $v = 0$,
$u = v_1$, $a = -9.8$ and $s = 2$ (taking up as positive):
$0 = v_1^2 + (2 \times -9.8 \times 2)$
$\Rightarrow v_1 = \sqrt{39.2} = 6.2609...$

Using $e = \frac{v}{u}$, where $v = v_1$, and $u = u_1$:
$e = \frac{6.2609...}{7.6681...} = 0.81649... = 0.816$ to 3 s.f.

b) Bounce 2:

From the symmetry of the vertical motion,
$u_2 = v_1 = 6.2609...$

$v = eu$, where $v = v_2$, $e = 0.81649...$ and $u = u_2$:
$v_2 = 0.81649... \times 6.2609... = 5.1120...$

Then $v^2 = u^2 + 2as$, where $v = 0$, $u = v_2$ and
$a = -9.8$ (taking up as positive):
$0 = 5.1120...^2 + (2 \times -9.8)s_2$
$\Rightarrow s_2 = 1.3333... = 1.33$ m (3 s.f.)

Q3 First find the first two rebound heights s_1 and s_2, then
set up the geometric progression.

Bounce 1:

Using $v^2 = u^2 + 2as$, where $v = u_1$, $u = 0$, $a = 9.8$ and
$s = 10$ (taking down as positive):
$u_1^2 = 2 \times 9.8 \times 10 = 196$
$\Rightarrow u_1 = \sqrt{196} = 14$

Using $e = \frac{v}{u}$, $v = eu$, where $v = v_1$, $e = 0.6$ and $u = u_1$:
$v_1 = 0.6 \times 14 = 8.4$

Then $v^2 = u^2 + 2as$, where $v = 0$, $u = v_1$ and $a = -9.8$
(taking up as positive):
$0 = 8.4^2 + (2 \times -9.8)s_1$
$\Rightarrow s_1 = 3.6$ m.

Bounce 2:

From the symmetry of the vertical motion,
$u_2 = v_1 = 8.4$

$v = eu$, where $v = v_2$, $e = 0.6$ and $u = u_2$:
$v_2 = 0.6 \times 8.4 = 5.04$

$v^2 = u^2 + 2as$, where $v = 0$, $u = v_2$ and $a = -9.8$
(taking up as positive):
$0 = 5.04^2 + (2 \times -9.8)s_2$
$\Rightarrow s_2 = 1.296$ m

So the rebound heights follow a geometric
progression with common ratio
$r = \frac{s_2}{s_1} = \frac{1.296}{3.6} = 0.36$, and a first term $a = 3.6$.

Use $s_n = ar^{n-1}$ to find the height of successive
bounces:
$s_3 = 3.6(0.36)^2 = 0.46656$ m
So the rebound height is less than 1 m following the
third bounce.

*Rather than finding s_1 and s_2, you could take the height that
the particle is dropped from as s_0, then use s_0 and s_1 to find
the common ratio.*

Q4 a) For the first bounce, using $e = \frac{v}{u}$, $v = eu$,
where $v = v_1$:
$v_1 = ue = ue^1$

From the symmetry of the vertical motion,
$u_2 = v_1 = ue^1$

Then using $v = eu$, where $v = v_2$, $u = u_2$:
$v_2 = e \times ue^1 = ue^2$

So $v_n = ue^n$.

b) For the first bounce, using $v^2 = u^2 + 2as$, where
$v = u_1$, $u = 0$, $a = 9.8$ and $s = H$ (taking down as
positive):
$u_1^2 = 2 \times 9.8 \times H \Rightarrow u_1 = \sqrt{19.6H}$

Using $e = \frac{v}{u}$, $v = eu$, where $v = v_1$, and $u = u_1$:
$v_1 = e \times \sqrt{19.6H} = \sqrt{19.6He^2}$

Then $v^2 = u^2 + 2as$, where $v = 0$, $u = v_1$, $a = -9.8$
and $s = h_1$ (taking up as positive):
$0 = (\sqrt{19.6He^2})^2 + (2 \times -9.8)h_1$
$\Rightarrow 19.6h_1 = 19.6He^2 \Rightarrow h_1 = He^{2(1)}$

For the second bounce, from the symmetry of the
vertical motion, $u_2 = v_1 = \sqrt{19.6He^2}$

$v = eu$, where $v = v_2$, $u = u_2$:
$v_2 = e \times \sqrt{19.6He^2} = \sqrt{19.6He^4}$

Then $v^2 = u^2 + 2as$, where $v = 0$, $u = v_2$, $a = -9.8$
and $s = h_2$ (taking up as positive):
$0 = (\sqrt{19.6He^4})^2 + (2 \times -9.8)h_2$
$\Rightarrow 19.6h_2 = 19.6He^4 \Rightarrow h_2 = He^{2(2)}$

So $h_n = He^{2n}$.

Q5 Using the expression from Q4 b), $h_n = He^{2n}$, where
$n = 3$, $e = 0.3$ and $h_3 = 0.2$ cm:
$h_3 = H(0.3)^6 = 0.2$
$\Rightarrow H = \frac{0.2}{0.3^6} = 274$ cm (3 s.f.) $= 2.74$ m (3 s.f.)

Q6 Using the expression from Q4 b), $h_n = He^{2n}$, the
common ratio for the geometric progression of
rebound heights, r, will be given by:
$r = \frac{He^{2(n+1)}}{He^{2n}} = e^{2(n+1)-2n} = e^2$.

The first term in the progression is the distance the
particle travels from hitting the plane the first time,
bouncing back up, then falling back down again to
hit the plane the second time (i.e. twice the height of
the first bounce).
So $a = 2He^2$.

Using the sum to infinity of the series:
$\frac{a}{1-r} = \frac{2He^2}{1-e^2}$.

So the total distance travelled is:
$$H + \frac{2He^2}{1-e^2} = H\left(1 + \frac{2e^2}{1-e^2}\right) = H\left(\frac{1+e^2}{1-e^2}\right)$$

Remember — to find the total distance travelled by the particle, you need to double the height of each rebound (to find the distance travelled between each impact with the plane), find the sum of these values, and then separately add on the height from which the particle was dropped initially.

Q7 Using the expression from Q6 for the total distance travelled:
$H\left(\frac{1+e^2}{1-e^2}\right) = 3$, where $H = 2.5$, so:

$\frac{1+e^2}{1-e^2} = 1.2 \Rightarrow 1 + e^2 = 1.2 - 1.2e^2$

$\Rightarrow 2.2e^2 = 0.2$

$\Rightarrow e = \sqrt{\frac{0.2}{2.2}} = 0.30$ (2 d.p.)

Q8 From the working for Q4 b) you know that:
$v_2 = \sqrt{19.6He^4}$, so in this case
$\sqrt{19.6(0.8)^4H} = 5.5$

$\Rightarrow H = \frac{5.5^2}{19.6 \times (0.8)^4} = 3.7679...$ m

Putting this into the expression from Q6:

Total distance travelled = $H\left(\frac{1+e^2}{1-e^2}\right)$

$= (3.7679...)\left(\frac{1+(0.8)^2}{1-(0.8)^2}\right) = 17.2$ m (3 s.f.)

4. Collisions and Energy

Exercise 4.1 — Kinetic energy and collisions

Q1 $e = \frac{v_B - v_A}{u_A - u_B}$

$\Rightarrow 0.2 = \frac{v_B - v_A}{12 - 0}$

$\Rightarrow v_A = v_B - 2.4$ ...[1]

$m_A u_A + m_B u_B = m_A v_A + m_B v_B$

$\Rightarrow (10 \times 12) + 0 = 10v_A + 15v_B$

$\Rightarrow 120 = 10v_A + 15v_B$ ...[2]

Substituting [1] into [2] gives:
$120 = 10(v_B - 2.4) + 15v_B \Rightarrow v_B = 5.76$ ms^{-1}

Substituting in [1] gives:
$v_A = 5.76 - 2.4 = 3.36$ ms^{-1}

Loss of K.E. $= (\frac{1}{2}m_A u_A^2 + \frac{1}{2}m_B u_B^2) - (\frac{1}{2}m_A v_A^2 + \frac{1}{2}m_B v_B^2)$
$= [(\frac{1}{2} \times 10 \times 12^2) + 0] -$
$\qquad [(\frac{1}{2} \times 10 \times 3.36^2) + (\frac{1}{2} \times 15 \times 5.76^2)]$
$= 720 - (56.448 + 248.832) = 414.72$ J $= 415$ J (3 s.f.)

Q2 a) $m_A u_A + m_B u_B = m_A v_A + m_B v_B$

$\Rightarrow (2 \times 3) - 5m = (2 \times -4) - 3m$

$\Rightarrow 14 = 2m \Rightarrow m = 7$ kg

b) Loss of K.E. =
$(\frac{1}{2}m_A u_A^2 + \frac{1}{2}m_B u_B^2) - (\frac{1}{2}m_A v_A^2 + \frac{1}{2}m_B v_B^2)$
$= [(\frac{1}{2} \times 2 \times 3^2) + (\frac{1}{2} \times 7 \times 5^2)] -$
$\qquad\qquad [(\frac{1}{2} \times 2 \times 4^2) + (\frac{1}{2} \times 7 \times 3^2)]$
$= (9 + 87.5) - (16 + 31.5) = 49$ J

Q3 $m_A u_A + m_B u_B = (m_A + m_B)v$

$\Rightarrow (5 \times 4) + (3 \times -2) = (5 + 3)v$

$\Rightarrow 14 = 8v$

$\Rightarrow v = 1.75$ ms^{-1}

Loss of K.E. $= (\frac{1}{2}m_A u_A^2 + \frac{1}{2}m_B u_B^2) - \frac{1}{2}(m_A + m_B)v^2$
$= [(\frac{1}{2} \times 5 \times 4^2) + (\frac{1}{2} \times 3 \times 2^2)] - [\frac{1}{2} \times (5 + 3) \times 1.75^2]$
$= (40 + 6) - 12.25 = 33.75$ J

Q4 First, find the speed of A before and after the collision by finding the magnitude of its velocities:
$u_A = \sqrt{6^2 + 2^2} = \sqrt{40} = 2\sqrt{10}$ ms^{-1}
$v_A = \sqrt{3^2 + 1^2} = \sqrt{10}$ ms^{-1}.

Now use conservation of momentum to find the speed of B following the collision:
$m_A u_A + m_B u_B = m_A v_A + m_B v_B$

$\Rightarrow (2 \times 2\sqrt{10}) + (3 \times 0) = (2 \times \sqrt{10}) + 3v_B$

$\Rightarrow 3v_B = 2\sqrt{10} \Rightarrow v_B = \frac{2\sqrt{10}}{3}$ ms^{-1}

Loss of K.E. $= (\frac{1}{2}m_A u_A^2 + \frac{1}{2}m_B u_B^2) - (\frac{1}{2}m_A v_A^2 + \frac{1}{2}m_B v_B^2)$
$= [(\frac{1}{2} \times 2 \times \sqrt{40}^2) + (\frac{1}{2} \times 3 \times 0^2)] -$
$\qquad [(\frac{1}{2} \times 2 \times \sqrt{10}^2) + (\frac{1}{2} \times 3 \times \left(\frac{2\sqrt{10}}{3}\right)^2)]$
$= [40] - [10 + \frac{20}{3}] = \frac{70}{3}$ J $= 23.3$ J (3 s.f.)

Using conservation of momentum in one dimension works here only because all the motion is in a single line — the velocity vectors are all proportional to each other. This method won't work if the motion isn't in a single line.

Q5 Call the 5 kg stone A and the 3 kg stone B.
Use conservation of momentum to find $\mathbf{v}_B$:
$m_A \mathbf{u}_A + m_B \mathbf{u}_B = m_A \mathbf{v}_A + m_B \mathbf{v}_B$
$5(4\mathbf{i} - 2\mathbf{j}) + 3(-3\mathbf{i} + 4\mathbf{j}) = 5(2\mathbf{i} + \mathbf{j}) + 3\mathbf{v}_B$
$\mathbf{i} - 3\mathbf{j} = 3\mathbf{v}_B$

$\Rightarrow \mathbf{v}_B = (\frac{1}{3}\mathbf{i} - \mathbf{j})$ ms^{-1}

Now find the magnitude of the velocities of A and B, so you can find the loss of K.E.:
$u_A = \sqrt{4^2 + (-2)^2} = \sqrt{20} = 2\sqrt{5}$ ms^{-1}
$u_B = \sqrt{(-4)^2 + 3^2} = 5$ ms^{-1}
$v_A = \sqrt{2^2 + 1^2} = \sqrt{5}$ ms^{-1}
$v_B = \sqrt{(\frac{1}{3})^2 + (-1)^2} = \frac{\sqrt{10}}{3}$ ms^{-1}

Loss of K.E. $= (\frac{1}{2}m_A u_A^2 + \frac{1}{2}m_B u_B^2) - (\frac{1}{2}m_A v_A^2 + \frac{1}{2}m_B v_B^2)$
$= [(\frac{1}{2} \times 5 \times \sqrt{20}^2) + (\frac{1}{2} \times 3 \times 5^2)] -$
$\qquad [(\frac{1}{2} \times 5 \times \sqrt{5}^2) + (\frac{1}{2} \times 3 \times \left(\frac{\sqrt{10}}{3}\right)^2)]$
$= [50 + 37.5] - [12.5 + 1.666...] = 73.3$ J (3 s.f.)

Q6 a) Call the engine A and the truck B.

$m_A u_A + m_B u_B = m_A v_A + m_B v_B$

$\Rightarrow 10\,000 u_A + 0 = 10\,000 v_A + (2000 \times 5)$

$\Rightarrow u_A = v_A + 1$ ...[1]

Loss of K.E. $= (\frac{1}{2}m_A u_A^2 + \frac{1}{2}m_B u_B^2) -$
$(\frac{1}{2}m_A v_A^2 + \frac{1}{2}m_B v_B^2)$

$2 \times 10^4 = [(\frac{1}{2} \times 10\,000 \times u_A^2) + (\frac{1}{2} \times 2000 \times 0)] -$
$[(\frac{1}{2} \times 10\,000 \times v_A^2) + (\frac{1}{2} \times 2000 \times 5^2)]$

$20\,000 = 5000 u_A^2 - 5000 v_A^2 - 25\,000$

$\Rightarrow u_A^2 - v_A^2 = 9$ ...[2]

Substituting [1] into [2] gives:

$(v_A + 1)^2 - v_A^2 = 9$

$v_A^2 + 2v_A + 1 - v_A^2 = 9 \Rightarrow v_A = 4$ ms^{-1}

Substituting in [1] gives:
$u_A = 4 + 1 = 5$ ms^{-1}

b) $e = \frac{v_B - v_A}{u_A - u_B} = \frac{5 - 4}{5 - 0} = 0.2$

Q7 Find the speed of A and B following the collision:

$e = \frac{v_B - v_A}{u_A - u_B}$

$\Rightarrow 0.4 = \frac{v_B - v_A}{6 - (-4)} \Rightarrow v_B = 4 + v_A$ ...[1]

$m_A u_A + m_B u_B = m_A v_A + m_B v_B$

$\Rightarrow (3 \times 6) + (4 \times -4) = 3v_A + 4v_B$

$\Rightarrow 2 = 3v_A + 4v_B$ ...[2]

Substituting [1] into [2] gives:

$2 = 3v_A + 4(4 + v_A)$

$-14 = 7v_A \Rightarrow v_A = -2$ ms^{-1}

Substituting in [1] gives:

$v_B = 4 + -2 = 2$ ms^{-1}

Initial K.E. $= (\frac{1}{2}m_A u_A^2 + \frac{1}{2}m_B u_B^2)$
$= (\frac{1}{2} \times 3 \times 6^2) + (\frac{1}{2} \times 4 \times 4^2) = 86$ J

Loss of K.E. $= 86 - (\frac{1}{2}m_A v_A^2 + \frac{1}{2}m_B v_B^2)$
$= 86 - (\frac{1}{2} \times 3 \times 2^2) + (\frac{1}{2} \times 4 \times 2^2) = 72$ J

Percentage of K.E. lost $= \frac{72}{86} \times 100\% = 83.7\%$ (3 s.f.)

Q8 Initial K.E. $= 18 + 48 = 66$ J

$\Rightarrow (\frac{1}{2}m_P u_P^2 + \frac{1}{2}m_Q u_Q^2) = 66$

$\Rightarrow [(\frac{1}{2} \times m \times 6^2 + \frac{1}{2} \times 2m \times (-2)^2) = 66$

$\Rightarrow 22m = 66 \Rightarrow m = 3$ kg

Final K.E. $= (\frac{1}{2}m_P v_P^2 + \frac{1}{2}m_Q v_Q^2)$

$18 = [(\frac{1}{2} \times 3 \times v_P^2 + \frac{1}{2} \times 6 \times v_Q^2)$

$\Rightarrow 12 = v_P^2 + 2v_Q^2$ ...[1]

$m_P u_P + m_Q u_Q = m_P v_P + m_Q v_Q$

$\Rightarrow (3 \times 6) + (6 \times -2) = 3v_P + 6v_Q$

$\Rightarrow 2 = v_P + 2v_Q \Rightarrow v_P = 2 - 2v_Q$ ...[2]

Substituting [2] into [1] gives:

$12 = (2 - 2v_Q)^2 + 2v_Q^2$

$12 = 4 - 8v_Q + 4v_Q^2 + 2v_Q^2$

$\Rightarrow 3v_Q^2 - 4v_Q - 4 = 0 \Rightarrow (3v_Q + 2)(v_Q - 2) = 0$

$\Rightarrow v_Q = -\frac{2}{3}$ OR $v_Q = 2$

Substituting these in [2] gives:

$v_P = \frac{10}{3}$ OR $v_P = -2$

The only possible values for the velocities of P and Q following the collision are $v_P = -2$ ms^{-1} and $v_Q = 2$ ms^{-1}. The other pair of values is not possible as it would require the particles to 'pass' through each other and continue moving in the same directions as before the collision.

Q9 Find the velocity of P before the collision:

$\mathbf{v} = \frac{\mathbf{s}}{t} \Rightarrow \mathbf{u}_P = \frac{20\mathbf{i} + 8\mathbf{j}}{4} = 5\mathbf{i} + 2\mathbf{j}$

$m_P \mathbf{u}_P + m_Q \mathbf{u}_Q = m_P \mathbf{v}_P + m_Q \mathbf{v}_Q$

$\Rightarrow 3m(5\mathbf{i} + 2\mathbf{j}) + m(-4\mathbf{i} + \mathbf{j}) = 3m(4\mathbf{i} + 3\mathbf{j}) + m\mathbf{v}_Q$

$\Rightarrow 15\mathbf{i} + 6\mathbf{j} - 4\mathbf{i} + \mathbf{j} = 12\mathbf{i} + 9\mathbf{j} + \mathbf{v}_Q$

$\Rightarrow \mathbf{v}_Q = -\mathbf{i} - 2\mathbf{j}$

Now find the speeds of P and Q before and after the collision:

$u_P = \sqrt{5^2 + 2^2} = \sqrt{29}$ ms^{-1}

$u_Q = \sqrt{(-4)^2 + 1^2} = \sqrt{17}$ ms^{-1}

$v_P = \sqrt{4^2 + 3^2} = 5$ ms^{-1}

$v_Q = \sqrt{(-1)^2 + (-2)^2} = \sqrt{5}$ ms^{-1}

Loss of K.E. $= (\frac{1}{2}m_P u_P^2 + \frac{1}{2}m_Q u_Q^2) - (\frac{1}{2}m_P v_P^2 + \frac{1}{2}m_Q v_Q^2)$

$\Rightarrow 42 = [(\frac{1}{2} \times 3m \times 29) + (\frac{1}{2} \times m \times 17)] -$
$[(\frac{1}{2} \times 3m \times 25) + (\frac{1}{2} \times m \times 5)]$

$\Rightarrow 84 = [(87m) + (17m)] - [(75m) + (5m)]$

$\Rightarrow 84 = 24m \Rightarrow m = 3.5$

Q10 $e = \frac{v_B - v_A}{u_A - u_B}$

$\frac{1}{4} = \frac{v_B - v_A}{2u - 0} \Rightarrow v_B = \frac{u}{2} + v_A$ ...[1]

$m_A u_A + m_B u_B = m_A v_A + m_B v_B$

$2mu + 0 = mv_A + mv_B$

$2u = v_A + v_B$ ...[2]

Substituting [1] into [2] gives:

$2u = v_A + \frac{u}{2} + v_A \Rightarrow v_A = \frac{3u}{4}$

Substituting in [1] gives:

$v_B = \frac{u}{2} + \frac{3u}{4} = \frac{5u}{4}$

Loss of K.E. $= (\frac{1}{2}m_A u_A^2 + \frac{1}{2}m_B u_B^2) - (\frac{1}{2}m_A v_A^2 + \frac{1}{2}m_B v_B^2)$

$= [(\frac{1}{2} \times m \times (2u)^2) + (\frac{1}{2} \times m \times 0^2)] -$
$[(\frac{1}{2} \times m \times (\frac{3u}{4})^2) + (\frac{1}{2} \times m \times (\frac{5u}{4})^2)]$

$= 2mu^2 - [\frac{9mu^2}{32} + \frac{25mu^2}{32}]$

$= 2mu^2 - \frac{17}{16}mu^2 = \frac{15}{16}mu^2$

Q11 For the first collision:

$$e_{AB} = \frac{v_{B1} - v_{A1}}{u_{A1} - u_{B1}}$$

$$0.4 = \frac{v_{B1} - v_{A1}}{u_{A1}} \Rightarrow 0.4u_{A1} = v_{B1} - v_{A1} \;...[1]$$

$$m_A u_{A1} + m_B u_{B1} = m_A v_{A1} + m_B v_{B1}$$

$$0.16u_{A1} + 0 = 0.16v_{A1} + 0.16v_{B1}$$

$$v_{A1} = u_{A1} - v_{B1} \;...[2]$$

Substituting [2] into [1] gives:

$$0.4u_{A1} = v_{B1} - u_{A1} + v_{B1} \Rightarrow 1.4u_{A1} = 2v_{B1} \;...[3]$$

For the second collision:

$$e_{BC} = \frac{v_{C2} - v_{B2}}{u_{B2} - u_{C2}}$$

$u_{B2} = v_{B1}$ and for the car to fall in the pocket, $v_{C2} = 1.6$

$$\Rightarrow 0.8 = \frac{1.6 - v_{B2}}{v_{B1} - 0} \Rightarrow 0.8v_{B1} = 1.6 - v_{B2} \;...[4]$$

$$m_B u_{B2} + m_C u_{C2} = m_B v_{B2} + m_C v_{C2}$$

$$0.16v_{B1} + 0 = 0.16v_{B2} + (0.03 \times 1.6)$$

$$\Rightarrow v_{B2} = v_{B1} - 0.3 \;...[5]$$

Substituting [5] into [4] gives:

$$0.8v_{B1} = 1.6 - v_{B1} + 0.3 \Rightarrow v_{B1} = \frac{19}{18} \text{ ms}^{-1} \;...[6]$$

Substituting [6] into [3] gives:

$$1.4u_{A1} = 2 \times \frac{19}{18} \Rightarrow u_{A1} = 1.5079... \text{ ms}^{-1}$$

So the initial K.E. of A must be:

$$\tfrac{1}{2}m_A u_{A1}^2 = \tfrac{1}{2} \times 0.16 \times (1.5079...)^2 = 0.182 \text{ J (3 s.f.)}$$

Exercise 4.2 — Kinetic energy and impulse

Q1 $I = mv - mu$

$$0.06\mathbf{i} + 0.09\mathbf{j} = 0.03\mathbf{v} - 0.03(2\mathbf{i} + 5\mathbf{j})$$

$$\Rightarrow 0.12\mathbf{i} + 0.24\mathbf{j} = 0.03\mathbf{v}$$

$$\Rightarrow \mathbf{v} = (4\mathbf{i} + 8\mathbf{j}) \text{ ms}^{-1}$$

Initial speed of marble:

$$u = |\mathbf{u}| = \sqrt{2^2 + 5^2} = \sqrt{29} \text{ ms}^{-1}$$

Final speed of marble:

$$v = |\mathbf{v}| = \sqrt{4^2 + 8^2} = \sqrt{80} \text{ ms}^{-1}$$

Increase in K.E. $= \tfrac{1}{2}mv^2 - \tfrac{1}{2}mu^2$

$$= (\tfrac{1}{2} \times 0.03 \times 80) - (\tfrac{1}{2} \times 0.03 \times 29)$$

$$= 0.765 \text{ J}$$

Q2 $I = mv - mu$

$$75\mathbf{i} - 100\mathbf{j} = 50\mathbf{v} - 50(8\mathbf{i} + 6\mathbf{j})$$

$$\Rightarrow 475\mathbf{i} + 200\mathbf{j} = 50\mathbf{v}$$

$$\Rightarrow \mathbf{v} = 9.5\mathbf{i} + 4\mathbf{j}$$

Initial speed of skater:

$$u = |\mathbf{u}| = \sqrt{8^2 + 6^2} = 10 \text{ ms}^{-1}$$

Final speed of skater:

$$v = |\mathbf{v}| = \sqrt{9.5^2 + 4^2} = \sqrt{106.25} \text{ ms}^{-1}$$

The skater's speed increases, so:

Increase in K.E. $= \tfrac{1}{2}mv^2 - \tfrac{1}{2}mu^2$

$$= (\tfrac{1}{2} \times 50 \times 106.25) - (\tfrac{1}{2} \times 50 \times 100)$$

$$= 156.25 \text{ J}$$

Q3 $I = mv - mu$

$$100\,000\mathbf{i} + 30\,000\mathbf{j} = 5000\mathbf{v} - 5000(500\mathbf{i} + 200\mathbf{j})$$

$$\Rightarrow 2\,600\,000\mathbf{i} + 1\,030\,000\mathbf{j} = 5000\mathbf{v}$$

$$\Rightarrow \mathbf{v} = (520\mathbf{i} + 206\mathbf{j}) \text{ ms}^{-1}$$

Final speed of rocket:

$$v = |\mathbf{v}| = \sqrt{520^2 + 206^2} = \sqrt{312836} \text{ ms}^{-1}$$

Final K.E. $= \tfrac{1}{2}mv^2$

$$= (\tfrac{1}{2} \times 5000 \times 312\,836)$$

$$= 7.8209 \times 10^8 \text{ J}$$

Q4 $I = mv - mu$

$$0.1\mathbf{i} - 0.15\mathbf{j} = 0.02(3\mathbf{i} - 5\mathbf{j}) - 0.02\mathbf{u}$$

$$\Rightarrow -0.04\mathbf{i} + 0.05\mathbf{j} = 0.02\mathbf{u}$$

$$\Rightarrow \mathbf{u} = -2\mathbf{i} + 2.5\mathbf{j}$$

Initial speed of shuttlecock:

$$u = |\mathbf{u}| = \sqrt{(-2)^2 + 2.5^2} = \sqrt{10.25} \text{ ms}^{-1}$$

Final speed of shuttlecock:

$$v = |\mathbf{v}| = \sqrt{3^2 + (-5)^2} = \sqrt{34} \text{ ms}^{-1}$$

Increase in K.E. $= \tfrac{1}{2}mv^2 - \tfrac{1}{2}mu^2$

$$= (\tfrac{1}{2} \times 0.02 \times 34) - (\tfrac{1}{2} \times 0.02 \times 10.25)$$

$$= 0.2375 \text{ J}$$

Q5 First find the velocity of the tennis ball just before it is hit:

Use $v^2 = u^2 + 2as$, where $a = -9.8 \text{ ms}^{-2}$ and $s = -2.5$ m

$$v^2 = 0 + 2 \times -9.8 \times -2.5 \Rightarrow v = \sqrt{49} = 7 \text{ ms}^{-1}$$

The ball is moving vertically downwards, so in vector form, the velocity is $\mathbf{v} = -7\mathbf{j}$

$I = m\mathbf{w} - m\mathbf{v}$ (where $\mathbf{w}$ is the velocity after impact)

$$3\mathbf{i} + 0.6\mathbf{j} = 0.06\mathbf{w} - 0.06(-7\mathbf{j})$$

$$\Rightarrow \mathbf{w} = 50\mathbf{i} + 3\mathbf{j}$$

Speed of ball before collision: $v = 7 \text{ ms}^{-1}$

Speed of ball after collision:

$$w = |\mathbf{w}| = \sqrt{50^2 + 3^2} = \sqrt{2509} \text{ ms}^{-1}$$

Increase in K.E. $= \tfrac{1}{2}mw^2 - \tfrac{1}{2}mv^2$

$$= (\tfrac{1}{2} \times 0.06 \times 2509) - (\tfrac{1}{2} \times 0.06 \times 49)$$

$$= 73.8 \text{ J}$$

Q6 K.E. after impulse is given by:

$$160 = \tfrac{1}{2}mv^2 = \tfrac{1}{2} \times 5 \times v^2 \Rightarrow v = 8$$

Velocity of the ball after receiving the impulse is:

$$\mathbf{v} = 8\cos30°\mathbf{i} + 8\sin30°\mathbf{j}$$

$$\Rightarrow \mathbf{v} = (4\sqrt{3}\,\mathbf{i} + 4\mathbf{j}) \text{ ms}^{-1}$$

(Both components are positive as the velocity is 30° above the positive unit vector i.)

$I = mv - mu$

$$= 5(4\sqrt{3}\,\mathbf{i} + 4\mathbf{j}) - 5(\sqrt{3}\,\mathbf{i} + 6\mathbf{j})$$

$$= (15\sqrt{3}\,\mathbf{i} - 10\mathbf{j}) \text{ Ns}$$

Review Exercise — Chapter 4

Q1 a) $\mathbf{I} = m\mathbf{v} - m\mathbf{u}$, so
$2\mathbf{i} + 5\mathbf{j} = 0.1\mathbf{v} - 0.1(\mathbf{i} + \mathbf{j})$
$2\mathbf{i} + 5\mathbf{j} = 0.1\mathbf{v} - 0.1\mathbf{i} - 0.1\mathbf{j}$
$0.1\mathbf{v} = 2\mathbf{i} + 5\mathbf{j} + 0.1\mathbf{i} + 0.1\mathbf{j} = 2.1\mathbf{i} + 5.1\mathbf{j}$
$\Rightarrow \mathbf{v} = (21\mathbf{i} + 51\mathbf{j}) \text{ ms}^{-1}$

b) $-3\mathbf{i} + \mathbf{j} = 0.1\mathbf{v} - 0.1\mathbf{i} - 0.1\mathbf{j}$
$0.1\mathbf{v} = -3\mathbf{i} + \mathbf{j} + 0.1\mathbf{i} + 0.1\mathbf{j} = -2.9\mathbf{i} + 1.1\mathbf{j}$
$\Rightarrow \mathbf{v} = (-29\mathbf{i} + 11\mathbf{j}) \text{ ms}^{-1}$

c) $-\mathbf{i} - 6\mathbf{j} = 0.1\mathbf{v} - 0.1\mathbf{i} - 0.1\mathbf{j}$
$0.1\mathbf{v} = -\mathbf{i} - 6\mathbf{j} + 0.1\mathbf{i} + 0.1\mathbf{j} = -0.9\mathbf{i} - 5.9\mathbf{j}$
$\Rightarrow \mathbf{v} = (-9\mathbf{i} - 59\mathbf{j}) \text{ ms}^{-1}$

d) $4\mathbf{i} = 0.1\mathbf{v} - 0.1\mathbf{i} - 0.1\mathbf{j}$
$0.1\mathbf{v} = 4\mathbf{i} + 0.1\mathbf{i} + 0.1\mathbf{j} = 4.1\mathbf{i} + 0.1\mathbf{j}$
$\Rightarrow \mathbf{v} = (41\mathbf{i} + \mathbf{j}) \text{ ms}^{-1}$

Q2 a) $\mathbf{I} = m\mathbf{v} - m\mathbf{u}$, so
$\mathbf{Q} = 2(-2\mathbf{i} + \mathbf{j}) - 2(4\mathbf{i} - \mathbf{j}) = -4\mathbf{i} + 2\mathbf{j} - 8\mathbf{i} + 2\mathbf{j}$
$\mathbf{Q} = (-12\mathbf{i} + 4\mathbf{j}) \text{ Ns}$

b)

$|\mathbf{Q}| = \sqrt{(-12)^2 + 4^2} = 12.6$ Ns (3 s.f.)

c) $\theta = \tan^{-1}\left(\frac{4}{12}\right) = 18.434...°$
Required angle $= 180° - 18.434...° = 162°$ (3 s.f.)

Q3 a) $m_A\mathbf{u}_A + m_B\mathbf{u}_B = m_A\mathbf{v}_A + m_B\mathbf{v}_B$, so:
$0.5(2\mathbf{i} + \mathbf{j}) + 0.4(-\mathbf{i} - 4\mathbf{j}) = 0.5(-\mathbf{i} - 2\mathbf{j}) + 0.4\mathbf{v}_B$
$\mathbf{i} + 0.5\mathbf{j} - 0.4\mathbf{i} - 1.6\mathbf{j} = -0.5\mathbf{i} - \mathbf{j} + 0.4\mathbf{v}_B$
$0.4\mathbf{v}_B = 1.1\mathbf{i} - 0.1\mathbf{j}$
$\Rightarrow \mathbf{v}_B = (2.75\mathbf{i} - 0.25\mathbf{j}) \text{ ms}^{-1}$
Speed $= |\mathbf{v}_B| = \sqrt{2.75^2 + 0.25^2}$
$= 2.76 \text{ ms}^{-1}$ (to 3 s.f.)

b) If they coalesce:
$0.5(2\mathbf{i} + \mathbf{j}) + 0.4(-\mathbf{i} - 4\mathbf{j}) = (0.5 + 0.4)\mathbf{v}$
$\mathbf{i} + 0.5\mathbf{j} - 0.4\mathbf{i} - 1.6\mathbf{j} = 0.9\mathbf{v}$
$0.9\mathbf{v} = 0.6\mathbf{i} - 1.1\mathbf{j} \Rightarrow \mathbf{v} = (\frac{2}{3}\mathbf{i} - \frac{11}{9}\mathbf{j}) \text{ ms}^{-1}$
Speed $= |\mathbf{v}| = \sqrt{\left(\frac{2}{3}\right)^2 + \left(-\frac{11}{9}\right)^2}$
$= 1.39 \text{ ms}^{-1}$ (to 3 s.f.)

Q4 Call the particles A and B. If $u_A = u$ then $u_B = -u$ (as it's going in the opposite direction at the same speed).
After the collision, $v_A = 0$ and $v_B = \frac{u}{2}$ (as it's going in the opposite direction to its original motion at half the speed).
$e = \dfrac{\text{speed of separation of particles}}{\text{speed of approach of particles}} = \dfrac{v_B - v_A}{u_A - u_B}$

$\Rightarrow e = \dfrac{\frac{u}{2} - 0}{u - (-u)} = \dfrac{\frac{u}{2}}{2u} = \dfrac{u}{4u} = \dfrac{1}{4}.$

Q5 a) For collision with a plane surface, $e = \frac{v}{u}$, so rebound speed $v = eu \Rightarrow v = 0.4 \times 10 = 4 \text{ ms}^{-1}$.

b) Call the particles A and B, so
$e = \dfrac{\text{speed of separation of particles}}{\text{speed of approach of particles}} = \dfrac{v_B - v_A}{u_A - u_B}$

$\Rightarrow 0.4 = \dfrac{v_B - v_A}{10 - (-12)} \Rightarrow v_B - v_A = 0.4 \times 22$
$\Rightarrow v_B - v_A = 8.8 \text{ ...[1]}$
Using the conservation of momentum:
$m_A u_A + m_B u_B = m_A v_A + m_B v_B$
$(1 \times 10) + (2 \times -12) = (1 \times v_A) + (2 \times v_B)$
$10 - 24 = v_A + 2v_B \Rightarrow v_A + 2v_B = -14 \text{ ...[2]}$
Equation [1] + equation [2] gives:
$3v_B = -5.2 \Rightarrow v_B = -1.7333... \text{ ms}^{-1}$.
Substituting in equation [1] gives:
$-1.7333... - v_A = 8.8$
$\Rightarrow v_A = -1.7333... - 8.8 = -10.5333... \text{ ms}^{-1}$.
So, to 3 s.f., the original particle's rebound speed is 10.5 ms^{-1}.

Q6 For the first collision, between A and B:
$e = \dfrac{v_B - v_A}{u_A - u_B} \Rightarrow \dfrac{1}{4} = \dfrac{v_B - v_A}{3u - 2u} \Rightarrow v_B - v_A = \dfrac{u}{4} \text{ ...[1]}$
And:
$m_A u_A + m_B u_B = m_A v_A + m_B v_B$
$(1 \times 3u) + (4 \times 2u) = (1 \times v_A) + (4 \times v_B)$
$3u + 8u = v_A + 4v_B \Rightarrow v_A + 4v_B = 11u \text{ ...[2]}$

Equation [1] + equation [2] gives:
$5v_B = 11u + \dfrac{u}{4} \Rightarrow 5v_B = \dfrac{45u}{4} \Rightarrow v_B = \dfrac{9u}{4}.$
Substituting in equation [2] gives:
$v_A + 9u = 11u \Rightarrow v_A = 11u - 9u = 2u.$
For the second collision, between B and C:
$e = \dfrac{v_C - v_B}{u_B - u_C} \Rightarrow \dfrac{1}{3} = \dfrac{v_C - v_B}{\frac{9u}{4} - u} \Rightarrow v_C - v_B = \dfrac{5u}{12} \text{ ...[3]}$
And:
$m_B u_B + m_C u_C = m_B v_B + m_C v_C$
$(4 \times \frac{9u}{4}) + (5 \times u) = (4 \times v_B) + (5 \times v_C)$
$\Rightarrow 4v_B + 5v_C = 14u \text{ ...[4]}$
4 × Equation [3] + equation [4] gives:
$9v_C = \dfrac{5u}{3} + 14u \Rightarrow 9v_C = \dfrac{47u}{3} \Rightarrow v_C = \dfrac{47u}{27}.$
Substituting in equation [3] gives:
$\dfrac{47u}{27} - v_B = \dfrac{5u}{12} \Rightarrow v_B = \dfrac{47u}{27} - \dfrac{5u}{12} = \dfrac{143u}{108}.$
So after both collisions:
A is travelling at $2u = \dfrac{216u}{108}$,

and B is travelling at $\dfrac{143u}{108}$,

which means that A is travelling faster than B in the same direction, so they should collide again.

Q7 Bounce 1:
Using $v^2 = u^2 + 2as$, where $v = u_1$, $u = 0$, $a = 9.8$ and $s = 1$:
$u_1^2 = 2 \times 9.8 \times 1 = 19.6 \Rightarrow u_1 = \sqrt{19.6} = 4.4271...$

Using $e = \dfrac{v}{u}$, $v = eu$, where $v = v_1$, $e = 0.5$ and $u = u_1$:
$v_1 = 0.5 \times 4.4271... = 2.2135...$

Then $v^2 = u^2 + 2as$, where $v = 0$, $u = v_1$ and $a = -9.8$:
$0 = 2.2135...^2 + (2 \times -9.8)s_1$

$\Rightarrow s_1 = \dfrac{2.2135...^2}{2 \times 9.8} = 0.25 \text{ m}.$

Bounce 2:

From the symmetry of the vertical motion,
$u_2 = v_1 = 2.2135...$
$v = eu$, where $v = v_2$, $e = 0.5$ and $u = u_2$:
$v_2 = 0.5 \times 2.2135... = 1.1067...$
$v^2 = u^2 + 2as$, where $v = 0$, $u = v_2$ and $a = -9.8$:
$0 = 1.1067...^2 + (2 \times -9.8)s_2$
$\Rightarrow s_2 = \dfrac{1.1067...^2}{2 \times 9.8} = 0.0625$ m.

Bounce 3:

From the symmetry of the vertical motion,
$u_3 = v_2 = 1.1067...$
$v = eu$, where $v = v_3$, $e = 0.5$ and $u = u_3$:
$v_2 = 0.5 \times 1.1067... = 0.5533...$
$v^2 = u^2 + 2as$, where $v = 0$, $u = v_3$ and $a = -9.8$:
$0 = 0.5533...^2 + (2 \times -9.8)s_3$
$\Rightarrow s_3 = \dfrac{0.5533...^2}{2 \times 9.8} = 0.015625$ m.

You could also answer this question using the fact that the height of the nth bounce is $e^{2n} = 0.5^{2n}$.

Q8 $e = \dfrac{v_2 - v_1}{u_1 - u_2} \Rightarrow 0.3 = \dfrac{v_2 - v_1}{3 - 0} \Rightarrow v_2 - v_1 = 0.9$ ...[1]

And: $m_1u_1 + m_2u_2 = m_1v_1 + m_2v_2$
$\Rightarrow (2 \times 3) + (3 \times 0) = 2v_1 + 3v_2$
$\Rightarrow 6 = 2v_1 + 3v_2 \Rightarrow v_1 + 1.5v_2 = 3$ ...[2]

Equation [1] + equation [2] gives:
$2.5v_2 = 3.9 \Rightarrow v_2 = 1.56$ ms^{-1}.

In equation [1]:
$1.56 - v_1 = 0.9 \Rightarrow v_1 = 1.56 - 0.9 = 0.66$ ms^{-1}.

Loss of K.E. $= (\frac{1}{2}m_1u_1^2 + \frac{1}{2}m_2u_2^2) - (\frac{1}{2}m_1v_1^2 + \frac{1}{2}m_2v_2^2)$

$= [(\frac{1}{2} \times 2 \times 3^2) + 0] - [(\frac{1}{2} \times 2 \times 0.66^2)$
$\quad + (\frac{1}{2} \times 3 \times 1.56^2)]$

$= 9 - 4.086 = 4.914$ J.

Q9 Using the impulse-momentum principle:
$I = m\mathbf{v} - m\mathbf{u}$, so
$-6\mathbf{i} - 2.5\mathbf{j} = 0.1\mathbf{v} - 0.1(30\mathbf{i} + 10\mathbf{j})$
$-6\mathbf{i} - 2.5\mathbf{j} = 0.1\mathbf{v} - 3\mathbf{i} - \mathbf{j}$
$0.1\mathbf{v} = -3\mathbf{i} - 1.5\mathbf{j}$
$\Rightarrow \mathbf{v} = (-30\mathbf{i} - 15\mathbf{j})$ ms^{-1}

The initial speed of the ball, $u = |\mathbf{u}| = \sqrt{30^2 + 10^2}$
$= \sqrt{1000}$ ms^{-1}
The final speed of the ball, $v = |\mathbf{v}| = \sqrt{(-30)^2 + (-15)^2}$
$= \sqrt{1125}$ ms^{-1}

So change in K.E. $= \frac{1}{2}mv^2 - \frac{1}{2}mu^2$
$= (\frac{1}{2} \times 0.1 \times (\sqrt{1125})^2) - (\frac{1}{2} \times 0.1 \times (\sqrt{1000})^2)$
$= 6.25$ J

Exam-Style Questions — Chapter 4

Q1 a) $I = m\mathbf{v} - m\mathbf{u}$, so
$3\mathbf{i} - 8\mathbf{j} = 0.4\mathbf{v} - 0.4(-6\mathbf{i} + \mathbf{j})$ *[1 mark]*
$3\mathbf{i} - 8\mathbf{j} = 0.4\mathbf{v} + 2.4\mathbf{i} - 0.4\mathbf{j}$
$0.4\mathbf{v} = 0.6\mathbf{i} - 7.6\mathbf{j}$ *[1 mark]*
$\Rightarrow \mathbf{v} = (1.5\mathbf{i} - 19\mathbf{j})$ ms^{-1} *[1 mark]*.

Speed is the magnitude of the velocity.

Drawing this as a right-angled triangle:

$|\mathbf{v}| = \sqrt{1.5^2 + 19^2}$ *[1 mark]*
$= 19.1$ ms^{-1} (to 3 s.f.) *[1 mark]*.

b) Using the triangle in part a), θ is the angle with $\mathbf{i}$, so:
$\theta = \tan^{-1}\left(\dfrac{19}{1.5}\right)$ *[1 mark]*
$= 85.5°$ (3 s.f.) below $\mathbf{i}$ *[1 mark]*.

Q2 Using the principle of conservation of momentum for the collision:
$m_1u_1 + m_2u_2 = m_1v_1 + m_2v_2$
Since marble 2 is stationary before the impact:
$(0.02 \times 2) + (0.06 \times 0) = 0.02v_1 + 0.06v_2$ *[1 mark]*
$\Rightarrow 0.02v_1 + 0.06v_2 = 0.04$
$\Rightarrow v_1 + 3v_2 = 2$ ...[1]
Since the collision is perfectly elastic, and so $e = 1$, the law of restitution gives a second equation:
$e = \dfrac{\text{speed of separation of particles}}{\text{speed of approach of particles}} = \dfrac{v_2 - v_1}{u_1 - u_2}$

$\Rightarrow 1 = \dfrac{v_2 - v_1}{2 - 0}$ *[1 mark]* $\Rightarrow v_2 - v_1 = 2$ ...[2]
Equation [1] + equation [2] gives:
$4v_2 = 4 \Rightarrow v_2 = 1$ ms^{-1} *[1 mark]*.
Substituting in equation [1] gives:
$v_1 + (3 \times 1) = 2 \Rightarrow v_1 = -1$ ms^{-1} *[1 mark]*.
So after the collision, both particles are travelling at a speed of 1 ms^{-1} (but the first particle is going in the opposite direction to its initial path).

Q3 a) Using the law of restitution for the collision between P and Q, where P is travelling at u and Q at $-u$ (i.e. in the opposite direction):
$e = \dfrac{v_Q - v_P}{u_P - u_Q} \Rightarrow \dfrac{3}{4} = \dfrac{v_Q - v_P}{u - (-u)}$ *[1 mark]*
$\Rightarrow \dfrac{3}{4} = \dfrac{v_Q - v_P}{2u}$
$\Rightarrow v_Q - v_P = \dfrac{3u}{2}$ ...[1]

Using conservation of momentum:
$m_Pu_P + m_Qu_Q = m_Pv_P + m_Qv_Q$
$2mu - mu = 2mv_P + mv_Q$ *[1 mark]*
$\Rightarrow 2v_P + v_Q = u$ ...[2]
Equation [2] − equation [1] gives:
$3v_P = -\dfrac{u}{2} \Rightarrow v_P = -\dfrac{u}{6}$ *[1 mark]*.
Substituting in equation [1] gives:
$v_Q - (-\dfrac{u}{6}) = \dfrac{3u}{2} \Rightarrow v_Q = \dfrac{4u}{3}$ *[1 mark]*.
Since P's velocity was initially positive, and is now negative, and Q's was initially negative but is now positive, the collision has reversed the directions of both particles *[1 mark]*.
$|v_Q| \div |v_P| = \dfrac{4u}{3} \div \dfrac{u}{6} = 8$,
so Q is now going 8 times faster than P *[1 mark]*.

b) For the collision with the wall,

$e_{wall} = \dfrac{\text{speed of rebound}}{\text{speed of approach}}$.

Q approaches the wall with a speed of $\dfrac{4u}{3}$ (from a)), so if v_{Qwall} is its rebound speed:

$e_{wall} = \dfrac{v_{Qwall}}{\frac{4u}{3}} \Rightarrow v_{Qwall} = \dfrac{4ue_{wall}}{3}$ **[1 mark]**.

Since Q collides again with P, v_{Qwall} must be greater than $|v_P|$, which is $\dfrac{u}{6}$ (from a)), so:

$\dfrac{4ue_{wall}}{3} > \dfrac{u}{6}$ **[1 mark]** $\Rightarrow e_{wall} > \dfrac{3u}{6 \times 4u}$

$\Rightarrow e_{wall} > \dfrac{1}{8}$ **[1 mark]**.

c) If $e_{wall} = \dfrac{3}{5}$, then (from b)):

$v_{Qwall} = \dfrac{4ue_{wall}}{3} = \dfrac{4u \times 3}{3 \times 5} = \dfrac{4u}{5}$ **[1 mark]**.

Q is now travelling in the same direction as P, which is still travelling at a speed of $\dfrac{u}{6}$ (from a)), and the particles have a coefficient of restitution of $\dfrac{3}{4}$, so using the law of restitution for the second collision between P and Q (taking the direction of motion of the particles as positive):

$e = \dfrac{v_P - v_Q}{u_Q - u_P} \Rightarrow \dfrac{3}{4} = \dfrac{v_P - v_Q}{\left(\frac{4u}{5}\right) - \frac{u}{6}}$ **[1 mark]**

$\Rightarrow \dfrac{3}{4} = \dfrac{v_P - v_Q}{\frac{19u}{30}}$

$\Rightarrow v_P - v_Q = \dfrac{19u}{40}$ ...[1]

Using conservation of momentum:

$m_Q u_Q + m_P u_P = m_Q v_Q + m_P v_P$

$\dfrac{4um}{5} + \dfrac{2um}{6} = mv_Q + 2mv_P$ **[1 mark]**

$\Rightarrow v_Q + 2v_P = \dfrac{17u}{15}$ ...[2]

Equation [1] + equation [2] gives:

$3v_P = \dfrac{193u}{120} \Rightarrow v_P = \dfrac{193u}{360}$ **[1 mark]**.

Substituting in equation [1] gives:

$\dfrac{193u}{360} - v_Q = \dfrac{19u}{40}$

$\Rightarrow v_Q = \dfrac{193u}{360} - \dfrac{19u}{40} = \dfrac{11u}{180}$ **[1 mark]**.

Since $v_Q = 0.22$ ms^{-1}:

$\dfrac{11u}{180} = 0.22$ **[1 mark]**

$\Rightarrow u = (0.22 \times 180) \div 11 = 3.6$ ms^{-1} **[1 mark]**.

Q4 Using the law of restitution for the collision between particles 1 and 2 gives:

$e = \dfrac{v_2 - v_1}{u_1 - u_2} \Rightarrow \dfrac{1}{4} = \dfrac{v_2 - v_1}{3u - 2u}$ **[1 mark]**

$\Rightarrow v_2 - v_1 = \dfrac{u}{4}$ ...[1]

Using conservation of momentum:

$m_1 u_1 + m_2 u_2 = m_1 v_1 + m_2 v_2$

$(2m \times 3u) + (3m \times 2u) = 2mv_1 + 3mv_2$ **[1 mark]**

$\Rightarrow 2v_1 + 3v_2 = 12u$ ...[2]

Equation [1] × 2 gives:

$2v_2 - 2v_1 = \dfrac{u}{2}$ ...[3]

Equation [2] + equation [3] gives:

$5v_2 = 12u + \dfrac{u}{2} \Rightarrow v_2 = \dfrac{25u}{2 \times 5} = \dfrac{5u}{2}$ **[1 mark]**.

Substituting in equation [1] gives:

$\dfrac{5u}{2} - v_1 = \dfrac{u}{4}$

$\Rightarrow v_1 = \dfrac{5u}{2} - \dfrac{u}{4} = \dfrac{9u}{4}$ **[1 mark]**.

Loss of kinetic energy =

$\left(\frac{1}{2}m_1 u_1^2 + \frac{1}{2}m_2 u_2^2\right) - \left(\frac{1}{2}m_1 v_1^2 + \frac{1}{2}m_2 v_2^2\right)$

$= \left[\left(\frac{1}{2} \times 2m \times (3u)^2\right) + \left(\frac{1}{2} \times 3m \times (2u)^2\right)\right] -$

$\left[\left(\frac{1}{2} \times 2m \times \left(\frac{9u}{4}\right)^2\right) + \left(\frac{1}{2} \times 3m \times \left(\frac{5u}{2}\right)^2\right)\right]$ **[1 mark]**

$= (9mu^2 + 6mu^2) - \left(\dfrac{81mu^2}{16} + \dfrac{75mu^2}{8}\right)$ **[2 marks]**

$= \left(15 - \dfrac{231}{16}\right)mu^2 = \dfrac{9mu^2}{16}$ J **[1 mark]**

Q5 a) For the collision between A and B, the law of restitution gives the following equation:

$e = \dfrac{v_B - v_A}{u_A - u_B} \Rightarrow e = \dfrac{v_B - v_A}{4u - 0}$ **[1 mark]**

$\Rightarrow v_B - v_A = 4ue$ ...[1]

Using conservation of momentum:

$m_A u_A + m_B u_B = m_A v_A + m_B v_B$

$4mu + 0 = mv_A + 2mv_B$ **[1 mark]**

$\Rightarrow v_A + 2v_B = 4u$ ...[2]

Equation [1] + equation [2] gives:

$3v_B = 4u(1 + e) \Rightarrow v_B = \dfrac{4u}{3}(1 + e)$ **[1 mark]**.

Substituting in equation [1] gives:

$\dfrac{4u}{3}(1 + e) - v_A = 4ue$

$\Rightarrow v_A = \dfrac{4u}{3}(1 + e) - 4ue = \dfrac{4u}{3}(1 - 2e)$ **[1 mark]**.

Since the coefficient of restitution must be between 0 and 1, and the coefficient of restitution between B and C is $2e$, then $0 \leq 2e \leq 1$

$\Rightarrow 1 - 2e \geq 0$ **[1 mark]**.

i.e. $v_A = \dfrac{4u}{3}(1 - 2e)$, where $u > 0$ and $1 - 2e \geq 0$.

So:

v_A cannot be negative **[1 mark]**, so the collision does not reverse the direction of A's motion **[1 mark]**.

b) After the collision, A is travelling at $\dfrac{4u}{3}(1 - 2e)$ and B is travelling at $\dfrac{4u}{3}(1 + e)$ (from a)).

In the time it takes B to travel a distance d, A has travelled $\dfrac{d}{4}$. So the speed of A must be a quarter of the speed of B **[1 mark]** i.e.

$\dfrac{4u}{3}(1 - 2e) = \dfrac{u}{3}(1 + e)$ **[1 mark]**

$\Rightarrow 4 - 8e = 1 + e$

$\Rightarrow 9e = 3 \Rightarrow e = \dfrac{1}{3}$ **[1 mark]**

c) Since $e = \frac{1}{3}$ (from b)), the speed of B as it approaches C is:

$\frac{4u}{3}(1 + \frac{1}{3}) = \frac{16u}{9}$ *[1 mark]*.

The coefficient of restitution between B and C is $2e = \frac{2}{3}$ *[1 mark]*.

So, using the law of restitution:

$2e = \frac{v_C - v_B}{u_B - u_C} \Rightarrow \frac{2}{3} = \frac{v_C - v_B}{\frac{16u}{9} - 0}$ *[1 mark]*

$\Rightarrow v_C - v_B = \frac{32u}{27}$ ...[1]

Using conservation of momentum:

$m_B u_B + m_C u_C = m_B v_B + m_C v_C$

$(2m \times \frac{16u}{9}) + 0 = 2mv_B + 4mv_C$ *[1 mark]*

$\Rightarrow v_B + 2v_C = \frac{16u}{9}$ ...[2]

Equation [1] + equation [2] gives:

$3v_C = \frac{80u}{27} \Rightarrow v_C = \frac{80u}{81}$ *[1 mark]*

Chapter 5: Statics

1. Moments and Equilibrium

Exercise 1.1 — Moments

Q1 Taking clockwise as positive:
Sum of moments = $(5\sin40° \times 4) + (3 \times 2) = 18.855...$
= 18.9 Nm (3 s.f.) clockwise

Q2 Taking anticlockwise as positive:
Sum of moments = $(10 \times 1) + (6\sin70° \times 2) -$
$(5 \times 0.5) = 18.776... = 18.8$ Nm (3 s.f.) anticlockwise

Q3 Taking clockwise as positive:
Sum of moments = $(1\sin25° \times 1.5) + (1.5g \times 2.5) -$
$(2.5\sin50° \times 4.5) = 28.765...$
= 28.8 Nm (3 s.f.) clockwise

Q4 Taking anticlockwise as positive:
$(25 \times 11\sin30°) - (8 \times 22\cos30°) = -14.920...$
= 14.9 Nm (3 s.f.) clockwise
This question has been done by resolving the distances
— you could've done it by resolving the forces instead.

Q5 Taking clockwise as positive:
$(13\sin20° \times 12) + (9\sin45° \times 5) - (8g\sin20° \times 5)$
$= -48.896... = 48.9$ Nm (3 s.f.) anticlockwise

Exercise 1.2 — Equilibrium

Q1 a)
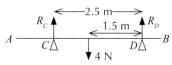

Taking moments about D:
$4 \times 1.5 = R_C \times 2.5$
$\Rightarrow R_C = 6 \div 2.5 = 2.4$ N

b) Resolving vertically:
$R_C + R_D = 4$
$\Rightarrow R_D = 4 - 2.4 = 1.6$ N

Q2 a)
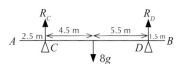

Resolving vertically:
$12 + R = 3g$
$\Rightarrow R = 17.4$ N

b) Taking moments about A:
$3g \times x = 17.4 \times 1.6$
$\Rightarrow x = 27.84 \div 29.4 = 0.947$ m (3 s.f.)

Q3
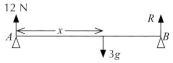

Taking moments about C:
$8g \times 4.5 = R_D \times 10$
$\Rightarrow R_D = 35.28$ N
Resolving vertically:
$R_C + R_D = 8g$
$\Rightarrow R_C = 78.4 - 35.28 = 43.12$ N

Q4 a)
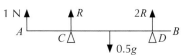

Let the reaction at C be R.
Then the reaction at D is $2R$.
Resolving vertically:
$1 + R + 2R = 0.5g$
$3R = 3.9$
$\Rightarrow R = 1.3$ N
So the normal reaction at C has magnitude 1.3 N and the normal reaction at D has magnitude 2.6 N.

b) Let x be the distance of the COM of the rod from A. Taking moments about A:
$(1.3 \times 1.6) + (2.6 \times 4.2) = 0.5g \times x$
$\Rightarrow x = 13 \div 4.9 = 2.65$ m (3 s.f.)

Q5 a) Taking moments about A:
$mg \times 2.7 = 20\sin80° \times 6$
$\Rightarrow m = 118.176... \div 26.46 = 4.466...$
$= 4.47$ kg (3 s.f.)

b) Resolving horizontally:
$T\cos\alpha = 20\cos80°$ **eqn1**
Resolving vertically:
$T\sin\alpha + 20\sin80° = mg$
$T\sin\alpha = 43.769... - 20\sin80°$
$\Rightarrow T\sin\alpha = 24.073...$ **eqn2**
Dividing **eqn2** by **eqn1**:
$\tan\alpha = 24.073... \div 20\cos80°$
$\Rightarrow \alpha = \tan^{-1}(6.931...) = 81.790...° = 81.8°$ (3 s.f.)

c) From **eqn1**:
$T = 20\cos80° \div \cos(81.790...°) = 24.3$ N (3 s.f.)

Q6 a) Resolving horizontally:
$T_1\cos75° = T_2\cos40°$
$\Rightarrow T_1 = \dfrac{T_2\cos40°}{\cos75°}$ **eqn1**
Resolving vertically:
$T_1\sin75° + T_2\sin40° = 2g$ **eqn2**
Substituting **eqn1** into **eqn2**:
$\dfrac{T_2\cos40°}{\cos75°}\sin75° + T_2\sin40° = 2g$
$T_2(\cos40°\tan75° + \sin40°) = 2g$
$\Rightarrow T_2 = 19.6 \div 3.501... = 5.597...$
$= 5.60$ N (3 s.f.)
Now using **eqn1**:
$T_1 = \dfrac{(5.597...)\cos40°}{\cos75°} = 16.566...$
$= 16.6$ N (3 s.f.)

b) Let x be the distance of the COM of the rod from A. Taking moments about A:
$2g \times x = (5.597...)\sin40° \times 2.4$
$\Rightarrow x = 8.634... \div 19.6 = 0.441$ m (3 s.f.)

Q7 a) Taking moments about the rod's COM:
$R \times 0.25\cos30° = 5.5 \times 0.4\cos30°$
$\Rightarrow R = 2.2 \div 0.25 = 8.8$ N

b) Resolving vertically:
$5.5 + 8.8 = mg$
$\Rightarrow m = 14.3 \div 9.8 = 1.46$ kg (3 s.f.)

Q8 a) Let l be the length of the rod.
Taking moments about B:
$11g \times (l - 13) = 42\sin38° \times l$
$107.8l - 1401.4 = (25.857...)l$
$(81.942...)l = 1401.4$
$\Rightarrow l = 17.102... = 17.1$ m (3 s.f.)

b) Resolving horizontally:
$T\cos\alpha = 42\cos38°$ **eqn1**
Resolving vertically:
$42\sin38° + T\sin\alpha = 11g$
$\Rightarrow T\sin\alpha = 11g - 42\sin38°$ **eqn2**
Dividing **eqn2** by **eqn1**:
$\tan\alpha = (11g - 42\sin38°) \div (42\cos38°) = 2.475...$
$\Rightarrow \alpha = 68.006...° = 68.0°$ (3 s.f.)

c) Using **eqn1**:
$T = 42\cos38° \div \cos(68.006...°) = 88.373...$
$= 88.4$ N (3 s.f.)

Q9 a) The wire at A makes an angle of $70° - 20° = 50°$ with the horizontal. The wire at B makes an angle of $45° + 20° = 65°$ with the horizontal.
Resolving horizontally:
$T_1\cos50° = T_2\cos65°$
$\Rightarrow T_1 = \dfrac{T_2\cos65°}{\cos50°}$ **eqn1**
Resolving vertically:
$T_1\sin50° + T_2\sin65° = 16g$ **eqn2**
Substituting **eqn1** into **eqn2**:
$\dfrac{T_2\cos65°}{\cos50°}\sin50° + T_2\sin65° = 16g$
$T_2(\cos65°\tan50° + \sin65°) = 16g$
$\Rightarrow T_2 = 156.8 \div 1.409... = 111.208...$
$= 111$ N (3 s.f.)
Now using **eqn1**:
$T_1 = \dfrac{(111.208...)\cos65°}{\cos50°} = 73.117...$
$= 73.1$ N (3 s.f.)

b) Let x be the distance of the COM of the rod along the rod from A. Taking moments about A:
$16g\cos20° \times x = (111.208...)\sin45° \times 10$
$\Rightarrow x = 786.362... \div 147.343... = 5.34$ m (3 s.f.)

Exercise 1.3 — Reaction forces

Q1 a) Taking moments about A:
$3g \times 2 = T \times 1$
$\Rightarrow T = 58.8$ N

b) Resolving vertically:
$T = 3g + R$
$\Rightarrow R = 58.8 - 29.4 = 29.4$ N

Q2 a) Taking moments about A:
$0.6g \times 0.4 = T\sin60° \times 0.6$
$\Rightarrow T = 2.352 \div 0.519... = 4.526...$
$= 4.53$ N (3 s.f.)

b)

Resolving horizontally:
$R_H = T\cos60° = (4.526...)\cos60° = 2.263...$ N
Resolving vertically:
$R_V + T\sin60° = 0.6g$
$\Rightarrow R_V = 0.6g - (4.526...)\sin60° = 1.96$ N

Using Pythagoras' theorem:
$R = \sqrt{(2.263...)^2 + 1.96^2} = 2.993...$
$= 2.99$ N (3 s.f.)
Using trigonometry:
$\theta = \tan^{-1}\left(\dfrac{2.263...}{1.96}\right) = 49.106...°$
$= 49.1°$ (3 s.f.) measured anticlockwise from the upward vertical.

Q3 a) Taking moments about A:
$(1.5g \times 0.6) + (0.5g \times 1.2) = T\sin20° \times 2.4$
$\Rightarrow T = 14.7 \div 0.820... = 17.908...$
$= 17.9$ N (3 s.f.)

b)

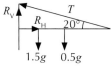

Resolving horizontally:
$R_H = T\cos20° = (17.908...)\cos20° = 16.828...$ N
Resolving vertically:
$R_V + T\sin20° = 1.5g + 0.5g$
$\Rightarrow R_V = 19.6 - 6.125 = 13.475$ N

Using Pythagoras' theorem:
$R = \sqrt{(16.828...)^2 + 13.475^2} = 21.558...$
$= 21.6$ N (3 s.f.)
Using trigonometry:
$\theta = \tan^{-1}\left(\frac{16.828...}{13.475}\right) = 51.314...°$
$= 51.3°$ (3 s.f.) measured clockwise from the upward vertical.

Q4 a) Taking moments about A:
$0.2g \times 0.1\cos\alpha = 1.2 \times 0.2\sin\alpha$
$0.196\cos\alpha = 0.24\sin\alpha$
$\tan\alpha = 0.816...$
$\Rightarrow \alpha = 39.237...° = 39.2°$ (3 s.f.)

b)

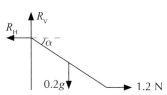

Resolving horizontally:
$R_H = 1.2$ N
Resolving vertically:
$R_V = 0.2g = 1.96$ N

Using Pythagoras' theorem:
$R = \sqrt{1.2^2 + 1.96^2} = 2.298...$
$= 2.30$ N (3 s.f.)
Using trigonometry:
$\theta = \tan^{-1}\left(\frac{1.2}{1.96}\right) = 31.476...°$
$= 31.5°$ (3 s.f.) measured anticlockwise from the upward vertical.

Q5 a) Let the distance from A to the COM be x.
Taking moments about A:
$(3 \times 0.1\cos35°) + (5 \times 0.7) = 0.8g \times x\cos35°$
$\Rightarrow x = 3.745... \div 6.422... = 0.5832...$
$= 0.583$ m (3 s.f.)

b)

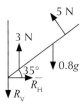

Resolving horizontally:
$R_H = 5\sin35° = 2.867...$ N
Resolving vertically:
$3 + 5\cos35° = 0.8g + R_V$
$\Rightarrow R_V = -0.744...$ N

Using Pythagoras' theorem:
$R = \sqrt{(2.867...)^2 + (0.744...)^2} = 2.962...$
$= 2.96$ N (3 s.f.)
Using trigonometry:
$\theta = \tan^{-1}\left(\frac{2.867...}{0.744...}\right) = 75.452...°$
$= 75.5°$ (3 s.f.) measured clockwise from the upward vertical.

R_V being negative means that it is acting upwards rather than downwards (as was initially assumed).

Q6 a) Let the distance from A to the COM be x.
Taking moments about A:
$(1.8g \times x) + (3.5\sin80° \times 7) = 95\cos71° \times 3.5$
$\Rightarrow x = 84.123... \div 17.64 = 4.768...$
$= 4.77$ m (3 s.f.)

b)

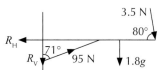

Resolving horizontally:
$R_H = 95\sin71° + 3.5\cos80° = 90.432...$ N
Resolving vertically:
$R_V + 1.8g + 3.5\sin80° = 95\cos71°$
$\Rightarrow R_V = 9.842...$ N

Using Pythagoras' theorem:
$R = \sqrt{(90.432...)^2 + (9.842...)^2} = 90.966...$
$= 91.0$ N (3 s.f.)
Using trigonometry:
$\theta = \tan^{-1}\left(\frac{90.432...}{9.842...}\right) = 83.788...°$
$= 83.8°$ (3 s.f.) measured clockwise from the downward vertical.

Q7 a) Taking moments about A:
$(110\cos30° \times 2) + (T\sin30° \times 4) = (1.75g \times 4) +$
$(2.25g \times 8)$
$\Rightarrow T = 54.474... \div 2 = 27.237...$
$= 27.2$ N (3 s.f.)

b)

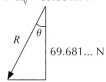

Resolving horizontally:
$R_H + (27.237...)\cos30° = 110\sin30°$
$\Rightarrow R_H = 31.411...$ N
Resolving vertically:
$R_V + 1.75g + 2.25g = (27.237...)\sin30° +$
$110\cos30°$
$\Rightarrow R_V = 69.681...$ N

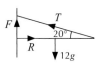

Using Pythagoras' theorem:
$R = \sqrt{(31.411...)^2 + (69.681...)^2} = 76.434...$
$= 76.4$ N (3 s.f.)
Using trigonometry:
$\theta = \tan^{-1}\left(\frac{31.411...}{69.681...}\right) = 24.265...°$
$= 24.3°$ (3 s.f.) measured clockwise from the downward vertical.

2. Friction and Limiting Equilibrium

Exercise 2.1 — Friction

Q1 a) Taking moments about A:
$12g \times 8 = T\sin20° \times 16$
$\Rightarrow T = 940.8 \div 5.472... = 171.919...$
$= 172$ N (3 s.f.)

b)

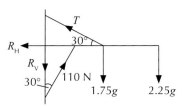

Resolving horizontally:
$R = T\cos20° = (171.919...)\cos20° = 161.551...$ N
Resolving vertically:
$F + T\sin20° = 12g$
$\Rightarrow F = 117.6 - (171.919...)\sin20° = 58.800...$ N
Using $F = \mu R$:
$58.800... = \mu \times 161.551...$
$\Rightarrow \mu = 0.36$ (2 d.p.)

Q2 a)

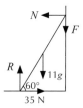

Resolving horizontally:
$N = 35$ N

b) Resolving vertically:
$F + 11g = R$
Taking moments about top of ladder:
$(11g\cos60° \times 3.5) + (35\sin60° \times 7) =$
$R\cos60° \times 7$
$\Rightarrow R = 400.826... \div 3.5 = 114.521...$ N
So $F = 114.521... - 11g = 6.721...$
$= 6.72$ N (3 s.f.)

c) $F = \mu N$
$6.721... = \mu \times 35$
$\Rightarrow \mu = 0.19$ (2 d.p.)

Q3 a)

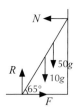

Taking moments about A:
$1.6g\cos20° \times 0.75 = N \times 1.1$
$\Rightarrow N = 10.046... = 10.0$ N (3 s.f.)

b) Resolving vertically:
$R + (10.046...)\cos20° = 1.6g$
$\Rightarrow R = 6.239... = 6.24$ N (3 s.f.)

c) Resolving horizontally:
$F = N\sin20° = (10.046...)\sin20°$
$= 3.435... = 3.44$ N (3 s.f.)

d) $F = \mu R$
$3.435... = \mu \times 6.239...$
$\Rightarrow \mu = 0.55$ (2 d.p.)

Q4

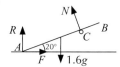

Resolving vertically:
$R = 10g + 50g = 60g$
Resolving horizontally:
$F = N$
If the ladder is on the point of slipping, then $F = \mu R$.
$\Rightarrow \mu R = N$
$\Rightarrow N = 0.3 \times 60g = 176.4$ N
Let x be the girl's distance up the ladder from the base.
Taking moments about base of ladder:
$176.4\sin65° \times 6 = (10g\cos65° \times 3) + (50g\cos65° \times x)$
$\Rightarrow x = 834.986... \div 207.082... = 4.03$ m (3 s.f.)

Q5 a)

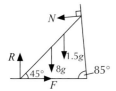

Taking moments about base of ladder:
$(8g\cos45° × 2) + (1.5g\cos45° × 3.5) =$
$N\sin40° × 4$
$⇒ N = 147.254... ÷ 2.571... = 57.272...$
$= 57.3$ N (3 s.f.)
Remember — the normal reaction always acts
perpendicular to the surface.

b) Resolving vertically:
$R = 8g + 1.5g + (57.272...)\sin5°$
$= 98.091...$ N
Resolving horizontally:
$F = (57.272...)\cos5° = 57.054...$ N
$F = \mu R$
$57.054... = \mu × 98.091...$
$⇒ \mu = 0.58$ (2 d.p.)

Q6 a)

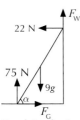

Resolving horizontally:
$F_G = 22$ N
Resolving vertically:
$75 + F_W = 9g$
$⇒ F_W = 13.2$ N
Taking moments about base of ladder:
$9g\cos\alpha × 2.4 = (22\sin\alpha × 4.8)$
$\qquad\qquad\qquad + (13.2\cos\alpha × 4.8)$
$148.32\cos\alpha = 105.6\sin\alpha$
$\tan\alpha = 1.4045...$
$⇒ \alpha = 54.550...° = 54.6°$ (3 s.f.)

b) $F = \mu R$
$F_W = \mu_W × 22$
$⇒ \mu_W = 13.2 ÷ 22 = 0.6$

c) $F_G = \mu_G × 75$
$⇒ \mu_G = 22 ÷ 75 = 0.29$ (2 d.p.)

Q7 a)

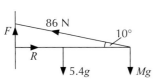

Resolving horizontally:
$R = 86\cos10° = 84.693...$N
Using $F = \mu R$:
$F = 0.55 × 84.693... = 46.581...$ N
Resolving vertically:
$46.581... + 86\sin10° = 5.4g + Mg$
$⇒ M = 8.595... ÷ 9.8 = 0.8770...$
$= 0.877$ kg (3 s.f.)

b) Let x be the distance of the COM from A.
Taking moments about A:
$(5.4g × x) + (Mg × 11) = 86\sin10° × 11$
$⇒ x = 69.724 ÷ 52.92 = 1.32$ m (3 s.f.)

Q8

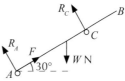

Let l be the length of the beam.
Taking moments about A:
$W\cos30° × 0.5l = R_C × 0.75l$
$⇒ R_C = \dfrac{\sqrt{3}}{2}W × \dfrac{0.5l}{0.75l} = \dfrac{\sqrt{3}}{3}W$ N
Resolving perpendicular to the beam:
$R_A + R_C = W\cos30°$
$⇒ R_A = \dfrac{\sqrt{3}}{2}W - \dfrac{\sqrt{3}}{3}W = \dfrac{\sqrt{3}}{6}W$ N
Resolving parallel to the beam:
$F = W\sin30° = \dfrac{1}{2}W$ N
Using $F = \mu R$:
$\dfrac{1}{2}W = \mu × R_A$
$⇒ \mu = \dfrac{1}{2}W ÷ \dfrac{\sqrt{3}}{6}W = \dfrac{1}{2} × \dfrac{6}{\sqrt{3}} = \dfrac{3}{\sqrt{3}} = \sqrt{3}$
$= 1.73$ (2 d.p.)

Usually, the coefficient of friction between a body and a
surface is between 0 and 1, but it can actually be any
number greater than 0 — as in this case.

Exercise 2.2 — Non-limiting equilibrium problems

Q1 a)

Taking moments about A:
$12g\cos55° × x = 30\sin57° × 2.5$
$⇒ x = 62.900... ÷ 67.452... = 0.933$ m (3 s.f.)

b) Resolving vertically:
$R + 30\sin2° = 12g$
$⇒ R = 116.553...$ N
Resolving horizontally:
$F = 30\cos2° = 29.981...$ N
Using $F ≤ \mu R$:
$\mu ≥ 29.981... ÷ 116.553...$
$⇒ \mu ≥ 0.26$ (2 d.p.)

Q2

The window cleaner is 6 m up the ladder.
Taking moments about base of ladder:
$(25g\cos68° × 4.5) + (76g\cos68° × 6) = N\sin68° × 9$
$\Rightarrow N = 2087.045... ÷ 8.344... = 250.105...$ N
Resolving vertically:
$R = 25g + 76g = 989.8$ N
Resolving horizontally:
$F = N$
Using $F ≤ \mu R$:
$N ≤ \mu × 989.8$
$\Rightarrow \mu ≥ 250.105... ÷ 989.8$
$\mu ≥ 0.25$ (2 d.p.)

Q3

Taking moments about A:
$(50\cos35° × 1) + (10\sin35° × 2) = N × 1.4$
$\Rightarrow N = 37.449...$
Resolving vertically:
$R + (37.449...)\cos35° = 50$
$\Rightarrow R = 19.323...$
Resolving horizontally:
$F + 10 = (37.449...)\sin35°$
$\Rightarrow F = 11.480...$
Using $F ≤ \mu R$:
$11.480... ≤ \mu × 19.323...$
$\Rightarrow \mu ≥ 11.480... ÷ 19.323...$
$\mu ≥ 0.59$ (2 d.p.)

Q4 a)

Let l be the length of the pole:
Taking moments about A:
$4g\cos60° × 0.5l = T\cos60° × l$
$\Rightarrow T = 2g = 19.6$ N

b) Resolving horizontally:
$R\sin40° = F\cos40°$
$\Rightarrow F = R\tan40°$
Using $F ≤ \mu R$:
$R\tan40° ≤ \mu R$
$\Rightarrow \mu ≥ \tan40°$, as required.

Review Exercise — Chapter 5

Q1

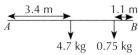

Taking clockwise as positive:
$(4.7g × 3.4) + (0.75g × 5.7) = 198$ Nm (3 s.f.)

Q2 a) Resolving vertically:
$43 + T = 13g$
$\Rightarrow T = 84.4$ N

b) Let x be the distance of the COM from A.
Taking moments about A:
$84.4\cos14° × 16 = 13g\cos14° × x$
$84.4 × 16 = 13g × x$
$\Rightarrow x = 1350.4 ÷ 127.4 = 10.6$ m (3 s.f.)

Q3 Let x be the distance of the COM of the beam from A.
Taking moments about A:
$40\sin30° × b = 5g\cos30° × x$
$20b = 24.5\sqrt{3}x$
$\Rightarrow x = \dfrac{20}{24.5\sqrt{3}}b = 0.471b$ m (3 s.f.)

Q4 a)

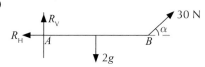

Taking moments about A:
$2g × 0.8 = 30\sin\alpha × 1.6$
$\sin\alpha = 0.326...$
$\Rightarrow \alpha = 19.066...° = 19.1°$ (3 s.f.)

b) Resolving vertically:
$30\sin\alpha + R_V = 2g$
$\Rightarrow R_V = 9.8$ N
Resolving horizontally:
$R_H = 30\cos\alpha = 28.354...$ N

Using Pythagoras' theorem:
$R = \sqrt{(28.354...)^2 + 9.8^2} = 30$ N
Using trigonometry:
$\theta = \tan^{-1}\left(\dfrac{28.354...}{9.8}\right) = 70.933...°$
$= 70.9°$ (3 s.f.) measured anticlockwise from the upward vertical.
The forces acting on the beam are symmetrical about the line of action of the beam's weight, so you could have answered this without doing any calculations.

Q5 a)

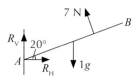

Taking moments about A:
$1g\cos20° × 0.4 = 7x$
$\Rightarrow x = 0.526$ m (3 s.f.)

b) Resolving vertically:
$R_v + 7\cos20° = 1g$
$\Rightarrow R_v = 3.222...$ N
Resolving horizontally:
$R_H = 7\sin20° = 2.394...$ N

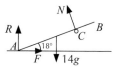

Using Pythagoras' theorem:
$R = \sqrt{(2.394...)^2 + (3.222...)^2} = 4.014...$
$= 4.01$ N (3 s.f.)
Using trigonometry:
$\theta = \tan^{-1}\left(\frac{2.394...}{3.222...}\right) = 36.613...°$
$= 36.6°$ (3 s.f.) measured clockwise from the upward vertical.

Q6

Taking moments about A:
$14g\cos18° \times 7.5 = N \times 13$
$\Rightarrow N = 75.279...$ N
Resolving vertically:
$R + (75.279...)\cos18° = 14g$
$\Rightarrow R = 65.604...$ N
Resolving horizontally:
$F = N\sin18° = (75.279...)\sin18° = 23.262...$ N
Friction is limiting, so, using $F = \mu R$:
$23.262... = \mu \times 65.604...$
$\Rightarrow \mu = 0.35$ (2 d.p.)

Q7 **a)**

Let l be the length of the ladder.
Taking moments about base of ladder:
$20g\cos60° \times 0.5l = N\sin60° \times l$
$49l = \frac{\sqrt{3}}{2}Nl$
$\Rightarrow N = \frac{98}{\sqrt{3}}$ N
Resolving vertically:
$R = 20g = 196$ N
Resolving horizontally:
$F = N$
Using $F = \mu R$:
$\frac{98}{\sqrt{3}} = \mu \times 196$
$\Rightarrow \mu = \frac{98}{196\sqrt{3}} = \frac{1}{2\sqrt{3}} = \frac{\sqrt{3}}{2(\sqrt{3})^2}$
$= \frac{\sqrt{3}}{6}$, as required.

b)

Let P be the horizontal force applied at the base of the ladder. P will be at its minimum value when friction is limiting (i.e. when F is at its greatest value).
Taking moments about base of ladder:
$(20g\cos60° \times 0.5l) + (60g\cos60° \times 0.75l)$
$\quad = N\sin60° \times l$
$269.5l = \frac{\sqrt{3}}{2}Nl$
$\Rightarrow N = \frac{539}{\sqrt{3}}$ N
Resolving vertically:
$R = 60g + 20g = 80g = 784$ N
Resolving horizontally:
$P + F = \frac{539}{\sqrt{3}}$
$P + \mu R = \frac{539}{\sqrt{3}}$
$P + (\frac{\sqrt{3}}{6} \times 784) = \frac{539}{\sqrt{3}}$
$\Rightarrow P = \frac{539}{\sqrt{3}} - \frac{392\sqrt{3}}{3} = \frac{147\sqrt{3}}{3} = 49\sqrt{3}$ N
$= 84.9$ N (3 s.f.)

Q8 **a)** Use the lengths given to draw a right-angled triangle. The length of the hypotenuse can be found using Pythagoras' theorem —
$\sqrt{1.2^2 + 0.9^2} = 1.5$

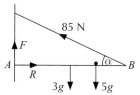

Using trigonometry:
$\sin\alpha = \frac{0.9}{1.5} = 0.6$ $\qquad \cos\alpha = \frac{1.2}{1.5} = 0.8$

Taking moments about A:
$(3g \times 0.6) + (5g \times x) = 85\sin\alpha \times 1.2$
$(3g \times 0.6) + (5g \times x) = 85 \times 0.6 \times 1.2$
$\Rightarrow x = 43.56 \div 49 = 0.889$ m (3 s.f.)

b) Resolving horizontally:
$R = 85\cos\alpha = 85 \times 0.8 = 68$ N
Resolving vertically:
$F + 85\sin\alpha = 3g + 5g$
$F + (85 \times 0.6) = 8g$
$\Rightarrow F = 27.4$ N
Using $F \leq \mu R$:
$\mu \geq 27.4 \div 68$
$\mu \geq 0.40$ (2 d.p.)

Exam-Style Questions — Chapter 5

Q1 a)

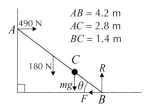

$AB = 4.2$ m
$AC = 2.8$ m
$BC = 1.4$ m

Taking moments about B:
$(mg\cos\theta \times 1.4) + (180\cos\theta \times 2.1)$
$= (490\sin\theta \times 4.2)$
Dividing throughout by $\cos\theta$:

$1.4mg + 378 = 2058\tan\theta = 2058 \times \frac{8}{11}$
$1.4mg = 1496.7... - 378 = 1118.7...$
$m = \frac{1118.7...}{13.72} = 81.539... = 82$ kg (to nearest kg)

[3 marks available in total]:
- *1 mark for taking moments about B*
- *1 mark for correct workings*
- *1 mark for the correct value of m*

b) Resolving horizontally:
$F = 490$ N
Resolving vertically:
$R = 180 + (81.539...)g = 979.090...$ N
As equilibrium is limiting, $F = \mu R$
so $(979.090...)\mu = 490$ N
$\Rightarrow \mu = 0.50$ (2 d.p.)
[5 marks available in total]:
- *1 mark for resolving horizontally*
- *1 mark for resolving vertically*
- *1 mark for using $F = \mu R$*
- *1 mark for correct workings*
- *1 mark for correct value of μ*

Q2 a)

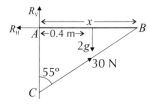

Taking moments about A:
$2g \times 0.4 = 30\cos55° \times x$
so $x = 7.84 \div 17.207... = 0.4556...$
$= 0.456$ m (3 s.f.)

[3 marks available in total]:
- *1 mark for taking moments about A*
- *1 mark for correct workings*
- *1 mark for correct value of x*

b) Resolving vertically:
$R_V = 2g - 30\cos55° = 2.392...$ N
Resolving horizontally:
$R_H = 30\sin55° = 24.574...$ N

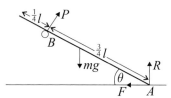

$|R| = \sqrt{(2.392...)^2 + (24.574...)^2} = 24.7$ N (3 s.f.)
$\tan\theta = \frac{24.574...}{2.392...}$
$\Rightarrow \theta = 84.4°$ (3 s.f.) measured anticlockwise from the upward vertical.
[5 marks available in total]:
- *1 mark for resolving vertically*
- *1 mark for resolving horizontally*
- *1 mark for correct workings*
- *1 mark for correct magnitude of R*
- *1 mark for correct direction*

Q3 a)

Taking moments about A:
$\frac{1}{2}l \times mg\cos\theta = \frac{3}{4}l \times P$
so $P = \frac{\frac{1}{2}lmg\cos\theta}{\frac{3}{4}l} = \frac{2}{3}mg\cos\theta$ N

[3 marks available in total]:
- *1 mark for taking moments about A*
- *1 mark for correct workings*
- *1 mark for getting required answer*
Mechanics is harder with algebra than with numbers, but once you've got the hang of it, doing it with numbers will seem a breeze.

b) $\sin\theta = \frac{3}{5}$ so $\cos\theta = \frac{4}{5}$
Using the result from part a) gives $P = \frac{8}{15}mg$
Resolving horizontally:
$F = P\sin\theta = \frac{8}{15}mg \times \frac{3}{5} = \frac{8}{25}mg$
Resolving vertically:
$R + P\cos\theta = mg$
so $R = mg - \frac{4}{5}P = mg - \frac{32}{75}mg = \frac{43}{75}mg$
You don't know if equilibrium is limiting, so using $F \leq \mu R$:
$\frac{8}{25}mg \leq \mu \times \frac{43}{75}mg$
$\Rightarrow \mu \geq \frac{24}{43} = 0.56$ (2 d.p.)
[6 marks available in total]:
- *1 mark for calculating $\cos\theta$*
- *1 mark for resolving horizontally*
- *1 mark for resolving vertically*
- *1 mark for using $F \leq \mu R$*
- *1 mark for correct workings*
- *1 mark for correct value of μ*

Q4 **a)**

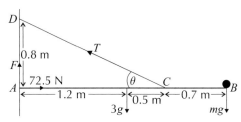

Resolving horizontally:

$T\cos\theta = 72.5$ N

$\tan\theta = \dfrac{0.8}{1.7}$

$\Rightarrow \theta = 25.201...°$

$\Rightarrow T = \dfrac{72.5}{\cos(25.201...°)} = 80.126...$

$= 80.1$ N (3 s.f.)

[4 marks available in total]:
- *1 mark for resolving horizontally*
- *1 mark for calculating θ or $\cos\theta$*
- *1 mark for correct workings*
- *1 mark for correct value of T*

b) From part a), $T\sin\theta = 72.5\tan\theta = \dfrac{580}{17}$

Taking moments about A:

$(3g \times 1.2) + (mg \times 2.4) = 1.7 \times \dfrac{580}{17}$

$23.52m = 58 - 35.28 = 22.72$

$\Rightarrow m = 0.9659... = 0.966$ kg (3 s.f.)

[3 marks available in total]:
- *1 mark for taking moments about A*
- *1 mark for correct workings*
- *1 mark for correct value of m*

c) Resolving vertically:

$F + \dfrac{580}{17} = 3g + (0.9659...)g$

$\Rightarrow F = 38.866... - 34.117... = 4.75$ N (3 s.f)

[3 marks available in total]:
- *1 mark for resolving vertically*
- *1 mark for correct workings*
- *1 mark for correct value of F*

Glossary

Acceleration
The rate of change of an object's **velocity** with respect to time.

Arc
Part of the edge of a circle.

Assumption
A simplification of a real-life situation used in a **model**.

Bead
A **particle** which has a hole in it through which a **string** or **wire** can pass.

Beam
A long, **thin**, straight, **rigid** body.

Centre of mass
The point at which a body's **weight** can be considered to act.

Centroid
The point where the **medians** of a triangle cross. Also the **centre of mass** of a uniform triangular **lamina**.

Coalesce
What happens when bodies join together as a result of a collision and move together with the same **speed** in the same direction.

Coefficient of friction
A number greater than or equal to zero which measures the effect of **friction** between an object and a surface.

Coefficient of restitution
A number between 0 and 1 which is equal to the ratio of the **speed** of separation to the speed of approach for two bodies colliding directly (or the ratio of the rebound speed to the speed of approach for a body colliding at right-angles with a **smooth**, fixed surface).

Component
The effect of a **vector** in a given direction.

Composite shape
A shape that can be broken up into standard parts, such as triangles, rectangles and **sectors** of circles.

Deceleration
An **acceleration** where the object's **speed** is decreasing.

Displacement
A **vector** measurement of an object's distance from a particular point.

Equilibrium
A state where there is no **resultant force** or **moment** acting on a body, hence the body is at **rest** (or moving with constant **velocity**).

External force
Any **force** acting on an object other than the **weight** of the object itself.

Force
An influence which can change the motion of a body (i.e. cause an **acceleration**).

Framework
A structure made from **rods** joined together or a **wire** bent to form a shape.

Friction
A frictional force is a resistive **force** due to **roughness** between a body and surface. It always acts against motion, or likely motion.

g
Acceleration due to gravity. g is usually assumed to be 9.8 ms^{-2}.

Gravitational potential energy
The potential energy a body has due to its height above a particular base level.

i
The horizontal **unit vector**.

Impulse (of a force)
The change in **momentum** of a body as a result of the **force** acting on it.

Inextensible
Describes a body which can't be stretched. (Usually a **string** or **wire**.)

j
A **unit vector** perpendicular to **i**, often taken to be vertical.

Kinematics
The study of the motion of objects.

Kinetic energy
The energy a body has due to its **speed**.

Lamina
A flat two-dimensional body whose thickness can be ignored.

Light
Describes a body which is modelled as having no mass.

Limiting equilibrium
Describes a body which is at **rest** in **equilibrium**, but is on the point of moving.

Magnitude
The size of a quantity.

Mechanical energy
The sum of the potential and **kinetic energies** of a body.

Median
A line drawn in a triangle from one vertex to the midpoint of the opposite side.

Model
A mathematical description of a real-life situation, in which certain **assumptions** are made about the situation.

Moment
The turning effect a **force** has about a pivot point.

Momentum
The product of a body's mass and its **velocity**.

Non-uniform
Describes a body whose mass is unevenly distributed throughout the body.

Normal reaction
The reaction **force** from a surface acting on an object. It acts at 90° to the surface.

Particle
A body whose mass is considered to act at a single point, so its dimensions don't matter.

Peg
A fixed support which a body can hang from or rest on.

Perfectly elastic collision
A collision for which the **coefficient of restitution** is 1, so there is no overall loss of **kinetic energy**.

Perfectly inelastic collision
A collision for which the **coefficient of restitution** is 0. The particles in such a collision will **coalesce**.

Plane
A flat surface.

Position vector
The position of a point relative to a fixed origin, O, given in **vector** form.

Power
The rate at which a **force** does **work** on a body.

Projectile
A body, projected into the air, which moves only under the influence of gravity.

Resolving
Splitting a **vector** up into **components**.

Rest
Describes a body which is not moving. Often used to describe the initial state of a body.

Resultant (force or vector)
The single **force/vector** which has the same effect as two or more forces/vectors added together.

Rigid
Describes a body which does not bend.

Rod
A long, **thin**, straight, **rigid** body.

Rough
Describes a surface for which a **frictional force** will oppose the motion of a body in contact with the surface.

Scalar
A quantity which has a **magnitude** but not a direction.

Sector
A portion of a circle bounded by two radii and an **arc**.

Smooth
Describes a surface for which there is no **friction** between the surface and a body in contact with it.

Speed
The **magnitude** of an object's **velocity**.

String
A **thin** body, usually modelled as being **light** and **inextensible**.

Tension
The **force** in a taut **wire** or **string**.

Thin
Describes a body which is modelled as having no thickness.

Thrust
The **force** in a compressed **rod**.

Trajectory
The path followed by a **projectile**.

Uniform
Describes a body whose mass is evenly spread throughout the body.

Unit vector
A **vector** of **magnitude** one unit.

Vector
A quantity which has both a **magnitude** and a direction.

Velocity
The rate of change of an object's **displacement** with respect to time.

Weight
The **force** due to a body's mass and the effect of gravity: $W = mg$.

Wire
A **thin** body often modelled as being **light**. It can be bent to form a shape.

Work
A measure of the energy transferred to or by a moving object by the **forces** causing or opposing motion.

Index

These are the formulas you'll be given in the exam, but make sure you know exactly **when you need them** and **how to use them**. You might also need some formulas from the C1, C2 and C3 formula sheets in M2. (In the exam, you'll be given a booklet containing the formula sheets for all modules).

Centres of Mass

For uniform bodies:

Triangular lamina:

$\frac{2}{3}$ along median from vertex

Circular arc, radius r, angle at centre 2α:

$\frac{r\sin\alpha}{\alpha}$ from centre

Sector of circle, radius r, angle at centre 2α:

$\frac{2r\sin\alpha}{3\alpha}$ from centre

As you can see, they don't give you many formulas for the M2 exam — you really do have to learn all the others by heart, I'm afraid.

MEM2T61